Theory and Research on the Causes of War

Theory and Research on the Causes of War

Edited, with an introduction by

DEAN G. PRUITT
State University of New York at Buffalo

RICHARD C. SNYDER
University of California at Irvine

PRENTICE-HALL, INC.

Englewood, Cliffs, N. J.

PRENTICE-HALL INTERNATIONAL, INC., *London*
PRENTICE-HALL OF AUSTRALIA, PTY. LTD., *Sydney*
PRENTICE-HALL OF CANADA, LTD., *Toronto*
PRENTICE-HALL OF INDIA PRIVATE LTD., *New Delhi*
PRENTICE-HALL OF JAPAN, INC., *Tokyo*

Current printing (last digit):
10 9 8 7 6 5 4 3 2 1

Library of Congress Catalog Card Number 70–75631

PUBLISHED WITH THE COOPERATION OF THE CENTER FOR RESEARCH ON CONFLICT RESOLUTION.

Printed in the United States of America

This volume is dedicated to LEWIS F. RICHARDSON and QUINCY WRIGHT, two imaginative and versatile scholars, who more than a generation ago showed how it might be possible for mankind's recurring hopes of peace to be matched ultimately by systematic knowledge of why wars occur.

Preface

While war has periodically been one of man's most serious problems, the range and significance of its impacts have grown to the point where today it may well be considered the major human problem. As the large-scale violence of contemporary war has become an increasing threat to basic values, an ever-growing number of scholars from a widening variety of disciplines have become involved in analyzing its causes and possible cures. Theory and research methodology have become increasingly sophisticated, to the point where the minimum conditions for a science of the causes of war may be said to exist.

The purpose of this volume is to provide a progress report on recent scholarly developments, particularly in the United States. To this end, twenty-two selected readings and seven introductory essays are presented.

The collection is divided into seven parts, each with an introductory essay. Part I discusses the nature of theory, as an abstract entity, and acquaints the reader with the particular research methods that have been developed in this field. Parts II through V represent the four major topics under which theories in this area can be classified. Parts II and III examine the forces (i.e., the factors) that impel states into war, Part II deals with the motives and perceptions underlying entry into war and Part III, with the patterns of change in motives, perceptions, and actions that precede war. Parts IV and V are devoted to conditions that constrain states from entering war, Part IV deals with military constraints and Part V, with non-military constraints. Part VI is devoted to the small but interesting, nontheoretical literature on statistical correlates of war. Finally, Part VII surveys several directions that can be taken in an effort to integrate the theoretical material and empirical findings presented in earlier sections.

The readings constitute a representative cross section of what the authors feel are the most valuable scholarly contributions made by American writers over the past ten years. About half are based on empirical studies and, hence, reflect the more scientific (or, as it is sometimes called, "behavioral") outlook of the modern day. The other half are theoretical contributions. Five of the readings are reprinted from the *Journal of Conflict Resolution*, which has been a preeminent, though not exclusive, publication outlet for scientific writings on the origins of war. An additional eight come from other publications. The remaining seven were especially prepared for this volume. Unfortunately many significant items from the past ten years had to be omitted from the readings because of space limitations. Wherever possible, reference is made to these in the introductory essays.

The introductory essays, taken as a whole, are intended as a broad survey of both old and new literature in this field, highlighting the various kinds of theories that have been proposed and describing their associated methods of inquiry. Though somewhat technical in content and presentation, it is hoped that all students and citizens wishing to probe the phenomena of war will find these essays challenging and comprehensible.

The editors began planning this book eight years ago, at a time when both were members of the International Relations Program at Northwestern University. At that time, the scientific approach to research on international conflict was in its infancy. So many good pieces of research have been done since then that the table of contents projected at that time has been almost totally discarded.

Thanks are due to members of the Northwestern International Relations Program who gave advice during the early stages, especially Professors Chadwick Alger, Harold Guetzkow and James A. Robinson (now at Ohio State University). Professors J. David Singer, of the University of Michigan, Glenn H. Snyder, of the State University of New York at Buffalo, and Charles A. McClelland, of the University of Southern California, made helpful comments on the manuscript at a later stage. Preparation of the book was sponsored by the Center for Research on Conflict Resolution, at the University of Michigan, which publishes the *Journal of Conflict Resolution*. That center will receive most of the royalties from the sale of the book.

Dean G. Pruitt
Richard C. Snyder

Foreword: Scope, Purpose, and Guidelines for the Reader

I

This book documents a revolution in our thinking: war and peace have, in the last decade, become respectable research topics for a significant number of social and behavioral scientists of varying disciplinary backgrounds who look at them as empirical phenomena to be explained. For the first time in history, we can speak of a "Peace Research Movement," characterized by rigorous empirical inquiry into the nature and origins of violence in international conflict.

Prior to the last decade, there was of course a substantial literature on war and peace, but much of it lacked the degree of sophistication associated with the intellectual viewpoint of modern science. Most theories of why wars start were overly simplistic. Systematic evidence supporting these theories was seldom presented. Rather, it was often assumed that we knew why wars occur and that the problem was one of persuading men to do the things necessary to get rid of them.[1] Much of the literature tended to be an appeal to reason, directed to governments and the publics that influence them. However desirable such appeals may have been, they did not add greatly to our understanding of violent conflict among nations.

Probably the most significant precursor to the Peace Research Movement was Quincy Wright's monumental two-volume *A Study of War*.[2] This presented war

[1] In the Twentieth Century until just recently the major schools of thought about how to get rid of war could be reduced to two interrelated notions: first, the attitudes of statesmen and citizens must change so that fighting is ruled out as a method of resolving conflict, and second, new international institutions must be built to regulate international conflict. The ingredients of peace were usually seen as good will, the discarding of weapons, and the development of a supranational authority.

[2] Wright, Q. *A Study of War*, Vols. I and II. Chicago: University of Chicago Press, 1942.

as a subject for empirical, interdisciplinary scholarship and demonstrated how demanding the scholarly task would be once one departed from clichés and long-standing assumptions. This landmark undoubtedly provided a challenge to those sufficiently qualified and patient to read it, but it was another fifteen years before one could see visible signs that the challenge had been taken up. In 1957, the Peace Research Movement was formally inaugurated in the scientific world with the founding of a new journal, the *Journal of Conflict Resolution, A Quarterly for Research Related to War and Peace.*

Other developments had their origin at the same time or shortly thereafter. In the latter half of the 1950's, a fresh line of thought—for the most part independent of the mainstream of international relations theory—developed around the nature of strategic encounters in a thermonuclear age. The unprecedented destructive potential of nuclear technology spawned a new concept, "deterrence," which became the focus of a vigorous set of analytical studies. In 1959, the Institute for International Order commissioned five monographs intended to identify the most significant research needs in the area of international conflict. University centers—most notably at Harvard, Michigan, Northwestern, Princeton, and Stanford—inaugurated research programs designed to improve methodology as well as initiate basic investigations of international conflict. In the same year, Project Michelson (see Selection 19), an interdisciplinary governmental research program on the nature of strategic deterrence, was inaugurated. These developments received considerable intellectual stimulation from the older field of international politics, which had broken out of its historical mold following the Second World War and had taken its first steps along what has been called "the long road to a general theory of international relations." Beginning with fresh perspectives from the writings of Morgenthau and Sprout—often called the "Realist School"—this field has become increasingly strong in both theoretical analysis and empirical methodology.

By 1960, John Lear, science editor of the *Saturday Review*, was heralding to the general public what he called the "science of peace."

II

Because the world has experienced repeated disillusionment over the failure of intellectual and political efforts to control international violence, it is necessary to add a note of caution to the chronicle just presented. We are by no means close to a mature science of international conflict, and the road is indeed long and rocky. Dramatic breakthroughs in the near future are highly unlikely (or if breakthroughs occur, they may not be recognized as such). Moreover, even when we reach our intellectual goal, the formidable task will remain of persuading national decision makers and their validators to act on the basis of principles derived from empirically validated theory. Nevertheless, a substantial foundation has been laid in the past ten years and, given adequate allocation of societal resources, it is reasonable to believe that significant advances will be made in the future toward an understanding of the conditions under which peace is maintained or war begins.

The purpose of this volume is to provide a reliable progress report on the present state of theory and research, in the United States, bearing on the *causes of war.* This purpose implies certain limitations. The works presented and discussed focus on the how and why of war but say little about the conditions of peace. This aspect of the general problem is surely worthy of attention but is not treated here because we believe that the study of the causes of war can be clearly bounded and therefore evaluated more easily, and because in many respects an understanding of why wars occur is a necessary preliminary to the development of an effective operational theory for avoiding them.

III

To draw up his own balance sheet of progress toward an understanding of the causes of war, the reader may wish to bear the following guidelines in mind as he reads:

1. *What kinds of questions are being asked in this research? Are the right questions being asked?* Examples of questions that are being asked are: What will be the rate and critical effects of nuclear proliferation? Do conflicts "spiral"? Is there a "point of no return" on the way to violence?

2. *How is war conceptualized by the various theorists? Are current conceptions of war adequate for theory building?* For example, is war regarded as a special case of alternative methods for waging and resolving social conflict in general? If so, what are the consequences for theory?

3. *What classes of variables are emerging as most significant in explaining international violence?* Are these "located" inside the nation? in individuals who act for the nation? outside in the international system or in relations among states? How do these variables affect the likelihood of war?

4. *Is there enough solid evidence to permit us to decide among, or reformulate, these competing hypotheses:*

a. War results from universal human characteristics (e.g., aggressiveness) *vs.* war results from rational calculations made by official decision makers.

b. Big wars come about because circumstances get out of the control of responsible decision makers *vs.* big wars are carefully planned phenomena and small wars will not grow into big ones if both sides want to avoid such a growth.

c. War results from a series of decisions which cumulatively reduce alternatives to one *vs.* war results from a conscious choice among several alternatives at a particular moment in time.

d. War grows out of impersonal "historical forces" *vs.* war grows out of the consequences of ambitions or goals of individual national leaders.

e. Violence inheres in the nation-state system (sovereignty, power motive) *vs.* violence results from errors of judgment on the part of decision makers.

5. *What research techniques and strategies are being used to find answers to questions and to build theory? How adequate are these techniques? What sorts of techniques need to be developed?*

Contents

PART THREE

Movement Toward War: From Motives and Perceptions to Actions

PART FOUR

Restraints Against the Use of Violence: Military Preparations

PART FIVE

Nonmilitary Restraints and the Peaceful Resolution of Controversy

PART SIX

The Incidence of War: Statistical Evidence

PART SEVEN

Toward an Integrated Theory and Cumulative Research

Theory and Research on the Causes of War

PART ONE

The Study of War: Theory and Method

INTRODUCTION

The main aim of this volume is to portray the current state of empirical research and theory regarding the causes of war and to acquaint the reader with relevant empirical methodology. But, before getting into this substantive material, it will be useful to begin with a few general reminders about the nature of, and justification for, scientific theory and methodology.

The Nature of Scientific Theory: Ideal and Reality

Scientific theory takes many forms, but an *ideal* form can be described which has received the endorsement of competent practitioners and philosophers of science. This ideal has been used, where possible, as a basis for organizing the introductory material in subsequent parts of the book and is reflected in the writings of most of the contributors. It can be described as follows.

All theory is composed of symbols or terms, the most important of which refer to *variables*, i.e., abstracted dimensions or properties of the real world. Good theory consists of a set of interrelated *theoretical propositions* concerning the relationship between two or more variables. An example of a theoretical proposition might be the familiar (and, in many cases, questionable) assertion that greater military preparedness on the part of one state reduces the likelihood that another state will launch a military attack against it. This proposition describes the relationship between two variables: the extent of military preparedness and the likelihood of military attack.

Most theoretical propositions describe a causal relationship (directional influence) between one or more *antecedent variables* and a *consequent variable*. Antecedent variables come first in the causal chain described in a proposition. For example, the proposition just stated contains one antecedent variable: the extent of military preparedness. Antecedent variables may alternatively be called *independent variables*, *factors*, *determinants*, or *causes*. Consequent variables come last in the causal chain. The consequent variable in the proposition stated above is the likelihood of military attack. Consequent variables are also sometimes called *dependent variables* or *effects*.

Good theory, in addition, usually says something about *intervening variables*, i.e., variables that occupy an intermediate position in the causal chain between antecedent and consequent variables. For example, the likelihood of military success as perceived by leaders of the second state might be treated as an intervening variable in the proposition presented above. In other words, this variable can be thought of as mediating the influence of the first state's military preparedness on the second state's likelihood of going to war. Intervening variables represent the *process* or *mechanisms* underlying the relationship between antecedent and consequent variables.

Good theory is usually *multidimensional* in the sense that each consequent variable is assumed to be a function of several antecedent variables. Hence, a sophisticated treatment of war should trace it to a variety of antecedent variables, some operating independently of one another and others interacting in a complex way. Good theory should also have considerable generality, i.e., the terms in the propositions should be broad enough to embrace many particulars.

A good theoretical proposition must be capable of passing an *empirical test* by which it is confirmed or disconfirmed. To make such a test, it is necessary that the terms in the proposition (or in another proposition that can be logically derived from it) be *operationalized*, i.e., translated into concrete forms that can be observed and, if possible, measured in the real world.

The ideal of theory just described obviously cannot be achieved quickly. In the early stages of development, theories often contain poorly defined terms that are not readily operationalized. Propositions may be quite vague, sometimes stating no more than the existence of an undefined relationship between two variables. Empirical tests may be wholly lacking at first, as in armchair speculation, or incomplete, as in generalizations derived from analysis of a single case study. Hence, the practical measure of whether an intellectual endeavor is "scientific" should rightly be whether it is *moving* toward the ideal described above rather than whether it has achieved this ideal.

Misconceptions that Impede the Development of Good Theory about the Causes of War

Not everyone agrees that it is either possible or fruitful to build scientific theory of the kind just described about the causes of war. This resistance is, in part, a product of five misconceptions which deserve a brief review.

Theory Is Impractical

A distinction is often drawn between theory and practice. Theory is assumed to be a product of the "ivory tower," interesting as a mental exercise but of little practical value. Since war is a practical problem, efforts to develop a theory of its causes are assumed to be a waste of resources.

Actually, the distinction between theory and practice is very misleading. All solutions to practical problems are based on some kind of theory. When fully developed, scientific theory has great practical application, as shown by the spectacular engineering advances that have been derived from discoveries in the natural sciences. A good theory of the causes of war would be an invaluable guide to preserving peace.

People who make invidious comparisons between theory and practice are often reacting to theory building in its undramatic earlier stages, when evidence is incomplete and applications have not been worked out. Yet one generation's Einstein, thinking while walking in the park, may develop the insights necessary for the next generation to master an important new source of physical power. Significant rewards will often be reaped in the long run by a society that is willing to tolerate what looks like unproductive activity in the early stages of theory development.

Many theories about the causes of war are admittedly only in primitive form today and hence appear to have little practical value. Yet the viability of our present civilization may well depend on the level of support given to theory building in this area.

It Is Not Possible to Generalize About the Causes of War

This argument assumes not that theory is impractical but that it is impossible because every war is different. According to this viewpoint, the only proper way to study the origins of war is to analyze individual historical cases of war for their unique elements. This argument, though seductive, can be easily refuted by examples from the physical or biological sciences. No two animals are exactly alike, and certainly not the flea and the elephant. Hence, one might argue that no valid generalizations can be stated that embrace both species. Yet the scientific disciplines of physiology, biochemistry, and genetics have proven this wrong. Science does not say that the flea and the elephant are the same thing but only that they are similar in certain ways, e.g., both are produced from the union of an egg and a sperm. Concomitantly, two wars, though not exactly the same, may have enough in common to permit the development of valid generalizations, e.g., both may have developed out of an arms race precipitated by one state's misperception of another's intentions.

War Is Inevitable

There are still many people who believe that war is inevitable. It is natural if not logical for such people to resist the expenditure of resources to study the factors leading to war, since this research seems to have no practical value. Arguments for the inevitability of war usually take one of three forms:

History Repeats Itself. Man has always had wars in the past and, therefore, will always have them in the future (Stockton, 1932). This argument can be refuted by pointing to historical examples of other deeply rooted institutions that have ceased to exist or nearly disappeared, e.g., slavery (Adler, 1944; Frank, 1962). One hundred and fifty years ago it might have been said, as it is now in the case of war, that men have always had slaves and will therefore always have them.

Survival of the Fittest. A second argument identifies war with the struggle for survival that contributes to evolution by ridding the world of unfit species. War is deemed inevitable on the assumption that the struggle for survival is a "law of nature." In addition to the teleological error of attributing a purpose to nature, this argument rests on a superficial analogy. War and the evolutionary struggle for survival are really not very similar. War involves direct fighting—physical conflict—whereas the struggle for survival is a matter of indirect competition for scarce resources. Far from ridding the world of less fit species in the fashion of evolution, war selectively destroys the best physical specimens, who are usually placed in the front lines of combat.

Nature of Man. A third argument is based on philosophical pessimism, the belief that man is basically evil. Man's evil nature is assumed to express itself periodically in violent behavior of which war is the most prominent manifestation. This argument is also questionable. Psychologists now reject the notion that aggression derives from a drive, like hunger, that builds up over time and seeks periodic release. Such a drive is not found among animals (Berkowitz, 1962); spontaneous aggression is quite rare in the animal kingdom. In addition, many individual humans and some entire societies (Kluckhohn, 1944) can be found that rarely or never engage in violent behavior. Violence appears to be a learned response to certain kinds of frustrating or hostile environments rather than an inevitable impulse deriving from "human nature."

In rejecting the three arguments just presented, the editors of this volume do not mean to imply that all kinds or levels of international *conflict* can necessarily be avoided. A world in which all conflict was avoided would probably be unhealthy, since conflict has a number of positive functions (Coser, 1956). The point is only that large-scale *violent* international conflict is not inevitable.

The Origins of War Can Be Traced to One Overriding Cause

Until recently, most writers on the causes of war have produced one-factor theories, i.e., theories that trace the origin of all wars to a single, paramount source. The one-factor approach to theory has generated some heated controversies, e.g., between those who advocate rational and those who advocate emotional origins, between those who stress the role of elites and those who stress the role of the masses, between those who implicate economic motives and those who implicate the distribution of military resources.

There is an analogy between this situation and a hypothetical group of ten-year-old children trying to explain the origin of stomach aches. One child stresses the difficulty of digesting certain kinds of food (e.g., green apples); another, the role of germs and illness; a third, the importance of general health; a fourth, the relationship to tiredness. In a sense, all the children are right. All the factors mentioned are antecedent to one or another form of stomach ache. But each child makes the error of overemphasizing the importance of one factor, i.e., of not developing a multidimensional theory of stomach aches.

Analogously, most one-factor theories of war deal with a significant variable but err in ignoring other significant variables. Some wars owe their origin largely to economic motives, others, to military imbalance. Still other wars are preceded by both kinds of factors or by neither. An adequate theory must weave together a variety of factors into a multidimensional framework. Within such a framework, it may of course be possible to assign a proportionately larger role to certain factors than to others.

A Single Cure Can Be Found for War

People who find only one cause for war are likely to advocate only one cure: universal socialism, universal brotherhood, world government, total disarmament, or standing firm at all times against the adversary. Such solutions usually seem so obvious to their proponents that the development of theory and systematic inquiry seem superfluous.

Some of these cures are highly controversial, e.g., universal socialism and standing firm at all times. Others such as world government, disarmament, and universal brotherhood would certainly prevent war if they could be achieved in the form envisioned by their proponents, but the problem clearly lies in the difficulty of achieving them. They suffer from all the usual problems of utopian proposals.

Many of the theories and findings presented in this volume carry implications concerning the cure for war, and some of these implications are developed in a few of the contributed articles. But a systematic effort to address this question is beyond the scope of the book. One thing is clear, however. The multidimensional nature of the theory that develops as one goes along in this volume implies a *multiple strategy* for coping with war, embracing a variety of approaches. It seems clear that, while devoting some resources to the pursuit of more utopian solutions such as disarmament and world government, men must also be practical about the present and devise a variety of strategies to prevent the development of war here and now.

Methods for Studying the Causes of War

Theories about the causes of war have traditionally been based on relatively unsystematic perusal of a narrow set of source materials dealing with historical wars. Recent years have witnessed an awakening of concern about research method, per se, and the development of many imaginative methodological innovations. The forerunner of this trend was the pioneering research of Quincy Wright (1942), which employed a variety of methods. The methods currently in use for studying international conflict will now be briefly described. Examples of their use will be presented throughout the rest of the book.

The Single-Case-Study Method

One approach to research is careful analysis of a single historical event or institution, e.g., a detailed study of the events leading up to the First World War or of the structure of the United Nations. An example of a single case study is the interpretation of events in the Japanese attack on Pearl Harbor by Russett (Selection 9). The case study approach is by no means new. Case studies have long been the bread and butter of political science. But a number of recent developments in this method merit comment.

Most case studies have been oriented toward the unique features of the event or institution studied. Because of this orientation, they have seldom contributed directly to the development of general, abstract theory. Yet, there is no reason why a researcher doing a case study should not use his data as a heuristic device to suggest general propositions about cause and effect. To do so is partly a matter of the researcher's attitude toward theory development. But it is also partly a matter of technique in the sense that the researcher who begins with an *explicit conceptual model* of the type of phenomenon under study is more likely to end up with a rich set of theoretical propositions than the researcher who plunges in with only implicit ideas about what he is looking for or with the aim of gathering "all the facts."

A conceptual model is basically a set of variables that are capable of being related to one another by the facts in the case under study. If the model is fruitful, it will help the investigator find relationships that he might otherwise overlook. Conceptual models are usually derived from earlier studies and bodies of theory about phenomena that are similar to the case under study. An example of the construction and use of such a model can be seen in a case study of the United States' decision to enter the Korean War (Snyder and Paige, 1958). The conceptual model in this case was a set of variables thought to affect the organization, processes, and outcomes of national foreign-policy making. The model was refined and extended somewhat as a consequence of data analysis in order to accommodate unanticipated findings. The capacity to make such changes is essential if a conceptual model is not to become a straight jacket. But these changes were made in a self-conscious attempt to carry through the initial intent to explore ways of building better theory in this realm of public policy making.

Innovations have also arisen in the way data are collected and presented in case studies. The traditional mode of research involved "(locating) and (pouring) over all available verbal records, noting down 'interesting' facts and gradually forming an impression of what happened and why" (Singer, 1965, p. 70). While such an approach to the case study still has its value, it can be supplemented in three ways: by the use of interviews, content analysis, and correlational procedures.

Interviews can be used to supplement written records in studies of current institutions and historical events that are sufficiently recent for some of the participants still to be alive. Interviews have two advantages over historical records as a source of information on a case: (a) They are more likely to be candid since the respondent can be reasonably assured of anonymity, and (b) they are more likely to contain the information desired by the investigator since he can frame the questions asked. Interviews were used by Snyder and Paige (1958) and have also been employed in studies of policy-making institutions by Alger (1961 and Selection 14) and Pruitt (1964). Discussions of interview methodology can be found in Kahn and Cannell (1957) and Richardson, Dohrenwend, and Klein (1965).

Content analysis is a technique for measuring variables that are latent in verbal material. It can be used with both historical documents and interview records. The procedure begins with category construction, i.e., the identification of variables, and the development of a set of operations for measuring them. The operations themselves involve two steps: (a) breaking the verbal material into elements, e.g., words or assertions, and (b) coding, i.e., assigning these elements to preconceived categories or points on a scale. The result is a tabulation of the number of items in each category or a set of averages from various scales.

The most extensive use of content analysis in the study of international conflict can be seen in the historical research by North and his associates (North et al., 1963, and Selection 5). Among the categories typically used in their research are "perception of capability," "perception of power," "perception of friendship," and "perception of hostility." For example, an item classified as a perception of hostility was a notation by Kaiser Wilhelm in 1914 in which he described British policy in this way, "She twists the noose of our political and economic destruction" (North et al., 1963, p. 44). In tabulating the analysis of documents from the six weeks prior to the First World War, these researchers found a superabundance of statements from German statesmen that fell into this category. From this, they inferred that hostility from other states was keenly felt in the German camp during this period.

In addition to North et al. (1963), useful guides to content analysis can be found in Berelson (1952) and Pool (1959).

If causal propositions are to be derived from a case study, some basis must be found for making inferences about cause and effect. Traditional studies have relied heavily on close observation of the order in which events occur plus common sense or theory borrowed from other fields. Verbal reports from participants who had some insight into the roots of their behavior have also been useful. Recent research has also employed *correlational procedures*. These permit a mathematical comparison of the pattern of change in one variable (e.g., hostile behavior of one state) with the pattern of change in another (e.g., hostile behavior of another state). The greater the similarity in pattern, the more likely it is that a causal relationship exists between the variables (or between each variable and a third common factor antecedent to both). North and his associates have also made extensive use of correlational techniques in analyzing a single case.

The Comparative-Case-Study Method

Single case studies have their place, especially in early research, as a source of ideas about possible causal propositions; but they also have their limitations. Many variables have a fixed value in a single case, e.g., the composition of the government of the United States during the decision to intervene in Korea. As a result, important correlations may be missed and important propositions not discovered. Even when variables take on a variety of values in a single case and sizable correlations emerge, it is often not wise to generalize beyond that case because of its many unique features.

A partial solution to these limitations is embodied in the method of comparative case studies, in which a "sample" of cases is gathered and the cases in this sample are compared with one another. The method employed for choosing a sample of cases should ensure variation on critical variables. For example, in a comparative case study of the causes of war, the sample should ideally include cases that led to war and cases that did not, so that the backgrounds of these two kinds of cases can be contrasted.

Two basic kinds of comparative case studies can be distinguished, small-sample and large-sample. Small-sample studies involve the comparison of only a few cases, often only two. Such studies frequently concentrate on only a few variables, which are studied in great depth with much attention to the processes interrelating them. Large-sample studies involve the comparison of many cases, often sixty to one hundred. Statistical methods are more likely to be used, often with computer support for the data analysis. Typically, a large number of variables are measured, and a big table is computed of intercorrelations among these variables. It is possible to generalize the findings from large-sample studies with greater assurance than from small-sample studies, because the unique elements of each case are more effectively submerged in the larger sample. Large-sample studies also permit the discovery of relationships between variables that are not intimately associated in time and place and whose relationship might, therefore, be overlooked in small-sample studies with their emphasis on process. On the other hand, large-sample studies are almost necessarily more superficial in the sense of permitting less care in the design of variables and less attention to the processes that link these variables.

Comparative case studies of international conflict have been done in the past by Schumpeter (1958) and Abel (1941), but traditional methods were used for developing and analyzing the data in the cases compared. Three examples that involve more modern methods are included in the present volume: (a) One, by Holsti, Brody, and North (Selection 5), is a small-sample study comparing two crises, one of which led to war (the First World War) and the other of which did not (the Cuban Missile Crisis). The other two examples involve large-sample techniques: (b) a comparison of twenty historical cases in six geographical regions designed to identify the antecedents of successful and unsuccessful deterrence of war between major powers by Naroll (Selection 11) and (c) a summary of several studies of the relationship between the incidence of internal and external war across large samples of states by Rummel (Selection 16).

The selection by Naroll is unique because the *sampling procedure* used for choosing the cases came very close to a random procedure. Random sampling enhances the confidence with which one can generalize to other cases that are similar to but not actually among the cases studied. The studies reported in the selection by Rummel are distinctive in the use made of *factor analysis*, a statistical method that reveals the dimensions underlying the relationship of many variables to one another.

The Inter-Nation Simulation Method

A striking, recent innovation in the study of international relations is a laboratory method developed at Northwestern University, the Inter-Nation Simulation technique (Guetzkow, 1959; Guetzkow et al., 1963).[1] This method makes use of an artificial world, built in the laboratory, consisting of a number of states, each with several policy makers. In each of a series of time periods, the policy makers in every state must make decisions about the internal allocation of resources and the conduct of foreign affairs. Many real-world strategies are available to the policy makers, including diplomacy, trade, aid, conventional war, nuclear war, and others. After each set of decisions, the policy makers get feedback from other states and the experimenter concerning the impact of their decisions. The nature of this feedback and other features of the simulation environment are derived from a complicated and sophisticated theory of internal and international affairs that produces "an operating environment for the decision makers that is designed to be isomorphic to the environment in which foreign-policy decision makers operate within the system of nations of the world" (Guetzkow et al., 1963, p. 104).

The Inter-Nation Simulation can be thought of as a working model of international relations, resembling in function the wind tunnel in aerodynamics. Like the wind tunnel, there is no *guarantee* that theoretical propositions based on the simulation can be validly generalized to real-life international affairs. But, to the extent that the theory underlying the simulation is valid, these propositions can be taken as *reasonable suggestions* of what may happen in real life. The theory underlying the simulation seems to have a good deal of face validity, but the ultimate test of this theory must eventually be an empirical one. Guetzkow and his associates are currently involved in a major effort to develop empirical evidence to test the validity of the simulation in a project entitled "Simulated International Processes."

An interesting contrast can be drawn between the Inter-Nation Simulation and the comparative-case-study method described above, from the viewpoint of *usefulness* for research on international conflict. There are points for and against the usefulness of each method.

[1]Several earlier all-man simulations of international relations were developed at places like the RAND Corporation and the Massachusetts Institute of Technology, but these have not achieved the prominence in research of the Northwestern version.

The comparative-case-study method has the advantage of greater realism, i.e., face validity. In other words, findings based on this method will probably make the investigator feel safer in generalizing about current international affairs. This does not mean that findings based on the comparative method are totally generalizable. There are differences between the modern era and historical eras that make generalization somewhat risky. Nor does it mean that findings based on the simulation method are clearly nongeneralizable. As mentioned earlier, the theory underlying this method has considerable face validity. But the comparative method appears to be superior to the simulation method in this respect.

The simulation method seems preferable as a research device to the comparative-case-study method in four other respects:

1. The simulation environment permits greater access to the events of international affairs and the policy makers responsible for them. Singer (1965, pp. 76–77) makes this point:

> Most of the relevant action takes place within the view of the researcher, or is recorded for him. Also the predictions, preferences and premises of the [policy makers] can be systematically tapped at the moment of decision, obviating reliance upon the ex post facto reconstruction and self-justification often found in memoirs and diaries.

2. The simulation method permits the investigator to create conditions of theoretical or prognostic interest that have not previously existed. The value of this can be seen in Brody's simulation study of the proliferation of nuclear weapons (Brody, 1963 and Selection 12). Such a study could not have been done on historical data since the conditions under investigation have never before existed.

3. The fact that he can manipulate the simulation environment makes it possible for the investigator to unravel cause and effect. When correlations are found in historical data, one can never be sure which variable is the "chicken" and which the "egg." But, in a simulation experiment, the investigator himself manipulates some of the variables. Subsequent events that are correlated with these manipulations can logically be construed as caused by them.

4. Since the environment of the simulation is less complex than that of historical case studies, relationships between variables may be found in the former environment that would be overlooked in the latter. In a sense, the comparative-case-study method places the investigator in the position that Galileo would have occupied had he tried to map the laws of gravity by waiting on a rough mountainside for boulders to break loose and roll downhill. If the boulders had fallen at all (see point 2 above), their course of descent would have been influenced by so many factors in addition to gravity—features of the terrain, contours of the rock—that he might never have discovered anything of an orderly nature. The simulation, on the other hand, has features of Galileo's inclined plane. It is possible that, in this simpler world, relationships will be seen more clearly.

In summary, there are advantages and disadvantages to the comparative case study and the Inter-Nation Simulation method; neither has a clear-cut advantage over the other. Rather, the investigator's choice of method must depend on such issues as the availability and richness of historical data relevant to his problem and the degree of ambiguity in these data with regard to cause and effect.

Reports on three simulation studies are included in this volume: (a) a report by Brody and Benham of a study by Brody on the effect of the proliferation of nuclear weapons on the international system (Selection 12); (b) a report on a study of what happens to the international system when one state achieves the capacity to delay nuclear retaliation, by Raser and Crow (Selection 10); and (c) a report on a study of the effect of crisis on national decision making, by Robinson, Hermann, and Hermann (Selection 6). In addition, an essay by Guetzkow is included (Selection 20) in which he urges that the Inter-Nation Simulation be regarded as a device for integrating theory and research on international relations.

Computer Simulation Method

A number of other methods have been developed for simulating international relations, most of which are summarized in Guetzkow et al. (1963).

Some of these methods involve *pure computer simulation.* In the Inter-Nation Simulation described above, human beings play the roles of national policy makers, and the experimenter's role is confined to defining the environment within which they are working. A pure computer simulation, on the other hand, is run without human beings. The experimenter provides the environment *and* defines a set of functions that reproduce typical human reactions to standard environments. The entire world is programmed on a large computer and "data collection" reduces to discovering the implications of the theoretical assumptions built into the computer program.

If valid theoretical assumptions about human nature and environmental reactivity are built into the program, pure computer simulation may be a useful device for discovering the implications of changes in the international environment whose effects are too complicated for the unaided human mind to trace through. But, given that man knows so little about the way in which policy makers make their decisions, one can mount a strong argument in favor of the Inter-Nation Simulation as opposed to the pure computer simulation as a device for making valid predictions. The Inter-Nation Simulation makes relatively few assumptions about how people behave but, instead, introduces real human beings into the policy-making roles. Furthermore, it permits gathering data about policy making that may be useful for theory building.

On the other hand, even if many of the assumptions are faulty, the very process of building a computer simulation may be a useful exercise inasmuch as it forces the researcher to face the problem of constructing an integrated theory and thereby reveals gaps in human knowledge.

An example of a computer simulation of the international system is described in Selection 18 by Abt and Gorden.

Small-Scale Laboratory Experiments

The Inter-Nation Simulation method described above is useful for learning about how people react to complex environments resembling international affairs. But it has the drawback of being big and expensive. For some problems, it may be possible to abstract a few of the most important features of the international environment and produce these in even simpler laboratory settings. For example, it may be possible to learn a lot about decision making under crisis by observing the behavior of groups of people solving difficult thought problems under instructions for simultaneous speed and accuracy. A long tradition of laboratory research on individuals and small groups exists in the field of psychology. Recent research on behavior in laboratory games (e.g., Deutsch, 1958; Deutsch and Krauss, 1960; Kelley, 1965; and Shure, Meeker, and Hansford, 1965) seems especially relevant to international conflict.

The arguments presented above to recommend use of the simulation technique as opposed to the comparative-case-study method can also be employed to justify use of small-scale laboratory experimentation. The problem of validly generalizing to international relations from such experiments is even more acute than in the case of simulation. But, where there are meaningful similarities beween real life and a small-scale laboratory setting, the latter is probably the best site for research because of the greater access that it affords to the behavior of the participants, the greater flexibility for creating relevant conditions and thus unraveling cause and effect, the greater likelihood of detecting relationships between variables, and, in addition, because of its lower cost.

Because of space limitations, no example could be provided in this volume of a laboratory study with implications for international conflict.

Survey Studies

Some problems in the study of international conflict can best be handled by public opinion surveys employing questionnaires. This kind of research is especially useful for assessing the nature and source of attitudes toward international affairs. Research on this topic is summarized in the introduction to Part II.

Extrapolation from Other Fields of Social Science

Often the phenomena examined by other social sciences are similar in important ways to the phenomena of international relations. For example, both negotiation and norms that regulate the methods used in the pursuit of conflict are found in marriage as well as in international politics. It follows that many of the findings from other branches of social science can be extrapolated to international relations, though, of course, the final proof of the value of such extrapolation necessitates empirical research on international relations itself. Examples of ideas about international conflict that were inspired by *psychological theory* can be seen in the selections by Pool (Selection 13) and Osgood (Selection 15).

In recent years, extrapolations from various fields, most notably sociology, have been integrated into what is coming to be called general *conflict theory* (see McClelland, 1962). This new interdisciplinary theory is in its early stages but is already being employed in the analysis of international conflict. Examples of the use of conflict theory can be seen in the selections by McClelland (Selection 7), Brody and Benham (Selection 12), and Alger (Selection 14).

Mathematical Models

As their understanding increases in complexity and their methods of measurement improve in precision, scientists tend to make increasing use of formal theoretical models, particularly those in which theoretical concepts and relationships are translated into mathematical terms and operations. This development is natural because mathematical notation permits greater precision in the statement of theoretical ideas and the derivation of their consequences. Furthermore, in some respects, mathematics is a richer language, involving more nuances than ordinary speech. Computer simulation is one kind of formal model which employs mathematical and logical relationships. The Inter-Nation Simulation also includes some mathematical features in the equations that are used to determine the results of national action. In addition, a few theorists have developed nonsimulative mathematical models of international conflict, i.e., models that state functional relationships between variables rather than unfolding relationships over time as do simulations. The most notable example is Richardson's (1960) model of the arms race. Selection 17 by Wesley presents a mathematical model from which predictions are generated that fit data about the incidence of war.

References

Abel, T., "The element of decision in the pattern of war," *American Sociological Review*, **6**(6), 853–859, 1941.

Adler, M. J., *How to Think about War and Peace*. New York: Simon and Schuster, Inc., 1944.

Alger, C. F., "Non-resolution consequences of the United Nations and their effect on international conflict," *Journal of Conflict Resolution*, **5**(5), 128–145, 1961.

Berelson, B., *Content Analysis in Communication Research*. New York: The Free Press, 1952.

Berkowitz, L., *Aggression: A Social Psychological Analysis*. New York: McGraw-Hill Book Company, 1962.

Brody, R. A., "Some systemic effects of the spread of nuclear weapons technology: A study through simulation of a multi-nuclear future," *Journal of Conflict Resolution*, **7**(4), 663–753, 1963.

Coser, L. A., *The Functions of Social Conflict*. New York: The Free Press, 1956.

Deutsch, M., "Trust and suspicion," *Journal of Conflict Resolution*, **2**(4), 265–279, 1958.

Deutsch, M., and R. M. Krauss, "The effect of threat upon interpersonal bargaining," *Journal of Abnormal and Social Psychology*, **61,** 181–189, 1960.

Frank, J. D., "Human nature and nonviolent resistance," *in* Q. Wright, W. M. Evan, and M. Deutsch, eds., *Preventing World War III: Some Proposals*. New York: Simon and Schuster, Inc., 1962.

Guetzkow, H., "A use of simulation in the study of inter-nation relations," *Behavioral Science*, **4**(3), 183–191, 1959.

Guetzkow, H., C. F. Alger, R. A. Brody, R. C. Noel, and R. C. Snyder, *Simulation in International Relations: Developments for Research and Teaching*. Englewood Cliffs, N.J.: Prentice-Hall, Inc., 1963.

Kahn, R. L., and C. F. Cannell, *The Dynamics of Interviewing*. New York: John Wiley and Sons, Inc., 1957.

Kelley, H. H., "Experimental studies of threats in interpersonal negotiations," *Journal of Conflict Resolution*, **9**(1), 79–105, 1965.

Kluckhohn, C., "Anthropological research and world peace," *in* L. Bryson, L. Finkelstein, and R. M. MacIver, eds., *Approaches to World Peace: A Symposium*, Conference on Science, Philosophy and Religion, New York, 1944.

McClelland, C. A., "The reorientation of the sociology of conflict," *Journal of Conflict Resolution*, **6**(1), 88–95, 1962.

North, R. C., O. R. Holsti, M. G. Zaninovich, and D. A. Zinnes, *Content Analysis: A Handbook with Applications for the Study of International Crisis*. Evanston, Ill.: Northwestern University Press, 1963.

Pool, I. de S., ed., *Trends in Content Analysis*. Urbana, Ill.: University of Illinois Press, 1959.

Pruitt, D. G., *Problem Solving in the Department of State*. Denver, Col.: University of Denver (Monograph Series in World Affairs), 1964.

Richardson, L. F., *Arms and Insecurity: A Mathematical Study of the Causes and Origins of War*. Pittsburgh, Pa.: The Boxwood Press, 1960.

Richardson, S. A., B. S. Dohrenwend, and D. Klein, *Interviewing: Its Forms and Functions*. New York: Basic Books, 1965.

Schumpeter, J., *The Sociology of Imperialism*. New York: Columbia University Press, 1958.

Shure, G. H., R. J. Meeker, and E. A. Hansford, "The effectiveness of pacifist strategies in bargaining games," *Journal of Conflict Resolution*, **9**(1), 106–117, 1965.

Singer, J. D., "Data-making in international relations." *Behavioral Science*, **10**(1), 68–80, 1965.

Snyder, R. C., and G. D. Paige, "The United States decision to resist aggression in Korea: the application of an analytic scheme," *Administrative Science Quarterly*, **3**(3), 341–378, 1958.

Stockton, R., *Inevitable War*. New York: Perth Press, 1932.

Wright, Q., *A Study of War*. Chicago: University of Chicago Press, 1942.

PART TWO

Motives and Perceptions Underlying Entry into War

INTRODUCTION

Most theories of the forces (factors) that impel states toward war can be reduced to formulations about the motives that lead men to involve their states in war, or to place them on the road toward war, and the perceptions underlying such motives. This introduction will be organized around three motivational and perceptual concepts that have received particular attention: (a) goals that can be advanced through war, (b) the perception of threat, and (c) hostility toward other states.

All three of these concepts are admittedly psychological in nature, and a question naturally arises concerning whose psychology is at stake, i.e., whose goals, perceptions, and hostility lead states into war? Answers to this question differ markedly, depending on the "unit of analysis" favored by a writer. Some writers avoid the question altogether, taking as their unit of analysis the state as a whole with its "national goals and capabilities." Others prefer a more analytical approach and refer, often rather vaguely, to the motives of "decision makers" or the "public." A third group of authors implicate specific interest groups, such as investors or munitions makers. Despite these differences in unit of analysis, all three kinds of authors share a concern with motivational and perceptual concepts and, hence, can be classed together for purposes of exposition.

Most of the literature in this area is speculative, so that little empirical evidence can be presented in this introduction.

Goals That Can Be Advanced Through War

An Inventory of Goals

Most authors who have written about the motives underlying the resort to war have been content to describe or list goals that appear to have played a part in the origin of historical wars. No wholly reliable method as yet exists for identifying such goals. One cannot fully trust the public statements of policy makers because they usually try to dress their actions in the most acceptable garments. Instead, one must mainly rely on inferential analysis and base one's conclusions on the "feeling that the argument somehow makes sense" (Rapoport, 1964, p. 13). Nevertheless, some writers probably have come close enough to the truth at times to make it worth reviewing their conclusions.

A distinction can be drawn between two kinds of goals that motivate conflict: *success-oriented* and *conflict-oriented* goals. Conflict that is produced by a desire for the fruits of victory, e.g., booty or dominion over the vanquished, can be said to have success-oriented goals. Conflict-oriented goals are satisfied by engaging in conflict, per se, whether victory is achieved or not, e.g., the desire for adventure or glory. Conflict that has its origins in success-oriented goals has sometimes been called "real" conflict in contrast to "induced" conflict, which has its origins in conflict-oriented goals (Mack and Snyder, 1957).

Success-Oriented Goals. War has been traced to a variety of *economic* goals, e.g., the desire for treasure, raw materials, means of production, trade routes, markets, outlets for investment, and places to settle population. *Political* goals have also been cited, e.g., the wish to regain territories formerly controlled, to achieve independence, to free oppressed groups in other countries, and to install or restore friendly governments in neighboring countries. Other authors have stressed *ideological* goals, e.g., spreading or destroying a religion, political philosophy, or economic system. *Punishment* motives are sometimes implicated, e.g., revenging an injury or insult, teaching another state a "lesson." Sometimes, violence appears to be initiated for the purpose of achieving greater *military security,* as in the Soviet war against Finland in 1939. Occasionally, a state fights a war in order to maintain or increase the *credibility* of its guarantees or threats in other areas. This appears to be one motive underlying American participation in the Vietnam War.

Many writers (e.g., Morgenthau, 1960; Organski, 1958; and Levi, 1960 and Selection 1) have stressed the importance of the search for *power* in their explanations of war and lesser forms of international conflict. Various definitions have been given of power, but in this context it seems to means the capacity to destroy, injure, deprive, thwart, or otherwise control another state, in short, the capacity to resolve future conflict in one's own favor. Thus present-day conflict is explained as a search for the capacity to win future conflict. "Elements" of power that can be achieved through international conflict include such things as economi resources, alliances, control of militarily strategic regions, and destruction enemy resources.

To explain war as an effort to achieve the means to win future conflict is simply to push the search for causes one step backward. One must then account for the concern about future conflict. On this issue, a controversy has developed. Some authors (e.g., Van Dyke, 1957, and Levy, 1960 and Selection 1) have argued that the search for power is motivated by the desire to achieve other kinds of goals in the future, such as economic and ideological goals. Others (Dunn, 1937, and Morgenthau, 1960) maintain that the search for power becomes an autonomous motive, i.e. that the capacity to win future conflict becomes a goal in itself, not subordinated to other goals. Both positions probably fit the facts under certain circumstances, but the nature of these circumstances is not well understood.

Conflict-Oriented Goals. Success-oriented goals can only be satisfied by the fruits of victory, while conflict-oriented goals are satisfied by the struggle, per se. Hence, to identify the conflict-oriented goals that can underlie war, one must look for the byproducts of war that may have positive value to society as a whole or to powerful groups within society. For example, war, at least in its early stages, generally intensifies *national dynamism.* Morale improves, people work harder for the common good, internal conflicts and rivalries diminish. The anticipation of such results may provide a rationale for supporting the entry of one's state into war. Fighting a war may also be a way of maintaining or regaining the *national honor,* a sense that one's nation is respectable. In addition, certain groups within a state always benefit from war. *Jobs* are available for workers in defense industries and *profits* for their owners. The *position* and *influence* of military and related governmental elites are likely to be strengthened in time of war. The anticipation of such outcomes may produce demands from certain groups for greater use of violence in relations with other states (Engelbrecht and Hanighen, 1934). Such demands may lead to war or may contribute to a movement toward war that is also impelled by success-oriented goals.

Theories of Imperialism

A list, such as the one just given, of the goals that contribute to the use of violence in international affairs is only the first step toward a motivational theory of war. A sound theory must also embody propositions about two issues: (a) the ways in which such goals develop and (b) the conditions under which war is elected as a method for achieving such goals. Little theory exists on the second issue other than the commonsense recognition that few goals in and of themselves produce war but that war grows out of a realization on the part of decision makers that violence is the most workable approach to a goal and that other alternatives are less attractive. A variety of theories have developed concerning the first issue, the roots of goals that can lead to war. Among the best known are those that attempt to account for *imperialism.*

Imperialism can be defined as a policy of unlimited geographical expansion. ˙ost theories of imperialism have focused on the historical period in the late ıeteenth century when the more powerful states of Europe annexed, by a series of military actions, most areas of the underdeveloped world. Only one of the major theorists, Schumpeter, has drawn his evidence from a broader historical spectrum.

The three most famous theories of imperialism will be summarized in this section. Fuller details on these and other theories can be found in Strachey (1960) and Winslow (1948).

Hobson's Theory. Hobson (1938, first published in 1902) based his theory on an analysis of British imperialism. He argued that in his day the British Empire imposed a heavy drain on England's economic, social, and moral resources. Since the nation as a whole did not benefit from the existence of the Empire, he assumed that special interest groups must have foisted the Empire on the body politic. The most likely suspects were those who derived benefit from the Empire, among them investors, financiers, certain manufacturers, exporters, shippers, members of the armed services and the Indian Civil Service, and educated groups whose sons might be able to find administrative jobs in the territories composing the Empire. Among these groups, he assigned a leading role to business interests seeking outlets for capital and goods.

Following up the last point, he suggested conditions under which the goal of unlimited expansion develops. He reasoned that imperialism develops during a period of economic imbalance, in which there is an *oversupply of both capital and goods* at home. Such an imbalance forces businessmen to seek outlets abroad; and, since foreign investments and markets generally need protection, these businessmen prevail on their government to seize and administer the territories in which they are conducting their operations.

As a solution to the problem of imperialism, Hobson recommended a reform of capitalism to prevent the development of an oversupply of capital and goods. His solution boiled down to placing the surplus capital in the hands of people at home who would use it to purchase the surplus goods, i.e., in the hands of workers and the government. Thus he recommended strengthening unions and imposing higher taxes on certain kinds of income.

Lenin's Theory. Lenin (1950, first published in 1917) leaned heavily on Hobson and on several earlier Marxist writers but added his own systematization. Like Hobson, he traced imperialism to an oversupply of capital. But he went beyond Hobson in asserting that imperialism would ultimately lead to major war between the great capitalist powers. He reasoned that the competition for colonies between these states would increase as the supply of underdeveloped regions of the world diminished. A major war might develop out of this competition, although it was possible instead that the states who were most powerful in any given period might come to an agreement about who possessed what. However, such an agreement could not last forever, since other capitalist nations who were outside of the agreement would eventually develop sufficient strength to challenge it. Major war would surely develop out of such a challenge. Lenin explained the First World War in terms of his theory, identifying the challenger as Germany.

Unlike Hobson, Lenin believed that imperialism was an inevitable outcome of capitalism in its mature stages and saw no cure for imperialism and world war other than the triumph of socialism. He argued that capitalism could not be reformed because the capitalists were so fully in control of their governments that they would be able to block all efforts at reform.

Schumpeter's Theory. Schumpeter (1955, first published in 1919; reviewed by Knorr, 1952) based his theory on a careful analysis and comparison of several past societies, including precapitalist societies, in which policies of imperialism developed. Like Hobson, he traced the support of this policy to a coalition of powerful political groups, including economic interests. But he argued that the major pressure for imperialism came from military and governmental circles whose authority and position in society depended on continued warfare. Thus he traced war to conflict-oriented rather than success-oriented goals.

For Schumpeter, the critical conditions that foster imperialism are those which create a large military machine and corresponding political organization, whose members then seek to maintain their position. Such institutions may have their origin in success-oriented conflicts, such as a war for independence. Once established, they tend to become self-perpetuating by constantly engaging their state in new war.

Schumpeter's solution to the problem of imperialism was markedly different from Lenin's. Schumpeter claimed that imperialism was an atavism (holdover) from precapitalist society and would eventually disappear as capitalism matured. He claimed that the spirit of capitalism is individualistic, democratic, and rational and that these traits would eventually make imperialism unwelcome in capitalist societies.

Critique of the Theories of Imperialism. The theories of imperialism just described have the defects of all single-factor approaches. They overstate the case for a particular explanation by ignoring other important factors. Hence, they are easily "refuted" by citing negative instances. For example, Lenin's claim to have explained the origin of the First World War has been seriously questioned by writers like Aron (1954) who show that the ferocity of competition for colonies among the major European states *declined* in the period just preceding the outbreak of this war. Schumpeter's picture of a military elite, spawned in one war and instrumental in producing the next, does not provide a close fit to German expansionism in the Second World War, which was guided by a political elite that came to power in peacetime.

On the other hand, if we are willing to look beyond the obvious defects in these theories, it may be possible to derive some useful ideas from them. For example, the causal mechanisms which they describe may be important in the case of certain kinds of wars. Thus, Schumpeter's picture of a governing elite whose position in society depends on preparation for and engagement in war is not inconsistent with what is known about roots of the Japanese war in Southeast Asia which culminated in an attack on the United States. Further theoretical advances are needed to specify the conditions under which such mechanisms operate.

Other Theories About the Sources or Goals Underlying War

Among the major rivals to the theories of imperialism described above are theories that trace violence-inducing goals to the *form of government* possessed by a state. Waltz (1959, pp. 120–121) presents the following summary statement about this diverse and contradictory literature:

> A world full of democracies would be a world forever at peace, but autocratic governments are warlike.... Monarchies are peaceful; democracies are irresponsible and impulsive, and consequently foment war.... Each of these formulations has claimed numerous adherents, and each adherent has in turn been called to task by critics and by history.

The development of goals that lead to war has also been traced to *uncertainty about tenure of power* among ruling elites. For example, Rosecrance (1963, p. 255) argues for the period between 1890 and 1918, "In Austro-Hungary, Germany and Russia where the position of the ruling elite was in jeopardy, aggressive military and political personalities came to the fore." Such goals are, presumably, in part conflict-oriented; i.e., elite groups assume that the preparation for and the conduct of war will cause the citizenry to rally around its government. In part, they may also be success-oriented; i.e., elite groups assume that they will gain internal prestige if they succeed in making conquests abroad. While the desire to resolve political instability may sometimes motivate elites to enter a war, the national dislocation resulting from political instability may also at times cause elites to feel that their state is too weak to succeed in war and hence cause them to shy away from involvement in it. In other words, there is no simple relationship between political instability and the likelihood of military involvement, an assertion that is supported by Rummel's (see Selection 16) failure to find any sizable correlation between these two variables in historical data. Rosecrance (1963) argues that a positive relationship between instability and belligerence will only be found in those states that have a "measure of social cohesion" (p. 305) and will be stronger in those cases where elites foresee a short, successful (and, hence, politically nondisruptive) military campaign.

Rosecrance also stresses the importance of ideological differences between states in the genesis of war. He argues, "the most violent forms of international conflict have usually been associated with divergences in elite ethos" (p. 280), citing in particular the period in European history between 1789 and 1814. Such divergences arouse both missionary zeal and the fear of internal ideological subversion, both of which can lead to the goal of overturning the political leadership of other states and thereby altering the religious, political, or economic systems in these states.

The development of national goals whose pursuit leads to war has also sometimes been traced to the perception of new opportunities for influence and conquest abroad. The concept of *power vacuum* is important in this regard. A power vacuum describes a geographical region that is militarily or politically weak and, hence, invites military or subversive incursion from abroad. Greece in 1946, South Korea in 1951, and the Congo in 1962 are possible examples. Power vacuums encourage ambition for control on the part of other states, either because control looks easy to establish or because it is feared that still other states will seek control. Power vacuums have often become the tinder boxes of war as states have vied for control over them.

Growth in perceived military and economic capability can also create among national leaders a sense of new opportunities for influence and conquest and, thereby, produce ambitions that set their state on a collision course with other states. Organski (1958) has cited this mechanism as a major determinant of both world wars, with German and Japanese industrialization heightening the ambitions of the leaders of these states and causing them to adopt expansionist policies. Past military success can also, of course, enhance perceived capability and raise ambitions.

If the perception of new opportunity can heighten national ambition, it seems reasonable to suppose that reduction in perceived opportunity will cause ambition to wane. Military deterrents are sometimes justified on this basis. For example, in his famous article advocating a policy of containing Russian expansionism, Kennan (1947) argued that the eventual outcome of the containment policy would be a reduction in Soviet aspirations for greater power in Europe. More recently, the United States has been making an effort to hold the line against communist take-overs in South Vietnam and Laos at least partially in an effort to reduce the motivation for war and revolution among communists in Asia and other parts of the underdeveloped world. A thorough analysis of military deterrence and the balance of power will be presented in Part IV of this book.

While subscribing to the notion that increased military capacity can cause a state to become more ambitious for influence over other states, Burton (1962) has questioned the companion assumption embraced by Kennan that blocking such ambitions will cause aggressive motivation to decline. He argues that resistance to a limited challenge from a state whose capabilities are growing will produce frustration and anger in that state and cause it to develop less-limited power needs that may make it more aggressive and dangerous in the long run. Thus, international instability results from an international system that provides no mechanisms for peaceful change to accommodate the desires of states whose military and economic capability is increasing.

To the present authors, it seems reasonable to suppose that Burton's theory is right under some circumstances and Kennan's containment theory is right under others. The most effective response to a challenge from a newly powerful state depends on the circumstances. Under some circumstances, peace is best preserved by giving in to the demands of an adversary to prevent the development of more dangerous goals in the future. Under other circumstances, one should oppose these demands so that the motives underlying them will disappear. But what are the appropriate circumstances for each kind of policy? There is clearly a theoretical gap at this point.

The Perception of Threat

The theories discussed in the last section attempt to account for the existence of certain success-oriented and conflict-oriented goals. For success-oriented goals to cause involvement in war, it is also necessary that they be seen by decision makers as *incompatible with* the goals of another state. Otherwise, there is no basis for conflict. There are two kinds of perceived incompatibility. The other state may be seen as an *obstacle* to the attainment of new goals; i.e., if we are intent on conquering one state, its ally may be seen as an obstacle to the attainment of our goal. Or the other state may be seen as a *threat* to continued achievement of an old, already realized goal; e.g., its military activity may be seen as a threat to our national security.

The first kind of incompatibility is prominent in theories that trace war to a scarcity of resources. Thus, as mentioned earlier, Lenin (1950) argued that war between the major European states became more likely as the supply of uncaptured potential colonies diminished. Rosecrance (1963, p. 234) argues, "The existence of large expanses still available [in the 18th century] for major actor appropriation helped to make extra-European expansion a safety value for European conflict."

The latter kind of incompatibility has received particular attention in recent years in discussions of the role of the *perception of threat* in the etiology of war. A synopsis of some of these discussions will now be presented.

Theories of Pre-Emptive and Preventive Attack

When the perception of threat leads directly to violence, we speak of *pre-emptive* or *preventive attack*. The purpose of such an attack is to deal the first blow before the other side has a chance to attack. The distinction between pre-emptive and preventive attack is relatively minor: a pre-emptive attack is based on the notion that the other side is about to begin a war, while a preventive attack is based on the assumption that war will begin at some time in the more distant future.

There is evidence that important wars of the past were initiated on a pre-emptive or preventive basis. For example, the German attack on Belgium and France in 1914, which came as a response to Russian mobilization, seems to have been based on the assumption that England, France, and Russia were about to initiate hostilities. Some writers have argued in recent years that a third world war, if it comes, is likely to have its beginning in a pre-emptive or preventive strike.

A number of recent books and articles (e.g., Kahn, 1960; Singer, 1962; Snyder, 1961; Schelling, 1960; and Schelling and Halperin, 1961 and Selection 3) have discussed the mechanisms underlying pre-emptive and preventive attack. The basic precondition for such an attack is the belief that the other party is going to start a war sometime in the future, i.e., that war is inevitable. Such a belief can lead to military action because it nullifies the most important restraints against the use of violence, fear of the cost of war and fear that a war will not be won.

When war is seen as inevitable, questions of feasibility and cost do not militate against the use of violence.

If, in addition, it appears that the cost or likelihood of winning a war can be materially improved by early launching of a surprise attack, such an attack becomes even more likely. The extent to which early, surprise attack is seen as advantageous depends in part on the vulnerability of one's own or the other party's military forces. The more vulnerable the other's forces, the more can be gained by surprise action. The more vulnerable one's own forces, the more can be lost by waiting for the other to attack. The perceived advantage of early military action also depends on the direction in which the distribution of military capability seems to be moving. The more rapidly the other party is gaining militarily, the greater is the apparent danger of delay and, therefore, the more attractive is preventive attack.

Preparation for War as an Antecedent to War

Perception of threats of a lesser magnitude than those just described often leads to defensive preparations, e.g., mobilizing troops, converting industries to the production of war materials, seeking allies, etc. Such preparations are usually heralded as efforts to avoid war by deterring the adversary and often have this effect (see Part IV). But, under some circumstances, military preparations in themselves can increase the probability of war.

There are various ways in which this can come about. The need to justify the expenditure on arms may through "psycho-logic" cause an increase in the perceived magnitude of threat to the point where a pre-emptive or preventive war is launched (Noel-Baker, 1958). Or preparation for war may elevate the social status of a military elite, which may then, according to Schumpeter's analysis, strive to preserve its status by stirring up foreign conflicts.

In addition, preparation for war usually changes goal priorities. Weakening the adversary becomes an important objective. Attempts must be made to block his procurement of goods, discredit him with potential allies, etc. Such action generally elicits resistance from the adversary, and the resulting conflict may eventually touch off a war that neither side really wants. The goal of weakening the adversary also usually stands in the way of developing functional and emotional ties with him that might otherwise act as restraints on violence (see Part V).

Finally, defensive preparations may be seen by citizens of the *other* state as evidence of threat, and so lead to all of the reactions just described on their side. If each side reacts to the other's military preparations with a new perception of threat and further military preparations, a vicious circle is born of the kind discussed in Part III.

Determinants of the Perception of Threat

The discussion in this section will be based on an analysis of the determinants of threat perception in international affairs published by one of the editors of this volume (Pruitt, 1965). This analysis rests on established psychological principles regarding perception, but supporting evidence from the realm of international affairs is admittedly scanty at present. The analysis postulates two sorts of antecedents for threat perception: evidence of threat and predispositions to perceive threat.

Evidence of Threat. For another state to be perceived as a threat, it must be seen as having both the *capability* and the *intent* to interfere with goal attainment (Singer, 1958 and Selection 2). Such perceptions are usually based, at least to some extent, on objective evidence.

Evidence of capability consists of such things as the possession of a large army. Such evidence is a two-edged sword. Not only does it contribute directly to threat perception, but it also is sometimes regarded as evidence of intent and thus contributes indirectly. The argument linking capability to intent usually goes as follows; "Why would they have all those arms if they didn't intend to attack us?" It seems to be very difficult for people to conclude that an adversary is arming out of fear of *their* armed forces.

Evidence of intent is also found in the circumstances surrounding the other state. During periods of controversy, the other state is usually assumed to have greater incentives for engaging in violence. The same is true during periods in which one's own or the other's military forces are highly vulnerable. For the reasons given above, such circumstances may be seen as raising the probability of pre-emptive or preventive war from the other side and hence as evidence of threat from the other side. Schelling (1960) has also suggested that knowledge that the other side expects an attack from us may be interpreted as evidence that the other side is likely to launch a pre-emptive or preventive attack.

Actions and statements from other states are also, of course, taken as evidence of intent. A number of writers (e.g., Phelps, 1963; Schelling and Halperin, 1961 and Selection 3; and Singer, 1962) have been concerned about the danger of *accidental war* based on mistaken intelligence about another state's actions or misinterpretation of such actions. Incidents that might falsely lead to the conclusion that the other side is about to launch (or is in the process of launching) an attack include such things as misinterpretation of objects on a radar screen, unauthorized or unintended launching of rockets from the other side, and actions of third parties aimed at throwing the blame on the other side (*catalytic war*).

Predispositions to Perceive Threat. Threat perception is often grounded in unambiguous and unassailable evidence; e.g., an army is approaching the border. But there are also many cases in which the evidence is not so clear-cut and in which the perception of threat is an inference, with all of the usual fallibility of inferences. Whether ambiguous evidence will lead to threat perception is determined by the *predispositions* of the perceiver. Predispositions to perceive threat take many forms. Some are general, embracing all sources and all types of threat; others are specific to one kind of threat, e.g., military attack; still others are specific to one source of threat, e.g., a certain foreign country.

Gladstone (1955) has shown through empirical research that some people have a general tendency to perceive threat, which leads them to be overly suspicious of other people and other states. Gladstone and Taylor (1958) suggest that such people may be making greater than average use of the defense mechanism of projection to protect themselves from recognizing their own hostile impulses. It is conceivable that some cultures may make greater use of projection than others and hence be more predisposed to the perception of threat.

The predisposition to perceive a certain kind of threat is probably enhanced by past experience with this kind of threat; e.g., people who have lived through bombing tend to overreact to minimal evidence that more bombs are coming. In addition, preparation for certain kinds of threat may, through a process of psychological justification, produce a predisposition to perceive such threats (Lerner, 1965; de Rivera, 1968). Hence, one might speculate that people or societies which engage in a great deal of military contingency planning or build elaborate military defenses tend to be especially alert to evidence of military threat. People who have a vested interest in institutions for coping with threats, e.g., Shumpeter's military elites, may be especially likely to find evidence of the existence of such threats.

The concept *distrust* is used when a predisposition is specific to a certain source of threat, e.g., a certain foreign country. Distrust of another state is usually based on unfavorable past experience with that state. The more acute and recent this experience, the greater the distrust is likely to be. This means that conflict with another state is a common source of distrust and, hence, of renewed conflict. By heightening distrust, conflict can engender conflict.

The notion that conflict can engender conflict is implicit in a concern that has frequently been voiced (e.g., Phelps, 1963, and Russett, 1962) that a political or conventional military crisis involving the great powers will heighten distrust to the point at which one side interprets minimal evidence as indicating that the other is about to launch a nuclear attack. A pre-emptive or preventive attack might result from such a situation.

Favorable experiences with another state often create trust, but this is not always the case. Conciliatory behavior by a distrusted adversary is sometimes, instead, treated as a sign of weakness. Holsti (1962) has demonstrated the operation of such logic in the results of a content analysis of six years of speeches by John Foster Dulles, former United States Secretary of State.

Trust is most likely to develop out of circumstances that cause states to become positively oriented toward each other's welfare (M. Deutsch, 1962), i.e., out of mutual dependence that motivates states to seek one another's good will (see Part V). Such interdependence may be based upon a trade agreement, a joint development plan, or a common enemy.

Ambiguity of Evidence. Two propositions can be stated about the relationships between predispositions and threat perception (Pruitt, 1965): (a) The stronger the predisposition to perceive threat, the more likely it is that threat will be perceived, and (b) the more *ambiguous* the evidence concerning another state's capabilities or intentions, the more impact will predispositions have on the perception of threat from that state. What determines the ambiguity of such evidence?

Some *kinds of evidence* are inherently more ambiguous than others. For example, as evidence of intent, military capability is often quite ambiguous, since a state may be arming for a variety of reasons.

A number of *conditions* increase the ambiguity of actions and statements and thereby increase the likelihood that threat will be falsely perceived. Ambiguity is greater, (a) the smaller the number of highly placed people who are well acquainted with the state being observed, (b) the poorer the capacity to empathize with citizens of the state being observed, and (c) the fewer and less adequate channels of communication that exist with members of the other state (Frank, 1968). Installation of the "hot line" between Washington and Moscow in 1962 is an example of an attempt to increase the number of channels of communication through which a seemingly threatening event (e.g., the accidental launching of a rocket) can be explained and hopefully made less ambiguous and, therefore, less liable to be misinterpreted under the pressure of cold-war mistrust.

Hostility Toward Other States

Traditional Theories of War as the Resultant of Hostility

In the 1930's and early 1940's, a group of behavioral scientists under the spell of psychoanalytic theory (Durbin and Bowlby, 1939; Tolman, 1942; Kluckhohn, 1944; May, 1943) began writing about the causes of war. Their analysis was based on an analogy to interpersonal violence, which is often an expression of hostile emotions even when it can be rationalized as goal-seeking behavior. On the basis of this analogy, they reasoned that international violence must have expressive roots, i.e., must arise from hostility toward other states.[1] They condemned as naive those theorists who traced war to rational (goal-oriented) considerations.[2]

These writers were never particularly explicit about whose emotions are responsible for war or how emotions become transformed into the decision to employ violence. But one gets the impression that they viewed hostility as a mass phenomenon permeating most levels of society and forcing national policy makers to launch an attack, willing or not.

The traditional psychoanalytic theory of scapegoating was employed by these theorists to explain the development of hostility toward other states. According to this theory, hostility develops whenever a person is frustrated, i.e., prevented from attaining his goals (Dollard et al., 1939). Ordinarily, hostility is expressed toward the agent of frustration. But, if this agent is protected by social norms, hostility

[1]The term actually used by these theorists was "aggressive impulses," but it seems to have the same meaning as "hostility" or "hostile emotions" (Berkowitz, 1962).

[2]Excerpts from these and related writers can be found in Bramson and Goethals (1964).

will be *displaced* (redirected) onto other, safer objects, the scapegoats. Thus, a man who is denied a pay raise by his employer may come home and yell at his wife. This theory of scapegoating has received considerable support in laboratory and field research on interpersonal relations (Berkowitz, 1962).

The extension of this theory to international relations is quite straightforward. Instead of being displaced onto another person, hostility may sometimes be displaced onto another state. Thus, hostility originating in frustrations experienced by the individual becomes translated into antagonism toward another state, which can contribute to a decision to employ violence against that state.

In some versions of this theory (e.g., Durbin and Bowlby, 1939), war seems nearly inescapable since it is attributed to the normal and presumably inescapable frustrations of everyday life. Other versions offer greater hope by tracing war to especially frustrating periods in the life of society as a whole, when "social and economic relations of life have been disrupted so that people feel bewildered, confused, uncertain, and insecure" (Duvall, 1947). Such frustrations can presumably be avoided if man can learn how to control the business cycle or solve other problems that produce mass frustration.

Criticism of "Hostility" Theories. A certain amount of evidence can be found to support the assumption that mass hostility produces war. In a number of historical cases, popular hostility toward another state has risen abruptly just prior to an attack on that state, a phenomenon that has sometimes been called *war fever.* However, a number of writers (e.g., Abel, 1941, and Bernard, 1958) have suggested that this evidence is misleading. On the basis of an empirical study of twenty-five past wars, the details of which are unfortunately not reported, Abel concluded that the decision to go to war is typically made by governmental elites well in advance of the outbreak of war and war fever. Abel argues that war fever results from propaganda produced by governmental elites to prepare their people for war and is not causally antecedent to war. The elites, not the masses, carry their states into war.

Even if we reject the role of *mass* hostility, it is still possible to assert with the psychologists that hostility *among elite decision makers* predisposes them to involve their nation in war. However, this position has also been attacked by authors who view war as rational behavior. On the basis of his twenty-five cases, Abel concludes that the decision to fight is always based on a careful weighing of probabilities and anticipation of consequences. "In no case," he writes (p. 855), "is the decision precipitated by emotional tensions, sentimentality . . . or other irrational motivations." Levi (1960) adds to this criticism the observation (for what it is worth) that Anthony Eden's memoirs reveal that the British campaign against Egypt in the Suez crisis was "undertaken on the basis of a fairly unemotional conclusion that British interests in the Suez Canal made it worthwhile" (p. 418).

A Modern Version of the Expressive Theory of War

One must be sympathetic with the critics just cited when they attack the traditional assumption that hostility is the *only* cause of war. To repeat a point made in the introduction to Part I, one-factor theories are inherently mistaken. Furthermore, these critics are undoubtedly on sound ground in asserting that war seldom erupts out of mass anger the way a fistfight erupts from a fit of temper and that mass anger is *often* a response to governmental manipulations. But to deny altogether the role of mass and elite hostility in the genesis of war seems to throw out the baby with the bath. What is needed instead is a more subtle version of the relationship between hostility and war and the source of hostility toward other states. Such a version has been developing in the literature of recent years. Empirical evidence for it is very insufficient, but it is in line with modern psychological theory.

Hostility and War. Hostility presumably works more subtly in the case of international conflict than in the case, say, of a fistfight between two gangs of boys. Rather than erupting in an angry display, hostility toward another state gently prods a decision maker toward a choice of harsher tactics and sharper words than he would otherwise use in dealing with that state. Hostility may close off certain alternatives that involve contributing to the other state's welfare. Hostility may reduce the capacity to empathize with the other state and the amount of communication with that state (Newcomb, 1947), both of which increase the ambiguity of the evidence concerning the other state and, therefore, the likelihood of perceiving it as a threat. Hostility may also prevent the development of an alliance with another state that would otherwise deter a third party from aggressive military action (see Part IV on military restraints.) These mechanisms can contribute to the likelihood of an eventual outbreak of violence as well as to the likelihood that a war will develop at any given time.[3]

The question of mass versus elite participation in national policy making is no longer posed as an "either–or." Both masses and elites are assumed to play a role, and the relevant question concerns the determinants of their relative weight. K. W. Deutsch (1957 and Selection 4) has suggested that their relative weight may differ from era to era. At times, public opinion may be quite pliable, permitting national leaders to encourage mass hostility toward another state "in order to marshal public support for [an] effective but costly foreign policy" (p. 201). However, once the enemy has been identified in the public thinking, public opinion sometimes becomes so inflexibly hostile that the government is forced to adopt harsher tactics toward the other state than are warranted by the situation.[4] The psychology of enemy identification has also been discussed by Gladstone (1959).

The role of hostility in elite decision making is easier to accept if it is realized that emotion and rational deliberation can operate side by side. A man who is influenced by emotion need not be livid and raging; he may seem cool and collected. Most of his behavior may be guided by rational deliberation while, at the same time, as was described above, hostility may be gently nudging him toward

---

[3]A concept closely related to hostility as used here is White's "black and white image." (White, 1965, 1968). Many of the points made in this paragraph are also made by White.

[4]Public opinion is by no means always of an emotional nature, but only the emotional elements are discussed in this section.

the adoption of harsher, less compromising tactics than he would otherwise adopt. He may rationalize such tactics by invoking quite reasonable goals such as "defending the national honor" or "punishing aggression." Such a subtle input of emotion, if continued over a period of time, can have an important impact on the course of events, especially if, as is likely to happen, it is magnified by the other side's reactions and the first side's counterreactions to those reactions.

Furthermore, despite what the critics have written, historical examples can be found in which it is reasonable to believe that emotion played a role in the decision to go to war. For example, in examining the private notes made by the German Kaiser in 1914 at the point of his decision to go to war, North and his collaborators (North et al., 1963, p.174) found the following highly emotional statement:

> The net has been suddenly thrown over our head and England sneeringly reaps the brilliant success of her persistently prosecuted purely anti-German world policy, against which we have proved ourselves helpless, while she twists the noose of our political and economic destruction out of our fidelity to Austria, as we squirm isolated in the net.

Sources of Hostility Toward Another State. The traditional displacement theory of the sources of international hostility is probably still worthy of some attention, but it needs updating. This theory has always been weak on the issue of why certain states are chosen as targets for displacing hostility and others are not. For example, if we accept the argument that German aggression in the 1930's arose in part from frustrations experienced by the average German as a result of the depression, we must still explain why this aggression was channeled toward England and France rather than Italy and Spain.

Recent laboratory research has provided some general information on the choice of target in interpersonal relations that is probably applicable to the special case of attitudes toward states. Berkowitz (1962) has shown that people tend to choose as the object on which to displace new hostility an individual or group toward which some hostility is already felt. Hence traditions of antagonism or a history of past conflict with another state probably increase the likelihood that it will become the target of displacement.

In addition, Duvall (1947) has suggested that the choice of a scapegoat can be directed by statements from national leaders, just as Hitler was able to channel German hostilities onto the Jews.

Although, as was just said, the displacement mechanism may be worthy of some attention, it can certainly not be considered the most important source of hostility toward another state. Considerably more important is perceived provocation from the other state, i.e., frustration *at the hands of that state* and the perception of that state as a threat.

An important question arises from this formulation: What determines the amount of hostility generated by a given level of perceived provocation? We can certainly assume that hostility is a positive function of the level of frustration or threat perceived. But what determines the steepness of this function? In some cases, the reaction to a given level of provocation is mild; in other cases, acute.

Some speculation exists on this issue, and also some empirical evidence, arising out of studies of personality correlates of individual differences in the way people feel their states should react to provocation from abroad. Such evidence is relevant to the issue of why states go to war to the extent that (a) people with certain personality structures tend to inhabit powerful positions in society or (b) states differ in the dominant personality makeup of their citizenry.

A number of writers, including Lerche (1956), have stressed the importance of *nationalism* as a determinant of the reaction to perceived provocation from other states. Nationalism can be defined as the love of one's state or "a focussing of attention, drive and positive emotion on the symbols of the nation" (Stagner, 1946, p. 404). The stronger this sentiment, the more hostility will be generated by experiences of frustration or threat from another state. Empirical evidence for this assertion has been found by Christiansen (1959) in a study of the relationship between personality and attitude toward foreign affairs in Norway. It follows that citizens of the newer states, where nationalism is often stronger, should react more violently to provocation from abroad.

Prior sentiment toward the other state may also determine the amount of hostility resulting from a given level of perceived provocation. Coleman (1957) has suggested that old hostility remaining from earlier incidents tends to interact with new hostility and cause an overreaction to what may sometimes seem a trivial provocation. Conversely, it is probable that frustration or threat from a state toward whom there are strong positive feelings will produce less hostility than would otherwise be expected. The hypotheses just stated are not directly supported by empirical evidence but are consonant with modern psychological theory.

To come back to the displacement theory of hostility toward other states, it seems reasonable to suppose that the reaction to perceived provocation is a function of the general level of frustration experienced by an individual. Provocative behavior identifies the other state as an appropriate target for displacement of hostility. The greater an individual's general level of frustration, the greater will be his potential for displacement once a target is found. Evidence supporting this supposition has also been developed by Christiansen (1959 and 1965). Christiansen found a correlation in Norwegian subjects between the extent to which an individual favors harsh reactions to provocation from other states and the extent to which he is in conflict about basic psychosexual impulses, an index of underlying frustration. It is interesting to note that the strength of this correlation was a function of nationalism. Hence, the more nationalistic an individual, the more likely he is to displace his anger onto other states when they have created a provocation.

These findings suggest that, in times of national crisis when many citizens are experiencing acute frustration, a state is likely to overreact to provocation from abroad and that this overreaction is particularly likely to occur if the citizens of the state are strongly nationalistic. However, as yet, no direct evidence has been developed concerning this proposition.

Conclusions

A number of motivational and perceptual factors (various goals, the perception of threat, and hostility) have been cited in this chapter, each of which conceivably plays a part in moving states toward war. Various propositions have also been stated about the antecedents of these motivational factors—the conditions under which they develop. Some of these propositions come from a study of war itself, others from parallels with well-documented research on human behavior in other situations.

Although provocative and hopefully important, the contents of this chapter fall considerably short of the ideal theory described in the previous chapter. Three deficiencies can be cited in the field of knowledge reflected in this chapter. First, the basic presentation of motivational factors lacks coherence. A list of factors that can contribute to the evolution of war is not a theory until something is said about how these factors interrelate and about the conditions that govern the relative importance of each factor as a cause of war. This deficiency will be partially remedied in the introduction to Part III, where a dynamic picture will be presented of the course of events leading toward war. Second, our understanding of the antecedents of these motivational factors is clearly rudimentary; much theoretical elaboration is obviously needed here. Third, and most important because it is a key to the other two deficiencies, it is clear that very little *empirical research* has been done on the motives underlying war. Most of the research cited in this chapter is based on speculation rather than empirical methodology. Yet empirical investigations are by no means out of the question in this area. Many of the propositions stated above could serve as the initial basis for an empirical study.

As an example, take Burton's (1962) proposition that blocking limited challenges from a state with newly developed military capabilities typically causes it to embrace less-limited power goals, which causes it to become more aggressive in the long run than it would otherwise be. If this proposition were explored with historical data, the investigator might construct a population of historical states whose economic and military capabilities, at one time or another, increased rapidly. An analysis of public pronouncements in that state and diplomatic notes from that state might then be made to assess changes in international goals, and an index might be made of the rapidity and extent to which these goals were satisfied by other states. Those states whose new goals were satisfied might then be compared with those whose new goals were frustrated. Comparisons could be made on such variables as the extent to which more general power needs emerge and such related phenomena as increased militancy and nationalism (as measured by content analysis of the mass media), diplomatic intractability (from analysis of diplomatic records), and military preparation (from analysis of budgetary records). Alternatively, a simulation method might be used in which systematic variations were made in economic and military capability and the willingness of other states to make concessions.[5] In both kinds of studies, as much interest would be centered on the cases in which the hypothesized relationship failed to develop as on the cases in which it developed, in an effort to determine the conditions under which the hypothesis is true and those under which it is false.

---

[5]The studies briefly sketched here are illustrative of the kind of research that might be done rather than definitive of what should be done to test this hypothesis. Other approaches to measuring the variables or to the whole design might well prove more productive.

References

Abel, T., "The element of decision in the pattern of war," *American Sociological Review*, **6**(6), 853–859, 1941.

Aron, R., *The Century of Total War*. Boston: Beacon Press, 1954.

Berkowitz, L., *Aggression: A Social Psychological Analysis*. New York: McGraw-Hill Book Company, 1962.

Bernard, J., "The sociological study of conflict," *in* UNESCO, *The Nature of Conflict*. Paris: UNESCO, 1958.

Bramson, L., and G. W. Goethals, eds., *War: Studies from Psychology, Sociology and Anthropology*. New York: Basic Books, Inc., 1964.

Burton, J. W., *Peace Theory*. New York: Alfred A. Knopf, Inc., 1962.

Christiansen, B., *Attitudes towards Foreign Affairs as a Function of Personality*. Oslo: Oslo University Press, 1959.

Christiansen, B., "Attitudes towards foreign affairs as a function of personality," *in* H. Proshansky and B. Seidenberg, eds., *Basic Studies in Social Psychology*. New York: Holt, Rinehart and Winston, Inc., 1965.

Coleman, J. S., *Community Conflict*. New York: The Free Press, 1957.

de Rivera, J. H., *The Psychological Dimension of Foreign Policy*. Columbus, Ohio: Charles E. Merrill Publishing Co., 1968.

Deutsch, K. W., "Mass communications and the loss of freedom in national decision-making: a possible research approach to interstate conflict," *Journal of Conflict Resolution*, **1**(2), 200–211, 1957.

Deutsch, M., "Psychological alternatives to war," *Journal of Social Issues*, **18**(2), 97–119, 1962.

Dollard, J., L. Doob, N. E. Miller, O. H. Mowrer, and R. R. Sears, *Frustration and Aggression*. New Haven, Conn.: Yale University Press, 1939.

Dunn, F. S., *Peaceful Change*. New York: Council on Foreign Relations, 1937.

Durbin, E. F. M., and J. Bowlby, *Personal Aggressiveness and War*. New York: Columbia University Press, 1939.

Duvall, S. M., *War and Human Nature*. Public Affairs Pamphlet 125, 1947.

Engelbrecht, H. C., and F. C. Hanighen, *Merchants of Death*. New York: Dodd, Mead and Co., 1934.

Frank, J. D., *Sanity and Survival: Psychological Aspects of War and Peace*. New York: Vintage Books, 1968.

Gladstone, A. I., "The possibility of predicting reactions to international events," *Journal of Social Issues*, **11**(1), 21–28, 1955.

Gladstone, A. I., "The concept of the enemy," *Journal of Conflict Resolution*, **3**(2), 132–137, 1959.

Gladstone, A. I., and M. A. Taylor, "Threat-related attitudes as reactions to communications about international events," *Journal of Conflict Resolution*, **2**(1), 17–28, 1958.

Hobson, J. A., *Imperialism: A Study* (rev. ed.). London: George Allen and Unwin, 1938.

Holsti, O. R., "The belief system and national images: a case study," *Journal of Conflict Resolution*, **6**(3), 244–252, 1962.

Kahn, H., *On Thermonuclear War*. Princeton, N. J.: Princeton University Press, 1960.

Kennan, G. F., "The Sources of Soviet Conduct," *Foreign Affairs*, **25**(4), 566–582, 1947.

Kluckhohn, C., "Anthropological research and world peace," *in* L. Bryson, L. Finkelstein, and R. M. MacIver, eds., *Approaches to World Peace: A Symposium*, Conference on Science, Philosophy and Religion, New York, 1944.

Knorr, K., "Theories of imperialism," *World Politics*, **4**(3), 402–421, 1952.

Lenin, V. I., *Imperialism: The Highest Form of Capitalism*. Moscow: Foreign Languages Publishing House, 1950.

Lerche, C. O., *Principles of International Politics*. New York: Oxford University Press, Inc., 1956.

Lerner, M., "The effect of preparatory action on beliefs concerning nuclear war," *Journal of Social Psychology*, **65**(2), 225–231, 1965.

Levi, W., "On the causes of war and the conditions of peace." *Journal of Conflict Resolution*, **4**(4), 411–420, 1960.

Mack, R. W., and R. C. Snyder, "An analysis of social conflict—toward an overview and synthesis," *Journal of Conflict Resolution*, **1**(2), 212–248, 1957.

May, Mark A., *A Social Psychology of War and Peace*. New Haven, Conn.: Yale University Press, 1943.

Morgenthau, H. J., *Politics among Nations*. New York: Alfred A. Knopf, Inc., 1960.

Newcomb, T. M., "Autistic hostility and social reality," *Human Relations*, **1**(1), 3–20, 1947.

Noel-Baker, P., *The Arms Race*. London: John Calder Publishers, Ltd., 1958.

North, R. C., O. R. Hosti, M. G. Zaninovich, and D. A. Zinnes, *Content Analysis*. Evanston, Ill.: Northwestern University Press, 1963.

Organski, A. F. K., *World Politics*. New York: Alfred A. Knopf, Inc., 1958.

Phelps, J., *Military Stability and Arms Control: A Critical Survey*. China Lake, Calif.: U.S. Naval Ordnance Test Station, 1963.

Pruitt, D. G., "Definition of the situation as a determinant of international action," *in* H. C. Kelman, ed., *International Behavior*. New York: Holt, Rinehart and Winston, Inc., 1965.

Rapoport, A., "Perceiving the cold war," *in* R. Fisher, ed., *International Conflict and Behavioral Science*. New York: Basic Books, Inc., 1964.

Rosecrance, R. N., *Action and Reaction in World Politics*. Boston: Little, Brown and Co., 1963.

Russett, B. M., "Cause, surprise, and no escape," *The Journal of Politics*, **24**(1), 3–22, 1962.

Schelling, T. C., "Arms control, proposal for a special surveillance force," *World Politics*, **13**(1), 1–18, 1960.

Schelling, T. C., and M. H. Halperin, *Strategy and Arms Control*. New York: Twentieth Century Fund, 1961.

Schumpeter, J., *The Sociology of Imperialism*. New York: Meridian Books, 1955.

Singer, J. D., "Threat perception and the armament-tension dilemma," *Journal of Conflict Resolution*, **2**(1), 90–105, 1958.

Singer, J. D., *Deterrence, Arms Control and Disarmament: Toward a Synthesis in National Security Policy*. Columbus, Ohio: Ohio State University Press, 1962.

Snyder, G. H., *Deterrence and Defense. Toward a Theory of National Security*. Princeton, N.J.: Princeton University Press, 1961.

Stagner, R., "Nationalism," *in* P. L. Harriman, ed., *The Encyclopedia of Psychology*. New York: Philosophical Library, 1946.

Strachey, J., *The End of Empire*. New York: Random House, 1960.

Tolman, E. C., *Drives toward War*. New York: D. Appleton-Century Co., Inc., 1942.

Van Dyke, V., *International Politics*. New York: Appleton-Century-Crofts, Inc., 1957.

Waltz, K. N., *Man, the State and War*. New York: Columbia University Press, 1959.

White, R. K., "Images in the context of international conflict: Soviet perceptions of the U.S. and the U.S.S.R.," *in* H. C. Kelman, ed., *International Behavior*. New York: Holt, Rinehart and Winston, Inc., 1965.

White, R. K., *Nobody Wanted War: Misperception in Vietnam and Other Wars*. Garden City, N. Y.: Doubleday and Co., Inc., 1968.

Winslow, E. M., *The Pattern of Imperialism*. New York: Columbia University Press, 1948.

1

WERNER LEVI

War and the Quest for National Power

A summary of the traditional theoretical position among political scientists that war has its origin in the quest for national power, which is a major occupation of states. This quest is necessitated by the absence, in the international system, of a supreme coercive agency which can guarantee protection to each state.

One of man's fundamental problems is to live in peace with his fellow men. He cannot live alone. Yet, in coexistence with others, conflicts inevitably arise. It is therefore characteristic of individuals, alone or organized in groups, to seek power for the satisfaction of their interests. Lest this lead to an eternal state of war, men organize themselves to reap the greatest benefit from cooperation and to reduce as much as possible conflict and strife. In particular, it is the minimum goal of social organization that the satisfaction of vital interests—usually bodily integrity and survival—should not lead to violent conflict but should, rather, be assured by peaceful methods or, failing these, by the application of supreme coercive power which is socially organized and usually vested in a central authority.

The social organization of the state[1] is intended to provide adequate means for peaceful adjustment of conflicts and to obviate the need for individual violence. Even when the means prove inadequate, the state simply does not permit violence—except as a matter of self-defense. The individual's personal accumulation of power is limited to most kinds of power short of physical force. As a compensation the state guarantees, as a minimum, the physical integrity and survival of the contestants in a conflict. This arrangement rests

An excerpt from "On the causes of war and the conditions of peace," *Journal of Conflict Resolution*, **4,** 411–420, 1960. Reprinted by permission of the author and that journal. The author is Professor of Political Science at the University of Hawaii.

[1]It should be understood throughout this article that "state" is used as a shorthand expression. It does not refer to any organism but rather, depending upon the context in which the word is used, to those making decisions on behalf of the people, those influencing these decisions, or all the citizens.

upon a habitual way of life and mental attitudes of the citizens indicating the existence of a community. The more complete the integration of the members into the community, the more successful.

In the international society, that loose association of states, the situation is basically different. Relations between states are ordered by routine practices and a vast network of international organizations promoting and regularizing the satisfaction of national interests. Much expedient cooperation exists between states, with well-established rules, regulations, and institutions. Innumerable conflicts of interest are resolved by accommodation and adjustment, either mutual or one-sided, depending upon the power relationship of the states involved. But this possibility is severely restricted because the society of states lacks an organized authority endowed with the legitimate supreme coercive power to guarantee the integrity and survival of each state, which is in turn merely an indication of the absence of any sense of solidarity among the peoples of the world. Every state is the guardian and guarantor of all its own interests. It must be ready to defend them at all times and for this purpose must possess power. In contrast to intrastate conditions, the possession of power cannot be limited to the non-physical kind because national interests may be threatened which a state wishes to defend by force. The time when such a vital threat may arrive is unpredictable, and the nature of the threat is unknown. Therefore, the quest for power becomes inevitably permanent, though not for this reason all-consuming. It is conditioned by its relation to the goals the state pursues, by its relation to the power of other states, by the capabilities of the state, by the intensity of the state's will to survive integer, and by the results of the interrelations of these factors.

The quest for power becomes a major occupation of the state and a standard by which most aspects of its life and activities are measured, no matter how relative the magnitude of the desired power may be. It can be granted that, as states usually assert for the diplomatic record, they do not seek power for its own sake; they do so merely as a means to the end of satisfying their needs. For the nature of power, they can argue with cogency up to a point, like that of money, allows it to be accumulated and stored, to be expended for a great variety of unforeseeable ends at a time of need (7, p. 7). But whatever the end of the search for power and whatever its qualifications and limitations, the possibility remains that it can itself lead to violent conflict. States may become rivals in vying for elements of power or in one attempting to become more powerful than the other. The paradox here is that the search for power, even if only to have it available for a future conflict of interests, may itself become a source of violent conflict. This is an unending process because power as such has become a vital interest to some states. The search for it becomes necessary to guard against the consequences of this search.[2] Thus, until another way is found to guarantee satisfaction of a state's interests, especially those it considers vital (or until states disappear), the possibility of violent conflict is a built-in feature of the nation-state

[2]The general ideas outlined here in regard to the role of power in international relations are old, although judging by recent debates raging around this subject, one may not think so. That states seek power to satisfy their interests was not discovered in the United States in the middle of the twentieth century. It was discussed in the pre-Christian era by such men as Kautilya in India and Mo Ti in China.

system in the modern world (5, 6).

This fact can easily enough explain the mutual suspicion among states and their potential hostility. Here is genuine conflict. No amount of good will among nations, understanding among peoples, elimination of stereotypes, or clarification of semantic difficulties can obliterate it. Better knowledge of each other among peoples may gradually lead to greater integration on the way to a community and thereby reduce the chances of violence as a solution of conflict; but it cannot abolish conflict (1). It is therefore quite erroneous to assume, as has often been done, that states have violent conflicts because their citizens are aggressive, militaristic, and nationalistic. It is often the other way around: citizens assume these characteristics or are being prepared for warfare because there are real conflicts between states which may have to be solved with violence. The vicious circle is that a potential threat to their state makes citizens bellicose, and their bellicosity makes them appear as a threat to other states. Under the prevailing system the citizen must live in anticipation of violence and take the necessary precautions, including readiness for war. Polls in many European and some American states showed that anywhere from one-third to three-quarters of the people consulted did not think it was possible to live in peace (2, pp. 125–216, question 3*a*).

This expectation of war does not, however, have to lead to war in accord with the assertion that "expectations determine behavior" (3, p. 15). For the expectation may produce behavior which either leads to its fulfilment or to its frustration. History is full of proof that governments have genuinely tried to avoid wars, knowing their potential existence. One of the reasons why they have sometimes failed is that they did not or could not choose the right means to avoid it. In a nation-state system, with the close identification of the citizen with his state, the anticipation of violence regularly leads the citizen to turn to his own community for increased security rather than to attempt integration with the threatening state for the sake of reducing the chance of violence (14, p. 19).

There are relations between states to which this general description does not apply. Not all states are hostile to each other, or, at any rate, not all consider every other state a potential threat to vital interests. Albania and Honduras are not anticipating violent conflict, nor are Norway and Great Britain, nor Canada and the United States. Such states either are not rivals for interest or power; or there is enough sentiment of community between them to obviate violence; or they repress violence for the sake of unity against a common enemy. They may still have conflicts of interest, but for a variety of reasons, including possibly the technical inability to be violent with each other or much simultaneous cooperation, they do not consider the use of violence. Such reasons may change, of course, or new causes may produce violence. Colombia was engaged in violent conflict with North Korea under United Nations action in the name of collective security. There was no reason for this in the direct relations between the two states, but for reasons sufficient to the Colombian government the violent conflict between the two states existed nevertheless, and very likely North Korea as such had very little to do with these reasons. As peace becomes increasingly indivisible and as technical developments enable—in the future—even small states to possess weapons which can reach any point on the globe and wipe out any state in the world, the chances for violent conflict between two states hitherto geographically, politically, and in every other way remote from each other, increase; just as—a compensating virtue—the chances for their integration and growth into a community also become greater. With such a community come the patterns of behavior facilitating peaceful solution of conflict and making the application of coercive power by the supreme authority only one of the means of conflict solution and an increasingly rare one. . . .

References

1. Bernard, Jessie, "The Sociological Study of Conflict." In International Sociological Association, *The Nature of Conflict.* Paris: UNESCO, 1957, 33–117.
2. Buchanan, William, and Cantril, Hadley, *How Nations See Each Other: A Study in Public Opinion.* Urbana: University of Illinois Press, 1950.
3. Cantril, Hadley (ed.), *Tensions that Cause Wars.* Urbana: University of Illinois Press, 1950.
4. Haas, Ernst B., and Whiting, Allen S., Jr., *Dynamics of International Relations.* New York: McGraw-Hill Book Co., 1956.
5. International Sociological Association, *The Nature of Conflict.* Paris: UNESCO, 1957.
6. Mack, Raymond W., and Snyder, Richard C., "The Analysis of Social Conflict—Toward an Overview and Synthesis," *Journal of Conflict Resolution,* 1 (1957), 212–248.
7. Nitze, Paul M., "Necessary and Sufficient Elements of a General Theory of International Relations." In William T. R. Fox, *Theoretical Aspects of International Relations.* Notre Dame, Indiana: University of Notre Dame, 1959.

2

J. DAVID SINGER

Threat Perception and National Decision Makers

A brief theory of the sources of the perception that another state is a threat to national security. Such perceptions are at the root of arms races and contribute to the likelihood of war (as will be argued in the third selection).

Prior to an examination of the threat-perception concept, the writer feels obligated to articulate such of his assumptions on the nature of international politics as might influence his subsequent treatment of the central problem in this paper. And, while none of these assumptions will be likely to win universal indorsement, it is beyond the scope of this paper to enumerate all the arguments and adduce all the evidence upon which they rest.

First, it is posited that we are operating today in a rather well-defined or "tight" bi-polar system, with the most crucial policy decisions being taken in Washington and Moscow.[1] Initiation, modification, encouragement, or obstruction may come from either set of allies, from the neutrals, or even from that sole and timid guardian of the *inter*national interest, the United Nations Secretariat; but, in the final analysis, it will be up to the Soviet Union and the United States either to perpetuate the present unstable equilibrium or to attempt to break out of it by a variety of means.

Second, it is assumed that the decision-making process in each of these powers is essentially a collective one. This is not to deny that the President or the First Secretary will in effect have the final word in their respective

An excerpt from "Threat perception and the armament-tension dilemma," *Journal of Conflict Resolution*, **2**, 90–105, 1958. Reprinted by permission of the author and that journal. The author is Professor of Political Science and Research Political Scientist (in the Mental Health Research Institute) at the University of Michigan.

[1]The writer would question Kaplan's (1957) classification of today's system as "loose bipolar" as overemphasizing the influence of the "universal actor" (UN), the "non-bloc actors" (neutrals), and the other bloc actors (Soviet and Western allies). Significantly, the "tight bipolar" model is characterized as having "a high degree of dysfunctional tension," and one which "will not be a highly stable or well integrated system."

governments or to suggest that there has not been a significant erosion of the collective leadership principle in the Kremlin in recent months. But it does posit the existence of a large and complex bureaucracy in each regime, responsible for collecting, interpreting, evaluating, and transmitting foreign-policy intelligence along the channels to the hierarchical apex. The implication here is that policy decisions are likely to be the result of consultation and compromise within each system rather than the whim or caprice of a single mind.[2]

The third, and perhaps most crucial, assumption is that the decision-makers on both sides, despite the welter of conflicting pressures, demands, and interests, are more concerned with the preservation (and extension) of national power than with the fulfilment of abstract political dogmas. It is contended, therefore, that the final determinant is, and will continue to be for some time, the elite's conception of national security,[3] not the ideological utterances of Marx or Locke, Lenin or Jefferson, Manuilski or Wilson. The formulation and articulation of an ideological position have their very real applications and, as such, may condition or modify but will not *determine* Soviet or American foreign policy; national security is the categorical imperative.[4]

On the basis of these assumptions, attention may now be directed toward the central question confronting those who intend either to survive within or to escape from the armaments-tension dilemma. This question might well be examined by reference to what Thomas and Znaniecki have called the "definition of the situation" (1947); this definition, as they see it, is the resultant of two sets of factors. First, there are the "objective conditions under which the individual or group has to act"; second, there are the "pre-existing attitudes" which operate to select, combine, and interpret the objective conditions, thus producing a somewhat subjective definition of the situation. Of such pre-existing attitudes, none is more central to world politics than that of ethnocentrism, a tendency which leads the citizen to "judge external phenomena in terms of his membership in a particular national group. The same item of behavior, objectively considered, has an entirely different meaning, depending on whether it is one's own or another nation which is responsible for it" (Klineberg, 1954, p. 556). From this powerful predisposition to suspect and distrust the people and governments of all other nation-states, a combination of recent events, historical memory, and identifiable sociocultural differences provides the vehicle by which thie vague out-group suspicion may be readily converted into concrete hostility toward a specific foreign power.

Now it may be argued that this tendency, while applicable to the masses, has little relevance to either the policy-making elite or the informed, attentive public. Admittedly, the phenomenon

---

[2]For a suggestive, but abstract, treatment of the foreign-policy decision-making process, see Snyder, Bruck, and Sapin (1954). Probably the most comprehensive discussion of the United States process is found in Snyder and Furniss (1954). Also valuable is Macmahon (1953). For the Soviet process, see Fainsod (1954) and Kulski (1954).

[3]This phrasing is used to distinguish the writer from those who might posit the existence of some *objectively* definable national interest.

[4]This would concur with the conclusion of most students of Soviet foreign policy (Fainsod, 1954; Kulski, 1954; Moore, 1950); but for the opposing emphasis see Huszar (1955) and Leites (1956).

may be less apparent among the educated and urbane career officers of a foreign ministry, but the wielders of ultimate political power are seldom of that background and frequently exhibit a xenophobia even more virulent than that of their followers. In addition and despite the fact that role does tend to mediate attitude and personality, the policy-maker is likely to manifest this hostility in its extreme form just because of the role which he *is* playing; he who is responsible for the protection of the nation from outside enemies is not likely to regard such potential sources of attack with either apathy or detachment. To the contrary, Soviet and American decision-makers view each other today with cold, calculating, suspicious hostility.

Superimposed on this basic hostility is the additional exacerbation of mutually ominous military capabilities. Not only does each elite attribute to the other a desire to increase its power and national security at the expense of the other, but each recognizes that the other has at its disposal an array of weapons and delivery systems which might be put to direct use when and if the potential gains appeared to justify the risks of retaliation. Aware of the possibility that the other may initiate either a limited or a total attack or politically exploit any strategic imbalance, each continues to drive harder for military superiority. (Parity will not suffice; there is the ever present danger of underestimation or major technological breakthrough.) And within this sort of perceptual framework, built of hostility plus capability, the inevitable consequence is that each elite will interpret the other's military capability as evidence of military intent. Failure to equate such capability with intent or unwillingness to infer design from physical capacity might produce disastrous national consequences; all error must be on the side of cynicism. In such a situation, proposals will be viewed as propaganda, criticisms as intimidation, and concessions as duplicity. The circularity and self-generating nature of the arms-tension pattern is manifest, and threat-perception is its prime ingredient. Thus is the "Richardson process" (Richardson, 1950) perpetuated and the feverish arms race nourished.

To summarize, it is contended here that threat-perception arises out of a situation of armed hostility, in which each body of policy-makers assumes that the other entertains aggressive designs; further, each assumes that such designs will be pursued by physical and direct means if estimated gains seem to outweigh estimated losses. Each perceives the other as a threat to its national security, and such perception is a function of both estimated capability and estimated intent. To state the relationship in quasi-mathematical form: Threat-Perception = Estimated Capability × Estimated Intent. The reasoning implicit in this capability-intent relationship is best illustrated by reference to two current military-psychological patterns. The British today maintain a relatively formidable military establishment, capable of rendering extensive damage to both the U.S.S.R. and the United States. While there is little threat-perception in Washington when these capabilities are assayed (almost no estimation of intent), the Kremlin regards that same potential with considerable alarm (high level of estimated intent). Conversely, the extreme hostility of the Egyptian government, because it is not coupled with significant military capability, has not produced any important level of threat-perception in Washington. In other words, as either capability or intent appears to approach the zero level, threat-perception tends to diminish.

References

Fainsod, M., *How Russia is Ruled.* Cambridge: Harvard University Press, 1954.

Huszar, G. B. de, *Soviet Power and Policy.* New York: Thomas Y. Crowell Company, 1955.

Kaplan, M., "Balance of power, bipolarity and other models of international systems." *American Political Science Review,* **51,** 684–695, 1957.

Klineberg, O., *Social Psychology.* New York: Henry Holt and Co., 1954.

Kulski, W. W., *The Soviet Regime: Communism in Practice.* Syracuse, N.Y.: Syracuse University Press, 1954.

Leites, N., *The Operational Code of the Politburo.* New York: McGraw-Hill Book Company, 1956.

Macmahon, A., *Administration in Foreign Affairs.* University, Ala.: University of Alabama Press, 1953.

Moore, B., Jr., *Soviet Politics—The Dilemma of Power.* Cambridge, Mass.: Harvard University Press, 1950.

Richardson, L. F., "Threats and security," *in* T. H. Pear, ed., *Psychological Factors of Peace and War.* New York: Philosophical Library, 1950.

Snyder, R. C., H. W. Bruck, and B. Sapin, *Decision-Making as an Approach to the Study of International Politics.* Princeton, N.J.: Princeton University Press, 1954.

Snyder, R. C., and Furniss, E. S. *American Foreign Policy.* New York: Holt, Rinehart and Winston, 1954.

Thomas, W. I., and F. Znaniecki, "The definition of the situation," *in* T. M. Newcomb and E. L. Hartley, eds., *Readings in Social Psychology.* New York: Henry Holt and Co., 1947.

3

THOMAS C. SCHELLING • MORTON H. HALPERIN

Pre-emptive, Premeditated, and Accidental War

A theoretical analysis of the perceptions underlying pre-emptive, premeditated, and accidental war. These perceptions are in large part a function of the vulnerability of strategic weapons. Various arms-control measures are described which can reduce the likelihood of these kinds of war.

The most mischievous character of today's strategic weapons is that they may provide an enormous advantage, in the event that war occurs, to the side that starts it. Both Russian and American strategic doctrines reflect preoccupation with the urgency of attacking in the event of evidence that the other is about to. The urgency is in the vulnerability of strategic weapons themselves, and of the communication and other facilities they depend on; the side that attacks first can hope to blunt the other's retaliation. Closely related is the advantage, in the event the other is already attacking, of responding quickly and vigorously—of being a close second if not first.

By itself this urgency would pose the danger of unintended war, a war provoked by ambiguous evidence of attack. The greater the urgency with which the decision must be made in the event of alarm, the greater the likelihood of converting false alarm into war itself. These dangers compound themselves: each side must be alert not only to the other's premeditated attack, but to the other's incentive to reach quick decisions in an emergency.

Hardly any other characteristic of weapons dramatizes so well that some of the danger of war resides in the very character of modern weapons. Hardly anything would be as tragically ironic as a war that both side started, each in the belief that the other was about to, each compelled by its expectations to

---

An excerpt from *Strategy and Arms Control*, New York: The Twentieth Century Fund, 1961. Reprinted by permission of the authors and the publisher. The first author is Professor of Economics and a member of the faculty of the Center for International Affairs at Harvard University. The second author is Deputy Assistant Secretary for Arms and Trade Control, International Security Affairs, Office of the Assistant Secretary of Defense of the United States of America.

confirm the other's belief that attack was imminent.

This danger does not depend on the belief that by striking quickly one may come off with a clean win. The comparison is not between initiating war and no war at all, but between initiating war and waiting for the other to initiate it. It may not be optimism that provides the dangerous incentive, but pessimism about the loss from failing to act in time. It is essentially "preventive war," improvised at a moment when war is considered imminent. *Pre-emptive* war is the term now in use for the case of war initiated in the expectation that attack is imminent.

At no time before in modern history did military technology make it so likely that the first moments of general war might determine its outcome. Whatever the Japanese expected from Pearl Harbor, it would have been a mistake to believe that they could foreclose an American victory by anything they might accomplish that one morning. In World War I, when nations were caught in the ponderous grip of mobilization procedures that provided advantage to the side that first started to mobilize, there may have been a slow-motion equivalent to nuclear attack. But in 1914 the difference between mobilizing half a day before the enemy and half a day behind was on a different scale of importance.[1]

The Incentive to Pre-empt

There are several ways that arms control might possibly help. One is to alter the character of the weapons themselves, especially their vulnerability to each other—their potency in foreclosing return attack. Whatever reduces the ability of weapons to achieve advantage by going quickly, and to suffer a great disadvantage by responding slowly, may reduce the likelihood of war.

A second approach is oriented towards the events that might precipitate pre-emptive decisions. Essentially, the urge to pre-empt is an *aggravating* factor: it converts a possibility of war into an anticipation of war, precipitating war. The pre-emptive advantage makes a suspicion of war a cause of war. If the actions, false alarms, accidental events, mischief or other occurrences that bring the pre-emptive urge into play can be minimized and damped, by cooperative arrangements or arms limitations, the danger of pre-emptive war may be reduced.

Third, arms control may possibly address itself to the decision process, and particularly to the expectations of each side about the other's actions or intentions on the brink of war. If cooperative arrangements can improve each side's intelligence about the other's preparatory actions, this may (but also may not) stabilize expectations. If each is able to reassure the other that it is not misinterpreting certain events as signalling the onset of war, dangerously compounding expectations may be averted. If each can avoid, in

[1]For a discussion of vulnerability in relation to the strategic balance see Bernard Brodie, *Strategy in the Missile Age* (Princeton: Princeton University Press, 1959); Herman Kahn, *On Thermonuclear War* (Princeton: Princeton University Press, 1960); Washington Center for Foreign Policy Research, *Developments in Military Technology and Their Impact on United States Strategy and Foreign Policy*, Study No. 8, December 1959, prepared for the Senate Committee on Foreign Relations, 86th Congress, 2d Session (Washington: U.S. Government Printing Office, 1959); Albert Wohlstetter, "The Delicate Balance of Terror," *Foreign Affairs* XXXVII (January 1959) 211–34 and his forthcoming book. For an analysis of the problem in the arms-control context see Thomas C. Schelling, "Surprise Attack and Disarmament," in *The Strategy of Conflict* (Cambridge: Harvard University Press, 1960) 230–54.

responding to the enhanced danger of war, actions and deployments that appear as preparations for attack, and can enhance the other's ability to perceive this, the interacting decisions that might explode into war may be damped.

Finally, it is likely that any forms of arms control that reduce the general expectation of war would reduce the urgency to pre-empt and the fear of each other's obsession with pre-emption.

The Incentive for Premeditated Attack

As far as major war is concerned, the incentive to initiate a premeditated attack is akin to the incentive towards pre-emptive attack. The reason is that with thermonuclear weapons on both sides, there might be little inducement in either case if it were not for the possibility of achieving, by taking the initiative, a substantial reduction in the other's ability or willingness to retaliate.

What creates the principal danger of premeditated attack is the same as with pre-emptive attack: the vulnerability of either side's retaliatory forces to an attack by the other. With a technology that permits an enormously potent weapon to arrive on an enemy target in a matter of minutes, the possibility is open that a well-coordinated surprise attack on the other side's own strategic forces might greatly reduce the size of these forces. By disrupting communications and disorganizing the victim's forces, the attacker can reduce the efficiency even of the weapons surviving; and they would have to be used against an attacker whose own defenses had the advantage of alertness and preparation. There is also the possibility that an attacker might hope to disarm the victim sufficiently to make retaliation appear futile.

Thus premeditated strategic attack by one major power against the other is largely a matter of the advantage of initiative and surprise. Collaborative measures to reduce this advantage, and to reduce thereby the incentive that either might have towards premeditated attack, might be an important supplement to the measures that we undertake unilaterally to assure our strategic forces against attack.

First, there may be measures that, taken jointly, would reduce the likelihood that the attacker could achieve *surprise*. Exchange of warning and intelligence facilities would be an example; and the original "open-skies" idea was oriented this way. In addition to warning arrangements, there might be limitations on weapons themselves, or on their use and deployment, designed to reduce their *capability for achieving surprise*. Limitations on the basing of weapons, or a requirement that they show up and be counted, might be of this sort. In other words, cooperative measures to improve intelligence and warning facilities, or cooperative measures with respect to weapons themselves designed to facilitate warning, might be considered.

Second, measures might be considered that would make weapons *less vulnerable even in the event of surprise*. Agreement to develop and to acquire weapons of a character relatively better for retaliation than for achieving surprise (as might have been the case if it had been possible to limit the accuracy of missiles) might reduce the incentives on both sides for initiating general war. Alternatively, since the advantage in striking first is largely in reducing or precluding a punitive return attack, measures to defend the homeland against incoming punitive weapons are complementary to offensive weapons of surprise attack. Thus abstention from active defense of cities (or, conceivably, from civil defense preparations) might increase the potency of each side's retaliatory forces in a manner analogous to the protection of the retaliatory forces themselves.

It has to be asked whether there is not some logical contradiction in both sides' wishing to eliminate the advantages that go with premeditated attack. Either one side is in fact interested in carrying out a well-coordinated attack on the other's strategic forces, or else not. If not, the measures appear superfluous. If so, there is at least one partner who is against the purpose of the agreement, and who either would not enter it or would do so only if he were certain that he could subvert it. Can there be a mutual interest in measures to frustrate premeditated attack?

For several reasons the answer can be "yes." It may be that neither side intends to attack but is uneasy about the other's intentions. It is thus obliged to develop military forces and to deploy them in a way that assumes the other side *may* attack; and it is obliged to react to ambiguous events as though the other side would indeed attack. If, then, neither in fact intends deliberate attack, there could be a good deal to gain by creating for both sides the reassurance that may accompany measures jointly taken to reduce the likelihood that either side, if it attacked, would succeed. In other words, since estimates of each other's *intentions* will necessarily be uncertain, measures reciprocally to reduce *capabilities* for preclusive attack may help both.

Second, even though neither side presently considers it wise or necessary to initiate general war, political events or technological change may alter the situation. But it may change either way: *either* we *or* the Russians may be the victim or beneficiary of technological break-through, of moments of military weakness, or of political incentives that override the fear of general war. Each of us may well be willing to relinquish capabilities in future contingencies on condition that the other side do likewise. (If a flip of a coin might give either of us the capability for successful attack it could look like a bad bet to both of us.)

Third, a main incentive—perhaps the overwhelmingly important motivation—towards premediatated attack on the other side's strategic forces would be a belief that war, sooner or later, is fairly likely, and that the *conservative* course would be to initiate it on the best possible terms. So-called "preventive war" considerations may be uppermost. This, in effect, is the "pre-emptive" urge in slow motion. The pre-emptive motive is the incentive to attack in the belief that the other is already attacking or is about to; the "preventive urge" has the same forestalling motives, but with respect to a war that is not yet imminent.

But the "preventive" and the "pre-emptive" urges can interact dangerously. The greater the "preventive urge" that either imputes to the other, the more probable it must expect an attack to be. The more alert it must itself then be to the need for a pre-emptive decision.

Furthermore, the preventive urges on both sides compound with each other. A powerful reason why one side might decide that a planned "preventive" attack was the only prudent action would be a belief that the other would sooner or later reach the same conclusion. The danger might be substantially deflated by measures that reduced the likely success of attack, by reducing both sides' *expectations* of attack.

The Danger of Accidental War

In current usage "accidental war" refers to a war that, in some sense, neither side intended, expected or deliberately prepared for. It includes war that might result from errors in warning systems or misinterpretations of tactical evidence. It includes the notion that a literal accident, such as the inadvertent detonation of a nuclear weapon, might precipitate war through misinterpretation, through expectation of the enemy's misinterpretation or through some sequence of automatic or semiautomatic responses and decisions. It includes the possibility of unauthorized provocative action by a pilot or bomber or missile commander; sabotage that inadvertently goes beyond its limited objectives; and plain mischief with or without the intended consequence of war. And it has come to include what is sometimes called "catalytic war"—a deliberate plot by some third country or countries, perhaps with nuclear weapons, to precipitate a war between the major powers (or just to precipitate a crisis, but with the consequence of war).[2]

"Accidental war" is sometimes used also to refer to mistakes in "brinkmanship," failure to foresee the consequences of military actions, or the accumulation of irreversible threats in the heat of a crisis. And it may refer to the particular occurrences or misunderstandings by which limited war explodes into general war.

The essential character of accidental war is that of a war initiated in the belief that war has already started or become inevitable. In most of the hypothetical cases of "accidental war," evidence is misread by one or both sides. (There is an important qualification: if both sides jump to the conclusion that instant war is inevitable, both sides may immediately make this conclusion "correct.")

It would not be accidents themselves, ambiguous spots on a radarscope, the mischief of a deranged bomber pilot, the sabotage, or the catalytic actions of third parties, that would *directly* bring about war. These occurrences provoke *decisions* that bring about war. The problem, therefore, is not solely one of preventing the "accidents"; it is equally, or more, one of forestalling the kinds of *decisions* that might lead to war as a result of accident, false alarm or mischief.

This idea of "accidental war" rests largely on the same premise that underlies pre-emptive war—that there is an enormous advantage, in the event war occurs, in starting it (or enormous advantage, in the event it seems to have started, in responding instantly) and that each side will be not only conscious of this but conscious of the other's preoccupation with it. It seems quite unlikely that war would be brought about by an electronic false alarm, by a mechanical accident, by the mischief of someone in a message center or on an airbase or by the provocative action of a third party, if there were not some urgency of responding before the evidence is in. The essence of a false alarm is that, if one fails to act upon it, it is seen to have been a false alarm. An accident is almost certain to be recognized as an accident, if war has not intervened meanwhile. And among all those who may have it in their power to bring about a provocative event that might precipitate the deci-

[2]For a discussion of accidental war see Thomas C. Schelling, "Meteors, Mischief, and War," *Bulletin of the Atomic Scientists* XVI (September 1960) 292–97; John B. Phelps *et al.*, *Accidental War: Some Dangers in the 1960's*, RP-6, The Mershon National Security Program, The Ohio State University, June 29, 1960.

sions that bring about war, very few, if any, would have the power to wage a persuasive imitation of war if the consequences of their actions could be assessed and analyzed for even a brief period of time. Thus "accidental war" is war that may be initiated on misinformation, incomplete evidence or misunderstanding, of a kind that could likely be cleared up were it not that the time to clear it up might seem a disastrous delay to a government confronted with the possibility that war has already started. "Accidental war" is, for the most part, pre-emptive war sparked by some occurrence that was unpredictable, outside the control of the main participants and unintended by them.

There are several ways that arms control might possibly help to reduce the danger of accidental war. An important one has been mentioned: reducing the urgency of quick action at the outset of general war. Cooperative or unilateral measures to improve the ability of each side's strategic forces to survive an attack, *and to remain under good command and control attack*, might slow down the tempo of decisions. Slowing down decisions on the brink of war not only means that either side, if it wishes to, can take more time to clear up whether or not the war has already started; it also means that each can impute less impetuous action to the other, and reduce thereby the need for its own quick reaction.

Measures to reduce the incidence of false alarm could be helpful. Exchange of warning facilities, of facilities for last-minute tactical intelligence, might reduce the incidence of false alarms by increasing the reliability of the warning system and improving the flow of evidence to each side. (Increased warning facilities might also increase the false-alarm rate; and some superficially attractive schemes for mutual warning probably could not communicate rapidly enough to be of use within the relevant span of time.) Agreements to limit the kinds of activities and deployments that might create misunderstandings or false alarms could also be helpful; even arrangements or activities that just improved each side's understanding of the other's behavior, facilitating discrimination between normal and abnormal traffic, might help.

And because the essence of this accidental-war problem is misunderstanding on one side or both, it is not out of the question that communications and other arrangements might be set up to facilitate direct contact between governments, of a sort that could clear up misunderstandings and provide certain assurances in an emergency.

Finally, to the extent that arms control helps to limit local war, or can reduce American and Soviet expectations of general war, the less likely it is that accidental occurrences will be construed as evidence of war.

PART THREE

Movement Toward War: From Motives and Perceptions to Actions

INTRODUCTION

The introduction and readings in Part II describe the motivational and perceptual forces underlying resort to war (goals, perceptions, and emotions) and give causal propositions concerning the sources of these forces. A dynamic element is still missing, however, from the full picture of forces leading toward war, i.e., a description and analysis of the *patterns of change* in motivation, perception, and consequent action that characterize international systems that are moving toward war. Through what stages do the motives, perceptions, and actions underlying war become intensified, and how can this sequencing of stages be explained? Part III will be devoted to this topic.

An analogy can be drawn between the material presented in Part III and a flow diagram in computer programming, which shows the sequence of steps through which a computational problem moves. In contrast, Part II on motives presents a more detailed description of certain key "subroutines," critical building blocks of the larger program. Ideally, the material in Part III should be logically deducible from the propositions in Part II, just as an entire computer program can be drawn up from detailed knowledge of all its subroutines. But this is not possible at present since the theory given in Part II is incomplete. Hence, to some extent, the material presented in Part III must stand on its own.

In contrast to the literature described and presented in Part II, which has been mostly speculative in nature, theorizing about the pattern of changes that lead to war has proceeded hand in hand with empirical research. Hence theory and research will be presented "side by side" in this introductory section.

A Natural History of Prewar Events

In his classic monograph on *Community Conflict*, Coleman (1957, p. 9) claims that, "The most striking fact about the development and growth of community controversies is the similarity they exhibit despite diverse underlying sources and different kinds of precipitating incidents." He goes on to describe a characteristic pattern of development.

Is it possible, in similar fashion, to describe a single pattern of development in relations between states prior to the outbreak of war—a definitive natural history of the coming of war?

The answer is probably both "yes" and "no." On the one hand, it would probably be unwise to try to encompass *all* prewar periods in a single pattern; there are just too many variants. Yet, on the other hand, there are striking similarities in more than a few historical cases, so that a pattern can be described that is *frequently* found. This pattern has been discussed by Gladstone (1959 and 1963), North and his associates (North, Brody, and Holsti, 1964; Holsti and North, 1965; and Selection 5), and others. It includes three features: rising tensions, rising military preparedness, and increasingly hostile actions. The same pattern is found for both parties to the developing conflict.

Usage of the term *tension* in literature on international relations in usually rather loose. In the present context, it summarizes most of the motivational constructs presented in the introduction to Part II: the perception that one's national goals are incompatible with those of another state; the perception of another state as a threat; fear, distrust, frustration, and hostility associated with another state.[1] These elements can be lumped together under a single rubric, tension, because they imply one another psychologically or have common roots.

North, Holsti, Zaninovich, and Zinnes (1963) have developed a number of techniques for measuring tension by content analysis of written materials. One method involves counting and grading for a given period of time all instances in which the perception of threat is mentioned in government records. By using this method, the *tension chart* shown in Fig. 1 was constructed, which shows how tension increased at about the same rate in the two great European alliances in the months just prior to the outbreak of the First World War. Holsti and North (1966) have validated this method of measurement against other indices of tension drawn from the economic world, e.g., the movement of gold, security prices, and the price of wheat futures, by showing that these indices exhibit the same pattern over the period of time represented in Fig. 1.

During periods of increased tension, the states involved often accumulate arms and otherwise prepare themselves for conflict. The process often takes on the character of a *preparedness race*, with the states vying for military supremacy.

As war approaches, the incidence and extremity of hostile actions and words

[1]So defined, tension can be treated as a "cause" of war because the term is shorthand for most of the motivational constructs presented in the introduction to Part II, including the more rational as well as the more emotional constructs.

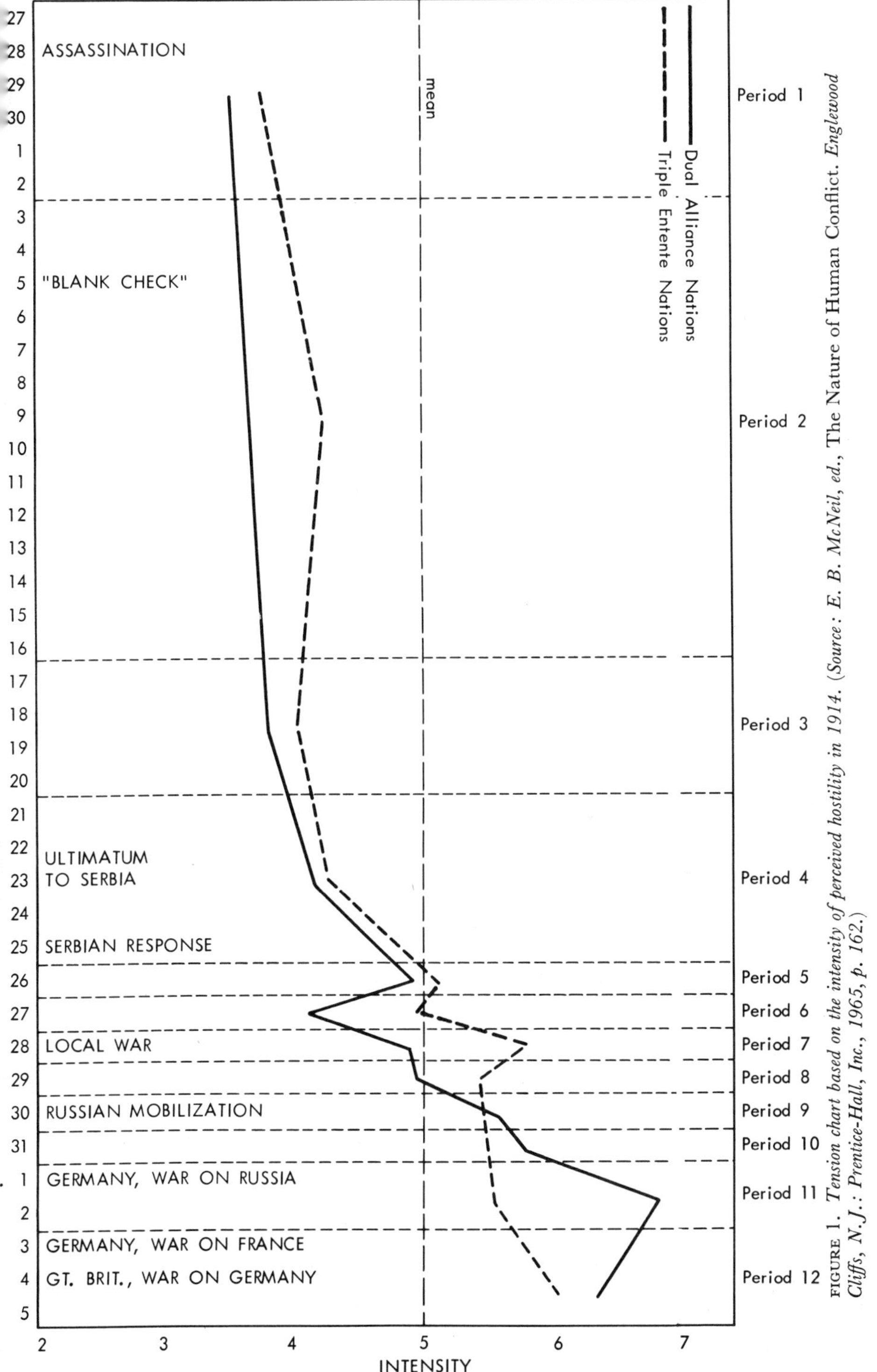

FIGURE 1. *Tension chart based on the intensity of perceived hostility in 1914.* (*Source: E. B. McNeil, ed.,* The Nature of Human Conflict. *Englewood Cliffs, N.J.: Prentice-Hall, Inc., 1965, p. 162.*)

on both sides frequently increases. The antagonists become more competitive and less accommodating in their dealings with one another. Negotiations become less productive. Favors are less often granted. Existing agreements and joint projects are abrogated one by one. Verbal abuse becomes shriller. Increasingly extreme tactics are employed in controversies.

Finally, the war begins.

Explanations for the Typical Prewar Pattern

What provides the impetus, the driving force, underlying the development of the pattern just described? Two theories exist. One theory attributes the development to the actions of a single state or coalition of states. The other attributes it to interaction between the two conflicting states or coalitions.

The Prewar Pattern as the Result of a Single State's Behavior

Most explanations of war hold explicitly or implicitly that the pattern just described is intensified by the behavior of a single state, the "aggressor." The aggressor is seen as taking the lead in exhibiting tension and as initiating hostile actions and military preparations. His opponent, the "victim," exhibits similar behavior, but as a *reaction* to the behavior of the aggressor. The aggressor's motivation is seen variously as arising from the possession of surplus capital and goods (Hobson, 1938, and Lenin, 1950), increasing national frustration (Duvall, 1947), etc. The victim's motivation is attributed to the perception of threat.

The Prewar Pattern as a Joint Product

Recently, several theorists have attributed the driving force behind the prewar pattern to an interaction between the two antagonists. The pattern is explained as a *vicious circle*, in which the behavior of each antagonist is a reaction to the other's just previous behavior. Both antagonists are seen as motivated by the perception of threat. The views of three writers who have taken this position will now be expounded.

Burton's Peace Theory. Burton's (1962) position (which has already been partially described in the introduction to Part II) grows out of the traditional viewpoint that traces international conflict to the leadership of a single state. But he adds the significant observation that the reactions of another state to the first state's provocation can materially affect the subsequent course of events.

The critical event that gets things started is a *change* in the world that has the effect of increasing the capability of state *R* (revolutionary) at the expense of state *S* (status quo); e.g., the development by *R* of the capability to manufacture products that challenge *S*'s established markets. When such a change occurs, *S* has a choice between adjusting to *R*'s challenge (e.g., withdrawing from certain markets) or resisting it (e.g., erecting tariff barriers against *R*'s products). Resistance by *S* constitutes a challenge to *R*, from which is likely to emerge hostility toward *S* and a renewed effort by *R* to achieve its aims. The result of such resistance is a vicious circle of challenge and counterchallenge, during which *R* becomes increasingly frustrated.

At some point, *R*'s frustration may become converted into a military posture, i.e., *R* begins to arm in an effort to bring force to bear on its claims. Quite naturally *S* will respond by arming, and an arms race begins, from which war is likely to develop. Once this development has occurred, there is no turning back because, for *R*, "the revolt against the status quo (has become) an end in itself rather than a means to the original purpose" (Burton, 1962, p. 60). Even if *S* is now willing to make the adjustment originally sought by *R*, *R* is not likely to be averted from its plunge toward war.

In summary, the progression toward war begins with an exchange of challenges, in which *R* attempts to reorganize the world in a limited way and is thwarted by *S*. Tensions build up in *R* to the point where *R* begins to arm and adopts a new unlimited goal of destroying *S*. At this point, the die is cast for war.

North's Theory of the Conflict Spiral. Though stressing the role played by both parties in the progression toward war, Burton distinguishes between the roles of *R* and *S*. The behavior of *R* is aimed at changing the status quo; that of *S*, at maintaining it. The frustration experienced by *R* is antecedent to the transition to an arms race. Other authors have gone even further toward discarding the traditional approach and have argued that the progression toward war depends on a vicious circle to which both sides make the *same* kind of contribution and which is governed by the perception of threat.

North and his associates have been the most persistent advocates of such a viewpoint. In a paper on the *conflict spiral*, they describe what they consider to be the typical chain of events through which "rising tensions and conflict escalation (lead) to war" (North, Brody, and Holsti, 1964, p. 1):

> If State *A*, either correctly or incorrectly, perceives itself threatened by state *B*, there is a high probability that *A* will respond with threats or hostile action. As state *B* begins to perceive this hostility directed toward itself, it is probable that *B*, too, will behave in a hostile (and defensive) fashion. This threatening behavior by *B* will convince *A* that its initial perceptions were correct, and *A* will be inclined to increase its hostile (and defensive) activity. Thereafter, the exchanges between the two parties will become increasingly negative, threatening and injurious.

War may eventually occur in a number of ways, but its chances are increased by the hostility, sense of threat, and atmosphere of crisis generated by such a vicious circle.

Richardson's Model of the Arms Race. Richardson (1960) viewed the mutual buildup of arms which often precedes wars as a vicious circle in which each side's increase in arms causes the other to perceive a greater military threat. Like North, he viewed the participants as making approximately equal contributions. He went further than other authors by devising a mathematical model to predict the precise course of the arms race. This model was presented in the form of differ-

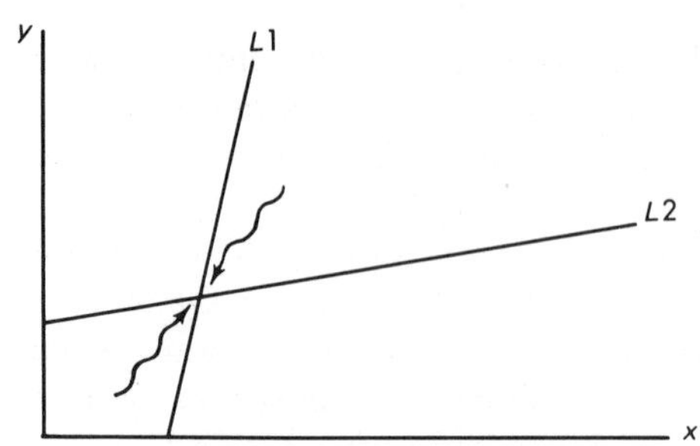

FIGURE 2. *Graphical representation of Richardson's model of the arms race. The arrows show how expenditures on arms approach a stable equilibrium point.*

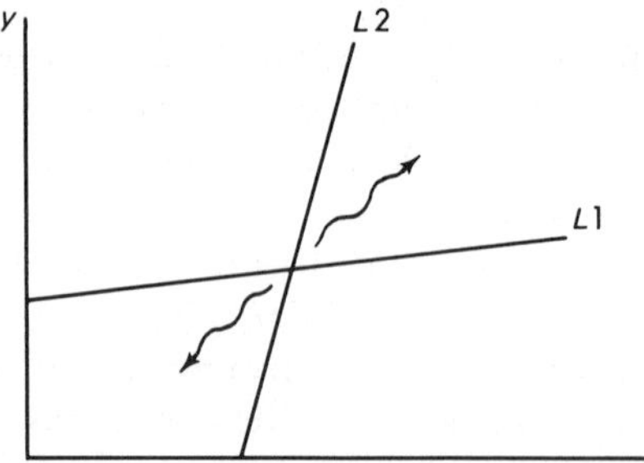

FIGURE 3. *Graphical representation of an arms race in which the equilibrium is unstable.*

ential equations, but the same material can be presented more simply in graphical form.[2]

In Fig. 2, dimension x represents state X's expenditure on arms, and dimension y represents state Y's expenditure. Line $L2$ shows the level of expenditure which the leaders of state Y would consider appropriate for every level of expenditure that state X might make. If their actual level of expenditure is below this line, the leaders of Y will spend more on arms; if above this line, existing armaments will be destroyed. Line $L1$ shows the level of expenditure considered appropriate by the leaders of state X for every level of expenditure made by state Y.

The equations for these two lines are as follows:

$$L1: \quad x = ay + g \text{ (X's expenditure as a function of Y's)}$$

$$L2: \quad y = bx + h \text{ (Y's expenditure as a function of X's)}$$

a (the slope of line $L1$ with respect to the y axis) is the *reaction potential* of state X, i.e., the amount by which the leaders of X feel it necessary to increase their expenditure for every unit of increase in the expenditure of state Y.

b (the slope of line $L2$ with respect to the x axis) is the reaction potential of state Y.

g (the intercept of line $L1$ on the x axis) is the level of expenditure that X would make if Y were disarmed. It is proportional to the "permanent grievances" felt by X against Y.

h (the intercept of line $L2$ on the y axis) is the level of expenditure that Y would make if X were disarmed.

At the point where the two lines intersect, both states are satisfied with their expenditure on arms. This point is comparable to an equilibrium in physics in that it can be stable or unstable. If stable, expenditures on both sides will always move to this point no matter where they begin. A deviation from the equilibrium point in whatever direction will be corrected. A stable equilibrium is shown in Fig. 2. If unstable, as in Fig. 3, expenditures will either increase or decrease

[2]The following material closely parallels an earlier presentation of Richardson's model by one of the authors (Pruitt, 1965).

indefinitely depending on where they start. Whether the equilibrium is stable or not depends on the slopes of lines $L1$ and $L2$ and thus on the reaction potentials: If the product ab is less than 1, the system will be stable; if equal to or greater than 1, it will be unstable. In addition, the smaller the product ab, the less will be spent on arms at the equilibrium point.

Richardson attempted to verify his model against data from the arms races of 1908 to 1914 and 1929 to 1939. He assumed that both races involved unstable equilibria of the type shown in Fig. 3, where each side feels militarily secure only if it adds more to its supply of arms than its neighbor just added. The model fit the data from 1908 to 1914 quite well but was less successful in fitting the data from 1929 to 1939. A contemporary effort to fit the model with data from the current arms race between the Western and Soviet blocs (Smoker, 1964) was also partially successful. Richardson's model and variations based on it have been used to help understand other vicious circles appearing in the relations between states by Rapoport (1960), Boulding (1962), and Pruitt (1965, in press).

Entry into War

War can come in various ways as a culmination of the prewar pattern just described. Sometimes it comes as the culmination of a plan developed at an earlier time by one of the states involved, the aggressor. In such cases, the prewar pattern is essentially an epiphenomenon, without status as a link in the causal chain. But often the heightened tension in the prewar period and the tactics that are adopted in response to this tension are causally antecedent to the coming of war. The states involved blunder into war, reluctantly choosing it at the last minute when there seems to be no alternative left (Commager, 1966).

Various things may happen at this last minute before a war. The sense of injury or frustration may reach such a height among the leaders of one state that they decide that war is the most profitable alternative. Attendant hostility among leaders or followers may hasten this decision, as in the United States' declaration of war against Spain in 1898, or a belief in the inevitability of war may become so great among the leaders of one state that they may decide to launch a pre-emptive or preventive war. This appears to have been the immediate German motivation for attacking France in 1914.

Sometimes war is preceded by a *threat* or series of threats. For example, in 1914, Russia first threatened war against Austria in an effort to stop the Austrian invasion of Serbia, and then Germany threatened war against Russia in an effort to stop the Russian mobilization. Threats against an adversary are insidious in this connection. They often look cheap, because little is lost if they succeed in bringing the adversary to terms. But they commit a state to go to war if the adversary refuses to be cowed and can thus introduce into an international crisis the volatile goal of preserving the national honor. Furthermore, threats may induce a sense of the inevitability of war in the adversary or his allies and thus encourage pre-emptive war, especially when backed up by credibility-building actions such as mobilization. Such appears to have been the case in 1914.

Though often resulting in war, the prewar pattern described in the last section by no means always leads to that conclusion. Sometimes it is arrested or even reversed. A theory is needed to explain why movement toward war is sometimes reversed while at other times it continues to a grim conclusion.

Deutsch (1957 and Selection 4) has suggested the following analysis of this issue. Assuming that neither party wants a war, war will be averted in an international crisis to the extent that the national policy makers can keep enough freedom of action always to have an *acceptable alternative* to war. Russett (1962) has gone further in the same line of reasoning, basing his theory on an analysis of the events leading up to the First World War. He distinguishes between two phases of an international crisis, the *point of surprise*, at which policy makers realize that there is a danger of war, and the *point of no escape*, at which they must make a definitive decision about action that reduces the number of future alternatives. He suggests that the likelihood of war depends on the amount of time elapsing between these two points. The more time that elapses, the more time will policy makers have to devise alternatives and think through implications; hence, the less likelihood there is that they will close off all alternatives but those that lead to war at the point of no escape. It follows that a "crisis in slow motion" is less likely to lead to war than a fast-moving crisis. The crisis preceding the First World War was a fast-moving crisis, perhaps because of the speed with which it was possible to mobilize and the importance that was accorded to striking first by national decision makers in both blocs (Rosecrance, 1963).

While the study of a single case, such as the crisis before the First World War, can lead to valuable theory if done by a conceptually minded scholar like Russett, comparison of such a case with its opposite, e.g., a crisis that did not lead to war, should be even more productive of theory. Such a study has been done by Holsti, Brody, and North (Selection 5). They compared the results of a content analysis of documents from the crisis preceding the First World War with the results of a similar analysis from the Cuban Missile Crisis, which did not lead to war. In both cases, they found a pattern of progressively rising tensions on both sides, but in the Cuban case the tension reached a peak and then fell off. They attribute the difference between these patterns to a number of factors, including the capacity in the Cuban case to empathize with the adversary, a desire not to humiliate the adversary unduly, the capacity for flexible military planning, and accurate perception of the level of violence embodied in the adversary's behavior.

Other Studies of Decision Making in Crisis

As defined by Hermann (1963), a *crisis* is a situation that involves a threat to major national goals when the time for decision is short and advance planning has been inadequate. The last stage in the progression of events leading to war often takes the form of a crisis for all parties concerned. Hence, a number of social scientists have begun theoretical and empirical research on decision making in crisis.

One of the earliest studies of governmental decision making in a crisis was an interview study of the United States' decision to enter the Korean War (Snyder and Paige, 1958). The object of this study was *not* to develop evidence to support generalizations, because a single case can seldom be used for this purpose. Rather, it was to develop a method for analyzing case studies of government decision making and to suggest a series of hypotheses about the effect of crisis that would be tested in later studies involving larger samples of cases (e.g., "The greater the urgency and the shorter the decision time, the fewer are the number of significantly differentiated alternatives," p. 362). A later interview study in the same program of research (Pruitt, 1964) was based on a sizable sample of cases and hence was capable of providing support for generalizations about crisis decision making (e.g., problem solving will be coordinated at a higher level of command the greater the perceived danger to national interests should a good decision not be made).

More recently, Robinson, Hermann, and Hermann (Selection 6) have employed an Inter-Nation Simulation setting for the exploration of some of the hypotheses developed by Snyder and Paige. This technique permitted gathering data on a number of cases, so that it was possible to develop support for generalizations about the effect of crisis. For example, support was found for the hypothesis stated earlier that time pressure produces a reduction in the number of alternative courses of action under consideration.

Other writers (Milburn, 1959; Snyder, 1961; Osgood, 1962) have made tentative deductions about the behavior of decision makers in crises from the findings in small-scale laboratory studies of the way men react to psychological stress. Under stress, men become more rigid, future time perspective tends to be foreshortened, decisions become more direct and impulsive, and behavior tends to be governed more by emotion and less by rational considerations. Given these findings, it seems reasonable to hypothesize that national policy makers will show impaired intellectual functioning under crisis. Some evidence in support of this hypothesis has been developed by Zaninovich (1964) in a content-analysis study of three East-West crises. This author found that, under high stress, policy makers tended to misinterpret and overreact to the reality situation, whereas under low stress they tended to "perceive and behave in a way which is commensurate with stimulus-events" (Zaninovich, 1964, p. 3 of "Summary").

None of the research just cited has demonstrated a direct link between crisis behavior and the decision to go to war. But some of the findings suggest mechanisms by which such a link may be established. If crisis causes policy makers to distort reality, entertain fewer alternatives, and become more rigid, impulsive, emotional, and short-sighted, it is not hard to believe that policy makers in crises will be more capable of making decisions that reduce their freedom of action to avoid war.

Escalation of War

The study of events that follow after the entry of a state into war is beyond the scope of this book. Nevertheless, it would be a mistake to fail to mention the phenomenon of *escalation*, i.e., the development of small wars into larger ones, since it is so much a feature of the modern day and sometimes involves the entry of other states into a formerly localized war. Literature in this area is quite scanty but does exist (Ackoff et al., 1966; Kahn, 1965; Wright, 1965).

Conclusions

The material presented in this part of the book provides a dynamic dimension to the study of the forces that compel states toward war. War is seen as a culmination of events that often involves an intensification of many of the factors described in Part II (called collectively tension) and a reduction in the number of available alternatives, frequently as a result of the time pressures and psychological rigidities associated with a crisis situation. Two contrasting types of theories have been advanced to explain this progression of events: one identifying as the agent of change a single dissatisfied state or bloc, and the other assigning equal responsibility to both states or blocs, each reacting in turn to the other's apparent provocation. A combination of these two types of theories has been proposed by Burton.

In comparison with the study of motives and perceptions leading to war (Part II), the study of movement toward war and of international crisis might seem to have a strong empirical underpinning. Yet it must be said that only a small beginning has been made in this area. Much research remains to be done. In particular, it seems desirable to use empirical measures, such as those developed by North, at an earlier stage in the progress toward war before a crisis has set in. This would make it possible, for example, to compare predictions from Burton's theory with those from the single agent of change and dual responsibility approaches.

References

Ackoff, R. L., et al. *Model Study of Escalation, Vol. I: Summary*. Philadelphia, Pa.: Management Sciences Center, University of Pennsylvania, 1966.

Boulding, K. E., *Conflict and Defense*. New York: Harper and Brothers, 1962.

Burton, J. W., *Peace Theory*. New York: Alfred A. Knopf, Inc., 1962.

Coleman, J. S., *Community Conflict*. New York: The Free Press, 1957.

Commager, H. S., "Can we control the war in Vietnam?" *Saturday Review*, Sept. 17, 25–27, 1966.

Deutsch, K. W., "Mass communications and the loss of freedom in national decision-making: a possible research approach to interstate conflicts," *Journal of Conflict Resolution*, **1**(2), 200–211, 1957.

Duvall, S. M., *War and Human Nature*. Public Affairs Pamphlet 125, 1947.

Gladstone, A. I., "The concept of the enemy," *Journal of Conflict Resolution*, **3**(2), 132–137, 1959.

Gladstone, A. I., "Relationship orientation and the processes leading toward war," *Background*, **6**(1), 13–25, 1963.

Hermann, C. F., "Some consequences of crisis which limit the viability of organizations," *Administrative Science Quarterly*, **8**(1), 61–82, 1963.

Hobson, J. A., *Imperialism: A Study*, rev. ed. London: George Allen and Unwin, 1938.

Holsti, O. R., and R. C. North, "The history of human conflict," *in* E. B. McNeil, ed., *The Nature of Human Conflict.* Englewood Cliffs, N. J.: Prentice-Hall, Inc., 1965.

Holsti, O. R., and R. C. North, "Comparative data from content analysis: Perceptions of hostility and economic variables in the 1914 crisis," *in* R. L. Merritt and S. Rokkan, eds., *Comparing Nations.* New Haven, Conn.: Yale University Press, 1966.

Kahn, H., *On Escalation.* New York: Hudson Institute, Series on National Security and International Order, 1965.

Lenin, V. I., *Imperialism: the Highest Form of Capitalism.* Moscow: Foreign Languages Publishing House, 1950.

Milburn, T. W., "What constitutes effective deterrence?" *Journal of Conflict Resolution,* **3**(2), 130–145, 1959.

North, R. C., R. A. Brody, and O. R. Holsti, "Some empirical data on the conflict spiral," *Peace Research Society (International) Papers,* **1,** 1–14, 1964.

North, R. C., O. R. Holsti, M. G. Zaninovich, and D. A. Zinnes, *Content Analysis.* Evanston, Ill.: Northwestern University Press, 1963.

Osgood, C. E., *An Alternative to War or Surrender.* Urbana, Ill.: University of Illinois Press, 1962.

Pruitt, D. G., *Problem Solving in the Department of State.* Denver, Colo.: University of Denver (Monograph Series in World Affairs), 1964.

Pruitt, D. G., "Definition of the situation as a determinant of international action," *in* H. C. Kelman, ed., *International Behavior.* New York: Holt, Rinehart and Winston, Inc., 1965.

Pruitt, D. G., "Stability and sudden change in interpersonal and international affairs," *Journal of Conflict Resolution,* in press.

Rapoport, A., *Fights, Games and Debates.* Ann Arbor, Mich.: The University of Michigan Press, 1960.

Richardson, L. F., *Arms and Insecurity: A Mathematical Study of the Causes and Origins of War.* Pittsburgh, Pa.: The Boxwood Press, 1960.

Rosecrance, R. N., *Action and Reaction in World Politics.* Boston: Little, Brown and Co., 1963.

Russett, B. M., "Cause, surprise and no escape." *The Journal of Politics,* **24**(1), 3–22, 1962.

Smoker, P., "Fear in the arms race: a mathematical study," *Journal of Peace Research,* **1,** 55–64, 1964.

Snyder, R. C., *Deterrence, Weapon Systems and Decision-Making.* China Lake, Calif.: U.S. Naval Ordnance Test Station, 1961.

Snyder, R. C., and G. D. Paige, "The United States' decision to resist aggression in Korea: the application of an analytic scheme," *Administrative Science Quarterly,* **3**(3), 341–378, 1958.

Wright, Q., "The escalation of international conflicts," *Journal of Conflict Resolution,* **9**(4), 434–449, 1965.

Zaninovich, M. G., *An Empirical Theory of State Response: the Sino-Soviet Case.* Ph.D. Dissertation, Stanford University, 1964.

4

KARL W. DEUTSCH

The Point of No Return in the Progression Toward War

A statement of the hypothesis that wars often come about because governmental decision-makers lose their freedom to choose alternatives other than going to war. At some point in time, the sequence of policies and actions reaches a "point of no return," and there is no way back to peace.

Governments frequently—though not always—decide to go to war when they believe themselves to be constrained by the lack of any acceptable political alternative to war. Their political decision-makers picture themselves to be in a situation in which international or domestic political pressures or the exigencies of some economic or military situation seem to leave them no other choice but war. If this were indeed a frequent situation—and part of the proposed research would be designed to test this possibility—then it seems worthwhile to study the flow of information by which these images of an implacable objective situation or of an implacable enemy or of an implacable domestic public opinion are being built up in the minds of the decision-makers. We should try to find out to what extent these images are realistic, that is, to what extent they do correspond to objective factors beyond their control; but we should also ask to what extent the actual state of the attitudes of the foreign country or of inflamed domestic public opinion has itself been produced by the flow of the communication process by which the basic "mental set"—the background for political perceptions of friendship or hostility—is being built up and by the further communications process through which latent attitudes of friendship or hostility are transformed into acute perceptions of a present conflict.

Governments, of course, may find it expedient to encourage this process in its early stages; they may even consider it essential, up to some unspecified point, in order to marshal public support for any effective but costly

---

An excerpt from "Mass communication and the loss of freedom in national decision-making: a possible research approach to interstate conflict," *Journal of Conflict Resolution*, **1**, pp. 200–211, 1957. Reprinted by permission of the author and that journal. The author is Professor of Government at Harvard University.

foreign policy. Robert Dahl has put the point clearly:

"The dilemma of the political leadership is this. Only if public opinion is fluid and undecided will the full range of theoretical alternatives be open; to the extent that public opinion hardens, alternatives are foreclosed. But because effectiveness in foreign policy depends finally upon the willingness of a nation to indulge in collective sacrifices, to rely on a fluid and indefinite public opinion is to substitute a reed for a sword."[1]

In order to be able to choose among several acceptable foreign-policy alternatives, any government must be able to command some significant portion of the income and manpower of its population. Dictatorships can compel a limited amount of such sacrifices in the face of public apathy; democracies will find it necessary, and even dictatorships find it expedient, to reduce or dispel this apathy by confronting their populations with the image of a single, sharply defined enemy and a single, clear-cut conflict. Yet, as these tactics are pursued and attitudes harden in proportion to the sacrifices demanded and sustained, the resulting policies and cumulative actions may pass the "point of no return." What began as an expedient may end as a trap, with all exits barred save those leading to catastrophe.

If it could be shown how governments lose their freedom of decision in the late stages of this process, it should be possible to alert these governments themselves, as well as the international community, to this mounting danger in its early stages. Just as it is often possible for United Nations personnel to patrol the physical borders of two adjacent states and to report any troop movements across them or even any threatening troop concentrations in their close vicinity, so it should be theoretically possible for the United Nations or some other international agency, as well as for agencies of the governments themselves, to patrol the borders of the mind. It should be possible to say whether the amount of attention given to a specific conflict area or to the image of a particular "enemy" country is reaching the danger point, in the sense that continuing hostile attention in the mass media may tend to harden public opinion to such a degree as eventually to destroy the freedom of choice of the national government concerned.

In some cases all the relevant phases of this process may occur within a single country, relatively independently of what the other country does, so long as it does not capitulate to the demands presented to it. In other cases it may involve the interplay of two or more countries in which information originating in each country may tend to aggravate further the hostile images and attitudes in the other.

In all such cases, however, it should be possible to construct an "early warning system," in regard to the mass-communication aspects of interstate conflicts; and it should also be possible to suggest some ways in which the media of mass communication could themselves be used by the national governments, either spontaneously or under the influence of the international community, in such a way as to soften and blur again these images in the public mind to a point at which the governments of the states in conflict would regain their freedom of decision and with it continuing opportunities for procrastination and eventual adjustment.

[1]Robert A. Dahl, *Congress and Foreign Policy* (New York: Harcourt, Brace & Co., 1950), p. 247.

5

OLE R. HOLSTI • RICHARD A. BRODY •
ROBERT C. NORTH

The Management of International Crisis: Affect and Action in American-Soviet Relations[1]

A case study of the Cuban missile crisis, employing content analysis of historical documents. This crisis is compared with the crisis of 1914 which led to the First World War. Differences are noted in the attitudes and approaches of policy makers, which may account for the fact that the former crisis was resolved peacefully while the latter escalated beyond the control of the participants.

In October, 1962, the first nuclear confrontation in history was precipitated by the establishment of Soviet missile sites in Cuba. For a period of approximately one week, the likelihood of a full-scale nuclear exchange between the United States and the Soviet Union was exceedingly high. Speaking of the events of the week of October 22, Attorney General Robert Kennedy recalled: "We all agreed in the end that if the Russians were ready to go to nuclear war over Cuba, they were ready to go to nuclear war, and that was that. So we might as well have the showdown then as six months later" (Alsop and Bartlett, 1962, 16).

An examination of the events immediately surrounding the crisis, analyzed in four rather distinct periods, offers a clear-cut case history of conflict that

This article appears in *Papers of the Peace Research Society (International)*, **2,** 1965, pp. 170–190, and the *Journal of Peace Research*, **3–4,** 1964, pp. 170–190. Reprinted by permission of the authors, the Peace Research Society (International) and the *Journal of Peace Research*. Ole R. Holsti is Associate Professor of Political Science at the University of British Columbia; Richard A. Brody is Associate Professor of Political Science at Stanford University; and Robert C. North is Professor of Political Science at Stanford University.

[1]This study was supported by the U.S. Naval Ordnance Test Station, China Lake, Calif., Contract N60530–8929, and is a revision of a paper delivered at the International Peace Research Society Conference at Ghent, Belgium, July 18 and 19, 1964, which appears under the title of "Measuring Affect and Action in International Reaction Models: Empirical Materials from the 1962 Cuban Crisis" in the Proceedings of that conference. Permission to republish has been granted.

escalated to the brink of war—and then deescalated. This pattern can be contrasted with the crisis during the summer of 1914 which spiraled into a world war.

During the 1962 pre-crisis period President Kennedy had been under considerable domestic pressure to take action against Cuba. In addition to attacks on Administration policy by Senators Capehart,[2] Bush, Goldwater, and Keating,[3] the Republican Senatorial and Congressional campaign committees had announced that Cuba would be "the dominant issue of the 1962 campaign." Public opinion polls revealed an increasing impatience with American policy toward Communist influence in the Caribbean. When the President arrived in Chicago on a campaign tour in mid-October, one "welcoming" sign said: "Less Profile—More Courage" (Wright, 1964, 184, 186).

There had been a number of rumors regarding the emplacement of Soviet missiles and troops in Cuba, but "hard" evidence was lacking; those most critical of Administration policy were not, in fact, willing to reveal their sources of information. Although Cuba had been under surveillance for some time, the first active phase of the crisis, from October 14 to October 21, began with the development of photographic evidence that Soviet missiles had indeed been located in Cuba. It was during this period that—according to President Kennedy—"15 people, more or less, who were directly consulted" developed "a general consensus" regarding the major decision to invoke a limited blockade (C.B.S., 1962, 2). Unfortunately for the purposes of this analysis, there are no publicly available documents written by either Soviet or American decision-makers for the period.

The second and third periods—October 22–25 and October 26–31 respectively—might be described as the "period of greatest danger of escalation" and the "bargaining period." The present paper is primarily confined to this time span, and is not concerned with the final period, during which the agreements reached between President Kennedy and Premier Khrushchev were assertedly carried out and in which further questions regarding verification were raised.

The period of most acute danger of escalation began with President Kennedy's address to the nation on October 22. The President announced:

> Within the past week unmistakable evidence has established the fact that a series of offensive missile sites is now in preparation on that imprisoned island. The purpose of these bases can be none other than to provide a nuclear strike capability against the Western Hemisphere.
>
> Additional sites not yet completed appear to be designed for intermediate-range ballistic missiles capable . . . of striking most of the major cities in the Western Hemisphere.
>
> This urgent transformation of Cuba into an important strategic base—by the presence of these large, long-range, and clearly offensive weapons of mass destruction—constitutes an explicit threat to the peace and security of all the Americas (*N.Y. Times*, Nov. 3, 1962, 7: 1).

The United States would, according to the President: (1) impose a "strict quarantine" around Cuba to halt the offensive Soviet build-up; (2) continue and increase the close surveillance of

[2]"He [President Kennedy] said to Mr. Khrushchev 'you go ahead and do whatever you want to in Cuba, you arm in any way you wish, and do anything you want to. We'll do nothing about it. . . .'" (N.B.C., 1964, 8).

[3]"I am sure the Administration must have been fully aware of what has been going on for the past month and yet they have remained silent on the threat to our security now festering in Cuba" (*Ibid.*).

Cuba; (3) answer any nuclear missile attack launched from Cuba against any nation in the Western Hemisphere with "a full retaliatory response upon the Soviet Union"; (4) reinforce the naval base at Guantanamo; (5) call for a meeting of the Organization of American States to invoke the Rio Treaty; and (6) call for an emergency meeting of the United Nations. At the same time he stated that additional military forces had been alerted for "any eventuality." James Reston reported "on highest authority" that,

> Ships carrying additional offensive weapons to Cuba must either turn back or submit to search and seizure, or fight. If they try to run the blockade, a warning shot will be fired across their bows; if they still do not submit, they will be attacked (*N.Y. Times*, Oct. 23, 1962, 1:4).

In accordance with the Joint Congressional Resolution passed three weeks earlier, the President signed an executive order on October 23 mobilizing reserves.[4]

In its initial response the Soviet government denied the offensive character of the weapons, condemned the quarantine as "piracy," and warned that Soviet ships would not honor it.[5] It was also reported that Defense Minister Malinovsky had been instructed to postpone planned demobilization, to cancel furloughs, and to alert all troops. Although the issue was immediately brought before the United Nations and the Organization of American States, the events of October 22–25 pointed to a possibly violent showdown in the Atlantic, in Cuba, or perhaps in other areas of the world. President Kennedy apparently expected some form of retaliation in Berlin. In this October 22 address he specifically warned the Soviet Union against any such move: "Any hostile move anywhere in the world against the safety and freedom of people to whom we are committed—including in particular the brave people of West Berlin—will be met by whatever action is needed."

The quarantine went into effect at 10 A.M. Eastern Standard Time on October 24.[6] At that time a fleet of 25 Soviet ships nearing Cuba was expected to test the American policy within hours. Statements from Moscow and Washington gave no immediate evidence that either side would retreat, although the Soviet Premier dispatched a letter to Bertrand Russell in which he called for a summit conference. The next day rumors of an American attack or invasion of Cuba were strengthened by the announcement by Representative Hale Boggs that, "if these missiles are not dismantled, the United States has the power to destroy them, and I assure you that this will be done" (*N.Y. Times*, Nov. 3, 1962, 6:1-2). At the same time American intelligence sources revealed that work on the erection of missile sites was proceeding at full speed.

The first real break in the chain of events leading to an apparently imminent confrontation came on October

[4]The deployment of military forces during the crisis is discussed in more detail in Joxe (1964), Knebel (1963), and LeMay (1963).

[5]William Knox, Chairman of Westinghouse Electric International, was told by Premier Khrushchev on October 24—the day the blockade went into effect—that "as the Soviet vessels were not armed the United States could undoubtedly stop one or two or more but then he, Chairman Khrushchev, would give instructions to the Soviet submarines to sink the American vessels" (N.B.C., 1964, 36).

[6]On the advice of Ambassador Stevenson, the blockade was postponed one day in order to give the OAS an opportunity to sanction it (Pachter, 1963, 31).

25 when twelve Soviet vessels turned back in mid-Atlantic. It was at this point that Secretary of State Dean Rusk remarked, "We're eyeball to eyeball, and I think the other fellow just blinked" (Alsop and Bartlett, 1962, 16). Shortly thereafter the first Soviet ship to reach the patrol area—the tanker *Bucharest*—was allowed to proceed to Cuba without boarding and search.

By the following day the crisis appeared to be receding somewhat from its most dangerous level. The Soviet-chartered freighter, *Marucla* (ironically, a former American Liberty ship now under Lebanese registry), was searched without incident and, when no contraband was discovered, allowed to proceed to Cuba. In answer to an appeal from Secretary General U Thant, Soviet Premier Khrushchev had agreed to keep Soviet ships away from the patrol area for the time being. President Kennedy's reply to the Secretary General stated that he would try to avoid any direct confrontation at sea "in the next few days." At the same time, however, the White House issued a statement which said: "The development of ballistic missile sites in Cuba continues at a rapid pace. . . . The activity at these sites apparently is directed at achieving a full operational capability as soon as possible" (*N.Y. Times*, Nov. 3, 1962, 11: 1). The State Department added that "further action would be justified" if work on the missile sites continued. Photographic evidence revealed that such work was continuing at an increased rate and that the missile sites would be operational in five days.

The "bargaining phase" of the crisis opened later in the evening of October 26. A secret letter from Premier Khrushchev acknowledged the presence of Soviet missiles in Cuba for the first time.[7] He is reported to have argued they were defensive in nature but that he understood the President's feeling about them. According to one source, "Never explicitly stated, but embedded in the letter was an offer to withdraw the offensive weapons under United Nations supervision in return for a guarantee that the United States would not invade Cuba" (*N.Y. Times*, Nov. 3, 1962, 6: 3).[8] A second message from Premier Khrushchev, dispatched twelve hours later, proposed a trade of Soviet missiles in Cuba for NATO missile bases in Turkey; the United Nations Security Council was to verify fulfillment of both operations, contingent upon the approval of the Cuban and Turkish governments.

In his reply to Khrushchev's secret letter of Friday evening, the President all but ignored the later proposal to trade bases in Turkey for those in Cuba. At the Attorney General's suggestion, the President simply interpreted Premier Khrushchev's letter as a bid for an acceptable settlement—as if the message regarding bases in Turkey had never been received (Hilsman, 1964, 21).[9]

---

[7]This is apparently the only written communication between the United States and the Soviet Union during the crisis period which is not publicly available (cf. Larson, 1963). President Kennedy filed the message—described as "panicky in tone and confused in content. . . so personal that it can hardly be called a diplomatic note"—among the most secret state papers (Pachter, 1963, 50).

[8]It was also on October 26 that "Mr. X" [Aleksandr S. Fomin], head of Soviet intelligence in the United States, approached John Scali of ABC News with essentially the same terms for a detente. This episode has been described in more detail in Hilsman (1964) and ABC News (1964).

[9]Pachter (1963, 68) develops the thesis that the message linking Turkey with Cuba was

As I read your letter, the key elements of your proposal—which seems generally acceptable as I understand them—are as follows:

1) You would agree to remove these weapons systems from Cuba under appropriate United Nations observation and supervision; and undertake, with suitable safeguards, to halt the further introduction of such weapons systems into Cuba.

2) We, on our part, would agree—upon the establishment of adequate arrangements through the United Nations to ensure the carrying out and continuation of these commitments—(a) to remove promptly the quarantine measures now in effect and (b) to give assurance against an invasion of Cuba (*N.Y. Times*, Nov. 3, 1962, 13: 4–5).

He added, however, that,

. . . the first ingredient, let me emphasize, . . . is the cessation of work on missile sites in Cuba and measures to render such weapons inoperable, under effective international guarantees. The continuation of this threat, or a prolonging of this discussion concerning Cuba by linking these problems to the broader questions of European and world security, would surely lead to an intensification of the Cuban crisis and a grave risk to the peace of the world (*Ibid.*).

In responding to Khrushchev's proposal to trade missile bases in Turkey for those in Cuba, a White House statement rejected that offer: "Several inconsistent and conflicting proposals have been made by the U.S.S.R. within the last 24 hours, including the one just made public in Moscow . . . . The first imperative must be to deal with this immediate threat, under which no sensible negotiation can proceed" (*N.Y. Times*, Nov. 3, 1962, 13: 3–4).

Despite the advent of negotiations, the situation was still dangerous. On October 27 an American U-2 reconnaissance plane had been shot down over Cuba, and several other planes had been fired upon. The Defense Department warned that measures would be taken to "insure that such missions are effective and protected." At the same time it announced that twenty-four troop-carrier squadrons—14,000 men—were being recalled to active duty. The continued construction on the Cuban missile sites, which, it was believed, would become operational by the following Tuesday, was of even more concern than attacks on the U-2's. Theodore Sorensen, speaking of the events of October 27, said, "Obviously these developments could not be tolerated very long, and we were preparing for a meeting on Sunday [October 28] which would have been the most serious meeting ever to take place at the White House" (N.B.C., 1964, 42).

On the following morning [October 28], however, Radio Moscow stated that the Soviet Premier would shortly make an important announcement. The message was broadcast in the clear to shortcut the time required by normal channels of communication.[10] Premier Khrushchev declared:

I regard with great understanding your concern and the concern of the United States people in connection with the fact that the weapons you describe as offensive

written prior to the secret note from Khrushchev, but that difficulties in communication caused them to be received in reverse order. The validity of this interpretation, which would absolve the Soviet Premier from the charge of trying to raise the ante during a nuclear poker game, cannot be determined from the available sources.

[10] "During the Cuban crisis, it took four hours, with luck, for a formal message to pass between Kennedy and Khrushchev. Any such message had to be carried physically from the head of state to the local embassy, translated, coded, transmitted, decoded on the other side, and carried to the other leader" (Bagdikian, 1963, 6).

are formidable indeed. . . . The Soviet Government, in addition to earlier instruction on the discontinuation of further work on weapons construction sites, has given a new order to dismantle the arms which you describe as offensive, and to crate and return them to the Soviet Union (*N.Y. Times*, Nov. 3, 1962, 14: 1).

The statement made no reference to the withdrawal of American missiles from Turkey.

In reply, President Kennedy issued a statement welcoming Premier Khrushchev's "statesmanlike decision." He added that the Cuban blockade would be removed as soon as the United Nations had taken "necessary measures," and further, that the United States would not invade Cuba. Kennedy said that he attached great importance to a rapid settlement of the Cuban crisis, because "developments were approaching a point where events could have become unmanageable."

Although Khrushchev stated that the Soviet Union was prepared to reach an agreement on United Nations verification of the dismantling operation in Cuba, Fidel Castro announced on the same day that Cuba would not accept the Kennedy–Khrushchev agreement unless the United States accepted further conditions, including the abandonment of the naval base at Guantanamo. But the critical phases of the Soviet–American confrontation seemed to be over. Despite the inability to carry out on-site inspection, photographic surveillance of Cuba confirmed the dismantling of the missile sites. The quarantine was lifted on November 21, at which time the Pentagon announced that the missiles had indeed left Cuba aboard Soviet ships.

I

What research questions does this sequence of events suggest? The crisis may be analyzed from several perspectives. From one point of view, it was a unique event, and not comparable to previous situations. In relation to either World War, the weapons systems of the adversaries were of incomparable magnitude. The nations, as well as their leaders, were different. Even the alerting and mobilizing of armed forces, which were so crucial to the escalation into war in the summer of 1914, resulted in a different outcome in October 1962. And certainly in its potential consequences, the Cuban crisis surpassed all previous cold war confrontations and, for that matter, any previous crisis in history. From this perspective the investigator may focus his attention on the unique characteristics of the situation.

The analyst of international relations may, on the other hand, examine the events of October 1962 in such a manner as to permit relevant comparisons with other crisis situations, both those resolved by war and those eventually resolved by non-violent means. Are there, for example, consistent patterns of behavior that distinguish the situations which escalate into general war—as in 1914—from those in which the process of escalation is reversed?

A conceptual framework developed for such analysis is a two-step mediated stimulus-response model (S — r : s — R), in which the acts of one nation are considered as inputs to other nations (Osgood and North, 1963). The nations are information-processing and decision-making units whose policies, in turn, can become inputs to other nations (Figure 1). The basic problem is this: given some action by nation B, what additional information is needed to account for nation A's foreign policy response?

Within the model, a stimulus (S)

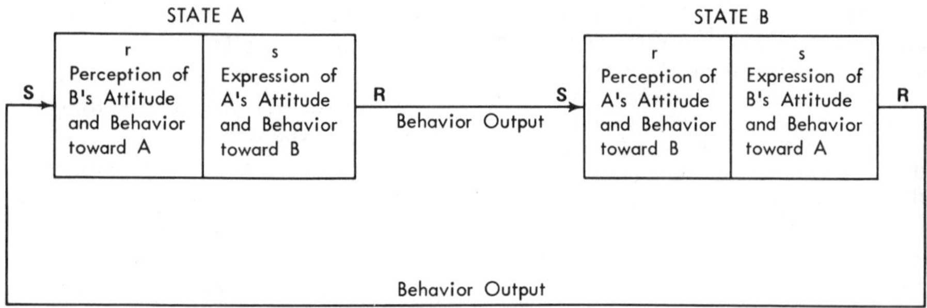

FIGURE 1. *The interaction model.*

is an event in the environment which two or more decision-makers may perceive and evaluate differently. A stimulus may be a physical event or a verbal act, which elicits a response (R) from another nation. For example, during the early autumn of 1962, the Soviet Union began erecting launching sites for medium range ballistic missiles in Cuba (R). Regardless of the Soviet motives or intent behind this act, it served as an input or stimulus (S) to the United States, which responded by a series of steps, including the naval quarantine of Cuba (R).

In the model the perception (r) of the stimulus (S) within the national decision system corresponds to the "definition of the situation" in decision-making models (Snyder *et al.*, 1962; March and Simon, 1958). For example, the Soviet missile sites in Cuba (S) were perceived by President Kennedy as a threat to the security of the Americas (r). Finally, the "s" stage in the model represents the actor's expression of his own intentions, plans, actions or attitudes toward another actor, which becomes an action response (R) when carried out. Both "r" and "s" carry evaluative and affective loadings.[11] Thus, irrespective of Russian intent, the Cuban missiles were perceived as a threat (r) by President Kennedy, who expressed American intent (s) to remove them from Cuba. This plan was put into effect by the quarantine (R), which then served as an input (S) to the Soviet decision-makers.

Operationally it would be much simpler, of course, to confine oneself to an analysis of actions (S and R) as do many classical formulations of international politics (Rosenau, 1964, 2). In some situations the one nation's actions may be so unambiguous that there is little need to analyze perceptions in order to predict the response of the other state; consider, for example, the American response to the Japanese attack on Pearl Harbor. Unfortunately, as Kenneth Boulding and others have pointed out, it is less clear that positive actions will lead to reciprocation.

In any case, not all—or even most—foreign policy behavior is unambiguous. For political behavior, what is "real" is what men perceive to be real. Boulding (1959, 120) has summarized this point succinctly:

> We must recognize that the people whose decisions determine the policies and actions of nations do not respond to the "objective" facts of the situation, whatever that may mean, but to their "image" of the situation. It is what we think the world is like, not

[11]A number of factors—including those of personality, role, organization and system—will affect the perceptual variables in the model. A further elaboration may be found in Holsti *et al.* (1964a), Ch. 1 and 2; and Brody (1966).

what it is really like, that determines our behavior.

At this point one might protest that well-trained statesmen will find little difficulty in interpreting the facts as they pertain to foreign policy. Yet one can cite example after example to the contrary. Consider, for example, the various interpretations—even among foreign policy professionals—which almost inevitably follow nearly every turn in Soviet policy. Such problems of interpretations are encountered at every point in the stream of decisions which constitute foreign policy, and *mis*perceptions may have behavioral consequences as "real" as more accurate perceptions do. Thus, since all decision-making is rooted in the perceptions of individuals, the model attempts to assess both objective and subjective factors. Other research has reinforced the belief that a model of interstate behavior must account for perceptual variables (North *et al.*, 1964; Holsti *et al.*, 1964b, 1968).

There have been serious doubts about the feasibility of quantifying perceptual and affective data, and the inclination, until recently, has been to emphasize "hard" variables and aggregate data.

As important as these objective data are, they may fail to take into sufficient account how human beings react. Moreover, objective data are usually compiled on an annual, quarterly, or monthly basis. While these indices may well be relied upon to reveal the trend toward an environment conducive to crisis (Richardson, 1960; Wright, 1957; K. J. Holsti, 1963; Deutsch, 1960)—such as Europe in 1914 or the Cold War since 1945—they may prove less useful for the intensive study of a short time period. Thus it is particularly important for the investigator who seeks to analyze short term changes in the international system—such as the crisis situation—to incorporate subjective data into his model.

II

The premise that the analysis of political behavior is enriched by the incorporation of perceptual data poses special problems for the student of international relations. Clearly the standard methods of attitude measurement—the personal interview, the questionnaire, or the direct observation of decision-makers in action—can rarely be used by the social scientist who seeks to study human behavior at the international level. What he needs are instruments for measuring attitudes and actions "at a distance." This is perhaps the primary rationale for settling upon the content analysis of the messages of key decision-makers—those who have the power to commit the resources of state to the pursuit of policy goals at the international level—as an important research tool.

Source materials used for the analysis of perceptions (s and r in the model) consist of 15 United States and 10 Soviet documents, a total of nearly thirty thousand words, from the ten-day period opening on October 22—the day of President Kennedy's address on the Cuban crisis—and closing on October 31. After relevant decision-makers had been selected, *all publicly available documents*, rather than a sample, were used. For example, President Kennedy, Secretaries Rusk and McNamara, Ambassador Stevenson, and Attorney General Kennedy were selected as the key American decision-makers. *The entire verbatim text of every available document* authored by these five persons during the ten-day period was included. These documents were subjected to analysis by means of the General Inquirer system of automated content analysis via the IBM 7090 computer (Stone, 1962; Holsti, 1964a;

Holsti *et al.*, 1964a). This analysis provided day-by-day ratings of each party's perceptions and intentions for six variables: positive affect (POS), negative affect (NEG), strength (STR), weakness (WK), activity (ATV), and passivity (PSV). In addition, the actions of each party were scaled on a dimension of degree of violence or potential violence.[12]

The perceptual data generated by the General Inquirer are combined with the scaled action data into the S – r: s – R model for the United States and the Soviet Union in Tables 1 and 2. The columns marked "S" and "R" in Tables 1 and 2 give a rank ordering of the degree of violence or potential violence in each party's actions over the ten days. United States actions are the responses (R) in Table 1 and the stimuli (S) to Russian actions in Table 2. Russian actions are the responses in Table 2 and the stimuli to American actions in Table 1. Looking at the action data alone, it is apparent that Soviet and American actions during the period are closely correlated; that is, the actions for both sides are most violent or potentially violent in the first three days, followed by a relatively steady decline through October 31. The Spearman rank-order correlation between Soviet and American actions ($r_s = .89$) is significant at the .01 level (Siegel, 1956). The correlation coefficient should not be interpreted to indicate that the level of violence in the actions of the two parties were of equal magnitude; the separate scaling of Soviet and American actions precludes such an inference. Rather, it indicates that as the level of violence in the actions of one party increased or decreased, the actions of the other party tended to follow a similar pattern.

[12]A more complete description of the research techniques may be found in the Methodological Appendix [following this Selection].

An examination of the perceptual data in Tables 1 and 2 reveals that the pattern of perceptions (r and s) was relatively consistent with the course of events—that is, Soviet and American actions (R and S)—surrounding the Cuban crisis.[13] There was a general tendency on the part of both Soviet and American decision-makers to perceive rather accurately the nature of each other's action, and then to respond in kind. In reading across Tables 1 and 2, we find that when the level of violence or potential violence in the actions of the other party (S) decline, there is a corresponding tendency for: (1) perceptions of the other party (r) to move away from the extreme negative end of the evaluative dimension; (2) statements of intent (s) to become more positive; and, (3) one's own actions to become less violent (R).[14] In each case October 25–26—previously identified as the point dividing two phases of the crisis—was the point at which mutual perceptions appeared to change. The rigidly negative-strong-active perceptions of the period of highest danger became somewhat modified at this point. Perceptions along the evaluative dimensions became more neutral and, in some cases, actually became positive. As one would expect, during the latter days of the crisis there was also an increase in perceptions of passivity. The potency dimension, on the other

[13]The reader may wonder why, in Table 2, the highest level of negative affect in the "s" sector of the model is found on October 28, the day of the Kennedy–Khrushchev agreement. This result is due primarily to President Kennedy's expressions of regret about an American weather airplane straying over Soviet territory; many of the words used by the President are "tagged" for negative affect in the General Inquirer dictionary.

[14]The empty rows in the perceptual (r and s) sectors of Tables 1 and 2 result from a lack of documents—meeting the criteria set forth earlier—on those days.

TABLE 1

Action and Perceptual Data—The United States

October 1962	Soviet Actions (S*)	U.S. Perceptions of Soviet Actions (r†)						U.S. Statements of Intent (s†)						U.S. Actions (R*)
		POS	NEG	STR	WK	ATV	PSV	POS	NEG	STR	WK	ATV	PSV	
22	3	1.3	33.5	37.2	5.5	16.2	6.3	11.9	11.2	29.5	4.4	31.8	11.2	2
23	1	0.3	30.3	26.1	3.6	32.3	7.4	11.6	9.7	35.7	2.0	35.7	5.3	3
24	2													1
25	5	17.8	15.6	31.1	0.0	24.4	11.1	16.0	9.0	21.0	5.0	32.0	17.0	4
26	6	13.5	8.1	21.6	2.7	35.2	18.9	30.3	0.0	30.3	3.0	12.1	24.3	5
27	4	10.7	16.1	21.4	8.9	19.6	23.3	24.3	1.7	28.6	6.7	22.7	16.0	6
28	7	25.3	13.4	33.3	2.7	18.6	6.7	16.4	21.7	23.1	3.7	21.7	13.4	7
29	8													9
30	9													10
31	10													8

*The values for S and R are *rank-order* figures: 1 is the highest level and 10 is the lowest level of violence or potential violence.

†The values for r and s are *percentages* of the total loading on the three dimensions.

TABLE 2

Action and Perceptual Data—The Soviet Union

October 1962	U.S. Actions (S*)	Soviet Perceptions of U.S. Actions (r†)						Soviet Statements of Intent (s†)						Soviet Actions (R*)
		POS	NEG	STR	WK	ATV	PSV	POS	NEG	STR	WK	ATV	PSV	
22	2													3
23	3	2.4	27.2	28.8	1.6	34.0	5.0	17.7	13.6	31.2	6.4	22.8	8.3	1
24	1	5.9	19.6	21.6	3.9	31.4	17.6	24.5	10.5	27.8	3.5	15.1	18.6	2
25	4	0.0	16.7	22.2	2.8	30.5	27.8	22.2	7.4	22.2	3.7	7.4	37.1	5
26	5	0.0	29.7	21.6	0.0	48.7	0.0	21.2	1.9	26.9	0.0	32.7	17.3	6
27	6	15.9	12.9	22.1	9.8	27.0	12.3	24.7	6.9	20.1	9.2	20.7	18.4	4
28	7	12.6	16.6	23.4	4.0	30.3	13.0	24.6	8.1	25.9	4.5	21.4	15.5	7
29	9													8
30	10													9
31	8													10

*The values for S and R are *rank-order* figures: 1 is the highest level and 10 is the lowest level of violence or potential violence.

†The values for r and s are *percentages* of the total loading on the three dimensions.

hand, remained predominantly on the strong side throughout the crisis period.

Spearman rank-order correlation coefficients across various steps in the model are presented in Table 3.[15] The evaluative dimension is the most sensitive to behavioral changes; the highest correlation coefficients are consistently those for positive affect (positive correlation with decreasing violence) and negative affect (negative correlation with decreasing violence).

Table 3 also reveals that there is a relatively close correspondence between the actions of the other party (S) and perceptions of the adversary's actions (r). By themselves these findings are hardly conclusive. When compared with a similar analysis of the crisis which escalated into World War I (Holsti *et al.*, 1964b, 1968), however, one interesting point emerges. In 1914, the leaders of the Dual Alliance (Germany and Austria–Hungary) consistently pursued policies with a higher level of violence or potential violence than did the members of the Triple Entente (England, France, and Russia). Over the crisis period as a whole, the actions of the Dual Alliance were significantly more violent ($z = 4.2$, $p < .001$). When the crisis was divided into twelve time periods, a Mann–Whitney U-Test confirmed the difference ($U = 31.5$, $p < .025$). A further analysis of the data disclosed that the only significant difference between the two alliances was in the S–r link; that is, between the actions of the other party and one's perceptions of them. German and Austro-Hungarian leaders consistently overperceived ($r > S$) the level of violence in the actions taken by members of the Triple Entente. British, French, and Russian leaders, on the other hand, underperceived ($S > r$) the level of violence of the

[15]Because there are no United States perceptual data for October 24, the average of the values of October 23 and 25 have been used for the purposes of calculating the correlation coefficients in Table 3.

TABLE 3

Spearman Rank-Order Correlations Across S–r: s–R Model

Soviet Perceptions of the U.S. (*r*)	*U.S. Action* (S) (*n* = 6)	*Soviet Action* (R) (*n* = 6)	*U.S. Perceptions of the Soviet Union* (*r*)	*Soviet Action* (S) (*n* = 7)	*U.S. Action* (R) (*n* = 7)
Positive	+.70	−.07		+.93	+.71
Negative	−.43	−.20		−.82	−.79
Strong	−.13	−.13		+.11	−.25
Weak	+.54	+.09		−.24	+.17
Active	−.43	−.20		−.18	−.14
Passive	−.31	+.03		+.18	+.32
Soviet Self-Perceptions (*s*)			*U.S. Self-Perceptions* (*s*)		
Positive	+.66	+.32		+.79	+.71
Negative	−.31	−.60		−.11	−.11
Strong	−.31	−.49		+.46	+.21
Weak	+.20	−.32		+.29	+.29
Active	+.37	+.14		−.86	−.71
Passive	−.37	+.03		+.79	+.54

actions of the Dual Alliance nations. The difference between the two coalitions in this respect was significantly different ($U = 32$, $p < .025$). In terms of the S – r : s – R model, this relationship between one coalition's actions (S), the other coalition's perceptions of those actions (r), and the resulting policies (R) was apparently the crucial one.

In the Cuban crisis, however, both sides tended to perceive rather accurately the nature of the adversary's actions and then proceeded to act at an "appropriate" level; that is, as the level of violence or potential violence in the adversary's actions diminished, perceptions of those actions increased in positive affect and decreased in negative affect, and the level of violence in the resulting policies also decreased. Thus, unlike the situation in 1914, efforts by either party to delay or reverse the escalation were generally perceived as such, and responded to in a like manner. Whether the different patterns of action and perception found in the 1914 and Cuban cases will be found consistently to distinguish crises that escalate and de-escalate can only be determined, of course, through continuing research.

III

Having utilized the S – r : s – R model to examine the pattern of Soviet and American interaction, it may be useful to attempt at least a partial explanation for the patterns with some comparisons with the 1914 crisis. Such an analysis will be concerned primarily with what might be called "styles of decision-making," and must of necessity be based on incomplete data. Although there are several accounts of the process by which American policy was formulated, such data with respect to the Soviet Union are much more fragmentary and inferential (cf. Kolkowicz, 1963; Horelick, 1964).

One major characteristic of Soviet policy during this period is clear. Unlike German leaders in 1914, Premier Khrushchev did not irrevocably tie his policy to that of a weaker—and perhaps less responsible—ally. The Cuban response to President Kennedy's address of October 22 was stronger and more unyielding than that of the Soviet Union. Premier Castro in fact ordered a general war mobilization *prior to* the delivery of the President's speech. The following day Premier Castro in effect left no room for either Cuba or the Soviet Union to maneuver: "Whoever tries to inspect Cuba must come in battle array! This is our final reply to illusions and proposals for carrying out inspections on our territory" (Draper, 1963, 42). Premier Khrushchev, on the other hand, like President Kennedy, almost immediately chose to interpret the crisis as one involving the United States and the Soviet Union alone.[16] In his correspondence with President Kennedy during October 26–28, it is also apparent that the Soviet Premier was unwilling to let the intransigence of Dr. Castro stand in the way of a possible solution of the crisis. In his letter of October 28, in which Khrushchev offered to withdraw the missiles, there was, in fact, no acknowledgment of the necessity to obtain Cuban agreement on the terms of the settlement.

American decision-making in regard to the missiles in Cuba was charac-

[16]In this respect, Soviet decision-makers differed markedly from those of Communist China, who referred to the events in the Caribbean as a Cuban–American issue. Further comparisons of Chinese and Soviet attitudes during the missile crisis may be found in Holsti (1964c).

terized by a concern for action based on adequate information. The resistance of the Administration against action—despite public pressure—until photographic evidence of the missile sites was available, has already been noted.[17] As late as Thursday, October 18, a series of alternatives was being considered pending more accurate information, and while the decision to institute a blockade was being hammered out, open discussion of the alternatives was encouraged. The President recalled that "though at the beginning there was a much sharper division . . . , this was very valuable, because the people involved had particular responsibilities of their own" (C.B.S., 1962, 4). Another participant in the decision-making at the highest level wrote: "President Kennedy, learning on his return from a mid-week trip in October, 1962, that the deliberation of the NSC [National Security Council] executive committee had been more spirited and frank in his absence, asked the committee to hold other preliminary sessions without him" (Sorensen, 1963, 60). Thus despite the very real pressure of time—the missile sites were to become operational by the end of the month—the eventual decision was reached by relatively open discussion. Group decision-making does not insure the emergence of sound policy, of course, but it does limit the probability of a decision performing a personality-oriented function (Verba, 1961, 103).[18]

Actually, it was not until Saturday, October 20—almost a week after the photographic evidence became available—that the general consensus developed. The President himself acknowledged that the interim period was crucial to the content of the final decision: "If we had had to act on Wednesday [October 17], in the first 24 hours, I don't think probably we would have chosen as prudently as we finally did, the quarantine against the use of offensive weapons" (C.B.S., 1962, 2–3).[19]

Another characteristic of the decision process in October 1962 was the very conscious concern for action at the very lowest level of violence—or potential violence—necessary to achieve the goals. Senators J. William Fulbright and Richard B. Russell were among those who urged immediate invasion of Cuba, a suggestion against which the President stood firm (N.B.C., 1964, 30).[20] According to Kennedy, the decision to impose a naval quarantine was based on the reasoning that:

> . . . the course we finally adopted had the advantage of permitting other steps, if this one was unsuccessful. In other words, we were starting, in a sense, at a minimum place. Then, if that were unsuccessful, we could have gradually stepped it up until we had gone into a much more massive

---

[17]McGeorge Bundy recalled that upon receiving the first news of the photographic evidence, "his [President Kennedy's] first reaction was that we must make sure, and were we making sure? And would there be evidence on which he could decide that this was in fact really the case" (N.B.C., 1964, 14).

[18]In this respect the contrast to many of the crucial decisions made in 1914 is striking. That the German Kaiser underwent an almost total collapse at the time he made a series of key decisions—the night of July 29–30—is evident from a reading of his marginal notes (Montgelas and Schücking, 1924).

[19]Despite the relative lack of speed—with the possible exception of the German army—with which European weapons systems could be mobilized in 1914, decision-makers in the various capitals of Europe perceived that time was of crucial importance—and they acted on that assumption (Holsti, 1964b). One can only speculate on the outcome had there been some delay in the making of such decisions in 1914.

[20]According to one top official, "invasion was hardly ever seriously considered" (*New York Times*, Nov. 3, 1962, 6: 3).

action which might have become necessary if the first step had been unsuccessful" (C.B.S., 1962, 4).[21]

By this step, no irrevocable decisions had been made—a number of options remained.

The concern of the President and his advisers with maintaining a number of options was based at least in part on an explicit distinction between threats and acts. The use of threats has become a more or less accepted tool of international politics in the nearly two decades of cold warring. The United States and the Soviet Union, on the other hand, had systematically abstained from direct violent action against each other. The desire to avoid killing Soviet troops was an important factor in the decision to refrain from an air strike against Cuba (N.B.C., 1964, 22). Instead the quarantine shifted the immediate burden of decision concerning the use of violence to Premier Khrushchev. Even if Soviet ships refused to honor the blockade, the initial American plan was to disable the rudders of the vessels, rather than to sink them (Bagdikian, 1963, 6).

The flexibility provided by a number of plans requiring less than the use of unlimited violence stands in marked contrast to the situation in 1914. One factor in the rapid escalation in 1914 was the rigidity of various mobilization plans. The Russian attempt to mobilize against only Austria was anathema to the Russian generals because no such formal plan had been drawn up. According to General Dobrorolski, "The whole plan of mobilization is worked out ahead to its final conclusion and in all its detail . . . once the moment is chosen, everything is settled; there is no going back; it determines mechanically the beginning of war" (quoted in Cowles, 1964, 343).

Similarly the Kaiser's last-minute attempt to reverse the Schlieffen plan —to attack only in the east—shattered Moltke, who replied:

That is impossible, Your Majesty. An army of a million cannot be improvised. It would be nothing but a rabble of undisciplined armed men, without a commissariat. . . . It is utterly impossible to advance except according to plan; strong in the west, weak in the east" (Moltke, *Erinnerungen*, quoted in Cowles, 1964, 348–49).

American decision-makers also displayed a considerable concern and sensitivity for the position and perspective of the adversary. This was a matter of deep concern in the development of the crisis. Unlike some of the key decision-makers in the 1914 crisis, those in October 1962 seemed to conceive a close relation between Soviet and American actions rather than two sides, each acting independently, *in vacuo*. Theodore Sorensen described the deliberation as follows: "We discussed what the Soviet reaction would be to any possible move by the United States, what our reaction with them would have to be to that Soviet reaction, and so on, trying to follow each of those roads to their ultimate conclusion" (N.B.C., 1964, 17).[22]

This sensitivity for the position of the adversary was apparent in a number of

---

[21]Robert Kennedy has revealed that the vote among the President's advisers was seven in favor of the naval quarantine to five for an air strike against the missile sites in Cuba (*San Francisco Chronicle*, Oct. 14, 1964).

[22]President Kennedy and others were aware of the possibility of misperception by their counterparts in the Kremlin, "Well now, if you look at the history of this century where World War I really came through a series of misjudgments of the intentions of others . . . it's very difficult to always make judgments here about what the effect will be of our decisions on other countries" (C.B.S., 1962, 3).

important areas. There was a concern that Premier Khrushchev not be rushed into an irrevocable decision; it was agreed among members of the decision group that "we should slow down the escalation of the crisis to give Khrushchev time to consider his next move" (N.B.C., 1964, 19). An interesting example of the President's concern emerges from his management of the naval quarantine: "The President ordered the Navy screen not to intercept a Soviet ship until absolutely necessary—*and had the order transmitted in the clear*" (Hilsman, 1964, italics added). There was, in addition, a conscious effort not to reduce the alternatives of *either* side to two—total surrender or total war. According to one participant, "President Kennedy, aware of the enormous hazards in the confrontation with the Soviets over Cuba in October, 1962, made certain that his first move did not close out either all his options or all of theirs" (Sorensen, 1963, 20–21). Sorensen added that:

> The air strike or an invasion automatically meant a military attack upon a communist power and required almost certainly either a military response to the Soviet Union or an even more humiliating surrender. . . . The blockade on the other hand had the advantage of giving Mr. Khrushchev a choice, an option, so to speak, he did not have to have his ships approach the blockade and be stopped and searched. He could turn them around. So that was the first obvious advantage it had. It left a way open to Mr. Khrushchev (N.B.C., 1964, 22).

Thus, unlike the 1914 situation, in which at least one ultimatum was worded so as to be incapable of execution, there was no demand which the Soviet Premier could not understand, none that he could not carry out, and none calculated to humiliate him unduly. During the summer of 1914, by way of contrast, there were numerous instances of failure on all three of these important points. The Austro-Hungarian ultimatum was deliberately worded in such a manner as to humiliate Serbia and to provoke rejection. The policy of the other powers, on the other hand, was hardly characterized by clarity. Russian decision-makers failed to communicate their initial desire to deter Vienna rather than to provoke Berlin. This was matched by England's inability to convey to German leaders their intention to intervene should the local conflict engulf the major continental powers.[23] And, in the culminating stages of the crisis, decision-makers in the various capitals of Europe made the very types of demands upon their adversaries—notably in regard to mobilizations—which they admitted they could not reciprocate.[24]

IV

In seeking to account for the differences between crises that escalate beyond the control of the participants and those that eventuate in a pacific resolution, perceptual variables have a demonstrable utility. A substantial difference between the 1914 and 1962 crises was the relative clarity with which tension-reducing moves were seen by

---

[23]The failure of communication was not, of course, solely attributable to the sender. The Kaiser, for example, consistently dismissed the warnings of his able ambassador in London, Prince Lichnowsky, in regard to the probable British policy should a major war break out on the Continent.

[24]For example, both the Kaiser and the Tsar demanded that the other stop mobilizing. Nicholas replied that, "it is technically impossible to stop our military preparations" (Montgelas and Schücking, 1924, 402). At the same time Wilhelm wrote: "On technical grounds my mobilization which had already been proclaimed this afternoon must proceed against two fronts, east and west" (*Ibid.*, 451).

the participants in the latter period; in the 1914 crisis this clarity was eroded by the tendency to imbue the potentially tension-reducing actions of the other alliances with hostile intent.

But this is only the beginning of analyses of international politics in crisis. To strictly account for the differences in outcome a great many more cases need to be studied—cases chosen to test the role of other plausible explanatory factors (weaponry, culture, etc.). But even these two cases may have furthered our understanding of the role of affect and action in the management of international crisis.

Methodological Appendix

The Stanford General Inquirer is programmed to measure perceptions—as found in written documents—along three dimensions: strength–weakness; activity–passivity; positive affect–negative affect. These dichotomized dimensions correspond to the evaluative, potency, and activity dimensions which have been found to be primary in human cognition in a variety of cultures (Osgood, Suci and Tannenbaum, 1957; Suci, 1957; Kumata and Schramm, 1956; Osgood, 1962). The dictionary thus reflects the assumption that when decision-makers perceive themselves, other nations, events—or any stimulus—the most relevant discriminations are made in a space defined by these three factors. The dictionary is used to measure changes in verbalized perceptions—the "r" and the "s" sectors in the basic model—in terms of frequency and intensity. The IBM 7090 can be programmed to analyze perceptual units defined in terms of the following elements: the *perceiver*; the perceived *agent* of action; the *action* or *attitude*; and the *target* of action. These components may be illustrated in a statement by President Kennedy (perceiver): "Soviet missiles (agent) threaten (action) all the Americas (target)." For the present analysis the computer has been instructed to measure the *action-attitude* component within a specified set of agent-target relationships involving the United States, Soviet Union, China and Cuba.

The scaling of action data (S and R in the model) was accomplished by the following technique. Three judges were given a set of cards concerning Soviet and American actions for the ten-day period October 22–31—the same period which encompasses all the publicly available documents by key Soviet and American decision-makers. Each action was typed on a separate card and these were then aggregated on a day-to-day basis. Thus each judge was given a set of cards for both United States and Soviet actions, each set being subdivided into ten periods. The judges were instructed to rank order the events—using the day as the unit of analysis—for the degree of violence or potential violence. The Soviet and American actions were scaled separately largely because of the disparity of available data; published chronologies of American actions during the crisis period are detailed almost to an hourly basis, whereas the action data for the Soviet Union are relatively sparse.

The level of agreement between each pair of judges for scaling both Soviet and American actions was:

Judge	*A*	*B*
B	.967	
	.939	
C	.800	.883
	.891	.842

The top figure is level of agreement for the scaling of Soviet action; the bottom figure is that for the scaling of United States action. All figures are significant at beyond the .01 level.

References

Alsop, Stewart, and Charles Bartlett, "In Time of Crisis," *The Saturday Evening Post*, Dec. 8, 1962, 15–20.

A.B.C. News, "John Scali, ABC News," Aug. 13, 1964.

Bagdikian, Ben H., "Press Independence and the Cuban Crisis," *Columbia Journalism Review*, Winter, 1963, 5–11.

Boulding, Kenneth E., "National Images and International Systems," *The Journal of Conflict Resolution*, **3,** 120–131, 1959.

Brody, Richard A., "Cognition and Behavior: A Model of Inter-State Relations," in O. J. Harvey, ed., *Experience, Structure and Adaptibility*. New York: Springer Publishing Company, 1966.

C.B.S. News, "A Conversation with President Kennedy," Dec. 17, 1962.

Cowles, Virginia, *The Kaiser*. New York: Harper & Row, Publishers, 1964.

Deutsch, Karl W., "Toward an Inventory of Basic Trends and Patterns in Comparative and International Politics," *American Political Science Review*, **54,** 34–57, 1960.

Draper, Theodore, "Castro and Communism," *The Reporter*, Jan. 17, 1963, 35–40.

Hilsman, Roger, "The Cuban Crisis: How Close We Were to War," *Look*, Aug. 25, 1964. 17–21.

Holsti, K. J., "The Use of Objective Criteria for the Measurement of International Tension Levels," *Background*, **7,** 77–96, 1963.

Holsti, Ole R., "An Adaptation of the 'General Inquirer' for the Systematic Analysis of Political Documents." *Behavioral Science*, **9,** 382–88, Oct., 1964a.

Holsti, Ole R., "The General Inquirer System Applied to Sino-Soviet Relations," Paper read at Conference of the American Psychological Association, Sept. 5, 1964c.

Holsti, Ole R., "Perceptions of Time, Perceptions of Alternatives, and Patterns of Communication as Factors in Crisis Decision-Making," Paper read at International Peace Research Conference, Chicago, Nov. 17, 1964b.

Holsti, Ole R., Richard A. Brody, and Robert C. North, *Theory and Measurement of Interstate Behavior: A Research Application of Automated Content Analysis*. Stanford, Calif.: Stanford University, 1964a (mimeograph).

Holsti, Ole R., Richard A. Brody, and Robert C. North, "Violence and Hostility: The Path to World War," Paper read at American Psychiatric Association Conference, Los Angeles, Calif., May, 1964b.

Holsti, Ole R., Robert C. North, and Richard A. Brody, "Perception and action in the 1914 crisis," *in* J. David Singer, ed., *Quantitative International Politics: Insights and Evidence*. New York: The Free Press, 1968.

Horelick, Arnold L., "The Cuban Missile Crisis: An Analysis of Soviet Calculation and Behavior," *World Politics*, **16,** 363–389, 1964.

Joxe, Alain, "La Crise cubaine de 1962—Entrainement contrôlé vers la dissuasion réciproque," *Strategie*, Été, 1964, 60–88.

Knebel, Fletcher, "Inside Story of the War We Never Fought," *in* "This World," Supplement of *The San Francisco Chronicle*, Feb. 10, 1963, 13–21.

Kolkowicz, Roman, "Conflicts in Soviet Party-Military Relations: 1962–1963," Rand Corp. Memo., RM-3760-PR, 1963.

Kumata, H., and Wilbur Schramm, "A Pilot Study of Cross-Cultural Methodology," *Public Opinion Quarterly*, **20,** 229–237, 1956.

Larson, David L., *The "Cuban Crisis" of 1962.*

Boston: Houghton Mifflin Company, 1963.

Le May, Curtis E., "Deterrence in Action," *Ordnance*, **47,** 526–528, 1963.

Levy, Sheldon G., and Robert Hefner, "Multi-dimensional Scaling of International Attitudes," Working Paper No. 201, Center for Research on Conflict Resolution, Nov. 1, 1962 (unpublished mimeograph).

March, James G., and Herbert A. Simon, *Organizations*. New York: John Wiley and Sons, Inc., 1958.

Montgelas, Max, and Walther Schücking, eds., *Outbreak of the World War, German Documents Collected by Karl Kautsky*. New York: Oxford University Press, 1924.

N.B.C., "Cuba: The Missile Crisis," Feb. 9, 1964.

New York Times, Oct.–Nov., 1962.

North, Robert C., "International Conflict and Integration: Problems of Research," *in* Muzafer Sherif, ed., *Intergroup Relations and Leadership*. New York: John Wiley and Sons, Inc., 1962.

North, Robert C., Richard A. Brody, and Ole R. Holsti, "Some Empirical Data on the Conflict Spiral," *Peace Research Papers*, **1,** 1964.

Osgood, Charles E., "Studies on the Generality of Affective Meaning Systems," *American Psychologist*, **17,** 10–28, 1962.

Osgood, Charles E., and Robert C. North, "From Individual to Nation: An Attempt to Make Explicit the Usually Implicit Process of Personifying International Relations," an unpublished manuscript (Urbana and Stanford, 1963).

Osgood Charles E., George J. Suci, and Percy H. Tannenbaum, *The Measurement of Meaning*. Urbana, Ill.: University of Illinois Press, 1957.

Pachter, Henry M., *Collision Course: The Cuban Missile Crisis and Coexistence*. New York: Frederick A. Praeger, Inc., 1963.

Rapoport, Anatol, *Fights, Games and Debates*. Ann Arbor, Mich.: University of Michigan Press, 1960.

Richardson, Lewis F., *Arms and Insecurity*. Pittsburgh, Pa.: The Boxwood Press, 1960.

Rosenau, James N., "Pre-Theories and Theories of Foreign Policy," Paper prepared for the Conference on Comparative and International Politics, Evanston, Ill., Northwestern University, Apr. 2–4, 1964.

San Francisco Chronicle, Oct. 14, 1964.

Siegel, Sidney, *Non-Parametric Statistics for the Behavioral Sciences*. New York: McGraw-Hill Book Company, 1956.

Snyder, Richard C., H. W. Bruck, and Burton Sapin, eds., *Foreign Policy Decision Making*. New York: The Free Press, 1962.

Sorensen, Theodore C., *Decision-Making in the White House*. New York: Columbia University Press, 1963.

Stone, Philip J., Robert F. Bales, J. Zvi Namenwirth, and Daniel M. Ogilvie, "The General Inquirer: A Computer System for Content Analysis and Retrieval Based on the Sentence as a Unit of Information," *Behavioral Science*, **7,** 484–494, 1962.

Suci, George J., "An Investigation of the Similarity between the Semantic Space of Five Different Cultures," Report for the Southwest Project in Comparative Psycholinguistics, 1957.

Verba, Sidney, "Assumptions of Rationality in Models of the International System," *World Politics*, **14,** 93–117, 1961.

Wright, Quincy, "Design for a Research Project on International Conflicts and the Factors Causing Their Aggravation or Amelioration," *Western Political Quarterly*, **10,** 263–275, 1957.

Wright, Quincy, "The Cuban Quarantine of 1962," *in* John G. Stoessinger and Alan F. Westin, eds., *Power and Order*. New York: Harcourt Brace & World, Inc., 1964.

6

JAMES A. ROBINSON · CHARLES F. HERMANN · MARGARET G. HERMANN

Search Under Crisis in Political Gaming and Simulation[1]

A study of the behavior of foreign-policy makers in crises, employing multiple runs of the Inter-Nation Simulation. Six hypotheses are tested, which were deduced from theories borrowed from several branches of the social and behavioral sciences.

Crisis

Crisis usually connotes a situation or event that threatens something about which someone cares greatly. The word belongs to the layman, not to the specialist. With few exceptions (e.g., Lasswell and Kaplan, 1950, pp. 242–243), social scientists have not defined crisis functionally or technically. Consequently, the term has several meanings (Miller and Iscoe, 1963; Wiener and Kahn, 1962). A number of current uses illustrate its connotations. For example, at least thirteen books in which crisis is the first word of the title were scheduled for publication within four months of 1964 (*Publishers' Weekly*, August 31, 1964, Vol. 186, No. 9, Title Index). The titles included crises in the humanities; crisis and response; crisis in medical education; and crisis of political imagination. To suggest the wealth of meanings

Especially prepared for this volume. James A. Robinson is Mershon Professor of Political Science and Director of the Mershon Center for Education in National Security at The Ohio State University; Charles F. Hermann is Assistant Professor of Politics at Princeton University; and Margaret G. Hermann is Assistant Professor of Psychology at Princeton University.

[1]This chapter is a revision of "Simulating Crisis Decision Making," prepared originally for a panel on "Foreign Policy and Affairs" at the Joint Meeting of the Institute of Management Sciences and the Operations Research Society of America, Minneapolis, October 7, 1964. Support for this research was provided by Contract N123(60530)32779A, Project Michelson, U.S. Naval Ordnance Test Station, China Lake, Calif. We are indebted to Wayman Crow and John Raser of the Western Behavioral Sciences Institute and to Lincoln Bloomfield and Barton Whaley of the Center for International Studies at the Massachusetts Institute of Technology for their splendid assistance in collecting the data presented in this chapter. Lucia Walton commented critically on an early version.

attached to the term, Hermann (1965, Chap. 1) documented that psychologists and sociologists frequently use crisis in technical papers as if it were synonymous with disaster, panic, stress, and tension.

Initially, we were interested in crisis in organizations that decide foreign policy (Hermann, 1963). Surveys of numerous decisions and relatively intensive studies of a few cases (Snyder, Bruck, and Sapin, 1962; Robinson, 1962, pp. 23–69) led us to consider crisis as one kind of decision situation or "occasion of decision" (Barnard, 1938).[2] From the rich and varied connotations of the term, we selected three that we denoted as *crisis*. In adopting a relatively technical definition, we undoubtedly surrendered some of the interpretive range of the looser term; but, what we lost in generality, we hoped to gain in precision.

For our research on crisis, we classified occasions of decision in three ways. First, a situation is either *anticipated* or *unanticipated*. The North Korean invasion of South Korea in June, 1950, was unanticipated by decision makers in Washington and other capitals (Snyder and Paige, 1958). Likewise, the discovery of Soviet missiles in Cuba in early October, 1962, apparently was not anticipated at the highest levels of American policy making. In contrast, one notes situations about which decision makers receive advance warning, as in the periodic extension and revision of trade-agreement legislation (Bauer, Pool, and Dexter, 1962).

Second, in this research, crisis situations were classified according to the degree of *threat* they presented to the decision-making unit. In international relations, one typically thinks of threats as involving potentially severe damage to the goals or objectives of the decision makers of a nation-state or to those of the authoritative decision makers of an international or regional organization. When, in 1948, the British notified the United States of their intention to withdraw economic support from Greece and Turkey, American foreign policy makers confronted a serious threat to their objectives in that area, namely, the preservation of national states independent of control by the Soviet Union (Jones, 1955). After North Korea invaded South Korea, the United States (and the United Nations) faced a threat to peace and to the integrity of their commitments to defend small countries on the perimeter of the Soviet Union.

A third characteristic of decision situations that we emphasize is the *time* available for responding. For example, American decision makers had approximately one week in which to decide whether to commit American troops to the defense of South Korea in the summer of 1950. On the other hand, three years earlier, in 1947, the American government spent approximately fifteen weeks in developing the Truman Doctrine to replace British support of Greece and Turkey.

In our research, we arbitrarily define crisis according to these three dimensions, or characteristics, of an occasion of decision. The most crisis-loaded situation is an unanticipated, major threat to objectives that compels decisino makers to respond almost immediately. The least crisislike, most routine situation is one that decision makers anticipate, that con-

[2]We forego a philosophic digression into the definition of situation or occasion. Those interested in pursuing this point are referred to Riker (1957).

tains little threat to any important goal, and that allows an extended period for response.

Three Studies Involving Political Gaming or Simulation[3]

This conception of crisis was developed for investigating hypotheses about decision making in which crisis was an independent variable. The hypotheses reported in this chapter involve relations between crisis, on the one hand, and search for information and alternatives, on the other. The data used for testing these hypotheses are drawn from three studies involving political gaming or simulation. The first, carried out at Great Lakes Naval Training Center in 1963, was directed by the authors. The political simulation used in this research was a modification of Inter-Nation Simulation. The second, conducted at the San Diego Naval Training Center in 1964, was directed by John R. Raser and Wayman J. Crow of the Western Behavioral Sciences Institute (WBSI). Again, Inter-Nation Simulation was used. The third, undertaken by the Center for International Studies at the Massachusetts Institute of Technology (MIT) in 1964, was directed by Lincoln P. Bloomfield and Barton Whaley. This study used a political-diplomatic game, or exercise.

[3]In this chapter we distinguish between political games and simulations. Both involve attempts to model or represent some aspects of political "reality," and each has potentially valuable uses. Our distinction depends on the existence of programmed relationships among some or all of the variables in the model of reality. A political game does not include programmed features; a simulation does. A political game always involves human players, but can be played on a computer. A more detailed comparison of the particular simulation and political game used in this analysis appears at the end of this section.

In designing the research at Great Lakes, we developed a "Post-Simulation Questionnaire" with which to gather data from participants. Through the cooperation of colleagues at WBSI and MIT, the same questionnaire was administered to participants in their studies. These three sets of data are used to test the same hypotheses. When results are similar among the three studies, we attach more confidence to the findings than we would if they differed radically or if they were based on only one of the studies. As the subsequent description of the research will indicate, the Great Lakes and WBSI simulations and the MIT game differ sufficiently that we are disinclined to attribute complementary findings to the similarities among the three political exercises.

The Great Lakes Study

To create crises (and complementary noncrises) and to study them as variables that affect decisions, we used Inter-Nation Simulation, a "man–computer" representation of factors and processes assumed to be critical in international relations (see Guetzkow, Alger, Brody, Noel, and Snyder, 1963). Inter-Nation Simulation emphasizes relations *between* and *among* units that correspond to nations. The units are complex enough, however, to be observed also for their intraunit or intraorganizational decision making. At Great Lakes Naval Training Center, we studied crises *within* national offices.

The circumstances of the research can be summarized briefly. We conducted eleven one-day simulations during the autumn of 1963. On each day, thirty different Navy petty officers acted as officials of six nations. Each nation had five positions: Central Decision Maker (head of government),

Internal Decision Maker (deputy chief of government), External Decision Maker (foreign secretary), Force Decision Maker (defense minister), and Aspiring Decision Maker (leader of the opposition).

Before the simulations were held, participating officers were given information about the Inter-Nation Simulation that included the "rules of the game," descriptions of the responsibilities of each office, and examples of the simulation forms and documents. When participants first reported for duty, we gave them 2½ hours' instruction and put them through an hour's practice. Then they began the first of six official one-hour decision periods during which they allocated basic resources, decided on investments or loans, engaged in conferences within their nation and with other nations, dispatched a delegate to an international organization, considered membership in a world bank, drafted military attack and response plans, and sent and received messages.

One of the most important experimental features was the method of introducing crises for the nations. We were not confident that the nations would create for themselves a sufficient number of crises, as we defined them, for statistical analysis. Therefore, it seemed necessary in each decision period to generate crises or to lay the ground for the quasi-natural development of crises in a later period. These prearranged interventions, planned, written, and timed in advance, were executed by the Simulation Staff and by confederate nations. They created occasions of decision by threatening goals or objectives of the experimental nations. Some threats were sprung without warning; others were hinted at or promised some time before actual invocation and could thus be regarded as anticipated threats rather than unanticipated threats. Some demanded response within fifteen minutes; others allowed as long as an hour for decision.

The WBSI Study

Inter-Nation Simulation was used also in the WBSI study, which included twelve separate runs. Each run had five nations with four decision makers each to fill the roles of Central Decision Maker, External Decision Maker, Force Decision Maker, and Aspiring Decision Maker. The participants, recruits who had just completed basic training at the San Diego Naval Training Center, participated for 4½ days, with 2 days devoted to learning and practicing the simulation and a half day to debriefing. The two days of experimental time were divided into twelve decision periods.

Unlike the Great Lakes study, the WBSI research did not concern crisis per se. It was undertaken to test hypotheses about some consequences of a nation's possessing "the capacity for delayed response" to a nuclear attack from another nation (see Raser and Crow, 1964). In the Great Lakes study, "contrived" situations of crisis and noncrisis were introduced at times determined in advance by the researchers. In the WBSI study, no such experimental interventions were made. Therefore, to the extent that crises developed, they did so "naturally."

The MIT Study

The MIT research used a political-diplomatic game (see Bloomfield and Whaley, 1965). Four or five teams are usually involved in the game, of which two represent the United States and Soviet Union. Other teams may depict individual nations or constellations of nations (e.g., Western Europe).

The number of players varies from team to team. The U. S. and Soviet teams normally contain five to seven members and play roles that coincide with roles of actual officials in high-level foreign-policy organizations in the American and Soviet governments. Other teams may be smaller. The total number of participants in a game is usually fifteen to twenty.

The data used in this chapter were obtained from two games played in 1964. In both, players were drawn from military, political, and research institutions closely associated with contemporary American defense policy making. These expert players received a booklet of materials several days in advance of the game. A single briefing prepared them to execute the procedures of the exercise. The games were played during a two-day period, with each move lasting about two hours.

The MIT study investigated "crisis management." Potential crises involving the United States were imagined, scenarios launched the event, and players responded with policy moves.

Some Ways in which the Inter-Nation Simulation and the Political-Diplomatic Game Differ

The MIT political-diplomatic game (MIT game) differs from Inter-Nation Simulation (INS) in several respects and thus provides a contrasting arena in which to test crisis hypotheses. First, INS nations and roles are abstractions and bear fictitious titles that correspond only conceptually to "real world" nations or roles. In the MIT game, nations and positions resemble more closely actual nations and roles in contemporary international politics.

Second, both INS studies begin with very brief descriptions of the state of the simulated world and allow the participants to interpret that world and make it their own. The MIT game opens with a detailed scenario of a realistic crisis (e.g., one involving the United States' sea-based deterrent weapons system).

Third, INS decisions are usually made in quantitative terms, and the results are calculated according to a set of arithmetic rules largely unknown to the participants and beyond the control of the Simulation Directors once the exercise begins. Decisions in the MIT game, on the other hand, are not calculated according to such formulas but rather are judged for appropriateness by the Control team, which consists of several knowledgable experts on the subject of the crisis. Control may also drastically change the time of the game being played and rewrite the scenario between periods or moves.

Fourth, INS research at Great Lakes and WBSI used participants who were not substantive specialists nor members of political elites. The MIT game is often played by relatively high-level policy makers from Washington and by specialists in research institutions.

Fifth, it is customary to distinguish the realism, qualitative character, and "unprogrammed rules" of the MIT game from the abstractions, quantitative symbols, and formal programs of INS. Games are usually manual exercises, while simulations are subject to computer manipulation. INS, although potentially a partial-computer activity, was manually calculated in the Great Lakes and WBSI runs.

Decision Situation and Search

We were interested in crisis as a decision situation because we had reason to believe that decision-making units respond differently to different kinds of situations. Although our theories of political decision making were not so refined that we knew precisely what differences to expect between international crisis and noncrisis, studies of individual decisions and other sources suggested some differences, especially with respect to search activities like the gathering of information and the construction of alternatives.

Some normative theories of decision making assume a linear relation between the amount of information and the number of alternatives available, on the one hand, and the quality of the prescribed decision, on the other. Similarly, much of the normative concern about crises and much of the effort to find ways of avoiding them have been predicated on the assumption that, in crises, search is forestalled and that, as a result, the rationality of choices is limited. In contrast to such theorizing, some experiments have shown that moderate stress produces creative decision making, including search, and induces more search and innovation than either absence of stress or presence of intense stress (e.g., Hare, 1962, p. 265). Like Berelson (1952) and Downs (1957), however, we do not necessarily assume that the more information or alternatives obtained, the better the decision will be.

The acts of searching for information and alternatives are aspects of the intelligence stage of any decision process (Lasswell, 1956). Even if judgment of the relative merits of outcomes based on differing amounts of search is reserved, the potential of the search variable to produce different kinds of policy outcomes makes it an important element in the analysis of decision making. Not only may the amount of search for information and alternatives affect policy, but crises, as compared with noncrises, may affect the degree of search. Thus, we have a chain of hypotheses in which crisis produces changes in amount of search, which in turn alters the nature of the policy outcome. The hypotheses explored in this chapter concern the first part of the sequence, the relationship between crisis and search.

Data on the hypotheses about search were gathered through a questionnaire administered to the participants at the termination of the trials or runs in the three studies. Each participant was asked to select two problem situations that involved him and originated outside his nation. For his first problem situation, the participant was instructed to choose one that he thought had the following characteristics: (1) It came as a surprise to his nation, (2) threatened a major goal or goals of his nation, and (3) imposed severe time pressures for response. These characteristics correspond to the three dimensions of our concept of crisis. After the participant selected a problem situation with these features, he was asked a series of multiple-choice questions about the situation. For his second problem situation, the participant was asked to choose one that did *not* contain these same three characteristics. This situation represents a noncrisis occasion of decision. The same multiple-choice questions were asked about the second problem situation.[4]

In the following six hypotheses, two types of search are differentiated. One type is search for alternatives, i.e., the attempt to seek different possible solutions or methods of handling the situation confronting the nation's decision makers. The other kind of

---

[4]Because of pretests of earlier versions of the questionnaire, the maximum number of respondents for Great Lakes is 123; for WBSI, 216; for MIT, 28. The absence of a response to a particular question results in a somewhat smaller sample on individual items. The questionnaire used in this analysis is reproduced in Hermann (1965, pp. 302–314).

search involves obtaining information necessary for making a decision and choosing among alternatives. On the basis of our observations about crises, some of which will be reviewed in examining the individual hypotheses, we expected that participants would report less search for alternatives in crisis, but more search for information. The time pressures associated with crisis would place a premium on all kinds of search activity (March and Simon, 1958). The often relatively small units involved in crisis decisions (Hermann, 1963) and the tendency of individuals to exhibit rigidity under stress (Driver, 1962) would reduce the ability to identify alternatives. Thus, with the limited time available, information would be sought to reduce the high degree of uncertainty associated with the crisis. The reduction in search for alternatives, as well as other features of crises, was hypothesized to decrease the number of alternative solutions actually considered by the decision makers as possible means of handling the situation. To evaluate these hypotheses in the three studies, the questionnaire data applicable to each relationship were subjected to statistical analysis.[5]

Hypothesis 1: *In crisis as compared with noncrisis, less search for alternative courses of action will be made.*

The first hypothesis involves search concerned with identifying alternatives. Some studies (e.g., March, 1962, p. 197) report that large organizations, such as those responsible for foreign policy, examine alternative courses of action sequentially rather than simultaneously. Under these conditions, confirmation of this hypothesis would mean that, in crisis, decision makers settle for one of the first alternatives they examine rather than consider one alternative after another. They search for a new alternative after disadvantages have been detected in the one under evaluation. A curtailment of alternative search may indicate that, under crisis, the ability of decision makers to assess alternatives critically decreases. Therefore, the need to reject an initial alternative and to continue searching is reduced. On the other hand, under the threat of crisis, decision makers may believe that no alternative open to their nation would be attractive, and their aspiration for a "highly favorable" solution and their motivation to search for such an alternative may thereby be lowered. In other words, the "satisficing" mechanism (Simon, 1957, pp. 241–273) may enter the crisis decision process at an early point and may result in the decision makers' increased willingness to accept one of the first alternatives that occurs to them.

The findings on hypothesis 1 are presented in Table 1. As in subsequent presentations of the data, Table 1 is subdivided into three sections, one section each for the Great Lakes, the WBSI, and the MIT results. The Great Lakes and WBSI data show that more participants shifted from "much search in noncrisis" to "little search in

[5]A type of chi-square, the McNemar test (Siegel, 1956, pp. 63–67), was used to accept or reject most of the hypotheses discussed below. This nonparametric test is designed to measure change in nominal data for two related samples. (Does a respondent when asked identical questions about a crisis and a noncrisis change his answer from one to the other?) In the tables accompanying the hypotheses, the critical change data are in the lower left- and upper right-hand cells. When one-half the sum of these two cells is less than 5, a binomial test (Siegel, 1956, pp. 36–42) has been used. With either test, a result was accepted as statistically significant if the p value was equal to or less than .05.

TABLE 1

Less Search for Alternatives in Crisis

		Great Lakes Crisis		WBSI Crisis		MIT Crisis	
		Much Search	Little Search	Much Search	Little Search	Much Search	Little Search
Noncrisis	Much Search	8	27	19	60	3	5
	Little Search	13	72	25	110	5	14
		$\chi^2 = 4.22$ $p < .05$		$\chi^2 = 13.60$ $p < .01$		$\chi^2 = .10$ Nonsignificant (n.s.)	

TABLE 2

Fewer Alternatives Perceived in Crisis

		Great Lakes Crisis		WBSI Crisis		MIT Crisis	
		Few Alternatives	Many Alternatives	Few Alternatives	Many Alternatives	Few Alternatives	Many Alternatives
Noncrisis	Few Alternatives	75	12	104	28	12	6
	Many Alternatives	28	6	58	22	4	5
		$\chi^2 = 5.62$ $p < .01$		$\chi^2 = 9.77$ $p < .01$		$\chi^2 = .10$ n.s.	

TABLE 3

More Search for Information in Crisis

		Great Lakes Crisis		WBSI Crisis		MIT Crisis	
		Much Search	Little Search	Much Search	Little Search	Much Search	Little Search
Noncrisis	Much Search	15	26	36	44	3	5
	Little Search	24	57	55	79	2	17
		$\chi^2 = .02$ n.s.		$\chi^2 = .81$ n.s.		Binomial Test n.s.	

crisis" (upper right-hand cell of each section) than shifted in the opposite direction (lower left-hand cells). Both the Great Lakes and the WBSI shifts are large enough to be statistically significant and, thus, to support the hypothesis. By contrast, the hypothesis is not confirmed by the MIT data, in which an equal number of people reported less and more alternative search in crisis. Two of the three sets of questionnaire data, then, supported the hypothesis.

Hypothesis 2: *In crisis as compared with noncrisis, fewer alternatives will be identified by the national decision makers.*

One might reason that, if search for alternatives is reduced in crisis (hypothesis 1), then fewer alternatives will be introduced in the crisis decision process. It is conceivable, however, that a substantial number of alternatives might be identified by the decisional unit without its conducting any formal search activity. The absence of alternative search may make the consideration of a large number of alternative courses of action unlikely, but clearly hypotheses 1 and 2 are not identical. Hypothesis 2 was advanced by Snyder and Paige (1958, p. 362) on the basis of their examination of the American decision to resist the invasion of South Korea in 1950. Furthermore, Holsti (1965, p. 374) found the decision makers in each alliance perceived the number of alternatives open to their coalition was significantly reduced in the crisis preceding the outbreak of World War I.

The results from the three studies, displayed in Table 2, repeat the pattern found for the previous hypothesis. In the simulations at Great Lakes and WBSI, the participants' shift from many alternatives in noncrisis to few alternatives in crisis is significantly greater than that in the opposite direction. The hypothesis is supported. In the MIT political game, however, the hypothesis is not confirmed.

Hypothesis 3: *In crisis as compared with noncrisis, search for information is more likely.*

We now turn to our other classification of search—that concerned with obtaining more information. We had reasoned that, given the limited response time allowed by crisis, the decision makers would make a substantial effort to search for information. This hypothesis was suggested by such research as Mack and Baker's (1961) study of unanticipated air-raid warnings and Wohlstetter's (1962) examination of the attack on Pearl Harbor. In both these crisislike illustrations, individuals devoted considerable time and energy to searching for information with which to confirm the nature of the situation they were experiencing. The surprise element incorporated in the crisis tended to generate disbelief and uncertainty, which in turn emphasized the need to gather more information before making a decision.

Contrary to our expectation, the hypothesis was not confirmed. As Table 3 shows, none of the questionnaire data supported the hypothesis.

To explain this unexpected result, we found it necessary to reexamine some of our assumptions about kinds of search and impact of crisis upon them. First, we had assumed that immediacy, by definition a part of any crisis, would place a premium on the total amount of search that could be undertaken by the decision makers. In other words, a feature of crisis would be a change in the normal search activities involved in the decision process. In Tables 1 and 3, however, the largest number of respondents in each of the three studies report little

TABLE 4

Less Information Search in Crisis Because of Pressures

		Great Lakes Crisis		WBSI Crisis		MIT Crisis	
		Well-Defined	Pressures	Well-Defined	Pressures	Well-Defined	Pressures
Noncrisis	Well-Defined	11	26	29	29	8	5
	Pressures	2	18	13	8	0	4
		$\chi^2 = 18.88$ $p < .01$		$\chi^2 = 5.36$ $p < .05$		Binomial Test $p < .05$	

TABLE 5

More Search for Information than Alternatives in Crisis

		Great Lakes Information Search		WBSI Information Search		MIT Information Search	
		Much Search	Little Search	Much Search	Little Search	Much Search	Little Search
Alternative Search	Much Search	9	12	24	20	2	6
	Little Search	29	71	66	104	2	16
		$\chi^2 = 6.24$ $p < .01$		$\chi^2 = 23.55$ $p < .01$		Binomial Test n.s.	

TABLE 6

Less Decision Confidence in Crisis

		Great Lakes Crisis		WBSI Crisis		MIT Crisis	
		Much Confidence	Little Confidence	Much Confidence	Little Confidence	Much Confidence	Little Confidence
Noncrisis	Much Confidence	34	48	51	96	12	12
	Little Confidence	16	22	26	42	1	1
		$\chi^2 = 15.01$ $p < .01$		$\chi^2 = 39.02$ $p < .01$		$\chi^2 = 7.69$ $p < .01$	

search in both noncrisis and crisis. The question can be raised: Did the conditions for failing to undertake search differ from noncrisis to crisis, particularly with regard to information search, or was our assumption wrong about the implications of crisis? Fortunately, from other data collected in the questionnaire, we were able to examine this issue. The following hypothesis was investigated.

Hypothesis 4: *If less search for information is made in crisis than in noncrisis, search is likely to be limited by pressures rather than made unnecessary because the situation is already well defined.*

This hypothesis was explored by means of a subanalysis of all the participants who reported little search for information in both crisis and noncrisis. (The individuals represented in the lower right-hand cell of each section of Table 3.) The reasons these persons gave for conducting little information search in noncrisis were compared with their reasons for little information search in crisis. Table 4 presents the results. In all three research enterprises, a definite shift occurred in the explanations advanced for failure to search. A statistically significant number changed from reporting sufficient information in noncrisis (the situation so well-defined that search was not required) to pressures preventing search in crisis. Although information search did not increase in crisis as compared with noncrisis, changed conditions for conducting information search were indicated in the participants' responses.

Even though the reasons for neglecting information search in crisis as opposed to noncrisis were consistent with our initial assumption, the differing effect of crisis upon information and alternative search did not appear as predicted. Alternative search declined in crisis, but information search did not increase. The pressure under which crisis decisions were made prevented much search activity. Given the limited effort devoted to search, might relatively more attention be devoted to information than alternative search? Our initial position led us to postulate the following hypothesis.

Hypothesis 5: *In a crisis, to the extent that search behavior occurs (defined as the sum of both search for information and search for alternative courses of action), the frequency of search for information will be greater than the frequency of search for alternatives.*

The data in Table 5 repeat a pattern we have seen before. In the Great Lakes and WBSI simulations, the hypothesis is supported by the statistics. A number of participants show differences in crisis between information and alternative search. Significantly more of the Great Lakes and WBSI participants report little search for alternatives and much search for information than the reverse. Among the MIT players, however, the number indicating the reverse of the behavior predicted by the hypothesis is slightly larger than the number supporting it. Again, the hypothesis is confirmed in two of the three studies.

At the beginning of this section, we stated that the hypotheses would be confined to the relationship between crisis and search, although we speculated that differences in search would affect policy outcomes. A final hypothesis drawn from the questionnaire data will provide the basis for one kind of speculation about the connection between search and outcomes.

Hypothesis 6: *In crisis as compared with noncrisis, the decision-makers' confidence in the ability of their decision to protect the affected goal is decreased.*

As indicated by the p values in Table 6, the hypothesis is statistically supported in the three studies in which the questionnaire was administered. The participants' confidence is lower in crisis that noncrisis.

This hypothesis does not directly involve search, but it may have implications for the variable we have been examining. We have seen that, although the relative amount of information search compared with alternative search increased in crisis, the pressures of the situation restricted both kinds of search. The limited amount of information and the reduced number of alternatives might be expected to reduce confidence in any decision that is made. This proposition illustrates the ways in which amount of information and alternative search could affect confidence in a policy regardless of its content. Other hypotheses may indicate how the substantive content of outcomes varies with the amount and type of search undertaken by the decision unit.

Finally, it can be noted that the attitude toward an outcome suggested by hypothesis 6 may influence search. After a decision has been made and a policy established, another type of search might be expected if decision confidence is low. Such search would attempt to seek approval and confirmation of the decision taken in order to reduce uncertainty and increase confidence.

All but one of the six hypotheses was confirmed in the questionnaire responses of the participants in the Great Lakes and WBSI simulations. Data from the MIT political game corresponded to those of the other two studies for three of the hypotheses. Ignoring for a moment the divergence of the MIT findings on the other three hypotheses, we can advance a rather coherent summary. Under crisis, both the search for alternative courses of action and the actual number of such alternatives considered by the political decision makers are reduced. There is some indication that search is restricted by the pressure of a crisis. Certainly pressure rather than a well-defined situation was the reason advanced for less information search in crisis. Although the absolute amount of information search does not expand in crisis, relatively more information search than alternative search occurs. The pattern of less alternative and information search in crisis may contribute to the finding that, in crisis, confidence in any policy decision is reduced.

Before we consider the implications of these findings for characterizing crisis as pathological or functional, attention must be directed to the three discrepancies between the MIT political game and the two simulations. Two types of explanation are available. The first is statistical; it argues that the differences should not be taken seriously, given the small number of individuals who completed the questionnaire in the MIT game. If the number of MIT respondents had approached the size of the Great Lakes and WBSI samples, the results might have been quite different. The other kind of explanation recognizes some difference between the simulations and the political game and their respective ability to reflect decision making in actual foreign-policy making organizations. Perhaps the use of participants in the MIT exercises who are experts in foreign policy in contrast to the enlisted Navy personnel used in the other studies accounts for the divergence. We have previously described other differences, any of which could be important. All the explanations of this type raise the need for "validity studies" in which these same hypotheses are explored with data from "real" international political crisis.

Crisis as Pathological or Functional

Several writers distinguish among kinds of crisis. Neustadt (1960, p. 186) differentiates *destructive* and *productive* crises in presidential politics. Snyder (1962) similarly observes different effects of crisis in defense policies. Our analysis of participant-selected simulation and game crises also supports the existence of destructive and productive types; or, alternatively, the analysis indicates that a crisis may be characterized by elements of both. A crisis may be an occasion for organizational malfunctioning but may at the same time contribute positively to the process and outcome of decision making.

The three studies certainly contain evidence for interpreting crisis as a form of pathological behavior. For example, the failure to search for alternative means of handling a crisis (hypothesis 1) may contribute to a situation in which only one or two alternatives are considered. As a consequence, an increased tendency to lower aspirations for the best possible response may occur at precisely the time when a decision of exceptional quality would be valuable for avoiding a grave and unusual threat.

Not only do decision makers report that they search for alternatives less in crisis, but they also perceive fewer alternatives available in such situations (hypothesis 2). Without adopting the position, "the more alternatives, the better," one is likely to regret choosing among a severely restricted range of choices when the consequences of action are important.

Some of the results, however, permit a more positive view of crisis than the pathological one. Social scientists now recognize positive as well as negative consequences of conflict (Coser, 1956; North, Koch, and Zinnes, 1960), a topic closely related to crisis. Perhaps the same perspective may be applied to crises. Without depreciating the uncertainties attached to decisions taken in response to basic threats in short response time and without warning, we think it worth acknowledging some more or less *rational* characteristics of decision activity observed in the simulated crises.

Evidence of rational behavior includes the propositions that search for information was not more likely in crisis than in noncrisis (hypothesis 3) and thus would not necessarily inhibit action; and that, when search was restricted, decision makers attributed nonsearch to pressures for action and did not delude themselves that the situation was clearly defined when in fact it was not (hypothesis 4). Moreover, the search in crises was more for information than for alternatives (hypothesis 5). Given a complicated response strategy, as in deterrence, such search seems quite appropriate; programmed alternatives may be available, but selection among them requires prior information about their relative appropriateness.

On the other hand, hypothesis 5 also has potential *negative* consequences. In some kinds of crisis, the greater search for information rather than for alternatives may be unfortunate. Like all occasions of decision, crisis situations involve uncertainty; information about vital factors is either unavailable or too costly to obtain. Excessive emphasis on search for information will not necessarily improve the factual bases of one's decision. Especially if the situation is one for which no programmed or prepackaged alternative responses have been prepared, failure to move from information search to alternative search may be disadvantageous.

That decision makers' confidence in their alternatives decreases in crises (hypothesis 6) may also have either negative or positive effects. If loss of confidence is associated with defensiveness, decision makers under crisis may be less open to sharing the basis of their decision with others. Hence, acquisition of further support may suffer. Moreover, rigidity conceivably could cause a decision unit to ignore *feedback* about the consequences of a decision and to create additional organizational difficulties, especially if the feedback were negative.

On the other hand, lack of confidence, if not associated with defensiveness and rigidity, may have the positive effect of motivating a unit to search for support by communicating more widely with allies and alliances. In addition, it may alert one to monitoring and appraising the execution of a decision and to keeping the decision up to date by altering it or terminating it to accommodate new developments.

These tentative suggestions about the relation of crisis to search constitute only illustrations of the implications of crisis for foreign-policy making. Both the further testing of formulations such as these and the wider exploration of crisis as a recurring phenomenon of global politics deserve to be included on the research agenda of applied social and political sciences.

References

Barnard, C. I., *The Functions of the Executive*. Cambridge, Mass.: Harvard University Press, 1938.

Bauer, R., I. de S. Pool, and L. A. Dexter, *American Business and Public Policy*. New York: Atherton Press, 1962.

Berelson, B., "Democratic Theory and Public Opinion," *Public Opinion Quarterly*, **16,** 313–330, 1952.

Bloomfield, L. P., and B. Whaley, "The Political-Military Exercise: A Progress Report," *Orbis*, **4**, 854–870, 1965.

Coser, L. A., *The Functions of Social Conflict*. New York: The Free Press, 1956.

Downs, A., *An Economic Theory of Democracy*. New York: Harper & Row, Publishers, 1957.

Driver, M. J., "Conceptual Structure and Group Processes in an Inter-Nation Simulation." Unpublished doctoral dissertation, Princeton University, 1962.

Guetzkow, H., C. F. Alger, R. A. Brody, R. C. Noel, and R. C. Snyder, *Simulation in International Relations*. Englewood Cliffs, N.J.: Prentice-Hall, Inc., 1963.

Hare, A. P., *Handbook of Small Group Research*. New York: The Free Press, 1962.

Hermann, C. F., "Some Consequences of Crisis Which Limit the Viability of Organizations," *Administrative Science Quarterly*, **8**, 61–82, 1963.

Hermann, C. F., "Crisis in Foreign Policy Making: A Simulation of International Politics." Unpublished doctoral dissertation, Northwestern University, 1965.

Holsti, O. R., "The 1914 Case," *American Political Science Review*, **59,** 365–378, 1965.

Jones, J. W., *Fifteen Weeks*. New York: The Viking Press, Inc., 1955.

Lasswell, H. D., *The Decision Process*. College Park, Md.: University of Maryland, Bureau of Governmental Research, 1956.

Lasswell, H. D., and A. Kaplan, *Power and Society*. New Haven, Conn.: Yale University Press, 1950.

Mack, R. W., and G. W. Baker, *The Occasion Instant: The Structure of Social Responses to Unanticipated Air Raid Warnings*. Washington, D. C.: Disaster Research Group of the National Academy of Sciences–Natural Research Council, 1961.

March, J. G., "Some Recent Substantive and Methodological Developments in Theory of Organizational Decision-Making," *in* A. Ranney, ed., *Essays on the Behavioral Study of Politics*. Urbana, Ill.: University of Illinois Press, 1962.

March, J. G., and H. A. Simon, *Organizations*. New York: John Wiley and Sons, Inc., 1958.

Miller, K., and I. Iscoe, "The Concept of Crisis: Current Status and Mental Health Implications," *Human Organization*, **22,** 195–201, 1963.

Neustadt, R. H., *Presidential Power*. New York: John Wiley and Sons, Inc., 1960.

North, R. C., H. E. Koch, Jr., and Dina A. Zinnes, "The Integrative Functions of Conflict," *Journal of Conflict Resolution*, **4,** 355–374, 1960.

Raser, J. R., and W. J. Crow, *Winsafe II: An Inter-nation Simulation Study of Deterrence Postures Embodying Capacity to Delay Response*. La Jolla, Calif.: Western Behavioral Sciences Institute, 1964 (mimeo).

Riker, W. H., "Events and Situations," *Journal of Philosophy*, **53,** 57–70, 1957.

Robinson, J. A., *Congress and Foreign Policy-Making*. Homewood, Ill.: Dorsey Press, 1962.

Siegel, S., *Nonparametric Statistics for the Behavioral Sciences*. New York: McGraw-Hill Book Company, 1956.

Simon, H. A., *Models of Man*. New York: John Wiley and Sons, Inc., 1957.

Snyder, R. C., "The Korean Decision (1950) and the Analysis of Crisis Decision-making." Paper delivered at Stanford University Conference on Decision Making in Crisis, Jan. 12–13, 1962.

Snyder, R. C., H. W. Bruck, and B. Sapin, *Foreign Policy Decision-Making*. New York: The Free Press, 1962.

Snyder, R. C., and G. D. Paige, "The United States Decision to Resist Aggression in Korea: The Application of an Analytical Scheme," *Administrative Science Quarterly*, **3,** 341–378, 1958.

Wiener, A. J., and H. Kahn, *Crisis and Arms Control*. Harmon, N.Y.: Hudson Institute, 1962.

Wohlstetter, Roberta, *Pearl Harbor: Warning and Decision*. Stanford, Calif.: Stanford University Press, 1962.

7

CHARLES A. McCLELLAND

The Acute International Crisis

A statement of the rationale for system interaction analysis of international crises and a discussion of hypotheses derived from the assumption that crisis behavior is a function of the social organization internal to a nation-state.

A judgment made by Karl Deutsch in 1957 has proved to be correct: "There are some indications that at the present time the problem of interstate conflicts is ripe for a concerted research attack, combining the methods of several of the social sciences. The aim of this research would be to develop techniques to do three things: to identify generally those conflict situations and states which are likely to lead to war; to evaluate particular conflict situations and the probable lines along which they are likely to develop if left to themselves; and to suggest further possible techniques for controlling or containing such conflict situations so as to prevent them from breaking out into war."[1]

I

So many probings into the general subject of conflict have been undertaken in the last few years that it should be emphasized that the hypothetical formulation which is to be developed here concerning international crises is but one alternative approach among several, dependent on the body of "new thought" on the subject of conflict. Starting with the ordinary apperception that acute crises are concrete phenomena of international history with distinct time and place boundaries, we are able now to pick and

An excerpt from an article by the same name in *World Politics*, 1961, 14, 182–204. Reprinted by permission of the author and the Center of International Studies at Princeton University, publisher of that journal. The author is Professor of International Relations at the University of Southern California.

[1]Karl W. Deutsch, "Mass communications and the loss of freedom in national decision-making: A possible research approach to interstate conflicts," *Journal of Conflict Resolution*, I (June 1957), 200.

choose from a number of research suggestions.

One of these suggestions is that an international crisis marks a turning point in a conflict and a period when major decisions are likely to be made.[2] The advent of studies which analyze such crucial times in international politics according to the conceptual schemes of decision-making promises important gains in knowledge of the "internal behavior of actors" on occasions when the purposes and procedures of states are revealed at their most fundamental level.[3] The data of crises may be reexamined under the hypothesis that the actions of decision makers may be narrowed progressively under the impact of mass communications and popular opinion until there can be no turning back from war.[4]

The conceptual framework of decision making[5] is extremely attractive for the analysis of crisis because it so readily encompasses many of the aspects of international conflict and crisis which were noted above. In addition, there is a possible framework of inquiry whose virtues are not so apparent and whose potential has been developed but little in the study of international relations. This is system interaction analysis.[6] Decision making and interaction analyses represent different investigative interests and preoccupations. A study of data such as that of an acute crisis can be focused according to one mode of analysis as well as the other.

The subject matter of the acute international crisis is almost ideal for the application of the interaction approach. Prominent international crises are complexes of events which can be dissected, up to a point, to yield numerous sequences of related acts. A crisis temporarily narrows the focus of international politics and accelerates events in the public view so that there is very little difficulty in tracing sequences of action in which Event A calls forth Event B which calls forth Event C, etc., until the track is finally lost. After a number of such sequences have been traced and studied, similarities or identities of form in some of them may appear.

The concept of conflict as a bargaining process leads one to expect that bargaining going on during intense crisis periods will appear in the details of the interaction. If there are "turning points" or important decisions in crises, these, too, will take shape under observations of the sequences. There is a possibility of learning a great deal about a "system" from the record of its performance, even in the absence of much knowledge about its main working parts: one need not always be concerned over the motives and capabilities of the "actors."

Without any reference to the setting

---

[2]Jacques Freymond, *The Saar Conflict, 1945–1955*, London and New York, 1960, p. xiv.

[3]Richard C. Snyder and Glenn D. Paige, "The United States decision to resist aggression in Korea: The Application of an Analytical Scheme," *Administrative Science Quarterly*, III (December 1958), 341–378; Allen Whiting, *China Crosses the Yalu: The Decision to Enter the Korean War*, New York, 1960; Bernard C. Cohen, *The Political Process and Foreign Policy*, Princeton, N.J., 1957.

[4]Deutsch, *op. cit.*, 200–211. See also Selection 4 in this volume.

[5]Richard C. Snyder *et al.*, *Decision-making as an Approach to the Study of International Relations*, Princeton, N.J., 1954.

[6]Robert Bosc, "La sociologie américaine des relations internationales," *Revue de l'action populaire*, CXLV (February 1961), 207–214; C. A. McClelland, "The function of theory in international relations," *Journal of Conflict Resolution*, IV (September 1960), 323–326, and references.

of the crisis or to its larger meanings in the politics of international relations, the coding of the events of a crisis in chains of interaction sequences makes possible the identification of patterns and the comparison of forms of crisis behavior. Almost immediately, inferences are drawn and labels for several kinds of sequences are brought to mind. In the due course of an analytical study, a mapping of the complete crisis from its dramatic initial "input" event to its tailing-off into the "normalcy" of routine international relations becomes possible. Studies which are limited to such charting and immediate analysis will have value in putting historical data to a new use and in developing limited explanations of an aspect of international behavior. The ambition is greater, however: we wish to cope with the matter of peace and war and with the problem of control, as Karl Deutsch has indicated.

The variations in international conduct must arise from one of three sources of variables or a combination of any of these at any given passage of history: from the traits and characteristics of the participating actors, from the effects produced by their contacts and interactions and from factors of the environment that are external to the first two sources. Our conception is, further, that information concerning conditions created at a certain moment by the effects of interaction and by factors of the environment is returned to the participating actors. The latter are presumed to receive and process such "output" information and to feed the processed results (as inputs) into the next phase of participation in the particular and relevant "system of action." It is the decision-making approach which inquires into the finer detail of the "internal" processing of the incoming streams of "outputs" and of the fabrication of new "inputs" to the system.

In this essay, the testing of a hypothetical structure against the interaction data cannot be reported but only promised for the future. The concluding section, therefore, sets forth no more than several propositions about certain overriding traits and characteristics of participating actors in a crisis system and about the course of the current series of crises between the poles of peace and war.

II

Our basic assumption is that the kind of social organization developed in a nation-state fundamentally conditions its crisis behavior.

With the exception of China, the nation-states that play dominating roles in international affairs in the present day are either in a final transitional phase or already equipped with advanced modernizing social organizations. The two chief protagonists of the cold war, the U.S. and Soviet Union, are, without question, in the advanced condition. The "principal actors" of contemporary international relations have become urbanized, secularized, and industrialized. Moreover, they have created and multiplied whole banks of social subsystems, marvelously intricate, intertwined and interdependent, within their national boundaries. These subsystems have a "high metabolism" and ceaselessly undergo change, modification, and reorganization. The services of large numbers of men with technical and specialized skills are required to keep the subsystems running and in order. Further, a great many persons must become habituated to performing services in different roles virtually as if they were standard replaceable parts of a complex mechanism. Modernizing societies favor and propagate social values which are instrumental and supportive of problem-solving activities.

The pull of domestic interests and practices and, with these, the concomitant system of emergent public values of a modernizing nation-state will cause the international environment to be perceived increasingly as a burden and distraction to the society. Relations with other countries and peoples may be acknowledged to be beneficial or, in some matters, essential for national survival, but the maintenance demands of the national organization set up strains in the contrary direction. The most desirable international situation would be one in which all goes smoothly, with minimum effort, minimum cost, minimum attention and maximum national benefit. A proper system of international relations would resemble the day-to-day operations of a well-run industrial plant or government bureau. Multitudes of difficulties and problems would be received and dispatched in the work-flow by specialists in handling such business, while the organization as a whole, buffered against shock, surprise, and major disruption, would continue its struggle for self-maintenance and self-organization.

The consequences which follow from this analysis are straightforward. An international system consisting of but two advanced modernizing nation-states as the actors would be one of progressively routine action whose crises would be of diminishing intensity and frequency of occurrence, assuming, of course, that the domestic social structures of each actor suffered no major breakdown or disruption. The system might be expected to evolve toward minimum action and a maximum regulation of the surviving relationships. International relations between the two nations would, in larger measure, become administrative.

It is not suggested, however, that the dominant mode of interacting behavior would shift necessarily. Conflict relations would not have to turn into collaboration or accommodation. On the contrary, if relations were founded primarily on competition, the competition would fall, more and more, into expected patterns and, perhaps, would be brought under self-enforcing rules of the game. It is even conceivable that chronic warfare could be waged under normal conditions and within controlled behavioral boundaries. It might well drift into the agonistic form which tended to develop in earlier centuries.[7]

When we approach the historical records of acute international crises and begin the analyses of interaction sequences, we shall be on the watch for signs of "routinizing behaviors" and for the rise of "standard" techniques for managing situations which, with passing of time, have become familiar types. The interaction patterns ought to show much evidence of bids countered by bids, claims countered by claims, stalemates, standoffs, postponements, and no-win, no-solution outcomes; barring upheavals in the system or environmental innovations, the general trend should be toward repetitions of such patterns of action but with a decreasing volume of interaction in succeeding crises (i.e., less action in the mobilization and demobilization of the crisis). If such phenomena appear in the record, they will be taken as evidence

[7]Johan Huizinga, *Homo Ludens: A Study of the Play-element in Culture*, Boston, 1950, ch. 5; Hans Speier, "The social types of war," *American Journal of Sociology*, XLVI (January 1941), 445–454.

in support of the hypotheses of the conservative behavior, the routinizing tendencies, and the spillover effects of crises in advanced modernizing nation-states.

The trend toward the routinizing of acute conflict operations and toward the growth of specialized skills of crisis demobilization can be interrupted and reversed in any of three predictable situations, however. First, under the competitive drive to preserve leadership and solidarity, the leading actors will tend to seek out new theaters and new forms for the interplay of their main-line conflict, with the possibility that unexpected control problems will arise. Secondly, the associated actors of the international system whose countries are in the labors of transformation of their social organizations, whether within or outside the coalitions, may create novel crisis situations in unfamiliar arenas. "Standard" demobilization techniques may then fail to work. Thirdly, the bipolar structure of the system may begin to crumble gradually, causing the principal actors to face the difficulties of reorienting their strategies and devising new control techniques.

In any of these eventualities, the duration and intensity of an acute crisis may be increased and the confidence in the demobilization of crises without general war may be decreased. The view may be ventured that crises connected with the third eventuality—the gradual crumbling of the bipolar system—will come closer to precipitating general war than any other. A further thought is that an abrupt and drastic reorganization of the international system into a new form might prove more favorable to the cause of the preservation of general peace than the process of gradual and piecemeal evolution toward the new system.

In the case of the present subject, there is now no reasonable basis for declaring that international crises will or will not occur more frequently or more violently during the coming decade than during the last ten years.[8] Intuition and past performances notwithstanding, it remains impossible to say whether the prospects of general war have become stronger or weaker according to the number of exposures to acute crises since the close of the last major war. We have emphasized above that historical behavior as complex and multi-dimensional as that of contemporary international relations should be examined in different perspectives and through several investigative approaches. We have chosen one among the many with no guarantee of its truth-producing efficacy.

[8]A field of study as future-oriented as international relations might be expected to give much attention to the bases of prediction, whether by officials, commentators, or scholars, but little attention is, in fact, given to the matter. For a discussion, see Hans H. Toch, "The perception of future events: Case studies in social prediction," *Public Opinion Quarterly*, XXII (Spring 1958), 57–66.

PART FOUR

Restraints Against the Use of Violence: Military Preparations

INTRODUCTION

Parts II and III have dealt with the forces and sequences of events that push states in the direction of war. The present section and the next will be concerned with forces that impose restraints on potential users of violence or facilitate the resolution of controversies before they reach the stage of violence.

Restraints are forces that reduce the attractiveness of violence. They operate by reducing the perceived likelihood or value of winning a war or by increasing the perceived likelihood or cost of unfavorable outcomes resulting from the use of violence. The best-known restraints are military, i.e., preparation for war on the part of one state in an effort to deter another from the use of violence. This section will deal mainly with two traditions in the literature on military restraints: theories about the balance of power and theories about nuclear deterrence. Much of Part V will be devoted to a discussion of nonmilitary restraints.

Again, as in Part II, our introductory comment will place much emphasis on the immense speculative literature about military restraints. But it will be possible to allude to a few empirical studies that represent the vanguard of a new movement whose aim is to test more adequately past speculations on this topic and to generate new propositions that are more solidly grounded in fact.

Balance of Power Theories

Balance of power has been called the "central theoretical concept in international relations" (G. H. Snyder, 1960, p. 21). Unfortunately, it is also one of the least precise. The present discussion will lean heavily on a recent book that makes a heroic and at least partially successful effort to clear away the fog surrounding this concept (Claude, 1962).

Distribution of Power as a Source of Stability

In the context of this discussion, the term *power* refers to military capability, "the elements which contribute directly or indirectly to the capacity to coerce, kill or destroy" (Claude, 1962, p. 6).

Given this definition and given the (admittedly problematical) possibility of at least rough measurement of the amount of power possessed by a state, one can make statements about the *way in which power is distributed*, at any given time, among the states or coalitions of states in the world or some region of the world. For example, one might say, "Most of the power is in the hands of two great alliances" or "The great nations are about equal in power." The way in which power is distributed has sometimes been called the balance of power, but it seems wise to reserve the latter concept and speak instead of the *distribution of power*.

Balance of power theories always contain some concept of *international stability*. (This term is often not used, the concept being embodied in descriptions of the *aim* or *function* of the balance of power.) However, the theories in this area differ substantially in the way they define stability. Two major varieties are found. Most writers refer to a condition in which no major state can establish hegemony over another. Thus Gulick (1955, p. 30), describing the historical European international system, writes, "The fundamental aim of the balance of power was to insure the survival of independent states." To a few writers, however (e.g., Wolfers, 1962), the concept refers to the absence of war or of substantial war. A variety of the second theme is the concept employed by Burton (1965, p. 56), a situation in which "no state or states can without good cause be an aggressor."

The two concepts of stability just described are not totally antithetical. A situation in which no state can conquer another is *likely* to be one in which every state refrains from war. On the other hand, war is not *necessarily* precluded in such a situation; hence, these concepts are not synonymous. Indeed, writers who adopt the former (survival of independent states) concept regard war as occasionally necessary to preserve stability. Thus, Claude (1962, p. 52) writes, "More often than not, scholars assert that the function of the (balance of power) system is to safeguard the independence of states . . . *even at the cost of war*" (italics added).

It seems reasonable to suppose that differences in the concepts of stability employed by various writers are a function of differences in the *values* held by these writers. In an earlier era, when war was generally regarded as a tolerable evil, the concept more often took the first form, i.e., preservation of the major international actors. Today, when war is almost universally viewed as a great misfortune, stability is more frequently used in the second meaning, i.e., the absence of war or major war. Apparently recognizing the tendency of this concept to "drift" in meaning as a function of changing values and the importance which this concept has had in the thinking of policy makers in every era, Rosecrance (1963, p. 231) has taken the novel approach of defining stability as a condition in which the "outcomes fall within limits generally 'accepted' by the major participants in the [international] system."

Regardless of the nature of their concept of stability, all balance of power theorists assume that stability is a function of the distribution of power. The most stable distribution is usually assumed to be that which ensures that any would-be aggressor will find ranged against him power adequate to defeat him. (A distribution that accomplishes this goal is also sometimes called a balance of power, but again it seems wise to reserve the term.) But what distribution accomplishes this result? Two answers have been given to this question: Some authors stress the stability of *equilibrium* (also sometimes called balance of power), i.e., a situation in which the major potential antagonists are approximately equal in power. Others emphasize the stability of a situation in which those states (or alliances) that are more satisfied with the status quo have a *preponderance* of power.

How Stable Distributions Develop

Though they have not always agreed on the nature of a stable distribution, balance of power theorists have usually agreed on the mechanisms that produce such a distribution. Stable distributions are thought to arise out of the *policies* of statesmen. Policies thought to lead to stability include the following:

1. Strengthening one's own military capability if potential adversaries strengthen theirs (Claude, 1962).
2. Making alliances with states that are threatened by strong adversaries and breaking alliances with states that have become overly strong or aggressive (Claude, 1962). A state that shifts its alliances in order to preserve a stable distribution of power is called a *balancer*.
3. Arranging compensations to other major states when one state becomes stronger (Gulick, 1955).
4. Avoiding, where possible, the destruction of a major state, even if it has been an aggressor (Kaplan, 1957), and returning conquered states to the family of nations with full status (Gulick, 1955). It can be argued that it is often unwise, from the viewpoint of stability, to destroy or alienate a former aggressor because that state may be needed in the future as an ally against a new aggressor.
5. Weakening a potential adversary through various strategies including military attack.

A number of *conditions* have also been cited that allegedly encourage the development of a stable distribution of power by facilitating the adoption and execution of the strategies just listed. These will now be presented.

A Large Number of Powerful States (Multipolarity). It has often been asserted (e.g., by Deutsch and Singer, 1964) that stability is a positive function of the number of independent, powerful states. The argument usually given for this assertion runs as follows: the more states there are, the greater the variety of alliances that can be formed; hence, the greater the likelihood that some coalition can be assembled to deter or, if necessary, defeat any would-be aggressor.[1] Kaplan (1957) has tried to be more precise about the number of states required and asserts that

[1]A multipolar world is also sometimes assumed to enhance the efficiency of certain nonmilitary restraints against war (see Part V).

a stable world requires the existence of at least five powerful states. Clearly, at least three are needed for a policy of shifting alliances to be feasible. A bipolar world, with only two major powers, has frequently been cited as dangerously unstable (e.g., by Huntington, 1958). Recently, however, Waltz (1964) has argued that a bipolar world may be more stable than a multipolar world because leaders in the major states take greater responsibility for deterring aggression, i.e., are more likely to adopt policies needed to provide stability, less likely to "pass the buck" to other states in the face of a challenge. Rosecrance (1966) has attempted to reconcile Waltz's point of view with the earlier theory of the value of multipolarity.

Freedom of Action Among Statesmen. Statesmen must have considerable autonomy to be able to execute the fine maneuvers involved in shifting alliances, compensating adversaries, and restoring former enemies to power. Their freedom is often hampered by surveillance and interference from citizens and elected representatives, which suggests that democracies may not always be able to play a full role in producing stable power distributions (Gulick, 1955).

Visibility and Measurability of the Elements of Power. The more visible and measurable the components of the power possessed by other states, the greater is the likelihood of mobilizing sufficient counterpower to deter these states (Lasswell, 1950).

The Absence of Extreme Hostility Between States. The more hostile the people in one state are toward another, the less likely are they to want their state to form a defensive alliance with it, arrange for it to receive compensation, or restore it to its former world position after it has been defeated (Gulick, 1955). Since these are among the policies that produce stable distributions of power, hostility can be an enemy of stability (see the introduction to Part II for a discussion of hostility).

Similarity of Outlook Among the Major States. The philosopher Kant first pointed out the importance of cultural similarity for the balance of power (Gulick, 1955). The more similar two states are in culture, the more friendly they are likely to be and therefore the more capable will they be of forming defensive alliances or, if they are antagonists, of imposing moderate peace settlements on one another. In addition, according to this point of view, cultural similarity facilitates the estimation of military strength in another state (see point 3) because military traditions are likely to be similar.

Claude has suggested that the term *balance of power* be used to describe a situation (or "system," in his terms) in which it is possible for all states to adopt and carry to fruition policies that produce stable distributions of power.

Stability Through Concession —Organski's Theory

Though preferring not to call himself a "balance of power theorist," Organski (1959) is in the tradition of writers who advocate the necessity of confronting a potential aggressor with a preponderance of power. He argues that war usually comes about when a frustrated state becomes so strong that an adequate preponderance of power cannot be brought against it. He is also interested in the occasional case in which war is averted under such circumstances. According to Organski, war can be averted only if other states make concessions to the state whose power is growing and thereby reduce its frustration to the point at which the cost of war overshadows the potential advantages of war. Such concessions, commonly called *appeasement*, are seldom popular. There is always a fear that they will add further military capability to an already powerful adversary and at the same time whet his appetite for more concessions. Yet appeasement, may, at times, be the only way to avoid war and may even produce long-term stability if the adversary's goals are limited. Organski's position in this regard is very similar to Burton's (1962), which was described in the introduction to Part III.

Organski suggests that the likelihood of making concessions to a growing state and, thereby, of averting war depends on three factors:

1. The speed with which the state is growing. The more rapid this growth is, the less time will other states have to adjust to the necessity for change.

2. The perceived likelihood that the growing state will become dominant. The more obvious it is that a state will eventually be very powerful, the more likely are other states to become resigned to making concessions.

3. The flexibility of statesmen to adjust to new situations.

In addition, a fourth condition might be added.

4. The level of hostility toward the growing state. The greater this hostility, the slimmer the chances are that necessary concessions will be made to it.

Balance of Power and War

As mentioned earlier, most balance of power theorists hold that the most stable distribution of power is that which confronts any would-be aggressor with a military force adequate to ensure its defeat. Such an assumption is quite reasonable (indeed it is tautological) if one's notion of stability is preservation of the major international actors. But, if one adopts the second definition of stability, i.e., the preservation of peace, it is necessary to go one step further in theory construction. States are clearly capable of beginning wars which they are not able to win. Indeed, the pages of history are strewn with examples of states that launched suicidal military ventures. Hence, for balance of power theory to form the basis for an adequate theory of the causes of war, it is necessary to inquire into the conditions under which the leaders of nations that are objectively faced with overwhelming odds will recognize or fail to recognize the futility of war and be governed by this recognition.

Several lines of evidence can be brought to bear on this question. In a content analysis of intimate German documents from the six weeks just prior to the start of the First World War, Zinnes, North, and Koch (1961) found little evidence of concern with military capability. Most of the attention of German policy makers appears to have been focused on evidence of hostility from other states. On the basis of this suggestive though by no means conclusive evidence, the authors of this study hypothesize that, in general, level of concern with military capability may be an inverse function of the degree of perceived hostility from other states.

When perceived threat becomes strong enough, national decision makers no longer engage in the careful weighing of capability that should precede any major national decision. A suicidal decision to enter war may conceivably result from such a situation, despite the existence of an objectively stable (in the first sense) distribution of power.[2]

Another line of evidence comes from a laboratory study conducted by Bass and Dunteman (1963) in which group members showed a persistent tendency to overestimate the strength of their own team in comparison with another team with which they were competing. If these findings can be generalized to international affairs, they suggest that, under some conditions, policy makers will overestimate the probability of victory for their own state and, hence, may go to war in a situation that is objectively stable in the sense that the power ranged against their state is adequate to defeat it. Future research on international conflict would do well to concern itself with the conditions under which policy makers overestimate the strength of their own states in this way.

Theories Concerning Nuclear Deterrence

Strictly speaking, the notion *deterrent* is synonymous with the concept restraint. Both terms refer to forces that reduce the attractiveness of alternatives involving violence. However, the term deterrent has been used almost exclusively to refer to strategic (high-yield) nuclear weapons which can be used to retaliate against an aggressor. For this reason, the term restraint has been used in this introduction in the more general sense.

A large, speculative literature concerning nuclear deterrence has evolved in the past ten years. Representative items include Brodie (1959), Brody (1960), Burns (1957), Hoag (1961), Kahn (1960), Kissinger (1957, 1965), Milburn (1959), Raser (1965), Schelling (1966), Singer (1962), G. H. Snyder (1960, 1961, and Selection 8), and R. C. Snyder (1961).

Nuclear weapons with their modern delivery systems have revolutionized strategic thinking. They are distinctive from earlier weapons in two ways: (a) They are capable of creating fantastic destruction, and (b) they can be delivered with high reliability to any place on earth. These two characteristics imply that a state possessed of a reasonably large and secure inventory of these weapons can count on being able to inflict terrible punishment on any state it chooses, *regardless of the military strength of that state.* Such has seldom, if ever, been the case in the past. It follows that a state which is contemplating attacking another state that has nuclear arms must reckon with the probability of absorbing immense destruction from a counterattack, even if the other state is weaker in overall strength. Hence,

[2]The Zinnes, North, and Koch (1961) findings might alternatively be seen as evidence that the German invasion of France in 1914 was a pre-emptive action in the sense used in the introduction to Part II of this volume. In other words, the German policy makers may have concluded at some point that war was inevitable. At this point, the question becomes not whether to go to war but when the war should begin. When such a question is posed, capability for war becomes a purely academic matter and is therefore not worth much discussion.

the possession of nuclear weapons by the other state can be a highly effective restraint against war, regardless of the overall distribution of power (military capability).

In a major war between two nuclear states, neither the stronger nor the weaker can emerge as the *victor* in the traditional sense of the term. The phrase *balance of terror* has been used to describe the conditions of mutual restraint that are likely to characterize relations between two nuclear states.

In addition to deterring attacks against states that have nuclear weapons, the very existence of these weapons seems to act as a damper on the use of conventional (nonnuclear) weapons in lesser confrontations. The reason for this is the fear that conventional warfare will escalate into nuclear exchanges. Nuclear states have encouraged this fear in some cases by threatening to retaliate with nuclear weapons if certain kinds of conventional attacks are made. For example, the United States has threatened to intervene with nuclear weapons if the Soviet Union initiates a major conventional attack against a NATO state.

Credibility of the Threat to Retaliate

By *credibility* is meant the extent to which a nation's threat to retaliate (or intervene on behalf of an ally) is believable. The issue of credibility is not really new, but it has received especial attention in the nuclear age because of the vulnerability of nuclear weapons to other nuclear weapons and the doubts that have been voiced about whether states will employ nuclear retaliation at the cost of total or partial annihilation.

A threat need not always be 100 per cent credible to be effective as a deterrent. The greater the damage that can be done to the adversary if the threat is carried out, the less credible need it be because the adversary will be less likely to take chances. Nevertheless, threats must have some credibility to be successful.

There are basically two kinds of credibility: credibility of capability and credibility of intent. The former can be defined as the extent to which a state seems capable of carrying out its threats; the latter, as the extent to which it seems willing to carry them out.

Credibility of capability is essential to what Kahn (1960) has called *Type I Deterrence*, deterrence of a direct attack. A direct attack on a nuclear state is likely to be aimed at its capability to retaliate, i.e., its nuclear weapons. For such an attack to be deterred militarily, it is necessary to demonstrate that enough of these nuclear weapons will survive such an attack to inflict unacceptable damage on the aggressor, i.e., to demonstrate credibility of capability. Singer (1962) has proposed six ways to reduce the vulnerability of retaliatory capacity and thereby increase this kind of credibility: increase the number of retaliatory weapons, disperse them over a greater region, place them at a greater distance from the adversary, move them more frequently, strengthen ("harden") their protective shieldings, and more adequately conceal them. In addition, measures that increase the capacity to detect an enemy attack before it arrives and to launch retaliatory weapons rapidly probably contribute to the credibility of capability.

Credibility of intent becomes a problem to the extent that a state would prefer not to do what it has threatened to do (Schelling, 1960). For this reason, it is an issue in what Kahn (1960) has called *Type II Deterrence*, military deterrence of extreme provocations, especially when such provocations come from a state with nuclear weapons. An example would be the American effort to prevent a Soviet attack on Western Europe through the threat of nuclear retaliation. If such an attack came, American decision makers might well prefer not to do what they had threatened to do, since this would invite certain nuclear counterretaliation against American cities. Yet, if Soviet decision makers believed that the United States was unwilling to counterattack under such circumstances, the threat would be hollow and ineffective. Hence, considerable attention has been given in the United States to the problem of establishing credibility of intent.

Various tactics have been devised for increasing the credibility of intent. Underlying each of these tactics is a theory about the conditions under which such credibility is established. Some of these tactics will now be described.

Demonstrating Resolve by Means of Harsh Actions and Stances. States often try to demonstrate their readiness to retaliate in one situation by taking harsh actions in another. For example, the vigor of the American reaction to the Russian challenge during the Cuban missile crisis can be seen, in part, as an effort to maintain the credibility of the American deterrent in other situations. In addition, when the danger of war seems great, states often mobilize their forces and show their strength in an effort to make it seem that they are poised for retaliation.

Enhancing the Apparent Seriousness of the Action to Be Deterred. A state is more likely to retaliate the greater the damage that has been incurred at the hands of an adversary. Hence, a general tactic for increasing credibility of intent is to arrange things so that it appears that the behavior to be deterred will constitute a serious and damaging challenge. For example, a state may announce publicly that certain kinds of behavior will be considered a serious challenge, as the United States has repeatedly done with respect to Russian occupation of West Berlin.

Another technique involves setting up a "trip wire." Things are arranged so that a minor usage of violence by an adversary necessarily damages vital interests of the state that is trying to establish its credibility. This in turn increases the likelihood of irrational behavior by that state. For example, the nuclear state may station some of its troops in a beleaguered region, as the United States has put troops in Berlin and the Soviet Union technicians in Cuba. Though it may be unreasonable to suppose that the Soviet Union will retaliate in the event of an American attack on Cuba per se, the chances of retaliation increase if such an attack kills Soviet technicians. Another trip-wire tactic involves the use of conventional weapons. An example will be found in the strategy of NATO, which involves the maintenance of sufficient conventional forces in Western Europe to create a large conventional war in the event of a Soviet attack employing conventional weapons. Though Soviet planners might believe that they could win such a war, they would also have to reckon with the possibility that a war of that size would create sufficient panic and irrationality in Washington to touch off the use of strategic nuclear weapons.

Increasing the Apparent Capacity to Endure Counterattack. To the extent that a state is capable of surviving a counterattack (i.e., a retaliation against its retaliation), it has less to fear if it implements a policy of retaliation with nuclear weapons. Concomitantly, the threat to retaliate should be more credible to the extent that the adversary can be made to believe that citizens of a state think they can survive a counterattack. Various schemes have been proposed to increase the apparent capacity to survive a nuclear war, most notably civil defense programs.

Automatizing Response. If retaliation can be made automatic, so that it cannot be averted once an attack is launched and if the opponent can be made to believe that it is automatic, full credibility will exist. No workable systems for automatizing nuclear retaliation have been seriously proposed, which is probably fortunate because of the danger that such a system may misfire. The principle of automatic response seems to create more problems than it solves.

Empirical Research on Credibility. Russett (1963) has performed an interesting small-sample comparative case study on the question of how a major power can make credible an intent to defend a smaller ally (the *pawn*) from attack by another major power. He used as a sample 17 cases of successful and unsuccessful deterrence between 1935 and 1961. He concludes that credibility of intent is a function of the "number of military, political, and economic ties between pawn and defender" (p. 107). Though sympathetic with his aim and general approach, Fink (1965) has questioned Russett's method and conclusions on several grounds including his operational definition of the concept *successful deterrence* and the possibility of alternative interpretations of his data. Fink's article represents one of the first thorough critiques of method in the study of international conflict and, as such, is an encouraging sign of approaching maturity for this field. In Selection 9 of this volume, Russett explores the reasons behind the failure of the United States' deterrent against Japanese aggression in 1941.

Problems with the Methods for Achieving Credibility

While retaliatory threats must have some credibility if they are to be successful, many of the methods for enhancing credibility may be inadvisable because they increase the likelihood of war in other ways. For example, when, in an effort to increase credibility, a state employs harsh tactics in lesser situations or mobilizes and exhibits its force, the adversary may mistakenly conclude that he is about to be attacked and launch a pre-emptive war. The institution of a large civil defense program may also increase the adversary's sense of threat and therefore the likelihood that he will pre-empt, by making it seem that the first state is willing to take the chance of war (Kahn, 1960, p. 158). Another example concerns a state that develops methods of launching its missiles rapidly in order to reduce the danger that its missiles will be destroyed on the ground in a surprise attack from an adversary. Such measures will increase its capacity to retaliate, and hence presumably the credibility of its deterrent. Unfortunately, such measures may, in addition, heighten the danger of accidental war, since rapid retaliation means less time to process information and, therefore, greater likelihood of misinterpreting ambiguous intelligence as evidence that an attack is on the way. (See Selection 4.)

The six basic methods for protecting nuclear weapons described by Singer (numbers, dispersal, distance, mobility, hardening, and concealment) probably have milder side effects. But even here there is some question in the light of evidence from a simulation study by Raser and Crow (Selection 10), which suggests that the capacity to delay nuclear retaliation may enhance a state's sense of its own power and, thereby, make it more likely to begin a war.

Stability in the Nuclear Age

In the modern deterrence literature, the term *stability* is usually taken to mean the avoidance of major war between the great powers.

Some discussions of this issue boil down to the proposition that stability will be maintained so long as all states maintain the credibility of their nuclear deterrents. Instability is identified with conditions that heighten the vulnerability of retaliatory forces and hence detract from the credibility of capability or the conditions that reduce credibility of intent. These discussions seem narrow, when one remembers that nuclear war can begin as a result of the mistaken belief that war is inevitable or as a result of irrationality at some point in the line of command governing the use of nuclear weapons.

Authors who take a broader view of the conditions underlying stability (e.g., Schelling, 1960, and Singer, 1962) have made a number of recommendations for *arms control* measures that reduce the likelihood that a state will perceive war as inevitable, by reducing the chance of accidental detonation of weapons, increasing the facilities for communication between potential antagonists, etc. Since hostility, suspicion, and irrationality—all potential breeding grounds for nuclear attack—are encouraged by participation in conventional war, it has also been proposed that a reduction in the frequency and intensity of conventional war will lead to a reduction in the likelihood of nuclear war.

One of the most important sources of instability in the forseeable future is likely to derive from the *proliferation of nuclear weapons*. The more states that have these weapons, the greater is the likelihood that somebody, somewhere will authorize their use. This prospect would be bad enough in itself, but, in addition, there is a danger that the resulting war will become general if it is not possible to pinpoint responsibility for the initial attack (Kobe, 1962). Negotiated agreements may be able to slow down the proliferation of nuclear weapons to some extent, but it seems reasonable to suppose that, in the long run, many more states will have these weapons. A thorough assessment of the immediacy and danger of nuclear proliferation will be found in Rosecrance (1964).

Though dangerous from the viewpoint of accidental war, proliferation of nuclear weapons could have a beneficial effect by causing the bipolar world community to fragment into smaller political units. Present trends in the world seem to be in this direction. As will be suggested in the introduction to Part V, such a fragmentation can produce new restraints against the use of violence by encouraging a "crazy-quilt" development of interlocking ties among states. Evidence of such a development was found by Brody (1963 and Selection 12) in a simulation study. As nuclear weapons proliferated in his artifical setting, bipolarity tended to disappear *and* overall hostility diminished. While accepting this evidence, it is also necessary to question whether the improved world atmosphere demonstrated by Brody can contribute enough to military stability to outweigh the greater danger of accidental war with the proliferation of nuclear weapons.

The point has already been made that the existence of nuclear weapons tends to reduce the likelihood of conventional warfare by inducing a fear of escalation in the minds of statesmen. We can rephrase this as follows: The existence of nuclear weapons increases conventional stability. But what is the relationship between conventional and nuclear stability? G. H. Snyder (1960, 1961) has suggested an inverse relationship: An unstable nuclear situation produces a stable conventional situation because statesmen fear to trouble the waters. But, to the extent that the nuclear situation can be made stable, conventional stability will reduce since statesmen need be less fearful of escalation.

Fear of the Costs of War

The success of nuclear deterrence and, to some extent, of conventional restraints is predicated on the potential aggressor's fear of the costs of war, i.e., his disutility for the dislocations and damages that war may bring to him. What determines the degree to which people fear the costs of war?

Several writers (e.g., Wright, 1942; Milburn, 1959) have suggested the importance of *war weariness* in determining the likelihood of war. According to this point of view, the more recent and more destructive a war is, the more fearful people will be of the costs involved in entering a new one. Thus the recency and destructiveness of a war may act as restraints against the employment of new violence.

The trouble with this argument is that the recency of war can cut both ways. While recent involvement in a war may make the citizens of a state more fearful of the costs of war, it may also make them more sensitive to evidence of the threat of war from other states. Such sensitivity can produce defensive efforts that lead to a cold war which may deteriorate into a hot one. The Soviet Union after the Second World War may be a case in point. War weariness alone should have made this state overly cautious in international affairs. But suspicion that her neighbors, especially Germany, would start a new war against her was at least partially responsible for a bolder foreign policy that sometimes ran the risk of producing a war.

Conclusions

The theories described in this introduction are all concerned with the restraints imposed by one state's military preparations on another state's decision about whether to go to war. Conspicuously absent from this introduction is a discussion of the restraints, if any, that are imposed by military preparations on the earlier stages of movement toward war, before the alternative of going to war has come under consideration. The reason for this gap is very simple; balance of power and deterrence theorists have paid relatively little attention to these earlier stages. The impact of military preparations on earlier stages of the process was discussed in the introduction to Part III; but the theories presented there included military preparations in the list of forces pushing states *toward* war. Yet it seems equally reasonable to suppose that, at times, the anticipation of eventually having to fight a war with a powerful adversary causes states to avoid harsher policies and more militant stances of the type that might hasten such a war; i.e., that military preparations or anticipated preparations sometimes slow down or even reverse the conflict spiral. There is clearly a theoretical and empirical gap here, which can be traced in part to a tendency of many theorists to focus narrowly on the decision to go to war. What is needed is research about the conditions under which military preparations enhance, as opposed to the conditions under which they dampen, the conflict spiral. A small theoretical effort in this direction is presented at the end of the introduction to Part VII.

As can be seen in the present introduction, theoretical work on military restraints has greatly outstripped empirical research. As a matter of fact, the first empirical study of this topic was published as recently as 1963 (Russett, 1963). The empirical selections in this part of the book are among the very few in existence. One would expect to find a great deal more empirical research on a topic of such great interest to national decision makers.

References

Bass, B. M., and G. Dunteman, "Biases in the evaluation of one's own group, its allies and opponents," *Journal of Conflict Resolution*, **7**(1), 16–20, 1963.

Brodie, B., *Strategy in the Missile Age.* Princeton, N.J.: Princeton University Press, 1959.

Brody, R. A., "Deterrence strategies: An annotated bibliography," *Journal of Conflict Resolution*, **4**(4), 443–457, 1960.

Brody, R. A., "Some systemic effects of the spread of nuclear weapons technology: a study through simulation of a multi-nuclear future," *Journal of Conflict Resolution*, **7**(4), 663–753, 1963.

Burns, A. L., "From balance to deterrence: a theoretical analysis," *World Politics*, **9**(4), 494–529, 1957.

Burton, J. W., *Peace Theory.* New York: Alfred A. Knopf, Inc., 1962.

Burton, J. W., *International Relations: A General Theory.* London: Cambridge University Press, 1965.

Claude, I. L., *Power and International Relations.* New York: Random House, 1962.

Deutsch, K. W., and J. D. Singer, "Multipolar power systems and international stability," *World Politics*, **16**(3), 390–406, 1964.

Fink, C. F., "More calculations about deterrence," *Journal of Conflict Resolution*, **9**(1), 54–65, 1965.

Gulick, E. V., *Europe's Classical Balance of Power.* Ithaca, N. Y.: Cornell University Press, 1955.

Hoag, M. W., "On stability in deterrent races," *World Politics*, **13**(4), 505–527, 1961.

Huntington, S. P., "Arms races: prerequisites and results," in: *Public Policy, 1958*. Cambridge, Mass.: Graduate School of Public Administration, 1958.

Kahn, H., *On Thermonuclear War*. Princeton, N. J.: Princeton University Press, 1960.

Kaplan, M., *System and Process in International Politics*. New York: John Wiley and Sons, Inc., 1957.

Kissinger, H. A., *Nuclear Weapons and Foreign Policy*. New York: Harper and Brothers, 1957.

Kissinger, H. A., ed., *Problems of National Strategy*. New York: Frederick A. Praeger, Inc., 1965.

Kobe, D. H., "A theory of catalytic war," *Journal of Conflict Resolution*, **6**(2), 125–142, 1962.

Lasswell, H. D., *A Study of Power*. New York: The Free Press, 1950.

Milburn, T., "What constitutes effective deterrence?" *Journal of Conflict Resolution*, **3**(2), 138–145, 1959.

Organski, A. F. K., *World Politics*. New York: Alfred A. Knopf, Inc., 1959.

Raser, J. R., *Guidelines for Understanding Deterrence Processes*. Technical Report to the Naval Ordnance Test Station from the Western Behavioral Sciences Institute, Dec. 15, 1965.

Rosecrance, R. N., *Action and Reaction in World Politics*. Boston: Little, Brown and Company, 1963.

Rosecrance, R. N., ed., *The Dispersion of Nuclear Weapons*. New York: Columbia University Press, 1964.

Rosecrance, R. N., "Bipolarity, multipolarity, and the future," *Journal of Conflict Resolution*, **10**(3), 314–327, 1966.

Russett, B. M., "The calculus of deterrence," *Journal of Conflict Resolution*, **7**(2), 97–109, 1963.

Schelling, T. C., *The Strategy of Conflict*. Cambridge, Mass.: Harvard University Press, 1960.

Schelling, T. C., *Arms and Influence*. New Haven, Conn.: Yale University Press, 1966.

Singer, J. D., *Deterrence, Arms Control and Disarmament: Toward a Synthesis in National Security Policy*. Columbus, Ohio: Ohio State University Press, 1962.

Snyder, G. H., "Balance of power in the missile age," *Journal of International Affairs*, **14**(1), 21–34, 1960.

Snyder, G. H., *Deterrence and Defense. Toward a Theory of National Security*. Princeton, N. J.: Princeton University Press, 1961.

Snyder, R. C., *Deterrence, Weapon Systems, and Decision-Making*. China Lake, Calif.: U.S. Naval Ordnance Test Station, 1961.

Waltz, K. N., "The stability of a bipolar world," *Daedalus*, **3,** 881–909, Summer, 1964.

Wolfers, A., *Discord and Collaboration*. Baltimore, Md.: The Johns Hopkins Press, 1962.

Wright, Q., *A Study of War*. Chicago: University of Chicago Press, 1942.

Zinnes, D. A., R. C. North, and H. E. Koch, "Capability, threat and the outbreak of war," *in* J. N. Rosenau, ed., *International Politics and Foreign Policy*. New York: The Free Press, 1961.

8

GLENN H. SNYDER

The Balance of Power and the Balance of Terror

A theory of the requirements for military stability in the nuclear age. A comparison is made between the traditional notion of "balance of power" and the modern conception of "balance of terror." The requirements for stability today are held to involve both kinds of balance. The analysis draws heavily on traditional deterrence theory, which is concerned with the effect of military preparations and the perception of these preparations on the likelihood of attack.

The venerable concept of the balance of power has lost stature among international relations theorists during the last 10 or 15 years, at any rate as a model for contemporary world politics. Many devotees of newer "modernist" or "behavioral" approaches allege that the balancing notion has been outmoded by intellectual progress; for them it is an intellectual antique with little or no descriptive or explanatory utility even for past international systems. Others who grant its historical validity argue that it has been outrun by history—in particular by the shift in world power distribution toward "bipolarity" after World War II, and by the heightened political importance of ideologies and mass public opinion; these circumstances deprive the international system of the pluralistic structure and flexibility in choosing and changing alliance partners, which are thought to have been necessary elements of the balance of power. For still others, the balance of power has been overtaken by technology; it is claimed that the development of nuclear weapons and long-range missiles has brought the balancing process to a halt and substituted a new and quite different regulator—that of nuclear

---

This article appears in *Proceedings of the New York State Political Science Association 1965* and Paul Seabury (ed.), *Balance of Power*, copyright © 1965 by the Chandler Publishing Company, San Francisco, California. Reprinted by permission of the author and the Chandler Publishing Company. The author is Professor of Political Science and Chairman of the Center for International Security and Conflict Studies at the State University of New York at Buffalo.

deterrence.[1] Implicitly disagreeing with the first two views, this article will challenge the last contention in particular. The balance of power theory is still generally valid and is still a useful model of at least certain important aspects of contemporary world politics. The new military technology has not terminated but only modified the balance of power process. It has superimposed a new system of equilibrium (the phrase "balance of terror" will serve) upon the old system which was based on nonnuclear capabilities. The two systems operate according to different tendencies and principles and can be separated analytically, but in practice they are inextricably mixed in a new balance of power in which elements of the old coexist with the new. I will attempt to compare the two subprocesses at certain salient points and then describe the nature of their interaction in an integrated process.

The Balance of Terror

There are "naïve" and "sophisticated" versions of the "balance of terror" or the nuclear strategic balance. The naïve view, the image held by relatively uninformed laymen, is simply that both sides are deterred from using nuclear weapons against the other by the fear of devastating retaliation. In this image, the targets of the nuclear strikes are cities. To initiate nuclear war would be to commit national suicide; hence a "balance" or "stalemate" exists.

The sophisticated version focuses on "counterforce" rather than "countervalue" (city) targeting. One or both sides could eliminate or drastically reduce the other side's retaliatory capacity by directing the first attack at the opponent's nuclear striking forces rather than at his cities. There are circumstances, theoretically at least, in which thermonuclear war initiated in this manner would be a rational act. According to this version, a "balance of terror" exists when neither side can, by executing a counterforce first-strike, reduce the opponent's retaliation to "acceptable" proportions. Or, to use the jargon of the trade, neither side has a "full first-strike capability," or (what amounts to virtually the same thing) both sides possess at least a "minimum strike-back capability"—*i.e.*, a residual capacity which, after the country had suffered the attrition of the attacker's first blow, could still inflict intolerable damage on the attacker's cities, population and economic assets in a retaliatory blow.

But the "sophisticated" version, as here defined, is not sophisticated enough. What, for example, is the criterion for defining the degree of retaliation that is "acceptable"? What purpose does the victim serve by retaliation against the attacker's cities, other than revenge? What motivates the attacker to strike in the first place; what purpose or political goal is served by a counterforce first-strike? Eliminating or reducing the victim's capacity to retaliate is not a purpose but a precaution. How is the war terminated after the initial strike and reprisal? What then determines the terms of settlement? What constitutes "victory" or "defeat"?

To make use of the sophisticated version for our purposes, it is necessary to return part way to the naïve image. I shall assert, somewhat heretically, that the *ultimate* function of

[1]For an early statement of this view, see Arthur Lee Burns, "From balance to deterrence," *World Politics*, IX (1957), 494–529.

nuclear weapons (especially the "strategic" variety) is either to destroy the enemy's cities and conventional war potential, or to support a threat to do so for purposes of blackmail or deterrence. To make this clear, it is convenient to start with a model of the balance of terror in its "pure" form. Assume two states, A and B, armed only with nuclear strategic missiles. Assume also that both states are expansionist—*i.e.*, that they both would like to subjugate all or part of the other if they could do so at acceptable cost.

In this model, the only means of subjugation is by nuclear blackmail. Blackmail, of course, cannot succeed as long as the opponent can make a "deterrent" counterthreat of devastating retaliation. But A, for example, may be able to blackmail B successfully if it can meet two requirements. First, it must be able to disarm B by a counterforce "firststrike" or at least be able to destroy enough of B's forces to restrict its retaliation to "acceptable" proportions. The criterion of "acceptability" is the amount of retaliatory damage to A which is just equivalent to the value which A places on B's capitulation to its demands. The demand may be for B's total capitulation or for some lesser concession. Secondly, A must maintain in reserve a force sufficient to blackmail B into conceding through the threat of "countervalue" or population destruction. Roughly, the necessary size of this force is measured by the value which A thinks B places on the things he is being asked to concede. If A fires all its forces in attempting to disarm B, it dissipates its blackmail or bargaining power and cannot achieve its political goal.

If A (or B, or both) can meet both of these requirements, the balance of terror is in disequilibrium. If both sides fall short of one or both requirements, an attack by either side is either futile or too costly and the balance of terror is in a state of equilibrium.

Note that A's initial counterforce strike is merely preliminary, undertaken only to put itself in a position to blackmail B. Counterforce strikes do not contribute *directly* to "winning the war," as is suggested in some of the current literature: they contribute only indirectly by improving the attacker's relative bargaining power—*i.e.*, his power to coerce the victim by the threat to strike at cities. And they contribute to this end *with high confidence* only if they are sufficient to reduce the victim's retaliatory capacity to below A's "acceptable" level. If B is left with residual forces higher than this level, he may be able to resist A's post-attack blackmail.

In the "real world," of course, A will have conventional forces; a combination of counterforce and countervalue strikes against B may so prostrate B as to make physical conquest possible and blackmail unnecessary. But such conquest would be the result of A's preponderance in the conventional balance after the nuclear exchange, and therefore falls under the heading of "interaction" between the two balances, which is discussed below.

Differences between the Conventional Balance and the Nuclear Balance

To compare and then integrate the two balancing systems, the first questions to be asked are: What is the nature of the "power" being balanced? What is the nature of "equilibrium" in each case? In traditional theory of (conventional) balance of power, the kind of power involved was the physical capability to take or hold territory.

Equilibrium was said to obtain when military capabilities and war potential on each side were roughly equal, so that neither side had the capacity to defeat the other in war and by so doing to change the territorial status quo. The preceding discussion shows that this is not the case in the nuclear "balance of terror." Nuclear weapons cannot, when employed, in and of themselves, take or hold territory. Physical conquest during or after a nuclear exchange requires the intervention of conventional forces. In the "pure" balance of terror, the political status quo can be changed only by political coercion—that is, by a process of blackmail supported by the threat of severe punishment. The status quo is preserved by "deterrence" supported by a similar threat. Thus the power that is balanced in the balance of terror is essentially "political power" rather than physical capabilities; capabilities enter in only as the threatened sanction supporting the political demand; not as an instrument for the direct physical achievement of political goals, as is usually the case in the traditional or conventional balance of power.

The balance of terror is more subjective in nature than the old balance of power. Whether "equilibrium" exists depends at least as much on factors "within the minds" of the opponents as upon an objective comparison of military capabilities. Subjectivity is obvious in the fact that equilibrium is defined in terms of "acceptability" of damage for both sides; what is acceptable depends on the values attached to the political stakes. Thus, in contrast to the old balance of power, in which the state of the equilibrium could be objectively—if roughly—determined by the uninvolved observer, such an observer can only intuitively guess at equilibrium in the balance of terror, since it depends principally on whether the gains to be made or losses to be avoided by striking first are less than the costs to be incurred—all as subjectively valued in the minds of the decision-makers.

The balance of terror is subjective in still another sense. The participants themselves, while presumably they can judge what is unacceptable damage for themselves, cannot be certain what is unacceptable for the opponent. Thus the determination of whether equilibrium exists is ultimately reduced to a guessing game about the opponent's values and intentions. There is therefore vast scope of disagreement or asymmetrical perceptions about the state of the balance and about the degree of political, military or technological change which would throw it "out of balance." For example, the balance may actually be in equilibrium, but one side may fear the other side *may* possess a full first-strike capability. Then the latter may achieve its political aims by bluff, whether these aims are of a deterrent or blackmail nature. In the obverse case—when the balance is in disequilibrium because one side can be provoked to strike first, but its opponent doesn't perceive this—the outcome could be war by "miscalculation."

Subjective considerations determine the "location" or "boundaries" of equilibrium within the spectrum of possible force ratios, but a comparison of relative capabilities is obviously still necessary for estimating whether equilibrium actually exists at any given time.

However, in sharp contrast to the traditional balance of power, the notion of quantitative equality between striking forces is totally irrelevant as a criterion for "balance." Equilibrium can exist when one side's offensive forces are far inferior to the other's, provided the inferior side's forces are relatively invulnerable to a counterforce strike and provided the forces surviving such a strike can penetrate the attacker's air defenses in sufficient numbers to inflict unacceptable damage. Or equilibrium might require having more striking forces than the opponent if one's own forces are highly vulnerable, and the enemy has a very good air defense and civil defense system. The essential criterion for equilibrium is a mutual capacity to inflict intolerable damage in retaliation, and this depends on a variety of technological factors in addition to numbers of delivery vehicles.

A corollary of this distinction is that, while a balance of conventional power can be said to exist only within a rather narrow range of relative capabilities on either side of strict equality, a balance of terror can exist within a wide range of force ratios. To illustrate: assuming relatively invulnerable offensive forces and rather important air-missile defense systems on both sides, side A, with 100 missiles, might be in a state of equilibrium against side B with 500 missiles; equilibrium might still obtain if side A were to increase its force to 1,000 missiles. In other words, even a tenfold increase by one side might not overturn the balance. The "range of equilibrium" would be the difference between the forces which A needs for a "minimum strike-back capability," and the forces it needs for a "full first-strike capability." This consideration has important implications for the *stability* of the balance of terror, to be discussed below.

Another important contrast between the two systems lies in the relative weight given to the functions of *deterrence* and *defense*. Both were functions of the pre-nuclear balance (and still are in today's conventional balance of power); but deterrence was secondary in the sense that it was an incidental consequence of an obvious capacity to defend territory successfully. It was also secondary in the sense that the primary purpose of balancing techniques—armaments, alliances, etc.—was to be ready to frustrate an expansionist state rather than to influence the intentions of that state. If deterrence failed, defensive war was considered to be a normal technique of the balancing process, a continuation of the process by violent means.

By contrast, the balance of terror centers heavily on the function of deterrence. Deterrence is achieved by the threat of devastating punishment or damage, not as a simple by-product of a capacity to defend territory or otherwise to frustrate the aggressor's aims. If deterrence fails, the system will have broken down completely; nuclear war cannot be considered a normal "technique" for adjusting or restoring the balance. This does not mean that it is not useful or wise to take measures in advance of war to mitigate the dreadful consequences of nuclear war, or even to "win the war" in some sense. In particular, it may be desirable (as the U. S. has done) to develop a "surplus" of offensive striking forces far beyond the amount needed for a deterrent equilibrium, in order to be able to destroy a maximum amount of the attacker's post-attack residual forces, while holding in reserve a powerful force for bargaining purposes. Such additional forces do not essentially disturb the equilibrium, unless they create a degree of preponderance which begins to approach a full first-strike capability.

Interactions in the "Mixed" Balance of Power

Nuclear and conventional balancing processes do not operate independently; they impinge on each other in various ways. The contemporary balancing process, in an overall sense, is a mixture of the two. Generally speaking, the entire system is in overall "balance" when either of two conditions exists. One is when each of the two subprocesses is "out of balance" but in different directions—*i.e.*, when one side preponderates in one component and the other side in the other. The other condition is when both conventional and nuclear balances are separately in equilibrium. If one is in balance and the other is not, the entire system is in a state of disequilibrium, at least with respect to any particular political issue. This is also the case when both processes are unbalanced in favor of one side.

To illustrate these somewhat cryptic remarks, let us turn away from our abstract model to the world of reality. We see a world of two nuclear powers (the Soviet Union, and the U. S.-Great Britain as a unit) which also have conventional forces; we also see two incipient nuclear powers and many non-nuclear powers. All possess conventional forces; some of them enjoy the protection of one or the other of the nuclear great powers.

That the latter enjoy the protection of the nuclear great powers means that the political function of nuclear weapons has been extended from strictly bilateral deterrence and blackmail between nuclear powers to that of deterring aggression against other (non-nuclear) countries. This function may require the nuclear protector to create an actual or apparent nuclear disequilibrium in his favor to make credible a determination to strike first if provoked by an attack on his allies. Short of this, concurrent with it, he can threaten the *limited* use of nuclear weapons in either a "tactical" or "strategic" manner.

The best example of interaction is the balance of power in Europe. Here, the Soviets preponderate in the conventional balance (although not so greatly as we thought a few years ago); while the U. S., as West Europe's protector, remains superior in nuclear forces. Yet it is doubtful whether the U.S. superiority, while quantitatively great, really constitutes a "full first-strike capability." If it did in its maximum sense—*i.e.*, if we could completely eliminate the Soviet nuclear forces in a first strike—it would be possible, theoretically, at least, to dispense with conventional forces in Western Europe. Total and obvious strategic nuclear disequilibrium would remove any need to even partially balance the Soviets at the conventional level. Conversely, if it were true that the U.S. obviously lacked a first-strike capability (meaning that we were clearly not willing to strike first in any circumstances), then this might reinstate the conventional balancing process in Europe in its full prenuclear dimensions—*i.e.*, it might well stimulate a build-up of conventional forces sufficient to hold successfully against a Red Army invasion.

That this has not occurred is due in part to the uncertainty of Soviet leadership as to whether equilibrium exists or whether the U.S. nuclear preponderance really amounts to disequilibrium. In other words, the Soviets may suspect that the U.S. has a full first-strike capability which could be activated if sufficiently provoked. Or they may believe that we are irrational enough to strike even when our force does not meet the objective requirements of such a capability. For in the case of deterrence (or blackmail) it is what the opponent thinks or fears that counts, and the U.S. nuclear superiority is great enough that the Soviet leadership no doubt fears some probability of a U.S. first strike in particularly tense or provocative circumstances. Considering the very great damage they would suffer if we did strike, a quite low probability in their calculations may be sufficient to deter.

Any remaining doubts which the Russians might have about our implicit threat of a strategic first strike are offset by the presence of tactical nuclear weapons in the hands of the NATO forces on the "central front" in West Germany. The American resolve in NATO to use these weapons, if necessary, to stop a Soviet invasion has been firmly declared and implemented by the rather thorough incorporation of their use into NATO's military plans and organization. It is no doubt highly credible to the Soviets that these weapons would be used if necessary, and, considering their own apparent belief that a tactical nuclear war in Europe could not remain limited, our tactical nuclear posture constitutes, in effect, a very credible threat of all-out nuclear war. Even if they were to assume that the *strategic* nuclear balance by itself was in a state of equilibrium, the tactical nuclear weapons would make it a rather unstable equilibrium. This instability is a potent deterrent of Soviet conventional provocations and reduces the need for balancing at the conventional level.

The function of the conventional NATO forces on the central front—apart from turning back small and medium-scale incursions—is further to enhance the credibility of nuclear deterrence by forcing the Soviets to undertake a major attack provocative enough to exceed the U.S. "threshold of nuclear response." Thus the overall balance of power in Western Europe is a function of three factors: the U.S. first-strike capability at the strategic nuclear level; the tactical nuclear threat; and the defense and deterrent effects of conventional forces. Each probably would be inadequate by itself, but the three together have created a mixed conventional-nuclear equilibrium which effectively deters Soviet aggression. The primary function of the tactical nuclear weapons is to form a "bridge" between a nonexistent conventional balance and a *possibly* extant strategic nuclear equilibrium. In other words, they assure the Soviets, in case they might otherwise have doubts, that a combined tactical-strategical nuclear imbalance in favor of the U.S. does exist.

We may turn the point around and note that during the period of the U.S. nuclear monopoly (strategic nuclear disequilibrium in our favor) we were deterred from capitalizing on this imbalance at least partly by the obvious Soviet superiority in the conventional balance which potentially enabled them to resist our nuclear pressure by credibly threatening to overrun Western Europe. An overall equilibrium obtained precisely because of a sharp disequilibrium in opposite directions in each of the two subcomponents.

Whereas in Europe conventional forces serve as auxiliary to the nuclear deterrent, in Asia the reverse is probably true. The obvious disequilibrium in the strategic nuclear balance between the United States and Communist China serves to deter the Chinese from openly committing their own conventional forces in internal wars (e.g.,

South Vietnam) and thus tends to create a conventional balance of power in Southeast Asia which might not otherwise exist. Alternatively, should the Chinese become involved with the United States in an overt conventional conflict, they probably would be deterred from committing enough forces to defeat the U.S. forces in fear of a U.S. nuclear response. Nuclear disequilibrium favoring the U.S. tends to limit our Communist opponents in Asia to a commitment of conventional forces which the U.S. and our allies can deal with successfully at the conventional level. In short, nuclear disequilibrium tends to promote conventional equilibrium or operational conventional preponderance for the United States.

When nuclear deterrence is extended to the protection of allies, the element of mutual assessment of *intentions* becomes critically important, much more so than in simple bilateral deterrence where the "credibility" of retaliation can more or less be taken for granted. In such "extended deterrence," the deterring side tries to create the impression that the balance of terror is out of balance in its favor or could be thrown into disequilibrium by sufficient provocation. He attempts to establish the "credibility" of his threat to strike first "all-out" or to initiate limited nuclear action. Estimates of relative capability are not irrelevant, but because of the essential subjectivity and hence uncertainty (in the opponent's mind) about what actually constitutes a "first-strike capability" for the deterrer, or about his willingness to run the risk of escalation, capability comparisons tend to be overshadowed by appraisals of the deterrer's apparent "resolve," "nerve," irrationality, gambling propensities and other subjective factors that bear upon his intentions. Paradoxically, it would seem that intent-perception has become more crucial in today's balance of power than in the pre-nuclear balance, even though (or perhaps, *because*) the physical capabilities have become many orders of magnitude more destructive.

Appraisals of intent not only are now more important, but important in a different way than in the old balance of power. In the latter, the relevant intentions were largely political in nature, centering on the question of *which* countries were likely to fight on either the offensive or the defensive side. It could reasonably be assumed that the countries which did participate in a war would do so to the full extent of their capabilities, but there was often considerable uncertainty about who would participate. With the emergence of bipolarity, the uncertainty about alliance partners drastically declined, but nuclear technology introduced a new form of intent-perception and a new form of uncertainty—that concerning what types of military capability the opponent was likely to use and what degree of violence he was willing to risk or accept.

One might say that this new kind of uncertainty has replaced the former uncertainty about alliance partners as a major source of stability in the balance of power. Or, to put it slightly differently, the implicit or explicit threat to "raise the ante" in order to avoid defeat has taken the place of the threat to recruit additional states to the defending alliance. Such a threat is more or less analagous to the practice of "holding the ring" in the old balance—when a state promised to be neutral if its ally were attacked by one country, but to come to its aid if it were attacked by two or more powers. In short, technology has to some extent provided a substitute for the political flexibility and stability which was lost to the balancing process when it shifted to a bipolar structure after World War II.

Stability

A careful distinction should be made between "equilibrium" and "stability" in both the conventional balance of power and the nuclear balance. The two terms often are erroneously used interchangeably. Equilibria in both balances can have varying degrees of stability; and it is even possible to have disequilibrium with relatively high stability, if the dominant side is not aggressively inclined and this fact is recognized by other members of the system.

In the traditional balance of power theory, the idea of stability usually referred generally to a supposed perpetual tendency of the system to maintain itself at or near a state of equilibrium. Deviations from equilibrium generated "feedback" forces which moved the balance back in the direction of equilibrium. Within this general notion, stability had at least three sub-dimensions which, so far as I know, were never precisely delineated. These were: the tendency or lack of tendency toward an arms race, tendencies either to stimulate or inhibit war, and the tendency of the process to preserve the independence of the major actors. Theorists tended to emphasize the third dimension; in fact, armament and warfare often were treated not as types of instability but as *methods* for preserving stability in the third sense, along with alliances and other techniques.

By contrast, the dimension of stability which receives most attention in the balance of terror, and by extension, in the contemporary balancing process as a whole, is the propensity of the system to produce war, the obvious reason being the possibility of *nuclear* war, the horrifying nature of which seems to outweigh all other considerations. How stable is the contemporary balance of power in this sense?

The basic criterion of stability in the balance of terror is the "distance" which both sides are from possessing a full first-strike capability. If neither side has forces which even approach this capacity—i.e., if both have a very strong "strike-back" capability, the balance of terror is very stable. If one or both are very close to having a first-strike capability, or actually do have it, the balance can be very unstable. It might be only moderately unstable if only one side possessed such a capability if that side were benevolent; but if both sides had it, fears of a first strike by the other, and consequent incentives to pre-empt, would be strong, even despite intrinsic benevolence on both sides.

Stability can be defined alternatively as the degree of economic, technological, or politico-military "shock" which the system can sustain without creating for one side or the other a capability and willingness to strike first. Economic shock (or degree of instability) refers to the amount of resource expenditure required for one or the other to acquire the *quantity* of forces required for a successful first strike—assuming a given technology. If neither side has the economic resources to produce such a capability, the balance is stable in this sense. Technological instability refers to the magnitude of the technological breakthrough (e.g., the degree of efficiency of an antimissile defense) which would create a sufficient first-strike force for either side. Politico-military instability means the extent of "provocation" by either side which would touch off a first strike by the other. The word "provocation" includes a wide variety of contingencies: being "backed into a corner" in a confrontation of threats and counter-threats, becoming involved in a limited conventional war which one is in danger of losing, suffering a limited nuclear strike by the opponent, becoming involved in an escalating nuclear war, and many others. Any of these events may drastically increase the potential cost and risk of *not* striking first and thereby potentially create a state of disequilibrium in the strategic nuclear balance. As noted earlier, whether equilibrium exists depends on the context of events; the "acceptability" of damage is calculated not only against the gains to be made by striking first but also against the *losses to be avoided*, in any particular set of circumstances.

Although these three criteria of stability-instability interact, it is my judgment that the balance of terror is currently most stable in the "economic" or resource sense, somewhat less stable technologically, and least stable according to the "politico-military" criterion. The apparently firm U.S. commitment to use nuclear weapons in the defense of Western Europe, if necessary, indicates that there are types of Soviet provocation at the lower levels of violence which could touch off a U.S. strategic first strike, or more likely, a tactical nuclear response, from which the war could escalate. It is hoped, of course, that the Soviets' recognition of the U.S. commitment will deter the provocation; that instability in this dimension will preserve a stable equilibrium in the overall balance of power. However, the risks of Soviet miscalculation and subsequent escalation which this commitment creates should not be underestimated and probably are the most serious potential sources of instability in the contemporary balance.

The point is often made in the strategic literature that the greater the stability of the "strategic" balance of terror, the lower the stability of the overall balance at its lower levels of violence. The reasoning is that if neither side has a "full first-strike capability," and both know it, they will be less inhibited about initiating conventional war, and about the limited use of nuclear weapons, than if the strategic balance were unstable. Thus firm stability in the strategic nuclear balance tends to destablize the conventional balance and also to activate the lesser nuclear "links" between the latter and the former. But one *could* argue precisely the opposite—that the greater likelihood of gradual escalation due to a stable strategic equilibrium tends to deter both conventional provocation and tactical nuclear strikes—thus stabilizing the overall balance. The first hypothesis probably is dominant, but it must be heavily qualified by the second, since nations probably fear the possibility of escalation "all the way" nearly as much as they fear the possibility of an "all out" first strike.

There is another stability hypothesis which is just the reverse—although not contradictory to—the one just described: a stable conventional equilibrium tends to increase the stability of the nuclear component of the balance. When both sides can defend themselves successfully at the conventional level, conventional aggression is likely to be deterred, and if it is not, there is little pressure on the defender to resort to nuclear action. But this one also has its obverse: it is sometimes argued that when the *status quo* side attempts to create a conventional equilibrium, the credibility of its nuclear theats is undermined since it might thereby indicate an unwillingness to initiate nuclear war by seeking to create an alternative to it. The potential aggressor might be then more willing to attack when he believes (perhaps mistakenly) that he has achieved a margin of conventional superiority. The first hypothesis tends to stress the effect of conventional balance in reducing the probability of escalation if war occurs; the second stresses the increased chances of the outbreak of war due to the apparently lower risk incurred by starting it.

When a great nuclear power places smaller non-nuclear countries under its nuclear protection (as a substitute for creation of a conventional equilibrium), one effect may be to reduce the stability of the strategic nuclear balance in the sense of stimulating an arms race. Nuclear deterrence of attacks on "third parties" theoretically requires a strategic nuclear capability approaching first-strike dimensions. Forces of this size may raise fears of an aggressive surprise first strike in the opponent's mind and therefore place psychological pressure on him to increase his nuclear force in order to strengthen his deterrence, perhaps to strengthen his chances of winning the war should his fears materialize, and, at the extreme, to develop a first-strike force himself to be in a position to pre-empt. This type of instability would be much weaker if the great nuclear powers were to limit themselves to bilateral mutual deterrence.

The nature of the "balance of power" process in a world of many nuclear powers is a challenging speculative problem which can only be touched upon here in connection with the question of stability. It is rather remarkable that the balance of terror is generally believed to be most stable when it is bipolar and least stable when it is multipolar, whereas the exact reverse was said to be true in the traditional theory of the balance of power. In the latter, bipolarity was said to be unstable because of the absence of a strong unattached power center (a "holder of the balance"), or of several centers, which could be recruited to block one of the "poles" which had developed marginal preponderance of capabilities and apparently aggressive intentions. A multiplicity of power centers would provide such balancing material and create uncertainty for an incipient aggressor as to the amount of power which would oppose his designs. A bipolar balance of terror is said to be relatively stable because only two power centers have the capacity to initiate nuclear war and because they are likely to be cautious in conflict situations which involve the danger of nuclear war. The major powers in the contemporary bipolar balance are said to be relatively "responsible" powers.

Many specific arguments have been advanced in support of the hypothesis that nuclear diffusion would greatly increase instability, but two in particular are probably the most influential. One is the "statistical argument": the notion that the more countries that have nuclear weapons, the more likely it is that some of these weapons will be fired, accidentally or otherwise, and the firing of nuclear weapons anywhere in the world may trigger a global holocaust. The other is the "irresponsibility argument": the idea that some of the countries which may acquire nuclear power will lack the caution and restraint which seems to characterize the nuclear great powers; they may threaten or use their nuclear weapons recklessly, perhaps because of domestic instability or simply a lack of concern for, or lack of comprehension of, the broader consequences of their actions.

The point is raised merely to note the striking difference between the two sets of stability hypotheses, not to analyze either, which would be far beyond the scope of this paper. The question of the stability or instability of a multipolar balance of terror is still moot; there are some reasons for believing it might be quite stable. Nor has the hypothesis concerning the conventional balance—that stability increases with the number of actors of comparable strength—been as yet subjected to rigorous empirical testing. Both are promising questions for future research. One suspects that the sharp dichotomy between the widely accepted views for each of the two cases would be considerably blurred by such investigation. Some questions may be pertinent. In the prenuclear system, for example, would it not be fairly plausible to assert that the greater the number of decision-making centers with the power to initiate major war, the greater the likelihood of war? In a multipolar nuclear system, might not the acquisition of nuclear weapons be conducive to a sense of caution and prudence? Somewhat in emulation of the Soviet Union vis-à-vis the United States, might not the new nuclear nations approach each other more carefully—as someone once put it, "like porcupines in love"? Might it not turn out that even a successful nuclear strike by one small power against another would so dissipate the winner's nuclear forces and result in such destruction to its own economy, that it would seriously lose position in both the nuclear and conventional balances of power and make itself vulnerable to attack or blackmail by third powers? And would this not then strengthen deterrence and enhance the general stability of the system? What would be the function of alliances in a world of many nuclear powers? The questions could be multiplied indefinitely, and the answers are certainly not obvious.

In Lieu of Conclusion

International relations theory and military-strategic analysis have been ignoring each other for too long. This essay has attempted to introduce a measure of integration, focusing on an idea which is common to both fields—that of equilibrium. Balance of power theory cannot embrace all phenomena of international politics, not even all military phenomena. Yet it has enjoyed a rather high degree of historical validation, as political theories go, and deserves to be rehabilitated, refined and renovated.

The foregoing analysis has tended to be logical rather than discursive, in accordance with my belief that the first priority task in the elaboration of a theory (at least some theories) is to clarify its logical core, which can then later be "softened" and brought closer to reality by empirical testing and less rigorous speculation. I am aware that categories such as "full first-strike capabilities," "equilibrium", and "acceptable damage" have been given a degree of precision here which they may not have in the minds of decision-makers; the real political world is far more subtle and complex. By way of example, I have tended to imply that mere preponderance in the balance of terror is politically useless unless it at least approaches a "full first-strike capability." Yet mere quantitative superiority in nuclear weapons does yield some political value. Krushchev evidently thought so when he sought to place missiles in Cuba, in order to improve the Soviet position in the nuclear balance, even though United States preponderance very probably did not amount to a first-strike capability, and the Cuban deployment would not have created one for the Soviets. Kennedy apparently thought so when he said that retention of the Russian missiles in Cuba "would have politically changed the balance of power; it would have appeared to [change it] and appearances contribute to reality."[2] Ancient ideas die hard; the notion that military preponderance means superior political power is so deeply ingrained that it continues to be believed and acted upon by both sides even though, in the strategic nuclear balance, it has little objective or logical basis. Further research would surely uncover many additional deviations which would serve to qualify and thus to enrich the logical analysis presented here.

[2]Quoted by Arnold L. Horelick in "The Cuban Missile Crisis," World Politics, XVI, No. 3, (April 1964) p. 376.

9

BRUCE M. RUSSETT

Refining Deterrence Theory: The Japanese Attack on Pearl Harbor[1]

A case study of the Japanese decision to launch the attack on Pearl Harbor, involving a decision-theoretical framework. This study is the second in a series aimed at understanding the conditions under which military deterrence succeeds or fails. The first study in this series, which involved a comparison of 17 cases, is described in considerable detail.

A Decision-Theory of Deterrence

The Japanese attack on Pearl Harbor represents one of the most conspicuous and costly failures of deterrence in history; as such it deserves careful examination to see if any general propositions can be extracted. A full investigation of the personalities and attitudes of the major participants in Japan's decision is quite beyond the scope of this article, although enough memoirs and official documents are available to permit an effort in this direction by other scholars. The purpose of the article is quite different: to show that in this and probably many other instances, a satisfactory explanation can be given largely without reference to idiosyncratic factors. The intent is to put the Japanese decision into the context of a more general theory of deterrence and to take a more explicit look at the foreign-policy making process than is sometimes done. Particularly, we want to examine some of the elements in common between this situation and other cases in the recent past. What is required is a theoretical framework that

---

An excerpt from "Pearl Harbor: deterrence theory and decision theory," *Journal of Peace Research*, 1967, 2, 89–106. Reprinted by permission of the author and that journal. The author is Associate Professor of Political Science and Director of the Political Data Program at Yale University.

[1]This article was written while I was Visiting Research Political Scientist at the Mental Health Research Institute of the University of Michigan. It was in part supported by a National Science Foundation grant to the Yale Political Data Program. I am grateful to Paul Hammond, Martin Patchen, J. David Singer, and Robert Ward for comments, and to Hal Christensen for some work in the archives of the Tokyo War Crimes Trial documents in connection with a graduate seminar at Yale University.

combines explanations on the level of the international system and the national decision-making system.

Some time ago I offered a model, derived from decision-theory, for analyzing the success or failure of nations' attempts to deter other nations from attacking smaller third parties.[2] The decision-theory model was cast in a utility-probability framework, in common with models suggested by several other writers.[3] It isolates certain variables in the mind of the formal decision-maker of a nation as he decides whether or not to attack a small nation which is to some degree under the protection of another power. The situation under scrutiny is one of deterrence in third areas (what Herman Kahn long ago labelled Type III deterrence), and has since the end of World War II been a major consideration of American policy-makers—how to prevent a Soviet (or Chinese) attack on allies or on exposed neutrals. Let us simplify for the moment to a single set of calculations in the mind of a single decision-maker. The prospective attacker must weigh the expected gains (utilities) to accrue from each of the following events:

1. W—an attack on the small nation, or pawn, which is countered by war on the part of the potential defender of that pawn; in other words, the utility—positive or negative—of having to fight a *war* with the major power;

2. A—an attack on the pawn which is not met by war with the defender; in other words, a successful act of *aggression*;

3. P—a decision not to attack the small nation. This outcome is in effect an aggregate of many possible courses of action; for simplicity, if somewhat inaccurately, we shall refer to it as *peace* or choosing not to attack at all.

P—the decision not to attack at all—is a choice fully under the control of the prospective attacker, and will occur or not, as he decides. The other two possible outcomes, however, are not fully under his control, and he can only estimate the likelihood that the defender will not go to war. Therefore he has to attach subjective probabilities to those two outcomes, and their utilities must be weighted by those probabilities. The utility of A must thus be discounted by whatever the attacker thinks is the probability (s) that he will actually get away with it, and the utility or disutility of W must similarly be weighted by its apparent likelihood (l-s in this simplified analysis). The final decision thus rests upon the relative values of two expressions: P (do nothing) on the one hand, and the summed utilities, weighted by their subjective probabilities, of A and W on the other. According to this formulation, the potential attacker will actually press ahead with his attack only if A times s plus W times l-s is greater than P. Since these are variables, of course, the same decision might be reached on the basis of quite different values in the formula. If the potential gains even from a successful attack (A) on the pawn are relatively low compared with "peace" (P), and the disutilities of a major war (W) are very great, even a small subjective probability that the defender will fight is enough to deter attack. On the other hand, the relative gains from a successful attack on the

[2]Bruce M. Russett, "The calculus of deterrence," *Journal of Conflict Resolution*, VII (1963), 97–109. I have changed the notation in order to make this presentation clearer.

[3]Related utility-probability models are employed by Daniel Ellsberg, *The Crude Analysis of Strategic Choice*, RAND Monograph P-2183 (Santa Monica, California: RAND Corporation, 1960); J. David Singer, "Internation influence: A formal model," *American Political Science Review*, LVII (1963), 420–430; and Glenn H. Snyder, *Deterrence and Defense* (Princeton, N.J.: Princeton University Press, 1961).

pawn might be quite high, but if the subjective probability of an unresisted attack were low, the aggression would still not be carried out. Thus the Chinese Communists, though they probably would value very highly the acquisition of Taiwan, have almost certainly been restrained by the high probability and disutility of a direct military confrontation with the U.S.

Now of course this model is grossly oversimplified, since a decision-maker is virtually always faced with a great variety of potential courses of action, not simply an attack/don't attack dichotomy, matched with a fight/don't fight choice by the potential defender. Nevertheless, each of these possibilities can, for analytical purposes, be thought of as aggregates of many shades of action. Another objection might be that political decision-makers certainly do not calculate utilities and probabilities in any precise way, though "strategic thinkers" and men versed in game theory may attempt to do so. But despite the fact that they may not try to put numerical values into an explicit model, decision-makers surely do weigh the probable costs and gains of various alternatives. Finally, the model is hardly operational as a predictor of events in international politics because of the extreme difficulties associated with any attempt to measure utilities and especially subjective probabilities. The problems are formidable in the laboratory, and virtually insuperable with real-world political leaders.[4] But despite the fact that we cannot actually measure even these implicit values with precision, the model will serve its purpose if it helps us identify relevant influences on a decision.

Empirical content was put into this model by a comparative study of 17 instances in the period 1935–1962 where a potential attacker threatened a smaller state that was to some degree under the protection of another power. By dividing those cases in which an attack was actually conducted from those in which the attacker drew back short of large-scale violent conflict, I was able to suggest several factors which seemed to be associated with successful deterrence and, in addition, to identify several which, though hypothesized in the national security literature to be relevant, seemed not to make a great difference in the outcome. Among other things, this *post hoc* experiment indicated that while military equality between the attacker and the defender was required at either the local or strategic level, military *superiority* by the defender, on either or both levels, was *not* a *sufficient* condition for deterrence. In terms of the above decision model, even though the potential disutilities of an attack might be very high to the attacker, these alone were not sufficient to restrain him. The other variables, and especially the attacker's subjective probability that the defender would actually fight, were highly relevant.

Pursuing this line of reasoning further, I found that certain characteristics of the *relationship* between the small state and the potential defender were far more closely associated with successful deterrence. Significantly, the existence or absence of an alliance or formal public commitment by the defender to protect the pawn was *not* one of these associated characteristics. In a large number of instances (Ger-

[4]Some experiments have, however, measured utilities and probabilities under laboratory conditions. *Cf.* Ward Edwards, "Utility and subjective probability: Their interaction and variance preferences," *Journal of Conflict Resolution*, VI (1962), 42–51, and the references cited there. Also useful is Robert M. Thrall, *et al.*, eds., *Decision Processes* (New York: John Wiley & Sons, Inc., 1954).

many's occupation of Austria, annexation of the remains of Czechoslovakia in 1939, the attack on Poland, and the American decision to cross the 38th parallel into North Korea among others), the attacker went ahead despite an explicit commitment, or he felt that the potential gains nevertheless compensated him for the risks.

I hypothesized that instead of worrying about a formal commitment the attacker would consider far more seriously some of the less formal bonds that might exist between defender and pawn when he assessed the probabilities that the defender would fight. Among these were (a) *military interdependence* (other than current alliance) such as the provision of arms and/or military advisors by the defender to the pawn; (b) *political interdependence*, which might include a former though no longer operative alliance as in fighting side-by-side in a previous war, or party and ideological ties like those between communist states; and (c) *economic interdependence*, which might include foreign investment but for which I chose, as a rough measure, to mean simply that exceptionally high proportions of their foreign trade are exchanged between them. With this approach I found important associations between the existence of these links and the success of deterrence. High military interdependence was the least powerful of the three, being found in seven of the eleven cases in which the attack was not deterred, as well as in each of the six instances in which it was. Political interdependence was twice as common in cases of successful as unsuccessful deterrence, and economic interdependence was almost *four* times as common—present to some degree in all of the "successes." The major hypothesis to which this led was: If other factors are equal, an attacker will regard a military response by the defender as more probable the greater the number of military, political and economic ties between pawn and defender. As summarized in the earlier paper:

> Strengthening these bonds is, in effect, a strategy of raising the credibility of deterrence by increasing the loss one would suffer by not fulfilling a pledge. It illustrates in part why the American promise to defend Western Europe, with nuclear weapons if necessary, is so credible even in the absence of overwhelming American strategic superiority. Western Europe is certainly extremely important because of its large, skilled population and industrial capacity. Yet it is particularly important to the United States because of the high degree of political and military integration that has taken place in the North Atlantic area. The United States, in losing Western Europe to the Communists, would lose population and industry, *and* the credibility of its pledges elsewhere . . . .
>
> The particular indices of economic, military, and political integration employed here are less important in themselves than as indicators of a broader kind of political and cultural integration, of . . . sympathy and loyalties, . . . trust, and mutual consideration . . . . Contact in some of these areas . . . tends to promote contacts of other sorts, and often produces mutual sympathies and concern for each other's welfare. . . .
>
> There is yet another way in which a defender may lose if he fails to honor his pledge. New Yorkers would sacrifice their own self-esteem if they failed to defend Californians from external attack; some of the same feeling applies, in lesser degree, to New Yorkers' attitudes toward Britishers. Though broad and intangible, this kind of relationship is nonetheless very real, and knowledge of it sometimes restrains an attacker. . . . [One cannot] put together a formula specifying precise values of the various elements of interdependence. But the more there are the stronger mutual interdependence becomes, and the greater is the attacker's risk in pressing onward.[5]

[5]Russett, *op. cit.*, pp. 107–109.

The Japanese Face a Dilemma

As we shall see, crucial elements in Japan's decision to attack Pearl Harbor were its need for the resources of Malaya and especially the Dutch East Indies, the realization that those resources could be obtained in sufficient quantity only by force and the conviction that the U.S. would declare war on Japan if those colonies were attacked, whether or not the Japanese themselves initiated hostilities with America. Japanese analysts reached the latter conclusion despite the absence of any American threat or promise.

The Japanese needed the resources of Malaya and the Dutch East Indies for military reasons. In 1940 fuel oil and scrap-iron were brought under the new National Defense Act of the U.S. as goods which could not be shipped out of the Western Hemisphere without an export license. Although commerce in these products with Japan was not cut off for another year, the threat of a raw-material scarcity to Japan was obvious. Following the freeze on Japanese assets in the U.S. of July 1941, and the consequent cessation of shipment of oil, scrap-iron and other goods from the U.S., Japan's economy was in most severe straits and her power to wage war directly threatened. Her military leaders estimated that her reserves of oil, painfully accumulated in the late 1930's when the risk of just such a squeeze began to be apparent, would last at the most two years. She was also short of rice, tin, bauxite, nickel, rubber, and other raw materials normally imported from the Netherlands Indies and Malaya. Negotiations with the Dutch authorities to supply these goods, plus extraordinary amounts of oil from the wells in Sumatra, had failed ostensibly on the grounds that the Dutch feared the material would be reexported to the Axis in Europe. The U.S., and the British and Dutch, made it quite clear that the embargo and freezing of assets would be relaxed only in exchange first for a return to the status quo in Indochina before July 1941 (in other words, Japanese withdrawal from air and naval bases there) and an agreement which would mean the end of the Japanese involvement in China and the abandonment of any right to station troops in that country. The purpose of the Western economic blockade was to force a favorable solution to the "China incident."

Under these conditions, the High Command of the Japanese navy demanded a "settlement" of one sort or other that would restore Japan's access to essential raw materials, most particularly oil. Without restored imports of fuel, the fleet could not remain an effective fighting force for more than a year and a half. While the Navy might have been willing to abandon the "China incident," it was utterly opposed to any long continuation of the status quo. Either raw materials supplies had to be restored by a peaceful settlement with the Western powers, or access to them in Thailand, Malaya, and the Indies, would have to be secured by force while Japan still retained the capabilities to do so.

If the Navy demanded either settlement or war, most members of the Japanese elite were opposed to any settlement which would in effect have meant withdrawal from China. The long war in China, begun in earnest in 1937 but tracing back to the seizure of Manchuria in 1931, was making little progress. Japanese forces had occupied most of the coast and most of China's industrial capacity, but with a trickle of American aid the Nationalist armies hung on in the interior. Yet no serious consideration was given to the possibility of peace with Chiang's government. To do so would have meant the end of all hopes of empire and even, so it was thought, of influence on the continent of Asia. Herbert Feis describes the reaction of moderate Foreign Minister Togo to the most forceful statement of American demands, on November 27, 1941: "Japan was now asked not only to abandon all the gains of her years of sacrifice, but to surrender her international position as a power in the Far East. That surrender, as he saw it, would have amounted to national suicide."[6]

In any case, the Army High Command simply would not have tolerated any abandonment of its position in China. Its own prestige and influence had been built up step by step during the war there, and its position in China became its power base in Japanese domestic politics. And the pursuit of the war had allowed the Army to achieve a degree of internal unity quite surprising in view of its earlier factional strife. General Tojo, by no means the most violent of Army war hawks, feared that any concession on the China issue would risk an actual revolt by extremist elements in the Army.[7] In fact, on the resignation of Prince Konoye's government in October 1941 Tojo had urged the appointment of Prince Higashi-Kuni as Premier, on the principle that should a settlement with the U.S. be decided upon only a member of the royal family would have a chance to control the Army and make peace. In the context of Japanese politics of the 1930's, when there had been several plotted *coups* and when one after another of the political leaders thought to be too conciliatory toward foreign elements were assassinated by extreme nationalists, this was hardly a far-fetched fear. Togo once characterized the Japanese internal political situation in these terms to Joseph Grew, American Ambassador to Tokyo, "If Japan were forced to give up suddenly all the fruits of the long war in China, collapse would follow."[8] And there was, after all, an attempted Army revolt in August 1945, when the Japanese government finally did accept the Allied terms of surrender.

Thus, to the various members of the Japanese decision-making system, and for somewhat different reasons, a peaceful settlement was utterly unacceptable.

Nevertheless, and here lay the dilemma, the Japanese were convinced that an attack on Malaya and the Dutch East Indies would be resisted militarily by the U.S. This conviction had to be based solely on inference. Yet it was a solid conviction, as shown by the otherwise inexplicable risk they took at Pearl Harbor.

Rather close links had been forged between the U.S. and the colonies of Malaya and the East Indies, bonds that were known to the Japanese and con-

---

[6]Herbert Feis, *The Road to Pearl Harbor* (Princeton, N.J.: Princeton University Press, 1950), p. 327.

[7]Lu describes vividly and convincingly the position of the Army on these questions. See David J. Lu, *From the Marco Polo Bridge to Pearl Harbor: Japan's Entry into World War II* (Washing- D.C.: Public Affairs Press, 1961).

[8]*Ibid.*, p. 304. *Cf.* the statement of the Japanese Minister of War at the cabinet meeting of October 12, 1941: "The problem of the stationing of the troops in China in itself means the life of the Army, and we shall not be able to make any concessions at all." Quoted in the memoirs of Prince Konoye, U.S. Congress, Joint Committee on the Investigation of Pearl Harbor Attack, *Pearl Harbor Attack: Hearings Before the Joint Committee*, 79th Congress, 1st Session (Washington, U.S. Government Printing Office, 1946), Part 20, p. 4009.

sidered to be of great importance. These ties, furthermore, closely resemble the kinds of links that we earlier indicated have been associated with the successful deterrence of attack on third parties. The Southwest Pacific area was of undeniable economic importance to the U.S.—at that time most of America's tin and rubber came from there, as did substantial quantities of other raw materials.[9] American political involvement in the area was also heavy. The U.S. was cooperating closely with the British and Dutch governments, and according to the Japanese evaluation, if the U.S. failed to defend the Indies it would lose its influence in China and endanger the Philippines.[10] Premier Tojo even referred in this context to the approval given Pan American World Airways to establish an air route between Singapore and Manila.[11]

Unilateral American actions to build up its military forces, both generally and in the Pacific in particular, were seen as evidence of aggressive intent.[12] But most convincing of all were the military ties apparently being established among the ABCD (American-British-Chinese-Dutch) powers. The U.S. was known to be supplying munitions and arms, including aircraft, not just to China but to British and Dutch forces in the Pacific. In cooperation with the British, Dutch, Australians, New Zealanders and the Free French (at New Caledonia) the U.S. had begun construction of a string of airfields to the Philippines. Furthermore, the U.S. had participated in staff conversations with British and Dutch military personnel at Singapore. The Japanese came to associate these conversations with an "Anglo-American policy of encirclement against Japan in the Southern Pacific Ocean."[13] This notion of encirclement appears time and again in Japanese official documents and memoirs. The freezing of Japanese assets by the U.S., British and Netherlands East Indies governments occurred on the same day, July 26, 1941. Although that act was in direct response to Japan's occupation of Southern Indochina, her leaders nevertheless saw it as the final link in their bondage.[14]

With these considerations in mind the Japanese leaders were faced with a true dilemma. An attack on the British and Dutch territories in the Pacific which was not resisted by the U.S. looked highly attractive, but highly unlikely. Much more probable was American resistance, and that promised substantial disutilities—a near-certain Japanese defeat. But the choice of a

---

[9]The economic importance of the area to the U.S. was not left to Japanese imagination. On July 11, 1940, Ambassador Grew pointed out to Foreign Minister Arita that in 1937, 15.8 per cent of the foreign trade of the Netherlands East Indies had been with the U.S. and only 11.6 per cent with Japan. He further emphasized the interest of the U.S. in continuing the open door there. See F. C. Jones, *Japan's New Order in East Asia: Its Rise and Fall, 1937–45* (London: Oxford University Press, 1954, p. 238) citing Cordell Hull, *The Memoirs of Cordell Hull* (New York: Macmillan, 1948), I, 895–896.

[10]*Cf.* The Japanese Foreign Office memorandum of early November 1941, International Military Tribunal for the Far East (hereafter cited as IMTFE), *Document* No. 1559A. Similar conclusions were expressed in the Liaison Conference meetings of October 1941, according to Robert J. C. Butow, *Tojo and the Coming of the War* (Princeton, N.J.: Princeton University Press, 1961), pp. 317–318.

[11]Butow, *op. cit.*, p. 225.

[12]IMTFE, *Transcript of Proceedings*, p. 36246.

[13]*Cf.* the Foreign Office memorandum so entitled, July 1941, IMTFE, *Defense Document* No. 1982. Foreign Minister Shigenori Togo in his memoirs (*The Cause of Japan*, New York, Simon and Schuster, 1956, pp. 84, 156, 163) repeatedly refers to the conversations this way.

[14]IMTFE, *Transcript*, p. 36273.

negotiated settlement with the U.S. was out of the question.

The only escape from the dilemma was by blunting one of its horns—to accept war with the U.S., but to attempt it under circumstances where the chances of victory were higher. Under these pressures Japan's leaders conceived what they considered to be a *pre-emptive* surprise attack on Pearl Harbor and seizure of the Philippines. In its military-industrial potential and its fleet in the Pacific the U.S. had a very powerful deterrent, but in terms of more recent terminology the latter was also highly *vulnerable*. Its vulnerability presented a third option with higher expected utilities.

For all the audacity of the strike at Hawaii, the aims were modest: to destroy, by tactical surprise, the existing offensive capabilities of the U.S. in the Pacific. The Japanese High Command hoped only to give its forces time to occupy the islands of the Southwest Pacific, to extract those islands' raw materials and to turn the whole area into a virtually impregnable line of defense which could long delay an American counteroffensive and mete out heavy casualties when the counterattack did come. As a result of their early success the Japanese naval and military chiefs extended this line a little farther than they had first meant to do, but their original intentions were not grandiose.

In deciding to attack Pearl Harbor the Japanese took what they fully recognized as a great risk. There is no doubt but that the Imperial government realized it could not win a long war with the U.S. *if the Americans chose to fight such a war*. Japanese strategists calculated that America's war potential was seven to eight times greater than their own; they knew that Japan could not hope to carry the war to the continental U.S. Admiral Yamamoto, the brilliant inventor of the Pearl Harbor attack plan, warned:

> In the first six months to a year of war against the U.S. and England I will run wild, and I will show you an uninterrupted succession of victories; I must also tell you that, should the war be prolonged for two or three years, I have no confidence in our ultimate victory.[15]

Without examination of the alternatives that the Japanese leaders seem to have perceived, this would appear to be a singularly foolish gamble. Certainly the element of wishful thinking was strong, and possibly the pressures of the situation were such that a limited element of "irrationality," in the sense of failure to examine properly the consequences of their act, was indeed present. (Though even here the "irrationality" label is not very helpful, and we are forced immediately to look for specific explanations. One might involve some careful hypotheses about the ways in which information may be distorted or its intake limited under duress. For example, a reduction in the number of facts considered seems to be a fairly common reaction to conditions of stress.) Because the proposed attack seemed an escape from the dilemma, it was grasped with more enthusiasm than it deserved. The Japanese never seriously considered exactly what would cause the U.S. to forgo crushing Japan, or how Japan might best create the proper conditions for a negotiated peace. Certain key elements, such as the probable effect of the Pearl Harbor attack on the American will to win,

---

[15]Quoted in Roberta Wohlstetter, *Pearl Harbor: Warning and Decision* (Stanford, Calif.: Stanford University Press, 1962), p. 350. General Suzuki, chairman of the Planning Board, had reported that Japan's stockpile of resources was not adequate to support a long war.

were left completely unanalyzed.[16] Japan's sole strategy involved dealing maximum losses to the U.S. at the outset, making the prospects of a prolonged war as grim as possible, and counting, in an extremely vague and ill-defined way, on the American people's "softness" to end the war.

A More Adequate Theory of Deterrence

Viewed from the perspective of the earlier study of the 17 cases of threatened aggression mentioned above, the Japanese might seem to have been adequately deterred from attacking the British and Dutch Pacific colonies. The U.S. had forged close bonds with these colonies resembling the kind that were earlier shown to be associated with the successful deterrence of attack on third parties. Why then did deterrence fail? Why did Japan not only attack the Indies anyway, but also directly attack the U.S. as well?

Recall the earlier formulation, which said that deterrence would succeed only if the utility of fighting a war times its apparent probability was less than the utility of no attack, i.e., of the status quo. While the option of attacking the colonies worked out, in Japanese thinking, to a most unattractive future, the status quo was also highly unpalatable. The poor prospects connected with both of these options (attacking the colonies and not attacking them) set the stage for the adoption of a third strategy of attacking the defender's vulnerable deterrent. Despite the great risks they doubtless saw in that strategy, it seemed to promise more gain or less loss than either of the former alternatives. Thus, once diplomatic negotiations revealed that the U.S. was not prepared to retract its demands for the Japanese withdrawal from China and Indochina, it became the clear and unanimous choice of the responsible Japanese officials. While they were well aware of America's potential strength and that the U.S. *could* win any war, they decided it might not *choose* to win a *long* war, and therefore picked the least unattractive course of action from a set of options few men would relish.

A general theory of deterrence must, therefore, very explicitly include all *three* (no attack; attack the pawn; attack the defender directly) of these gross options whenever it attempts to deal with deterrence of an attack on a third party rather than simply deterrence in a purely bilateral situation. Anything less is inadequate for theory and dangerous for policy. In assessing utilities and subjective probabilities, the crucial variables will include the nature and strength of the *ties* between defender and pawn; the *strength* of the defender's deterrent, both in a local and in a strategic sense; and the *vulnerability* of that deterrent to surprise attack. And excessive attention by the defender to deterring an attack on an ally or client state can result merely in failing to deter, or rather in encouraging, an attack upon itself. If the attacker is also very dissatisfied with the status quo, a lesson for modern policy merits remembrance—one should avoid presenting an opponent with options which are *all* highly unpalatable to him.[17]

---

[16]Apparently these seemingly obvious questions were simply not asked. See for example General Suzuki's report of his meeting with the former premiers on November 29, 1941, IMTFE, *Transcript*, p. 35223. See also the material presented by Stephen S. Large, *The Japanese Decision for War: How Rational?* (Ann Arbor, Mich.: University of Michigan, M. A. Thesis, 1965), pp. 46–48.

[17]As, for example, President Kennedy was careful to do both during the Cuban missile crisis and in his later praise of Khrushchev's "statesmanlike decision."

10

JOHN R. RASER · WAYMAN J. CROW

A Simulation Study of Deterrence Theories[1]

A study of the effect of the capacity to delay nuclear retaliation on international politics and the likelihood of war, employing multiple runs of the Inter-Nation Simulation. This study provides an empirical check on the validity of certain hypotheses put forward by deterrence theorists.

This paper reports a study on the impact of a specific weapons system characteristic on the structure of deterrence. It includes (1) a brief definition of deterrence, and (2) a short discussion of several nuclear deterrence strategies and their instabilities and hazards. (3) It describes a theoretical model based on hypotheses derived from the deterrence literature, as to how an invulnerable retaliatory force characterized by "capacity to delay response" might affect an international system. (4) It reports the results of tests of these hypotheses in an Inter-Nation Simulation.

Definition of Deterrence

Deterrence is a process which prevents unacceptable behavior in another by promising to *punish* him for unacceptable actions or to *deny* him success. Both methods have been used in international relations. For example, the custom of holding hostages and the Roman decimation policy guaranteed that unacceptable actions would result in the loss of something valued. The "balance of power" system in 19th century Europe, on the other hand,

Reprinted from *Proceedings of the International Peace Research Association Inaugural Conference*, Assen, The Netherlands: Royal VanGorcum Ltd., 1966, by permission of the authors and the publisher. John R. Raser is Research Fellow and Project Director at the Western Behavioral Sciences Institute at La Jolla, California, and Visiting Research Political Scientist at the Mental Health Research Institute of the University of Michigan (1967–1968). Wayman J. Crow is Associate Director of the Western Behavioral Sciences Institute.

[1]This is a much condensed version of a research report entitled: "WINSAFE II: An Inter-Nation Simulation Study of Deterrence Postures Embodying Capacity to Delay Response," Western Behavioral Sciences Institute, La Jolla, Calif., July 31, 1964. The research was supported in part by Naval Ordnance Test Station Contract N123(60530)35639A.

was an attempt to deter by *denial*; in essence, it promised to face any potential aggressor with a defensive coalition so strong as to *deny* him any possibilities of success.

Deterrence Strategies

Prior to 1945, nations relied chiefly on deterrence-by-denial. Nuclear weapons have now rendered that policy obsolete, *if the act to be denied is a nuclear attack*, for effective *defense* against attack by nuclear-armed supersonic bombers and missiles is all but impossible. However, *punishment* by nuclear retaliation is comparatively cheap and fairly certain of success.

Confronted by a world in which several nations possess nuclear weapons and at least minimum delivery capability, and by the likelihood that more nations will join the "club," the nuclear powers are of necessity committed to mutual deterrence by promise of punishment or, in Churchill's phrase, a "balance of terror." Peace is to be maintained by reciprocal threat, each nation promising the others that attack will bring retaliation of such magnitude as to offset any possible gains. Aggressions short of attack within the nation's boundaries are to be deterred by fear that *any* conflict can escalate into thermonuclear war; if that fails they are to be met with conventional or even nuclear tactical forces.[2]

Examination of this strategy, however, shows that it may not only fail to prevent war, but may even *increase* its possibility. Which nation is the deterrer, which the deterred? Each sees his own preparations as defensive and the other's as aggressive. The following illustration shows how war could be precipitated.

America considers herself to be on the defensive, but how might this posture be seen by a "defensive" antagonist? Not long ago, the United States retaliatory force was so vulnerable to surprise attack that it almost certainly could not have weathered one and carried out its mission. Knowing this, an opponent might logically conclude that since the United States' force was clearly useless for retaliation, it must be intended for a first strike. Had he not better pre-empt the initiative and himself strike first? But the United States, anticipating this chain of logic, might well decide that she should strike first in order to deny him the possibility of a first strike designed to prevent her first strike . . . and so on . . . . This is an unstable situation, unstable in the sense that the "defensive" system designed to prevent war might of itself actually precipitate it.[3]

In recognition of this possibility, a new deterrence strategy has been developed, based on the doctrine that it is not *gross* nuclear capability which effectively deters, but only that *portion* of it that can survive a surprise attack and effectively retaliate.[4] The United States implemented this strategy with

---

[2]An exceptionally clear summary of the development of deterrence doctrine in the United States may be found in William Kaufmann, *The McNamara Strategy*, New York, Harper & Row, 1964, especially in Chaps. 1 and 2.

[3]For discussions of this problem see G. Snyder, *Deterrence and Defense: Toward a Theory of National Security*, Princeton, N. J., Princeton University Press, 1961; Schelling, T. C., *The Strategy of Conflict*, Cambridge, Mass., Harvard University Press, 1960; Brodie, B., *Strategy in the Missile Age*, Princeton, N. J., Princeton University Press, 1959; Morgenstern, O., *The Question of National Defense*, New York, Vintage Books, 1961.

[4]Wohlstetter, A., "The Delicate Balance of Terror," *Foreign Affairs*, **37,** 211–234, 1959, provided the first concise statement of this problem.

SAC "alerts," designed to convince her opponents that she would not wait for impact, but would retaliate on *warning*. However, the possibilities for false interpretations of "warning" signs, the need for "hair trigger" responses, and the demand for instant decisions by local commanders, could, it is clear, result in accidental war. These inherent dangers are compounded when manned bombers are supplemented with vulnerable and unrecallable missiles.

A related approach to deterrence maintains that if intelligence reports seem to indicate that the opponent is *preparing* an attack the "defender" could then strike first (a "pre-emptive" first strike) and cripple the aggressor's forces. This is a new form of the old doctrine of deterrence-by-denial, and is one aspect of counter-force strategy. But this leads to mutual fear of mutual misapprehension—side A fears side B may *think* side A is about to launch a first strike, in fear of side B's anticipated first strike . . . and so on . . . .

Even if these strategies should not lead to war, they create other difficulties; e.g., the constant *fear* of surprise attack or of accidental war, expensive arms races, the continuing necessity for a state of national "alert," and the necessity to act belligerently in order to convince an opponent of the nation's *will* to strike on warning. Foreign policy must be geared to maintaining those alliances and base-rights which insure the most advantageous strategic position. Continuing threats to kill *en masse*, and the continuing possibility of being killed *en masse*, may erode the nation's value system.

All of these problems have been frequently discussed; but the proposed solutions—preventive war, comprehensive arms control, unilateral or multilateral disarmament—seem to be either unacceptable or unachievable. Strategists are therefore searching for other ways to stabilize deterrence and eliminate some of its drawbacks.

Theorists of deterrence have proposed that stability is primarily a function of the *invulnerability* of the retaliatory system; that is, its capacity to survive and to retaliate overwhelmingly, after a surprise attack of any magnitude. It is thought that such invulnerability would both eradicate the first-strike premium and eliminate the probability of accidental war, inherent in the strategy of strike-back-on-warning. Possession of an invulnerable retaliatory force, however, provides a new strategic possibility—that of refraining from immediate strike-back, and delaying the retaliatory blow in order to deliver it later at a time and in a manner of the "defender's" choosing. Secretary of Defense McNamara advocated such a force and such a strategy when he testified before the House Committee on Armed Services, February 23, 1961:

> In this age of nuclear-armed intercontinental ballistic missiles, the ability to deter rests heavily on the existence of a force which can weather a massive nuclear attack, even with little or no warning, in sufficient strength to strike a decisive counter-blow. This force must be of a character which will permit its use, in event of attack, in a cool and deliberate fashion and always under the complete control of the constituted authority.

Such a capability has been termed "capacity to delay response" or for convenience, "CDR." Some theorists have reasoned that if one nation is known to possess this capacity, the stability of the deterrence situation will be increased.[5] Can this be confirmed?

[5]Those who have been closest to this terminology are: Richard C. Snyder, *Deterrence, Weapons Systems, and Decision-Making*, N.O.T.S. TP 2769, China Lake, Calif., Oct. 1961; T. E. Phipps, "Need for Staying Power of the FBM Submarine System, N.O.T.S., Memo, Nov. 28, 1961; and T. W. Milburn, "Capacity to Delay Response," memo to authors, April, 1963.

From discussions of invulnerability in the literature, it becomes apparent that what invulnerability actually does is to create a "package" of options constituting a CDR; these options are enumerated below. In general it is presumed in the deterrence-literature that a CDR will change other nations' perceptions of the nation which acquires it, and affect the interactions within the international system. However, much of the literature is ambiguous and contradictory as to the *nature* of this effect. It therefore seemed worthwhile to codify the options arising from invulnerability, to develop a series of hypotheses as to the effect of these options in an international system, and to test the hypotheses in the Inter-Nation Simulation. In short, we have attempted to explicate and test that which is implicit and untested in the literature, in order to ascertain whether CDR would indeed increase the stability of the deterrence situation.

Capacity to Delay Response

The Capacity to Delay Response requires (a) a weapons-system capable of withstanding the most devastating blow or series of blows, and of retaliating decisively (*weapons-invulnerability*); (b) a command, communications, and information-gathering organization capable of surviving such a blow and, despite it, of gathering and evaluating information, and planning and executing a chosen retaliation (*command-and control-invulnerability*); and (c) recognition of, and ability to accept, delay as a possible response strategy (*response-flexibility*).

A nation achieving these three capabilities (a "CDR-nation") would acquire certain options, briefly stated as follows:

A. It need not retaliate immediately upon the occurrence of unexplained or ambiguous events, or upon *warning* that attack is on the way.
B. It need not retaliate immediately upon attack, the source of which is unknown.
C. Since it need not retaliate on warning of attack, it need not promise to do so.
D. It is not under pressure to strike first (pre-emptively) to avoid loss of its retaliatory force.
E. Since a CDR nation has more time to make the decision to retaliate, it can better centralize and rationalize its decision-making process.
F. It need not retaliate on a pre-programmed basis, but can retarget its retaliatory forces after attack.
G. Since it can delay retaliation, a CDR-nation can establish responsibility for the initiation of nuclear war.
H. Since it can choose its time, it can retaliate when the attacker's defenses are weak.
I. Since it need not empty its arsenals, or lose them, it can retain deterrence-capability after attack.
J. Since the technical requirements for effective surprise attack may overlap those for CDR, a CDR-nation might be able to strike first more effectively.
K. Since it need not retaliate reflexively a CDR-nation can deliberate its response and thus might not retaliate at all.

The literature suggests that consequences for the international system will flow from the known possession of these options by one nuclear nation. That is: *Changes will be effected in an international system by the known existence of these options whether or not an occasion arises for exercising them.*

The remainder of this paper focuses on the interrelated effects for an international system arising simply from the knowledge that *one* nation has these options.

Theoretical Model

A detailed theoretical model was constructed, predicated on the options listed above and the hypotheses derived from them. The hypotheses, and the ways they are linked, were drawn from more than two hundred writings on deterrence strategy. There is also experimental evidence (to a certain extent contradictory) substantiating some of the linkages in the model diagrammed in Figure 1.

The reasoning in the deterrence-literature is, of course, much more detailed than is presented here.[6] What follows, however, should suffice to acquaint the reader with the background for the choice of the hypotheses and the development of the theoretical model.

Options E, F, G, H, I, and J—that is, those relating to more rational decision-making, post-attack retargeting, fixing responsibility for nuclear initiation, continued deterrence, and first-strike capability—may have the effect of making the CDR-nation appear stronger to others, while at

[6]The foregoing reasoning was drawn from more than 200 writings on deterrence, much of which had already been put in propositional form by Richard C. Snyder in his *Deterrence, Weapons Systems, and Decision-Making*, *op. cit.* A selected list of other writings which have been particularly important would include: Amster, W. "Design for Deterrence," *Bull. Atomic Science*, **12,** 164–165, 1956; Backus, Commander P. H., "Finite Deterrence, Controlled Retaliation," *U.S. Naval Institute Proceedings*, **85,** 323–331, March 1959; Brodie, B., "The Anatomy of Deterrence," *World Politics*, **11,** 173–179, 1959; Brody, R. A., "Some Systemic Effects of the Spread of Nuclear Weapons Technology: A Study Through Simulation of a Multi-Nuclear Future," *J. Conflict Resolution*, **7**(4), 662–787, Dec. 1963; Brower, M., "Controlled Thermonuclear War," *New Republic*, July 30, 1962; Brower, M., Nuclear Strategy of the Kennedy Administration," *Bull. Atomic Sci.*, **18,** 34–41, 1962; Burns, A. L., "The International Consequences of Expecting Surprises," *World Politics*, **10,** 512–536, 1958; Buzzard, Rear Admiral Sir Anthony, "Massive Retaliation and Graduated Deterrence," *World Politics*, **8,** 228–237, 1956; Deutsch, M., "Some Considerations Relevant to National Security," *J. Soc. Issues*, **17,** 57–68, 1961; Gartoff, R. L., *Soviet Strategy in the Nuclear Age*, New York, Praeger, 1958; Halle, Louis J., "Peace in Our Time? Nuclear Weapons as a Stabilizer," *The New Republic*, Dec. 28, 1963, pp. 16–19; Halperin, M. H., "Nuclear Weapons and Limited War," *J. Confl. Resolution*, **5,** 27–29, 1961; Kahn, H., *On Thermonuclear War: Three Lectures and Several Suggestions*, Princeton, N.J., Princeton University Press, 1961; Kaplan, M. A., "The Calculus of Nuclear Deterrence," *World Politics*, **11,** 20–43, 1958; Kaufmann, W.H., *The Requirements of Deterrence*, Memo No. 7, Princeton University, Center of International Studies, 1954; Kobe, D. H., "A Theory of Catalytic War," *J. Confl. Resolution*, **6,** 125–143, 1962; Leghorn, R. S., "The Problem of Accidental War," *Bull. Atomic Scientists*, **14,** 205–209, 1958; McClelland, C. A., ed., *Nuclear Weapons, Missiles, and Future War: Problem for the Sixties*, San Francisco, Chandler, 1960; McNaughton, J. T., *Arms Restraint in Military Decisions*, Speech prepared for delivery at Int. Arms Control Symposium, Univ. of Michigan, Ann Arbor, Dec. 19, 1962; Milburn, T. W., *Capacity to Delay Response*, April 1963, typed memo to the authors; Milburn, T. W., "The Concept of Deterrence, Some Logical and Psychological Considerations," *J. Soc. Issues*, **17,** 3–12, 1961; Milburn, T. W., "What Constitutes Effective Deterrence?" *J. Confl. Resolution*, **3,** 138–145, 1959; Morgenstern, O., *op. cit.*, New York, Vintage Books, 1961; Pepitone, A., and R. Kleiner, "The Effects of Threat and Frustration on Group Cohesiveness," *J. Abnormal Psychol.*, **54,** 192–199, 1957; Pilisuk, M., "The Hostile Enemy: A Factor in Credible Deterrence," Ann Arbor, Univ. of Michigan, 1961, ditto; Pruitt, Dean G., "Threat Perception, Trust and Responsiveness in International Behavior," Center for Research on Social Behavior, Univ. of Delaware, Newark, Delaware, Technical Report No. 11 for the Office of Naval Research, Washington, D. C., Contract No. Nonr-2285 (02), January 9, 1964; Russett, B. M., "The Calculus of Deterrence," *J. Confl. Resolution*, **7,** 97–109, 1963; Schelling, T. C., "Bargaining, Communication, and Limited War," *J. Confl. Resolution*, **1,** 19–36, 1957; Schelling, T. C., *op. cit.;* Sherwin, C. W., "Securing Peace Through Military Technology," *Bull. Atomic Sci.*, **12,** 159–164, 1956; Singer, J. D., "Threat Perception and the Armament-Tension Dilemma," *J. Confl. Resolution*, **2,** 90–105, 1958; Singer, J. D., *Deterrence; Arms Control, and Disarmament: Toward a Synthesis in National Security Policy*, Columbus, Ohio, University of Ohio Press, 1962; Snyder, G. H., *op. cit.*, Wohlstetter, A., *op. cit.*

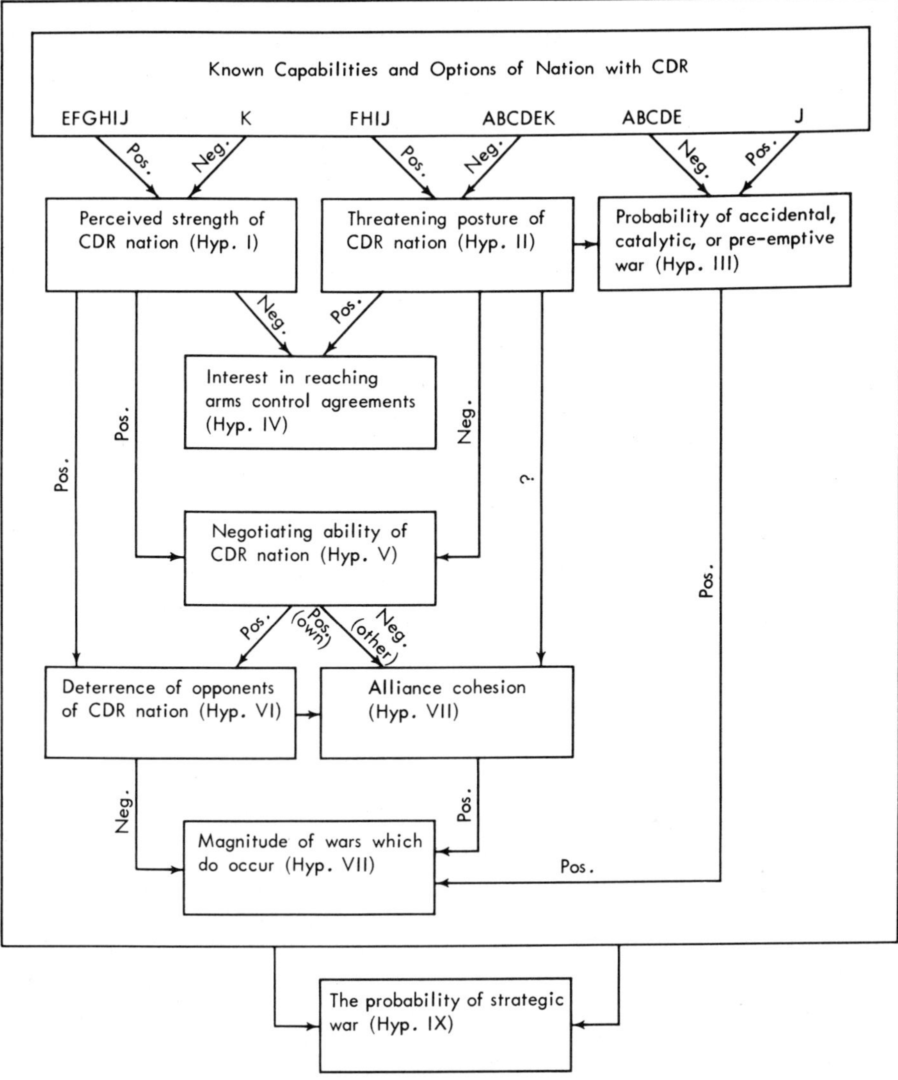

FIGURE 1. *Model underlying the simulation study of the capacity to delay response.*

least one Option, K—relating to the increased possibility that the nation may not respond at all—, may make it appear weaker.

Some of the same options, specifically F, H, I, and J, may also make the nation appear more threatening, while Options A, B, C, D, E, and K—that is, those relating to responses to ambiguous events, to attacks from unknown sources, to promises to retaliate on warning, to the temptation to pre-empt, to rational decision-making, and to the increased possibility that the nation might not retaliate at all—may make it less threatening to others.

"Perceived strength" and "threat," then, constitute the first two dependent variables.

The knowledge that one nation possesses Options A, B, C, D, and E—those relating to responses to ambiguous events, to attacks from unknown sources, to promises to retaliate on warning, to temptations to pre-empt, and to rationalized decision-making—may cause changes in the system such that accidental, catalytic, and pre-emptive ("unintended") wars will become less probable, while Option J, giving the nation greater first-strike effectiveness, may make such wars more probable.

Changes in the "strength" and "threat" variables should have a variety of related consequences for the system.

Thus, it is proposed, if the CDR-nation feels itself stronger, it should be less interested in arms control agreements, if it feels weaker, its interest should increase; while interest of other nations is directly correlated with the CDR-nation's threat. The "strength" and "threat" variables should also affect the CDR-nation's ability to negotiate: if it is seen as stronger but less threatening, it should be better able to negotiate, and if it is seen as weaker but more threatening, it should be less able to negotiate.

Negotiating ability as well as perceived strength should affect a nation's deterrence-capability—i.e., better negotiating ability should better enable a nation to offer its opponents alternative courses of action, or to solve critical conflicts. In turn, the effectiveness with which a nation can deter its opponents, combined with its threat and negotiating ability, should influence the cohesion of all alliances in the system.

The CDR-nation's deterrence-capability, the cohesiveness of all alliances in the system, and the likelihood of "accident" or "pre-emption" should combine to influence the escalation, and thus the magnitude of any wars which do occur.

Finally, it is proposed, the perceived strength and threat, the probability of accidental, pre-emptive and catalytic war, the interest in arms control agreements, negotiating ability, deterrence-effectiveness, alliance cohesion, and likelihood of escalation, should all interact in such a way as to affect the probability of strategic war. The hypotheses based on these lines of reasoning are given in the Results section.

Methodology

Because of its flexibility and because it can provide a wealth of data, the Inter-Nation Simulation was chosen as the research tool with which to test the hypotheses contained in the theoretical CDR model. Since the INS has previously been described in detail,[7] only a brief outline will be presented here.

The INS is a laboratory "game," composed of a number of simulated "nations," each with different parameters, constituting an "international" system. Each nation includes a mathematical model of the major economic and political variables operating in a nation-state; human "decision-makers" (the participants) and "resources," which the participants allocate to accomplish their goals. The international system has itself certain resources and relationships with respect to trade, aid, communication, espionage, alli-

[7]Guetzkow, Alger, Brody, Noel, and Snyder, *Simulation in International Relations*, Englewood Cliffs, N.J., Prentice-Hall, Inc., 1963. See also, Verba, Sidney, "Simulation, Reality, and Theory in International Relations," *World Politics*, **16**(3), 490–520, April 1964.

ances, treaties, war, etc. To test the CDR hypotheses, the "world" was so structured that false warnings, accidental firings, surprise attacks, and attacks from unknown sources were possibilities. Strategy choices as to timing of responses, promises to retaliate for attacks on allies, promises to respond on warning or not to respond until after impact, were all available. In short, the possibilities and uncertainties confronting the players were as similar as possible to those faced by real world decision-makers.

In the present study, the "world" consisted of five nations divided, at the start, into two alliance-blocs. One consisted of UTRO, a rich and powerful nuclear nation, allied with two small non-nuclear nations, ALGO and INGO. The other consisted of a powerful nuclear nation, OMNE, and a somewhat smaller non-nuclear nation, ERGA. All nations except INGO were members of an international organization, the I.O.

At the start of play, the participants were given a history of their "world" —a long record of war and conflict, inter-bloc suspicion and hostility, unsuccessful efforts at arms control, unrest and revolution within some nations. In short, the aim was to create, as the starting condition, a bi-polar, Cold War world—a simplified version of the post-World War II situation.

The data were obtained from 12 replications, or "runs"; each run consisted of twelve 70-minute periods, and required three days of play.

Subjects, i.e., the national decision-makers, were recruits at the Naval Training Center in San Diego, California, awaiting transfer to special schools. For each run, 20 recruits (out of about 1600) were selected on the basis of educational level, General Classification Test scores, and "boot" camp performance. After two days' orientation, each subject was randomly assigned to one of the nations and to a role within his nation as Central Decision Maker, Aspiring Central Decision Maker, External Decision Maker, or Decision Maker for Force.

The level of involvement was intense. There were all-night sessions in the Base library, and statements such as, "this has been the most important experience of my life . . ."; perspiring palms and foreheads, nervous tics, tears of frustration, and two fights, testified to the sense of reality experienced by the participants.

The research-design contained two conditions—CDR and non-CDR. In the latter, all nuclear weapons-systems were vulnerable; in the CDR condition, *one* nation, OMNE, obtained invulnerability as a research-and-development payoff, and an editorial in the *World Times* (a dittoed newspaper issued each period) pointed out the options, to insure that their existence was known to all. The CDR condition ended when an R & D payoff gave UTRO a "detection system." The conditions were manipulated in the course of the study as follows:

	PERIODS		
	1–3	*4–7*	*8–12*
6 runs	Non-CDR	CDR	non-CDR
6 runs	CDR	non-CDR	CDR

The participants thus served as their own controls, reducing the variability arising from personality differences among decision-makers. Since this design gave equal importance to shifts from non-CDR to CDR, and from CDR to non-CDR, it was possible to examine what happened when the CDR-nation gained or lost its invulnerability.

Results[8]

Hypothesis I: *Omne will be perceived as stronger (weaker) with CDR than without it.* The perceived strength of the CDR nation was operationally defined as the combined ratings of all participants on the following periodically distributed questionnaire item:

Rate each of the *nuclear* nations (including your own if you are a nuclear nation) on the following scales. (Place the first letter of the name of the nuclear nation in the space in which it belongs. You may place more than one nation in the same space.)

______	______	______	______
extremely weak militarily	quite	slightly	neither

______	______	______
slightly	quite	extremely strong militarily

The number of shifts in the direction of the hypothesis was compared with that of shifts toward the counter-hypothesis, and the statistical significance obtained with a sign test.[9] Omne was seen as stronger after gaining CDR ($p < .0001$), and weaker after its loss ($p < .0005$). It was decided, therefore, that: *when Omne had a known CDR she was perceived as stronger than when she did not.* Apparently Options E, F, G, H, I, and J were more important in the minds of the participants than was Option K.

Analyses of the interactions on a nation-by-nation-basis yielded a highly interesting and unexpected result. When Utro's perceptions of Omne's strength were compared with Omne's own perceptions of her strength, it was found that while Omne saw herself as stronger when she gained CDR ($p < .0006$), she did not see herself as weakened by its loss, though all the other nations did. Generalizing from this result, it may be that a powerful nation readily sees a weapons breakthrough as increasing its strength, but does not see nullification of the breakthrough as decreasing its strength.

Why is this? Nothing was found in the literature of international politics to suggest such a phenomenon. Do nations readily see augmentations to their strength, but find it difficult to recognize losses? While the answer appears to be "yes," on the basis of the data, it is not intuitively obvious and certainly seems worth exploring.

This unexpected result raised an interesting second question. If a nation readily sees additions to its strength, but is reluctant to recognize losses, then might there not be a mirror-reaction in an opponent—that is, might not the opponent fail to perceive additions to the strength of another nation, but be quick to recognize any losses? Should this be the case, it would logically complement, and tend to verify, the first finding. It would be expected in our study, then, that Utro would fail to see Omne's gain of CDR as adding to her strength, but would clearly see its loss as decreasing her strength. And so it proved. Utro did not significantly change her rating of Omne when the latter obtained CDR, but did indeed see her as weaker upon its loss ($p < .009$). Thus the postdiction was confirmed. These results suggest that changes in national strength may give rise to three types of reactions:

---

[8]The data reported here are only a small portion of the complete study which used content analysis, detailed studies of each world by observers, examination of world events, and player evaluations, in addition to the scale data reported here. The different types of data reinforce one another quite consistently.

[9]See Siegel, S., *Non-Parametric Statistics for the Behavioral Sciences*, New York: McGraw-Hill Book Company, 1956. pp. 63–83. The .05 level (two-tailed) of rejection was used, with .1 considered a strong trend.

1. The nation experiencing these changes tends to perceive only its gains in strength and not its losses.
2. The primary opponent fails to recognize additions to the other nation's strength, but readily perceives its losses.
3. The nations less directly involved are able to perceive changes in strength more accurately.

Hypothesis II: Omne will be more (less) threatening with CDR than without it. Its threat was operationally defined as the combined ratings of all participants on four 7-point scale items: "extremely cautious—extremely rash"; "extremely belligerent—extremely peaceful"; "extremely threatening—extremely reassuring"; and "extremely likely—extremely unlikely to precipitate war." Data were gathered and treated as for Hypothesis I.

On gaining CDR, Omne was seen as *more* likely to precipitate war ($p < .02$), and on losing it, as *less likely* to do so ($p < .04$); as *less cautious* ($p < .03$), on gaining CDR; as *less rash* ($p = .007$), on losing it. On the peaceful–belligerent scale there was no shift when Omne gained CDR, but a strong trend ($p = .1$) toward seeing her as *more belligerent* when she lost it. There was a strong trend towards the threat-end of the threat–reassurance scale when Omne gained CDR ($p < .08$), but no shift when she lost it.

Summarizing the results of these four ratings, it was decided that: *Omne was seen as more threatening with CDR than without it.*

It should be recalled from Figure 1 and from the list of CDR options that Hypothesis II was drawn from two sets of relationships between certain of the options and "threat." A nation possessing CDR could be seen as *more* threatening due to Options F, H, I, and J, all of which increase its ability to wage war effectively. Conversely, it was proposed that Options A, B, C, D, E, and K would serve to decrease the threat posed by the nation possessing CDR, since it would be seen as less apt to precipitate war by accident or design (A, B, D); it could have a more rationalized decison-making process (E); it need not act belligerently to maintain the credibility of its deterrent (C); and it might be seen as unlikely to use its nuclear force at all (K). On the basis of the results it was concluded that in the INS, the options which increased war-waging capability were dominant. It is, of course, possible that the participants simply ignored the options, and that in a cold war system, if one belligerent is seen as gaining strength, it almost automatically becomes more threatening.

Hypothesis III: Accidental, pre-emptive, and catalytic war will be less (more) likely when Omne has CDR.

Data to test this hypothesis were obtained by comparing the participants' responses under CDR and non-CDR conditions, to two scenarios:

(1) "If, as the situation now stands, a nuclear weapons impact occurred in the nuclear power of your bloc, it might mean several things. It might mean that some nuclear forces had exploded by accident, but if so, the opposing bloc might assume that you would believe it to have been the first wave of an attack from him and he might feel it wisest to hit you before you struck back at him. It might be a missile launched from one of the smaller powers who had obtained nuclear weapons secretly, and who hoped to make the great nuclear powers go to war with one another in order to enhance his own position. It might be the first wave of an attack from an opponent of which you had received no warning. If such an event did occur, *what would be your recommended response*

for your bloc? Your recommendation should be made on the basis of how likely you feel that this would be an intentional strike rather than an accident, on how you feel the opponent would respond to such an event, on the basis of what your condition would be after accepting a first strike, and on your ability to prevent the opponent from hitting you if you do strike immediately with an attempted disarming blow."

____________a. No military response.
______________b. Military response.

(2) "If, as the situation now stands, you received unverifiable but apparently well-founded intelligence reports that the other bloc was in the process of preparing to launch an all-out nuclear strike against you, what would be your recommended response for your bloc? Your recommendation should be made on the basis of how believable you would consider such information, given the current state of the world, on what your condition would be after accepting a first strike, and on your ability to prevent their hitting you by striking first with an attempted disarming blow."

____________a. No military response.
______________b. Military response.

When Omne gained CDR, a significant number of participants ($p < .05$) shifted from "military" to "no military" response; when Omne lost CDR the shifts were in the opposite direction ($p < .01$ on the first scenario, and $p < .001$ on the second).[10] The decision was that: *accidental, pre-emptive, and catalytic wars were less likely when Omne had CDR than when she did not.*

This hypothesis was drawn from two sets of related options: since Options A, B, C, D, and E decrease the likelihood that the CDR-nation will act inappropriately, the probability of "unintended" wars will be decreased; however Option J designating increased capability of waging pre-emptive war, may actually increase the probability of such wars, since the nation possessing this option might be more likely to exercise it; furthermore other nations' anxiety concerning this, might evoke behavior that itself would increase the probability of such wars. On the basis of the results, it was concluded that the Options A through E were dominant and that Option J did not importantly influence the situation.

Hypothesis IV: Interest in arms control agreements will be less (greater) when Omne has CDR than when she does not. To test this hypothesis data were drawn from subjects' responses on a 7-point scale ("extremely important—extremely unimportant") to the following item:

Indicate how important you feel it is, given the present state of the world, that arms control or disarmament agreements be reached.

Data were treated as for Hypotheses I and II. It was predicted in the model that the outcome would depend on changes in the "strength" and "threat" variables. Since Omne perceived herself as strengthened when she gained CDR, the model predicted that she would be less interested in arms control agreements. There was a weak trend in this direction ($p = .13$, one-tailed), but she did not shift toward greater interest when she lost CDR. This is as expected, since she did not see herself as weakened. The prediction that if other nations saw Omne as stronger and more threatening they would be more interested in arms control agreements was also partially confirmed: interest was significantly greater ($p = .01$) when Omne gained CDR, though scarcely changed ($p = .25$) when she lost it.

Hypothesis V: Omne's known possession

[10] The McNemar test for the significance of changes was used for this dichotymous choice data. For a description see Siegel, *op. cit.* pp. 63–67.

of CDR will enable her to negotiate more (less) adequately. It was reasoned that perceptions of the CDR nation as stronger and less threatening would enchance its negotiating ability, and conversely. Because Omne was seen as both stronger and *more* threatening, no prediction could be made.

Bales Interaction Analysis[11] was carried out for all I.O. meetings and on a random sample of written messages. Indices of "task orientation," "difficulty of communication," and "expressive-malintegrative acts" were developed for interpreting the Bales scores on this communication flow, with respect to negotiating ability. The gain or loss of CDR did not significantly affect any of the indices, or result in any consistent trends. The hypothesis that there is a relation between CDR and negotiating ability was therefore rejected.

Hypothesis VI: Omne's known possession of CDR will increase (decrease) her deterrence capability. According to the model, if Omne is seen as stronger, and if she is better able to negotiate, her opponents will be more effectively deterred. Omne was indeed seen as stronger but since her negotiating ability was not affected, the prediction can be made, but with somewhat less confidence. Nevertheless, the results tend to indicate that CDR did increase Omne's deterrence-capacity. Responses to the following scenarios were gathered and treated as for Hypotheses I, II, and IV:

(1) If, as the situation now stands, the nuclear power of the other bloc should begin moves which threaten to result in a loss of prestige and power for your bloc, *how great would this threatened loss have to be* before you would recommend that your bloc respond with military action? Your recommendation should be made on the basis of what you feel may be accomplished at the present time through the use of military force; on the basis of comparative power positions and whether you think you could win a war; and on the basis of how successful you feel that negotiations might be in preventing such moves.

Extremely great loss ____ ____ ____ ____ Quite minor loss

(2) If, as the situation now stands, waging war with the other block seems to you to be the best means for accomplishing military, political, economic, or moral ends, *how important would these ends have to be* before you would recommend war as the course of action for your bloc? Your recommendation should be made on the basis of what you feel may be accomplished at the present time through the use of military force, on the basis of your comparative power positions and whether you think you could win a war, and on the basis of how successful you feel that negotiations might be in accomplishing such ends.

Extremely important ____ ____ ____ ____ Of minor importance

There was a strong trend for Omne's opponents to be more deterred when she gained CDR ($p = .08$, one-tailed, on the first scenario and $p = .07$ on the second). There was a strong trend ($p = .09$) on the first scenario, and a significant shift ($p = .02$) on the second scenario, towards Omne's opponents' being less deterred when she lost CDR. It was concluded that *when Omne had CDR there was a strong trend for her opponents to be more deterred.*

Hypothesis VII: Omne's known possession of CDR will reduce (increase) alliance cohesion. The model predicted that alliance-cohesion would change as a function of changes in the threat of the CDR-nation, its negotiating ability, and/or its deterrent-capacity. However, evidence in the literature as to

[11]Robert F. Bales, *Interaction Process Analysis*, Ann Arbor, University Microfilms, Inc., 1962, gives a detailed description of the twelve categories to which message units may be assigned. We used comparisons among the number of message units assigned to different categories to arrive at the indices named.

these linkages is contradictory. Brody's INS studies indicate that alliance cohesion is *positively* correlated with outside threat, while Pepitone and Keliner, in a small-group laboratory, found a *negative* correlation between "group cohesion and outgroup threat."[12] The consequences of deterrent effectiveness for alliance-cohesion are also in dispute; in some discussions of NATO it is assumed that more effective deterrence will increase alliance-cohesion, while in others it is assumed that the resulting sense of security might weaken alliances. Since in this study CDR did not effect Omne's negotiating ability, that factor had to be omitted. For all these reasons, it was impossible to predict how alliance-cohesion would change as a function of CDR.

Alliance-cohesion was measured in three ways. (1) Changes with the gain and loss of CDR in the ratio of inter-bloc to intra-bloc messages were calculated for each run to provide an "index of differentiation"; no significant results were obtained (sign test) for either alliance, and no consistent trends emerged. (2) Data were obtained from 7-point scales indicating how friendly the decision-makers felt toward their allies, and how friendly they believed their allies felt toward them; data were handled as for Hypothesis I. Results were not significant, though the level of friendliness among allies tended to decrease slightly when Omne had CDR. (3) Data on the ratio between the number of positive, supportive, and friendly messages exchanged within a bloc and the number of negative messages were obtained by Bales Interaction Analysis and an "index of solidarity" calculated for each run. CDR was not correlated with a change in the Omne alliance, but the opposing alliance was significantly *less* cohesive ($p < .05$, two-tailed; Wilcoxen Matched Pairs Signed-Ranks Test).[13] Since significant results were obtained on only one of the three measures, it was decided to reject the hypothesis that CDR affects alliance-cohesion.

Hypothesis VIII: When Omne is known to have CDR, any wars that occur will be more (less) limited. It was predicted that as an outcome of Omne's increased deterrence-capacity, the slightly lessened alliance-cohesion, and the reduced likelihood of "unintended" wars following the advent of CDR, wars would be *more* limited.

This was not the case. Wars occurred in seven of the twelve runs; during non-CDR conditions the average conventional attack involved 755 FC's, and the average nuclear attack involved 7 FN's ("FC" and "FN" designate one unit of conventional and nuclear force, respectively). During CDR conditions, size of conventional attacks rose to 1000 FC's, while that of nuclear attacks rose to 66 FN's. Though the attack-N was too small for statistical treatment, the conclusion seems inescapable that in the INS, at least, there was strong correlation between Omne's possession of CDR and *increased* magnitude of wars. This outcome directly contradicts that predicted by the model, and the assumptions in the deterrence-literature. Discussion of Hypothesis IX will elucidate this result.

Hypothesis IX: Omne's known possession of CDR will decrease (increase) the probability of strategic war. As was discussed earlier, it is the hope of deterrence strategists that the likelihood of strategic war will be *reduced* as a consequence of a nation's known possession of CDR. If it is assumed, however, that more frequent and heavier attacks and the

[12]Brody, R. A., *op. cit.*, and A. Pepitone and R. Kleiner, *op. cit.*

[13]Pages 75–83 of Siegel, *op. cit.*, described this test.

replacement of conventional by nuclear fire-power indicate a greater likelihood of strategic war, then, in the INS at least, it must be concluded that strategic war was *more* likely when Omne had CDR.

During non-CDR conditions, Omne launched 4 attacks against others, while Utro launched 3. But when Omne had CDR, she launched 13 attacks and Utro launched 8, 5 of them against Omne, all but one retaliatory. It is clear that Omne was primarily responsible for the increase in number of sizeable nuclear wars. It was concluded that *strategic war was much more probable when Omne had CDR, primarily because Omne was more belligerent and aggressive and more ready to make war when she had CDR.* This conclusion is supported not only by the increase in number and size of wars during CDR conditions, but by others' perceptions of Omne, and her own self-perceptions, as measured on the "threat" scales. There is further evidence from Omne's responses to the scenario used to measure willingness to engage in military action to reach national goals: after obtaining CDR, Omne's willingness significantly ($p < .05$) increased.

Conclusions

The most important conclusion to be drawn from this study is that one whole aspect of the effect of a capacity-to-delay response has been neglected by the theorists; *what is the effect of invulnerability and the consequent capacity-to-delay response on the nation's sense of its own strength, on its aggressiveness, and on its willingness to engage in war to achieve national goals?*

It may be that because most of the theorists are American, and are discussing *American* invulnerability, such speculations simply do not occur to them. But while one may generalize from *any* simulation to the real world only with great caution, the results from this INS study strongly suggest that this is an aspect of invulnerability which should not be ignored.

The unexpected and thought-provoking results obtained in this study vindicate the use of the experimental approach for investigating highly complex social phenomena. At the same time, they highlight the need for validity studies, so that we may know to what extent such results can be generalized. Simulation models need to be made more isomorphic to the "reality" with which we are concerned; and we need to learn more about how age, experience, intelligence, personality, and cultural differences affect the participants' behavior. Work is steadily going forward with respect to both these questions at Northwestern University, at the Western Behavioral Sciences Institute, and at other centers for simulation study. The cultural factors are being examined in a variety of ways: for example, the study reported here has been replicated in Mexico City and in Tokyo.[14] Efforts are under way to develop an international scholarly community which can, through cooperative research with simulation and other techniques, furnish crucial insights into complex world problems.

---

[14]The results of the Mexico City replications are reported in "A Cross-Cultural Simulation Study," by Wayman J. Crow and John R. Raser, La Jolla, Calif., Western Behavioral Sciences Institute, Oct. 31, 1964. In general, the results on the hypotheses were the same as with the American participants. The Mexicans, however, exchanged far more messages, concentrated much more energy on the international interaction, neglected their internal economies, did not engage in arms races, emphasized the importance of the International Organization, and shared power more with subordinates. The results of the Tokyo study are not yet available as of the time of writing.

11

RAOUL NAROLL

Deterrence in History[1]

A comparative case study of the effectiveness of deterrence, based on a systematically drawn sample of cases from 2,000 years of history. An assessment is made of the adequacy of several hypotheses from deterrence theory. Because of the sampling method used, the generalizations supported by the study hopefully transcend cultural differences.

This paper presents a preliminary report of a cross-historical survey. The survey tested thirty hypotheses about factors associated with frequency of warfare, territorial growth, and territorial stability. The two most conspicuous states of several major world civilizations were studied in seventeen cases; in three other cases, the Swiss confederation was studied. The entire enterprise was a pilot study, intended to try out the cross-cultural survey method of anthropology on a comparative study of history.

Space does not permit adequate description of the method of study here. Particular centuries were chosen on the basis of accessibility of data; but, within each century, always the particular, randomly chosen decade, 76 to 85 (e.g., 1476 to 1485 A.D.) was studied. Great care was taken to define the concept of major civilization, or *paidea*: A *paidea* was defined as a culture or group of cultures in which professional teachers of adults carried out instruction from a body of literature originally written in a given script. Thus, civilizations were classed in terms of the bodies of literature used by their professors (priests, *gurus*) to give formal instruction to adult students. Formal statistical tests established that observed correlations were not artifacts of similarities between states studied which were neighbors in either time or space; in other words, the linked-pair method for the solution of Galton's problem (Naroll, 1964a) was applied in three dimensions, two dimensions of space and one of time. Also, in order to seek consistent reporting bias in the sources and hence spurious correlations reflect-

---

Especially prepared for this volume. The author is Professor of Anthropology and Chairman of the Center for Comparative European Studies at the State University of New York at Buffalo.

[1]This research was suggested by Dr. T. W. Milburn and supported by a series of contracts with the Naval Ordnance Test Station, China Lake, Calif., as part of Project Michelson.

ing errors in source material, five data quality-control factors were used: (a) year of publication; (b) proximity of source author to event reported; (c) degree of association of author with state whose fortunes were being studied; (d) degree of sympathy expressed by author for that same state; and (e) classification of source as primary or secondary (see Naroll, 1962). All these matters are discussed at length in a forthcoming volume (Naroll, Bullough, and Naroll, 1969).

In that forthcoming volume, we also set forth detailed definitions of the concepts used in the study. Again, space does not permit their discussion here. These definitions sought to pin down exactly what sorts of statements in the sources would be taken to imply what sorts of conclusions about the behavior of the state being studied. For example, one of the three dependent variables was the frequency of war. Frequency of war was measured by the number of months in which the conspicuous state studied was at war during the decade in question. Just what did we mean by *war*? How did we decide when a war started and when it stopped? We used more than 750 words to answer those questions, and we stated 21 formal definitions of related concepts.

Frequency of Warfare

One of the leading problems of this study was the problem of war frequency. This problem has widely interested theoreticians in international relations in recent years. Two opposing schools of thought have grown up on the question. One of these, the arms-race school, holds that military preparations tend to make wars more likely. The other, the deterrence school, holds that, on the contrary, military preparations tend to make wars less likely, at least among those states on a defensive stance.

The arms-race theory has been a favorite topic in recent years, and there is a large body of literature on it. The point of view that military preparations tend to make war more likely has been expressed by Quincy Wright (1942, Vol. 2, 690–691), Arthur Lee Burns (1959, pp. 326–342), Mulford Sibley (1962), J. David Singer (1962, pp. 169–171), Henry A. Kissinger (1957), Sidney Lens (n.d.), and D. F. Fleming (1962), among others. These men all hold that, in an arms race, each side strives for military superiority. It is not enough to have parity, for the dangers of underestimating the rival and of his achieving a technological breakthrough still remain. Each side may interpret his rival's capability as a sign of intent. Thus, the arms race becomes circular and self-generating and continues to grow more dangerous. Since the deterrent cannot remain truly stable, no real security is gained by an arms race. There seems to these men only one resolution to the problem and that is through some system of arms control or disarmament.

The deterrence theory holds, on the contrary, that military preparations make for peace by forcing would-be aggressors to count the cost. This point of view has been expressed in one form or another by P.H. Backus (1959, pp. 23–29), Glenn H. Snyder (1959, p. 457; 1960, pp. 163–178; 1961, pp. 10–15, 43–45, 286, 287, 289), Arthur T. Hadley (1961), Charles G. McClintock and Dale J. Hekhuis (1961, pp. 230–253), Thomas W. Milburn (1959, pp. 138–145), Oskar Morgenstern (1960), Herman Kahn (1962, pp. 22–55), Dexter Perkins (1960), and Lawrence S. Finkelstein (1962), among a large group of others. In addition, Richard Brody (1960, pp. 443–457) and Richard C. Snyder and James A. Robinson (1961) have abstracted much literature on deterrence. The advocates of deterrence argue that it reduces the probability of enemy attack by making clear the net loss or lower net gain that the attack would bring. They point out that there is no defense against a nuclear war, and, consequently, our best hope is for a stable, credible deterrent. For a deterrent to be stable it must be invulnerable, so that increased effort against it would be futile. The advocates of this point of view feel that mutual invulnerability would stabilize the arms race, resulting in a so-called balance of terror. This balance would then presumably allow conflicts to shift to limited wars and to an eventual stabilization and finally to reduction of war. Since all these aspects are negative, there has been developing a feeling that positive aspects of deterrence should be employed also wherever possible to reinforce the negative aspects (Milburn, 1959; Richard C. Snyder and James A. Robinson, 1961, p. 133; Glenn Snyder, 1960, p. 163). Positive deterrence might be accomplished by providing the aggressor with an area where he can practice harmless aggression or where he can win prestige. Alliances and treaties, trade agreements, sharing of new scientific gains with the aggressor are cited as examples of positive deterrence. Since the recent findings of learning theory show that punishments alone do little to change the basic motives of behavior, but that punishment combined with reward can be effective in changing behavior, the proponents of positive deterrence think that further study should be given to the use of positive deterrence as a supplement to negative.

Deterrence and War Frequency

This study embodied four specific tests of the deterrence hypothesis. The basic data for these and other tests are shown in Table 1, and the tests themselves are shown in Table 2. (a) The study contrasted those periods in which the "Conspicuous State" was on a defensive stance and had larger armed forces than did its "Conspicuous Rival" with those periods when it did not. (The variable in question is "Strength, D.S.") (b) It contrasted those periods in which the conspicuous state, while on a defensive stance, had more mobile armed forces than did its conspicuous rival with those periods when it did not ("Mobility, D.S."). (c) It contrasted those periods in which the conspicuous state, while on a defensive stance, had better quality armed forces than those of its conspicuous rival with those periods when it did not ("Quality, D.S."). (d) It contrasted those periods in which the conspicuous state, while on a defensive stance, had extensive fortifications with those periods in which it did not ("Fortifications, D.S."). In all four of these tests, it was predicted, in accordance with the deterrence hypothesis, that wars would be less frequent during the periods when the conspicuous state, while on a defensive stance, enjoyed the specified military advantages than during other periods. None of these predictions was confirmed by the correlation with "Months of War."

Whether the conspicuous state took a defensive or aggressive stance (see under "Defensive Stance") was also unrelated to frequency of war. It follows that peace-loving nations are no less likely to be involved in war than warlike nations. Hence, one must conclude that it takes only one nation to make a war, not two nations, a conclusion offering no comfort whatever to advocates of unilateral disarmament.

If anything, armament tends to make war more likely. Thus, the proposals for bilateral disarmament made by Presidents Eisenhower and Kennedy on behalf of the United States and by Chairman Khrushchev on behalf of the Soviet Union in the hope that such steps would make war less likely do receive some modest empirical support from the present study. The correlations between months of war and the "S.I." variables (stance immaterial, i.e., coded for all conspicuous states, whether on defensive stance or not) suggest, without adequately demonstrating, that, in the past, civilized societies with better quality or more-mobile armed forces or heavily fortified frontiers have been engaged in war *more frequently* than those without.

It might, of course, be argued that even these modest results are theoretically unexciting, since the correlations in question might be explained as resulting from a tendency for nations actually at war or expecting war soon to make better military preparations than other nations. However, the present study does *not* seem to bear out this line of reasoning. If warfare frequency were the cause and military preparations the effect, we should expect the various types of military preparations to be correlated with each other. But, as Table 2 shows, the four military preparation traits, in fact, seem to have little or no relationship with each other. This fact is less surprising when the sampling design of the present study is considered. This study selected that state in a given *paidea* (major civilization) which, for a predesignated period, was most conspicuously involved in conflicts with other states and called it the conspicuous state. Next, the study selected the other state in or near the *paidea* in question which seemed most often to be involved in rivalry, either diplomatic or military, with the conspicuous state and called this other state its conspicuous rival. Consequently, it can be said that, concerning apparent need for armed forces, this study involved little variance: nearly all the conspicuous states had obvious need for armed forces to protect themselves against possible attack by their conspicuous rivals. That is to say, our survey of history indicates that leading civilized societies have usually lived in danger of war and few statesmen of such societies have ever been in a position to neglect their nation's armed forces in good conscience. (The most striking exception seems to be China during the last few decades of the first century B.C., when the great Hun enemy seemed thoroughly pacified and no other serious rivals were in sight.)

In a parallel study, a cross-cultural survey of primitive tribes (Naroll, 1964b, p. 26), similar results were found. In that study, a low positive correlation was found between war frequency, on the one hand, and military obstacles and military readiness, on the other.

Cultural Exchange and War Frequency

There is little formal discussion of the cultural-exchange point of view in anthropological or international-relations theory. Yet, it seems to be widely influential today on both sides of the iron curtain and, for decades, if not centuries, has figured prominently in after-dinner speeches welcoming distinguished visitors from abroad. The proponents of cultural exchange dislike war and seem to think that mutual cultural understanding between nations makes war between them less likely. Apparently the proponents of cultural exchange see war as an outgrowth of ethnocentric prejudice and suppose that the dispelling of prejudice by first-hand contact would make for peace.

A skeptic might point out that,

TABLE 1

Trait Data

Columns:	1	2	3	4	5	6	7	8	9	10	11	12	13	14	15
Line Number	Decade Beginning	Conspicuous State	Conspicuous Rival	Sampling Order	Report Number	Months of War	Territorial Gain	Territorial Instability	Defensive Stance 718	Strength, S.I. A701	Strength, D.S. B701	Mobility, S.I. A702	Mobility, D.S. B702	Quality, S.I. A703	Quality, D.S. B703
	Europe														
1.	225 B.C.	Rome	Carthage	19	25	49	34	60	A	P	A	A	A	A	A
2.	25 B.C.	Rome	Parthia	13	23	37	57	49	P	P	P	A	A	P	P
3.	176 A.D.	Rome	Marcomanni-Quadi	7	16	49	49	36	P	A	A	P	P	P	P
4.	376	Rome	Visigoths	3	12	55	40	49	P	A	A	A	A	P	P
5.	576	Byzantines	Persia	15	26	66	61	58	O	O	O	A	A	P	O
6.	1276	France	England	5	13	37	40	48	P	A	A	A	A	A	A
7.	1376	England	France	11	21	66	34	60	O	A	A	A	A	P	O
8.	1576	Spain	Netherlands	9	18	66	38	51	P	P	P	P	P	P	P
9.	1676	France	Netherlands	1	10	51	60	53	A	P	A	A	A	P	A
10.	1776	England	France	17	28	55	34	62	P	P	P	A	A	A	A
	Switzerland														
11.	1376	Swiss Confed.	Kiburg	2	14	45	61	58	P	P	P	A	A	P	P
12.	1476	Swiss Confed.	Burgundy	16	30	44	61	58	A	A	A	A	A	P	O
13.	1576	Swiss Protestant	Swiss Catholic	6	19	37	49	36	P	A	A	A	A	A	A
	Russia														
14.	1476	Muscovy	Novgorod	12	24	42	63	68	A	P	A	P	A	P	A
	Saracens														
15.	776	Abbasids	Byzantines	18	31	56	50	37	A	P	A	O	A	P	A
	China														
16.	125 B.C.	Former Han Dynasty	Huns	14	27	66	59	53	A	P	A	A	A	P	A
17.	25 B.C.	Former Han Dynasty	Huns	20	32	37	50	36	A	P	A	A	A	P	A
18.	776 A.D.	T'ang Dynasty	Tibetans	8	20	52	49	36	P	P	P	A	A	A	A
19.	1076	Sung Dynasty	Tanguts	10	22	49	49	36	A	P	A	O	A	O	A
20.	1376	Ming Dynasty	Yunnanese Mongols	4	15	39	60	55	A	P	A	A	A	A	A

NOTES

Column 6, Months of War

Entry is value of Z, where:

Y = number of months of war in the decade

$X = 2 \text{ arcsine } \sqrt{(Y/100)}$ (i.e., twice the arcsine of the square root of one one-handredth)

S = standard deviation of the X scores

$\overline{X}$ = mean of the X scores

$Z = 50 - 10[(X - \overline{X})/S]$

Column 7, Territorial Gain

Entry is value of Z, computed as in Column 6, where:

Y = percentage of territorial gain or loss enjoyed or suffered by the conspicuous state from or to its conspicuous rival or its allies during the decade studied, with gain considered a plus score and loss a minus score

X = arctangent $\sqrt{Y}$ (arctangent

16	17	18	19	20	21	22	23	24	25	26	27	28	29	30	31	32	33	34	35	36	37
Fortifications, S.I. A704	Fortifications, D.S. B704	Propinquity 712	Prestige 713	Previous Conflict 714	Natural Barriers 715	Capital City 716	Announcements A705	Surprise B705	Alliances A706	Active Diplomacy A707	Intense Diplomacy B707	Benefits A709	Cultural Exchange A708	Trade B708	General Exchange C708	Experience of Ruler A710	Youth of Ruler B710	Unbridled Ruler C710	Hereditary Monarchy D710	Civil War 711	Centralization 717
A	A	P	A	P	P	P	P	A	A	P	A	A	A	O	A	O	O	A	A	A	A
A	A	P	P	P	P	A	O	O	P	P	P	A	A	P	P	A	P	A	A	O	P
P	P	P	P	P	P	P	A	A	P	P	P	P	P	P	P	A	A	A	O	P	P
O	O	P	P	P	A	P	A	P	A	P	P	P	P	P	P	A	A	A	A	A	P
P	O	P	A	P	P	A	P	A	O	P	A	A	A	A	A	A	O	O	A	O	P
P	P	P	A	P	A	P	O	O	O	P	P	P	A	P	P	A	P	A	P	P	A
P	O	P	A	P	A	P	P	A	O	P	A	A	A	P	P	A	A	A	P	P	A
A	A	A	P	A	P	A	P	A	P	P	A	P	A	A	A	P	A	A	P	O	P
P	A	A	P	A	A	P	A	A	A	P	P	O	P	A	P	P	P	P	P	A	P
A	A	A	P	P	P	P	P	A	A	P	P	A	P	A	P	P	P	P	P	P	A
P	P	P	P	P	A	P	A	P	P	A	A	A	P	P	P	O	O	A	A	A	A
P	O	A	A	A	P	O	P	A	O	A	A	A	P	A	P	O	O	A	A	O	A
O	O	P	A	A	A	O	O	O	P	P	P	A	O	O	O	O	O	A	A	A	A
A	A	P	A	P	A	P	P	A	A	A	A	P	P	A	P	P	P	P	P	O	P
P	A	P	P	P	P	A	A	P	A	P	P	P	A	O	A	A	P	P	P	P	A
P	A	P	A	P	P	A	O	O	A	A	A	P	A	O	A	P	P	P	P	A	P
A	A	P	P	P	P	A	O	O	A	A	A	P	A	O	A	A	P	P	P	A	A
P	P	P	A	P	P	P	O	O	P	P	P	P	A	O	A	A	A	P	P	P	A
P	A	P	A	P	P	A	A	P	A	A	A	P	A	A	A	A	P	P	P	A	A
A	A	P	P	A	P	A	A	A	A	A	A	A	P	A	P	P	A	A	A	A	A

NOTES

Column 8, Territorial Instability

Entry is value of Z, computed as in Column 6, where:

Y = percentage of territorial gain or loss, as in Column 7 but with both gain and loss considered plus scores

$X = \sqrt{\ln Y}$ (square root of natural logarithm)

N.B. The foregoing transformations were selected heuristically because they produced quasi-normal distributions, which satisfactorily resembled the normal distribution in skewness and kurtosis, according to the Geary-Pearson tests of normality (Geary and Pearson, n.d.).

Other Columns:

P = Trait present
A = Trait Absent
O = No data on trait

TABLE 2

Correlations and Significance Levels

	Months of War A732	Territorial Gain A730	Territorial Instability A731	Defensive Stance 718	Strength, S.I. A701	Strength, D.S. B701	Mobility, S.I. A702	Mobility D.S. B702	Quality, S.I. A703	Quality, D.S. B703	Fortifications S.I. A704	Fortifications, D.S. B704	Propinquity 712	Prestige 713
Months of War A732	......	.08	–.25	–.03	.07	.12	.13	.26	.36	.14	.32	–.18	–.21	–.09
Territorial Gain A730	......	......	.21	–.35	.27	–.09	.00	–.22	.39	–.04	.21	–.03	.08	.00
Territorial Instability A731	......	......	......	–.13	.12	.10	.01	–.22	.08	.01	.30	–.29	–.31	–.14
Defensive Stance 718	......	......	.09	......	*–.30	*.39	–.10	.12	–.03	*.39	–.06	.40	.03	.05
Strength, S.I. A701	......	......	......	.053	......	*.20	–.14	.05	–.13	–.10	*–.25	*–.37	.07	.15
Strength, D.S. B701	......	......	......	......	......	......	–.13	–.01	.04	.29	–.12	.05	–.13	.21
Mobility, S. I. A702	......	......	......	......	......	......	......	*.47	*.09	.18	–.06	–.17	.06	.00
Mobility, D.S. B702	......	......	......	......	......	......	.018	......	*–.01	*.32	.10	–.01	–.04	*.13
Quality, S.I. A703	.08	.05	......	......	......	......	......	......	......	*.30	.12	–.02	.07	.15
Quality, D.S. B703	......	......	......	.020	......	......	.074	......	.058	......	.11	.15	.13	*.33
Fortifications, S.I. A704	.10	......	......	......	.088	......	......	......	......	......	......	*.33	–.02	–.23
Fortifications, D.S. B704	......	......	......	.026	.057	......	......	......	......	......	......	......	*.05	.03
Propinquity 712	......	......	......	......	......	......	......	......	......	......	......	......	......	–.12
Prestige 713	......	......	......	......	......	......	......	......	......	......	......	......	......	......
Previous Conflict 714	......	......	......	......	......	......	......	......	......	......	......	......	.032	......
Natural Barriers 715	......	......	......	......	......	......	......	......	......	......	......	.051	......	......
Capital City 716	......	......	.09	......	.088	......	......	......	......	......	......	......	......	......
Announcements A705	......	......	.004	......	......	......	......	......	......	......	......	......	.051	......
Surprise B705	......	......	.03	......	......	......	......	......	......	......	......	......	......	......
Alliances A706	......	......	......	.003	......	.036	......	......	......	.036	......	.027	......	......
Active Diplomacy A707	......	.004	......	.043	......	......	......	......	......	......	......	......	......	......
Intense Diplomacy B707	......	......	.025	.044	......	......	......	......	......	......	......	......	......	......
Benefits A709	......	......	.015	......	......	......	.08	......	......	......	......	......	......	......
Cultural Exchange A708	......	.10	.08	......	......	......	......	......	......	......	......	......	......	......
Trade B708	......	......	......	.045	......	......	......	......	......	.067	......	......	......	......
General Exchange C708	.05	......	.04	......	.054	......	......	......	......	......	......	......	......	......
Experience of Ruler A710	......	......	.005	......	.092	......	......	......	......	......	......	......	.036	......
Youth of Ruler B710	......	......	......	......	......	......	......	.095	......	......	......	......	......	......
Unbridled Ruler C710	......	......	......	.044	.017	......	......	......	......	.020	......	......	......	......
Hereditary Monarchy D710	......	......	......	......	......	......	......	......	......	......	......	......	......	......
Civil War 711	......	.06	......	......	......	......	......	......	......	......	......	......	......	......
Centralization 717	.08	......	.10	......	......	......	.068	......	.017	.060	......	......	......	......

The upper right half of this table shows coefficients of correlations. The first three columns and lines are of quantitative variables (see Table 1); the remaining columns and lines are of qualitative variables. The coefficients of correlation between two quantitative variables are product moment coefficients; between one quantitative and one qualitative variable are point biserial coefficients; between two qualitative variables are phi coefficients. Phi coefficients marked with asterisks were computed from contingency tables in which one empty cell occurred by adding unity to each of the four cells.

The lower left half of this table shows one-tailed probabilities. That is to say, the table shows the probability of obtaining this unlikely a relationship in one direction (plus or minus) only. Each of these then gives the probability of obtaining the particular result actually obtained, or one even less likely, if in fact the two variables are not related and the result is a mere chance freak of sampling or other random factor. Needless to say, since many of these results were not predicted

Previous Conflict 714	Natural Barriers 715	Capital City 716	Announcements A705	Surprise B705	Alliances A706	Active Diplomacy A707	Intense Diplomacy B707	Benefits A709	Cultural Exchange A708	Trade B708	General Exchange C708	Experience of Ruler A710	Youth of Ruler B710	Unbridled Ruler C710	Hereditary Monarchy D710	Civil War 711	Centralization 717
.15	.18	–.10	.33	–.07	–.11	.29	–.21	.11	–.27	–.17	–.40	.14	–.29	.17	.30	.25	.34
–.22	.02	–.34	–.33	.03	.03	–.58	–.22	–.07	.31	–.33	.10	.22	.20	.21	–.26	–.44	.29
–.04	–.24	.31	.69	–.52	–.33	–.15	–.45	–.52	.37	–.26	.42	.62	.07	–.17	–.19	–.10	.18
–.10	–.08	.25	–.12	–.12	*.53	.41	.41	–.03	.00	*.39	.25	–.14	–.16	–.41	–.13	.30	–.05
–.02	.30	*–.25	.12	–.10	–.12	–.17	–.15	–.04	–.07	–.33	*–.29	*.26	.05	*.38	.14	–.14	–.07
–.05	.08	–.12	.04	–.17	.45	.08	.03	–.07	.07	–.12	.11	–.03	–.05	.10	.11	.10	–.08
.11	–.10	–.12	–.10	*.04	.08	–.16	.05	*.27	.03	.04	–.14	.08	–.13	.14	*.12	*.12	*.29
.00	*.02	.14	–.20	*.02	*.26	*.02	–.13	*.11	–.12	–.15	.12	–.10	*–.30	*–.08	*–.03	*.10	*.21
–.02	.07	–.15	.04	*.02	–.14	–.10	–.15	.12	–.07	–.04	–.11	.03	.02	–.04	–.04	.02	*.38
–.10	.07	–.09	.02	.02	.45	.07	–.04	.10	.08	.45	.19	–.07	–.12	*–.39	–.30	.16	.38
–.02	–.11	.05	–.26	*.18	.00	–.05	.05	.05	.05	.14	.09	–.31	.11	–.05	.01	.12	.05
*.05	–.15	*.33	*–.11	–.05	*.42	.03	.19	–.02	–.03	*.45	.11	*–.25	–.23	–.19	.14	.30	–.30
.43	.03	.05	–.16	*.15	–.12	.03	.08	.02	–.21	*.30	–.05	*–.38	–.18	.05	–.05	.12	.03
.00	.00	–.01	–.43	.07	–.07	.00	.20	–.05	.28	.02	.15	.03	–.14	.06	.06	.08	.10
......	–.06	.05	–.16	.15	.00	–.06	–.06	.16	–.21	*.30	–.05	*–.38	.18	.15	.10	*.17	–.12
......	......	*–.42	.00	–.02	.10	.01	–.07	–.08	–.22	–.27	*–.38	.10	–.05	.10	–.10	–.03	.06
......	.011	......	–.06	.01	–.05	.20	.24	.05	.37	.26	.44	–.13	.05	–.05	–.08	.19	.01
......	......	......	......	*–.38	.17	.00	–.30	–.23	–.14	–.18	.00	.08	.04	.06	–.08	.13	–.14
......	......	......	.035	......	.17	–.02	.02	.22	.07	.20	–.02	*–.27	*.24	–.01	.12	–.04	–.07
......	......	......	......	......	......	.20	.13	–.03	.05	.37	–.05	–.12	–.46	–.39	–.14	.10	–.03
......	......	......	......	......	......	......	*.47	.04	–.12	.19	–.10	–.17	–.05	–.12	–.10	*.34	.06
......	......	......	......	......	......	......	......	.06	.03	.27	.19	–.13	.05	–.06	–.03	.35	–.02
......	......	......	......	......	......	......	......	......	–.09	–.08	–.23	.05	.02	.37	.56	.33	.18
......	......	.057	......	......	......	......	......	......	......	.02	*.52	.33	–.14	–.01	–.18	–.02	.03
.070	......	......	......	......	......	......	......	......	......	......	.20	*–.43	.12	*–.36	–.06	.12	–.14
......	.017	.031	......	......	......	......	......	......	......	......	......	.03	–.14	–.32	–.14	.02	–.03
.036	......	......	......	......	......	......	......	......	.092	.027	......	......	–.14	.08	.03	–.18	.13
......	......	......	......	......	.052	......	......	......	......	......	......	......	......	.33	–.14	–.18	–.05
......	......	......	......	......	.059	......	......	.045	......	.049	.088	......	......	......	*.50	–.08	–.10
......	......	......	......	......	......	......	......	.008	......	......	......	......	......	......	......	*.31	.10
......	......	......	......	......	......	.042	.084	......	......	......	......	......	......	......	.063	......	–.03
......	......	......	......	......	......	......	......	......	......	......	......	......	......	......	......	......	......

in advance, since many of the relationships predicted in advance were not in fact found, and since most of the correlations observed did not attain statistical significance, these particular probabilities cannot be taken at face value. The probabilities of product moment coefficients were computed by using the standard error of these coefficients and entering a normal distribution table; of point biserial coefficients, by using Student's t distribution; and of phi coefficients, by obtaining the exact probabilities (Fisher's exact test) from the tables of Lieberman and Owen (1961). Two kinds of probabilities were omitted: (1) those greater than 0.10; (2) those between two variables whose relationship was an artifact of coding definitions, e.g., between Strength, Defensive Stance (B701) and Defensive Stance (718) in general. D.S. means Defensive Stance, and S.I. means Stance Immaterial.

among civilized societies, cultural differences are considerable and these differences include important inconsistencies in value systems. Consequently he might think that peaceful intercourse would actually strengthen ethnocentric feelings, instead of weakening them, by reinforcing certain cultural stereotypes.

However, the results of this study offer some support to the cultural-exchange theory. General cultural exchanges are negatively related to warfare frequency as predicted in advance. Unilateral bestowal of benefits was also expected to be negatively related to warfare frequency; it proved instead to have a low and nonsignificant positive correlation. Furthermore, mere trade was not related to war frequency.

These predicted results contrast with the absence of similar results from a similar test in the cross-cultural survey of primitive tribes (Naroll, 1964b, p. 24). Perhaps this contrast may arise from the fact that many primitive people, more often than civilized ones, tend to fight most frequently with nearby neighbors who have a common culture, i.e., speak mutually intelligible dialects of the same language and share a common value system and a common set of manners and customs.

Diplomacy and War Frequency

There may well be some relationship between activity of diplomats and frequency of war: The more active the diplomats are, the more frequent is war. If so, perhaps the most attractive explanation would seem to be to suppose that diplomatic activity is a symptom of trouble, especially among nations of medieval and ancient times which did not regularly exchange diplomatic missions. This too seems to be the most plausible explanation for the positive correlation between the issuance of an ultimatum and the frequency of war; an ultimatum presumably is a symptom of serious trouble.

War Frequency and Characteristics of the Regime

Apparently, older rulers (over forty-four years of age at the beginning of a decade) are more likely to be involved in war than younger rulers; hereditary rulers, than elective or self-appointed ones; and states with greater centralization of political authority, than those with lesser. Since these three characteristics of the regime are not intercorrelated but instead are unrelated (see Table 2), perhaps the most plausible explanation might be that a ruler who regards his status in the state more possessively is more likely to become involved in war. Another way of putting the same idea might be to say that a ruler who is relatively more conscious of his *status*, in Pierce's sense (Pierce, 1956), than of his *role* is more likely to be involved in war. Pierce means, by status, the claims a given social position has upon society and, by role, the claims society has upon the incumbent. In this sense, a ruler's status consists not only of his perquisites of office but also his power, his ability to use the machinery of the state to further his personal ends. His role consists of the functions he performs on behalf of the state.

Possible Sources of Spurious Correlation

Galton's problem (Naroll, 1961) presents no difficulties here. No tendency was evinced for successive periods of time in the same cultural tradition to resemble each other in the frequency of warfare involving the conspicuous state; nor was there any tendency for contemporaneous neighboring cultural traditions to resemble each other in this respect.

However, there are two suggestions of possible reporting bias by the historians used as our sources of information. Primary sources showed a very slight tendency to report warfare more frequently than did secondary sources and a very strong clear tendency to report the bestowal of benefits by (or to) the conspicuous state upon (or from) the conspicuous rival more frequently than did secondary sources.

Historians writing within 100 years of the events described, whether primary sources or secondary sources, showed a considerably greater tendency to report wars more frequently than historians writing more than 100 years later. Such earlier historians displayed a similar tendency to report the bestowal of benefits more frequently than did later historians.

In addition, historians who had some associations with the conspicuous state tended to report wars less frequently than those without such associations; however, such historians had no parallel tendencies in reporting other traits which might help explain any of the substantive correlations between the frequency of warfare and the other traits.

Territorial Growth

Characteristics of Armed Forces

As predicted, both size (i.e., number of men) and quality rating of armed forces proved positively related to territorial growth. These results parallel those from the cross-cultural survey (Naroll, 1964b, p. 28) that military preparedness and military technology among primitive tribes tend to be correlated with territorial growth. The present study suggests that quality is more important than quantity.

Capacity for Delayed Response

This study suggested that capacity for delayed response is positively related to territorial growth. Where capital cities are within 300 miles of the frontier, societies are less likely to expand, more likely to contract, than when they are farther away. True, one might conceivably explain this by supposing that societies with contracting territories are more likely to have frontiers within 300 miles of *any* point of their interior, but the sampling method, seeking the most conspicuous state in each of the *paideas* or traditions studied, introduced a selective preference for larger, stronger states and thus makes such an explanation less plausible. States with capitals within 300 miles of the frontier in this study include the Roman Empire in 225 B.C., in 176 A.D., and in 376 A.D.; France in 1276 and 1676; England in 1376 and 1776; Russia in 1476; the Swiss Confederation in 1376; and China under the T'ang Dynasty in 776; of these ten, fully seven had been recently expanding rather than contracting.

On the other hand, there proved to be no correlation between territorial growth and the presence of either natural barriers or artificial fortifications.

Diplomatic Factors

Diplomatic activity seems again to be a symptom of trouble among the societies of our cross-historical sample. There is a high and clearly significant negative correlation between the relative frequency of diplomatic activity and territorial growth.

Conspicuous states whose intentions are announced likewise seem to tend to be states in trouble. The announcement of intentions (for example by ultimata) is also negatively related to territorial growth.

Similarly, societies on a defensive stance apparently tend to be societies in trouble, for defensive stance is likewise negatively correlated with territorial growth. However, this relationship could well be a coding artifact, since societies under attack are coded as societies on a defensive stance.

Other Factors

Societies undergoing civil war seem likely to lose territory to outsiders. In two cases, territorial loss was suffered by the conspicuous state through successful rebels establishing an independent nation in a portion of the empire of the conspicuous state. In order to avoid coding artifacts, one of these cases (Spain, 1576 to 1585) was simply not counted either way; the other (England, 1776 to 1785) was counted as a case of loss because the Gordon Riots constituted a brief civil war, tending to weaken the British war effort but not themselves depriving Britain of territory.

Active trade between conspicuous state and conspicuous rival is likewise associated with territorial loss by the conspicuous state. Possibly this relationship might reflect a neglect of military preparations by a trade-oriented society.

However, cultural exchanges between conspicuous state and conspicuous rival are associated with territorial gain on the part of the conspicuous state.

Possible Sources of Spurious Correlation

Galton's problem presents no difficulties here. No tendency was evinced for successive periods of time in the same cultural tradition to resemble each other in territorial gain, nor was there any tendency for contemporaneous neighboring cultural traditions to resemble each other in this respect.

However, there are two suggestions of possible reporting bias in primary or secondary sources. Historians associated with the conspicuous state displayed a slight tendency to report territorial gains more frequently than territorial losses, and such historians were also slightly more likely to ascribe larger armed forces to the conspicuous state and to report cultural exchange between it and its conspicuous rival.

Historians writing more than 100 years after the events in question also displayed a slightly greater tendency to report territorial gain by the conspicuous state, and such historians were also slightly more likely to report announcements of intentions by the conspicuous state and to report capital cities closer to national frontiers.

Territorial Instability

Capacity for Delayed Response

Both natural barriers on the frontier and fortifications tend to be associated with the absence of territorial change. These relationships were predicted in advance, and both support the hypothesis that greater capacity for delayed response tends to stabilize the frontier of a state enjoying such capacity. Similarly, states whose capital cities are more than 300 miles from their frontiers have greater territorial stability than those whose capital cities are closer. (It is relevant to note that capital cities tend to be closer to frontiers with natural barriers than to frontiers without natural barriers and, further, that when capital cities are close to the frontier, fortifications are more often found.)

Time and Space Factors

Conspicuous states enjoy greater territorial stability when their conspicuous rival is a geographical neighbor with a common land frontier than when it is not. Situations in which the intentions of the conspicuous state are announced well in advance seem to be situations of territorial instability, while wars which begin unannounced as surprise attacks seem to be situations of territorial stability.

Diplomatic Factors

Conspicuous states enjoy greater territorial stability when they have allies than when they do not. Intensity of diplomatic activities is likewise associated with territorial stability, but, to some extent, this might be a coding artifact; diplomacy was coded as relatively intense when some kind of diplomatic agreement on any matter whatever was reported, in contrast to those periods in which no negotiations were reported or, if any, then no agreements were reported.

Cultural Exchanges

Benefits unilaterally conferred by the conspicuous state upon the conspicuous rival or vice versa tend to occur during periods of little territorial change. However, cultural exchanges tend to occur during periods of greater territorial change, as does general exchange (defined as either cultural exchange or trade or as both).

Experience of Ruler

Rulers who have had more than nine years of service as such at the beginning of the decade being studied become involved in less territorial change than those with less experience. This result suggests that perhaps more experienced rulers (regardless of age) tend to be more cautious, to take fewer risks, and hence to gain or lose smaller territorial stakes.

Possible Sources of Spurious Correlation

Galton's problem arises in considering territorial instability. Contemporaneous societies adjacent in space *do* tend to resemble each other in territorial instability. If such societies were actually rival geographical neighbors, this finding would be a mere coding artifact; but no two of the contemporaneous conspicuous states in our sample were in fact rivals during any decade studied. Rather, this relationship is best explained by the hypothesis that certain historical periods were more territorially unstable throughout large parts of Eurasia than were other such periods. However, only one of the substantive traits related to territorial instability also had the characteristic of tending to occur similarly among contemporaneous societies adjacent in space: cultural exchange. This result likewise is plausibly explained by the notion that, throughout large parts of Eurasia during particular centuries, cultural exchange was more frequent than during other centuries. Consequently, the correlation between cultural exchange and territorial instability may wholly or partly reflect mere coincidence of time rather than actual functional relationships between cultural exchange and territorial instability.

Several characteristics of historical sources likewise proved related to the reported amount of territorial instability. Historians publishing since 1850 tended to report more territorial changes than those publishing earlier. Primary sources tended to report fewer territorial changes than did secondary sources, and authors writing within 100 years of the events described likewise tended to report fewer territorial changes than authors writing later. These three classifications are, of course, related conceptually to one another; most primary sources are written within 100 years of the events described and first published before 1850. Suspicion falls somewhat upon reports of fortifications, which may tend to be reported by secondary sources slightly oftener than by primary sources. Suspicion falls strongly upon announcements of intention, which recently published books mention more frequently than books published before 1851; and there are slight tendencies toward reporting bias reflected in the publication date in reports of general exchange.

Historians associated with the conspicuous state seem slightly less likely to report territorial changes than those not so associated. Such historians also seem slightly less likely to report alliances and unilateral benefits and are slightly less likely to be associated with states whose conspicuous rivals are geographical neighbors or have natural barriers on their frontiers.

Policy Implications

To what extent is a comparative study of history relevant to international relations today? Its relevance is obviously limited by two factors. First, modern nuclear weapons pose an unprecedented threat to enemy cities. While, in former times, cities were often destroyed and their inhabitants all slaughtered, yet such disasters were comparatively rare and hence low-probability risks in the eyes of decision makers. Today, at the outset of a full-scale nuclear war, the complete destruction of the cities of both contestants seems so likely as to amount to a virtual certainty. This unprecedented danger introduces a new factor never before present in the minds of decision makers.

Second, our cross-historical survey deals with probabilities only, with correlational tendencies. There is never any assurance that, even if circumstances remained unchanged, the general correlational tendencies would hold good in any particular future case. Our cross-historical survey produces nomothetic results, but our statesmen at any given time are faced with an idiographic problem. In other words, our results may tell us what usually happens in circumstances of a given sort, but our statesmen, at any given time, are concerned with what is going to happen in a single, particular, unique situation.

For these reasons, statesmen must obviously continue to rely first of all on their experienced subjective judgments about the particular situations they face at particular times. Nevertheless, the results of this kind of cross-historical survey are relevant and useful to them. If such results do not yield clear and simple predictions, they do show the direction in which the pull of the current is set, the direction in which, other things being equal, the trend of events is likely to take. Studies like these cannot solve the statesman's problem for him, but they can help him think.

Certainly statesmen must consider as best they can the unprecedented threat to cities which modern nuclear weapons pose. One lively possibility they have been considering is the possibility that nuclear weapons offer too grave a threat to be used again. Just as both sides were prepared to use poison gas in World War II but never did, (with one small exception), so nuclear weapons may conceivably never again be used in combat. If not, then wars fought with conventional weapons presumably will resemble the wars fought in the past with respect to the variables considered in the present study. But, even if on the contrary nuclear weapons are used, statesmen can consider to advantage the lessons of past history studied impersonally and statistically. True, they must in any particular case ask themselves in what way the introduction of nuclear weapons has altered the situation, but it is still useful to have as a baseline for their thinking the pattern which wars have followed in the past.

Clearly, it would be unwise for statesmen to make comparative historical studies their master, to follow only the policies indicated by such studies, and to leave out of account all the special circumstances of the time (including not only nuclear weapons but the personalities of the leading rival statesmen and the specific strategic and tactical situations). But I submit that it would be equally unwise to leave entirely out of account the findings of comparative historical studies. The present preliminary attempt seems to me evidence that such studies are needed for national security planning and that their results ought to be taken into consideration along with all other relevant factors. They are worth a line or a paragraph in a National Security Council estimate of the situation.

Deterrence and Peace

This study, like the parallel cross-cultural survey (Naroll, 1964b, p. 35), indicates that, in the very long run, preparation for war does not make peace more likely. It does not seem to make much difference either way; but, if it does make any difference at all, it is slightly in the direction of making war *more* likely than peace.

Military Preparedness and Territorial Growth

This study, again like the parallel cross-cultural survey (Naroll, 1964b, p. 35), found evidence supporting the "common-sense" attitude that military preparations tend to favor territorial growth. Better-quality armies, larger armies, and greater capacity for delayed response through remoteness of capital cities from frontiers all seem positively related to territorial expansion.

Cultural Exchange and Peace

While the cross-cultural survey of primitive tribes found no support for the hypothesis that peaceful cultural exchanges made war less likely (Naroll, 1964b, 38), this study of higher civilizations, in contrast, did find some support for this hypothesis. These results are consistent with the notion that peaceful economic, intellectual, or family ties tend to make war less likely and, also, with the notion that bestowal of unilateral subsidies often has its intended effect of securing peace with the recipient.

References

Backus, P. H., "Finite deterrence, controlled retaliation," *United States Naval Institute Proceedings*, **85,** 23–29, 1959.

Brody, Richard A., "Deterrence strategies:

An annotated bibliography," *Journal of Conflict Resolution*, **4,** 443–457, 1960.

Burns, Arthur Lee, "A graphical approach to some problems of the arms race," *Journal of Conflict Resolution*, **3,** 326–342, 1959.

Finkelstein, Lawrence S., "Defense, disarmament and world order," *Behind the Headlines* (published by the Canadian Institute of International Affairs), **22**(1), 1962.

Fleming, D. F., *Does Deterrence Deter?* Philadelphia: American Friends Service Committee, 1962.

Geary, R. C., and E. S. Pearson, *Tests of Normality*. London: Biometrika Office, n.d.

Hadley, Arthur T. *The Nation's Safety and Arms Control*. New York: Viking Press, Inc., 1961.

Kahn, Herman, "The arms race and some of its hazards," in: Mendlevitz, Saul H., ed., *Legal and Political Problems of World Order*. New York: Fund for Education Concerning World Peace through World Law, 22–55, 1962.

Kissinger, Henry A., *Nuclear Weapons and Foreign Policy*. New York: Harper and Row, Publishers, 1957.

Lens, Sidney, *Revolution and Cold War*. Philadelphia: American Friends Service Committee, n.d.

Lieberman, Gerald J., and Donald B. Owen, *Tables of the Hypergeometric Probability Distribution*, Stanford, Calif.: Stanford University Press, 1961.

McClintock, Charles G., and Dale J. Hekhuis, "European community deterrence: Its organization, utility and political feasibility," *Journal of Conflict Resolution*, **5,** 230–253, 1961.

Milburn, Thomas W., "What constitutes effective deterrence?" *Journal of Conflict Resolution*, **3,** 138–145, 1959.

Morganstern, Oskar, "Effective and secure deterrence: The oceanic system," *Journal of the Royal Canadian Air Force Staff College*, 1960.

Naroll, Raoul, "Two solutions to Galton's problem," *Philosophy of Science*, **28,** 15–39, 1961.

Naroll, Raoul, *Data Quality Control*. New York: The Free Press, 1962.

Naroll, Raoul, "A fifth solution to Galton's problem," *American Anthropologist*, **66,** 863–867, 1964a.

Naroll, Raoul, "Warfare, peaceful intercourse and territorial change: A cross-cultural survey," mimeographed, 1964b. (A highly condensed version appeared as "Does military deterrence deter?" *Transaction*, **3,** 14–20, 1966.)

Naroll, Raoul, Vern R. Bullough, and Frada Naroll, *Twenty Deterrence Histories: A Cross-Historical Survey*. Albany, N.Y.: State University of New York Press, 1969.

Perkins, Dexter, "Peace and armaments," *Virginia Quarterly Review*, **36**(4), 1960.

Pierce, Albert, "On the concepts of role and status," *Sociologus, N. S.*, **6,** 750–755, 1956.

Sibley, Mulford, *Unilateral Initiatives and* Disarmament. Philadelphia: American Friends Service Committee, 1962.

Singer, J. David, *Deterrence, Arms Control, and Disarmament*. Columbus, Ohio: Ohio State University Press, 1962.

Snyder, Glenn H, *Deterrence by Denial and Punishment*. Princeton, N. J.: Center of International Studies, 1959.

Snyder, Glenn H, "Deterrence and power," *Journal of Conflict Resolution*, **4,** 163–178, 1960.

Snyder, Glenn H, *Deterrence and Defense*. Princeton, N. J.: Princeton University Press, 1961.

Snyder, Richard C., and James A. Robinson, *National and International Decision-Making*. New York: The Institute for International Order, 1961.

Wright, Quincy, *A Study of War* (2 vols.) Chicago: University of Chicago Press, 1942.

12

RICHARD A. BRODY • ALEXANDRA H. BENHAM

Nuclear Weapons and Alliance Cohesion[1]

A theoretical analysis and experimental study of the effect of the proliferation of nuclear weapons on the cohesiveness of alliances. Multiple runs of the Inter-Nation Simulation were employed in the experimental study.

Introduction

The interest of students of society in the military aspects of international politics is not a new phenomenon. Historians at least as far back as Thucydides have chronicled the military-political transactions of states, and they have raised the reporting of these transactions to a high art. Political analysts at least as far back as Machiavelli have been willing to acknowledge processual contiguities between war and politics. Von Clausewitz's dictum, "War is to be regarded not as an independent thing, but as a political instrument," is essentially paralleled in the writings of such political philosophers as Hobbes, Marx, and Lenin.

The acknowledgment of an intimate connection between war and politics signals a recognition that military preparation, strategy, and level of capability (one kind of power) are data of consequence in the analysis of international relations. This impression is reinforced by the priority given these items as "bases of power" by the authors of international-relations texts.

Further evidence of this interest can be drawn from the burgeoning literature on many facets of contemporary military-political problems, e.g., deterrence, disarmament, arms control, or the "cold war."

The thirty-odd books and articles on deterrence strategies analyzed by the senior author (Brody, 1960) now represents a small fraction of the total literature. The literature on the so-called "*N*th-Country Problem" alone is now nearly as extensive as that on *all* aspects

---

Especially prepared for this volume. Richard A. Brody is Associate Professor of Political Science at Stanford University and Alexandra H. Benham is a graduate student in the Department of Political Science at Stanford University.

[1]This is an abridgement of a larger study published by the senior author in the *Journal of Conflict Resolution* (Brody, 1963). The scope of the present paper precludes supporting its conclusions with the data available in the larger study.

of deterrence a few years ago. If the magnitude of writing is an index of interest, there is high interest in this topic. What can be said of the content?

Some Key Assumptions in the Deterrence Literature

Writers on deterrence have been primarily concerned with behavior in the dyad. The explicit units of analysis, i.e., the constituents of this dyad, are the United States and the Soviet Union. The bloc allies of these two nations are generally seen as acting through the bloc leaders in matters which concern the primary international interaction system. Underlying this point of view, are two implicit postulates: (a) "If the Soviet Union is deterred, so are its allies," and (b) "if the United States deters, its allies do not provoke." Thus, cohesion of the two bloc alliances is assumed.

There is of course a literature which holds this cohesion problematical (e.g., Wolfers, 1959; Knorr, 1959; Brzezinski, 1960; Modelski, 1960; Osgood, 1962), but, by and large, there has been little overlap between it and the deterrence literature.

The concentration of focus on the U.S.–U.S.S.R. dyad is not without rationale, given a desire to understand the contemporaneous international system. As a statistical metaphor, the behavior of these two national actors is a major source of variance of the behavior of the entire system. To postulate this state of affairs, however, it is not necessary to agree with Morgenstern's contention (1961, p. 208), "the fundamental tendency toward bipolarity will remain a characteristic of the power game . . . ."

With certain notable exceptions, writers on deterrence have not looked beyond the thermonuclear dyad. The tendency among those who *have* examined the $2 + N$ nuclear-power world has been to multiply the sources of danger in the present conflict system by N, i.e., to essay the Nth-country problem *qua* problem. They reason essentially in the following manner: "There are serious problems facing the two major powers, e.g., the stability of the deterrent relationship, the potential for accidental war, and the difficulty of achievement of a disarmament *rapprochement*; these problems will be exacerbated with an increase in the number of nations with control over nuclear weapons."

Inventory of Propositions About the *N*th-Country Problem Extant in the Literature

In order to support the above characterization of the reasoning on this topic, a sample of representative propositions drawn from the literature will be presented here. The presentation of these propositions without comment should not be construed to mean that the authors are satisfied about their "truth status." Some of them are mutually contradictory, a fact which emphasizes the need for empirical research. The hypotheses to be specifically explored in this study will be stated later on in this section, at which time some parallels between propositions from the literature and the hypotheses under examination will be indicated.

A. Propositions Which Predict Problems Occasioned by the Spread of Nuclear Weapons

1. The spread of nuclear military capability will almost certainly decrease the stability of deterrence systems. The greater the number of nations that possess the capability of launching a nuclear strike, the greater [will be] the probability that

there will be a strike (Brown and Real, 1960, p. 25).

2. According to the "statistical theory," the probability of a global thermonuclear war increases as the number of nuclear powers increases, because (a) the larger the number of these powers, the greater the probability [is] that nuclear weapons will be used in some conflict (both because of more opportunities and a greater chance of irresponsibility); and (b) if nuclear weapons are used in the conflict, the risk of its expanding into a global war is greater than if the conflict remained non-nuclear (Iklé, 1960, p. 391).

As a counterhypothesis the following is offered:

3. The counterargument [to the "statistical" argument] is that the diffusion of nuclear capability might make the involvement of major powers in global conflicts appear to be more risky and hence render it less likely. In other words, *N*th-country capabilities might either help to deter local aggression altogether or they might help to isolate local conflicts (Iklé, 1960, p. 391).

B. Proposition about National Motives for Attaining Independent Nuclear Capability

A nation may be attracted toward a nuclear development of its own . . . not only because nuclear weapons mean power, honor, and a fuller sovereignty in general in our time, but also because in particular a nation so equipped can now itself make the key decisions, to defend itself with these weapons and pull its allies into the fight (Miller, 1959, p. 37).

C. Propositions about Effects of the Spread of Nuclear Weapons on the International System

1. We might foresee a world in which gradually more powers became independent nuclear powers in their own right . . . . [On] assuming that the control exercised by a bloc over its constituent members would be very tight, it would seem likely that the process would come to an end in a very rigid world of separate, autarchic, nuclear powers having very little to do with each other . . . . If you can "standoff" every other nation in the world, there is not a pressing necessity to be connected with someone else who can do so, too (Burns, 1958, p. 38).

2. Two limiting states of military art can be imagined which in the circumstance of the late twentieth century would come near to dictating policy: (1) the invention of a very cheap make-it-yourself, all-purpose deterrent would invite every nation to be isolationist in military affairs, fragmenting such alliances as NATO and the Warsaw Pact . . . [and] (2) the opposite situation, in which an adequate deterrent weapon-system had become so expensive that only the superpowers or very large blocs would afford it . . . , would almost prescribe a world alignment much like that which obtained, say, about 1956–58 (Burns, 1961, p. 188).

3. It has been argued that nuclear diffusion must prove destabilizing for the reason that nations acquiring nuclear weapons either would actually be in a more independent position than before or would at least feel that they enjoyed a greater degree of independence. According to this argument, nuclear diffusion may therefore be expected to have a disruptive effect on the cohesiveness and unity of the major alliance systems—particularly the Western alliance system (Tucker, 1962, p. 13).

As counterhypotheses the following propositions are offered:

4. A measure of independent [nuclear] strength for each of the NATO allies is likely to contribute to the cohesiveness of alliance . . . (Hilsman, 1959, p. 168).

5. Within one bloc, the wider distribution of nuclear weapons poses great problems to the bloc: if the control over the weapons is unconditionally given to some of its members, the bloc is less firm as an entirety . . . , nevertheless, the members will still be held together by common fears, ideals, interests, and treaties, the

real force binding them is the existence of the superpower around which the bloc is formed . . . [and] the fundamental tendency toward bipolarity will remain a characteristic of the power game (Morgenstern, 1961, pp. 206–208).

6. A nuclear arsenal under national control [is not] a means of becoming independent of big power tutelage . . . . *N*th countries [will] continue to be dependent on the support of a major nuclear power (Kissinger, 1961, p. 242).

In this study we shall focus on this last set of propositions (C.1 through C.6) as most fundamental to the structure of international relations.

The Approach to this Study

The approach taken in this study stems from the assumption that to conceive of the *cold war* as a pattern of interaction is a useful heuristic. The cold war can be thought of as a system of action with certain describable regularities—interaction processes—which serve to define it as a steady state.

Proceeding from this heuristic, we may ask the question: *If one characteristic of the cold-war system—the number of nations with nuclear capability—is changed, will the system survive or will a new steady state emerge?* If the nuclear differential is crucial to the interaction pattern we call the cold war, then we should expect that the spread of nuclear weapons (the *N*th-country situation) would alter the pattern of interaction. Our working hypothesis is that a marked change in the number of nuclear nations will be reflected in a marked (i.e., "step-level") change in the cold-war system; a new steady state will result.

A Model of the Cold-War System

In gross terms, the cold-war system can be described as *bipolar*, i.e., there are two major centers of military and economic power toward which other nations are attracted. The reasons for attraction in a given direction would include historic and economic ties, fear of suzerainty being established by one superpower or the other, the actual presence of one or the other major power's troops at the end of World War II, and a feeling of being threatened by one or the other nuclear power.

Moreover, while nations exist outside of either alliance system, in many respects the bipolarity may be considered "tight." Nations which avoid alliance with either bloc do so at the price of reduced international influence, at least in the military sense. Given the absence of a third force, in many significant respects the future of the bipolarity becomes the future of the entire system (King, 1959, p. 113).

Between the blocs, there has developed a state of high threat[2] and, at least conceptually, antecedent to this threat are mutual perceptions of hostility. Where the object of focus is charged with negative affect, as in the case here, behavior tends to take the forms of aggression or avoidance (Frank, 1958). Threat and hostility, thus, tend to reinforce each other.

This *threat-hostility* cycle feeds into interbloc relations: As hostility increases, communication decreases; as communication decreases, hostility increases (Newcomb, 1947, p. 73). It also feeds into intrabloc relations. The presence of perceived out-group hostility, and consequently the perception of threat, tends to reinforce the dependency relationship within the blocs and to increase intrabloc cohesive-

[2]This was originally specified as "tension." However, attempts to meaningfully operationalize tension as an intervening variable proved futile, so "threat" was substituted for tension in the analysis.

ness. This dependency also stems, in part, from the nuclear disparity between the superpower which heads the alliance and the other member nations.

The combination of dependence and cohesion has produced blocs which are more or less hierarchically organized; i.e., authoritative decisions tend to flow from the bloc leader rather than from other bloc members. We should expect a hierarchical bloc to exhibit properties associated with a *wheel* communication net; i.e., the modal lines of communication are those between members and the leader (Wolfers, 1959). We should expect that nonhierarchical blocs would have more or less *all-channel* communication nets; i.e., no member is more central than any other in the communication system (Guetzkow and Simon, 1955).

In summary, the cold-war system is composed of two hierarchically organized bloc alliances with the leading nations in the blocs possessing a virtual monopoly of nuclear strike and counterstrike capability. Moreover, there is threat-generating hostility between the blocs, which reinforces cohesion within the blocs and which itself is reinforced by this cohesion. The relationship within the blocs is one of dependency born of necessity. In part, the dependency relationship is due to the hostility of the nuclear armed leader of the opposing bloc and in part to the nuclear disparity within the alliance. It is in this context that the effects of the spread of nuclear weapons will be essayed and explored.

The Cold-War System and the Spread of Nuclear Weapons

It has already been asserted that the result of an increase in the number of nuclear nations, in the above described system, will be a marked change in the cold-war steady state.

In two respects, the relationship of each nation vis-à-vis its own alliance and toward the other alliance can be expected to be changed by the achievement of independent nuclear capability: (1) in a reduction of the dependency on the bloc leader, and (2) in a reduction in the level of perceived out-group threat. Other changes in the system follow from these changes.

As the former nonnuclear power increases its capacity to retaliate in kind, the credibility of the opposing bloc-leader's aggressiveness is reduced. Reduced also, it is hypothesized, is the willingness of the former nonnuclear power to remain part of an alliance which it feels no longer functions for its protection, at lease to the extent of the costs involved in maintaining the alliance (Morgenthau, 1959, p. 185). In addition, achievement of nuclear parity may bring into question the equitability of the existing hierarchy. As the nuclear base of power increases for the former nonnuclear bloc members, their willingness to remain in a subordinate decision-making role should decrease.

The capability of decisional independence and the increased unwillingness to remain subordinate in the bloc (i.e., increased dissatisfaction with the hierarchical structure of the bloc) will, it is hypothesized, lead to an increase in intrabloc threat. Coupled with reduced perceived out-group threat, the increase in intrabloc threat should lead to a marked reduction in the cohesion which previously characterized the bloc-alliance system (proposition C.3, above). The attractiveness of membership will be lessened, particularly membership under a hierarchical structure. The alliances may survive this traumatic input, but they will not survive it unchanged.

The expected change is the fragmentation of the blocs (proposition C.2, above). Whether the steady state which emerges will look like Kaplan's *balance of power system* (1957, p. 30 ff) or *unit veto system* (1957, p. 50 ff) will depend on decisions which are occasioned by the spread. If national strike forces are maintained, the system will probably resemble the unit veto model. If, however, spread is followed by disarmament, the balance of power model will probably describe the system. In either case, where there were two power centers, there will now be multiple power centers (proposition C.1, above).

In summary, the expected change in the cold-war system is the fragmentation of the blocs which comprise it. This (step-level) change will be prompted by the increased independence of the formerly nonnuclear national actors after they achieve nuclear capability; the increased sense of independence and a lowering of the perceived threat from the opposing bloc will lessen the intrabloc cohesion and eventuate in the predicted fragmentation.

Research Design

The development of what is hoped is a coherent analytic model of the effects of the spread of nuclear weapons does not eliminate the problem of alternative formulations and mutually contradictory hypotheses.[3] The problem of finding a means of evaluating the plausibility of alternative formulations remains with us.

Deprived as we are of on-going crucial natural experiments, we are left with the choice of waiting for the *N*th-country situation to evolve in actuality; working with the three extant, approximate cases, i.e., the British, French, and Chinese developments (Rosecrance, 1964); *or* trying to reproduce artificially the cold-war system and then experimentally inducing the spread of nuclear capability.

In the final analysis, the confirmation or disconfirmation of the model will depend upon the effects of nuclear diffusion in the *real* world; in this sense, we have no choice but to wait for the situation to evolve. But, if our interest is in evaluating the plausibility of the model *prior* to the actual occurrence, substitutes for a full-blown crucial natural experiment must be sought.

The two available alternative approaches—case studies of extant developments and simulation—are by no means mutually exclusive enterprises. The paucity of case material augurs ill for the exploration of the *N*th-country situation with any statistical model in mind, although these cases can be productive of hypotheses and offer potential reality checks for ideas and measuring tools developed in the simulation. Since at this time they can furnish only suggestive evidence, gaming remains as a potentially useful approach.

The particular gaming approach employed, the Northwestern Inter-Nation Simulation (hereafter, INS), was chosen because it was felt that it was flexible enough to offer a reasonable prospect of providing a model world in which the spread of nuclear weapons could be examined.[4]

The INS is comprised of a system of interacting units, where the units are teams of individuals. The unit actors

[3] In formulating our model, we have sided with those predicting a lessening of cohesion within the bloc (propositions C.1, 2, 3 *supra*) but compare propositions C. 4, 5, 6.

[4] For full-blown discussions and descriptions of the INS, the reader should see Guetzkow (1959); Brody and Noel (1960); and Guetzkow, Alger, Brody, Noel, and Snyder (1963).

are styled *nations*. The individuals who act for the nation are its *decision makers*. In the particular form of the INS used in this study, INS-8,[5] the participants were 357 North Shore and North Chicago high-school students. Each of the seventeen replications which comprise INS-8 covered four half-days of real time, twelve periods of simulation time. Decision makers were asked to make domestic and international decisions—i.e., to commit their nations to courses of action—in a bipolar binuclear seven-nation simulation world. Information about the structure of the international system was kept to a minimum; the entire scenario was contained in a three-paragraph "World Perspective." The development of the nations and the international system beyond starting time t_0 was almost entirely the product of the participants' decisions, the principal exception being the experimentally introduced spread of nuclear weapons.

The INS is an operating model of the international system;[6] prototypical classes of international behavior exist in the model. Thus, a nation may remain at peace or engage in war. Moreover, wars may be limited or total; a nation may trade with other nations and seek or give foreign aid; alliances may be formed for a variety of reasons and with differing degrees of cohesion; international organizations may be founded or foundered. Several media of international communication are available: written messages, face-to-face conferences, international organization, and a "world press."

The following section presents the results of the exploration of the theoretical model through INS-8.

Exploration of the Model

In exploring the theoretical model posited above, by means of INS, it seems reasonable to ask the following questions:

The fundamental question is: Is the international system different before and after the spread of nuclear weapons?

More particularly: If there is a change in the system, what is its relationship to the hypothetical model? That is to ask, is the cold-war system established? Do we get two blocs which relate to each other and have an intrabloc structure, as predicted? Is the prespread system tightly bipolar? If the cold war does emerge, does it fragment under the impact of the spread of nuclear weapons?

It is really necessary to answer the second set of questions first, by the examination of the hypotheses contained in the theoretical model. The answer to the more general question follows from this examination; its answer will serve as a summary evaluation of the model.

The verbal model of the cold war and the impact upon it of the spread of nuclear weapons implies a set of *conditions* and *linkages* between conditions. The conditions are predictions about differentials in perceptions, attitudes, needs, and relations within and between blocs. The linkages specify *relations*

[5]The INS-8 was an emendation of the earlier exploratory and classroom runs of the simulation (runs INS-1 through INS-8), altered to allow representation of the theoretical model of the cold war and the spread of nuclear capability. For a detailed description, see Guetzkow, Brody, Driver, and Beach (1960).

[6]Since, in INS, we have a laboratory situation, the experimentor is provided direct access to decision makers. This access makes possible the employment of standard techniques of attitude assessment. Data from these instruments and data generated by the operation of the system will be used in the exploration of the hypothetical model outlined above.

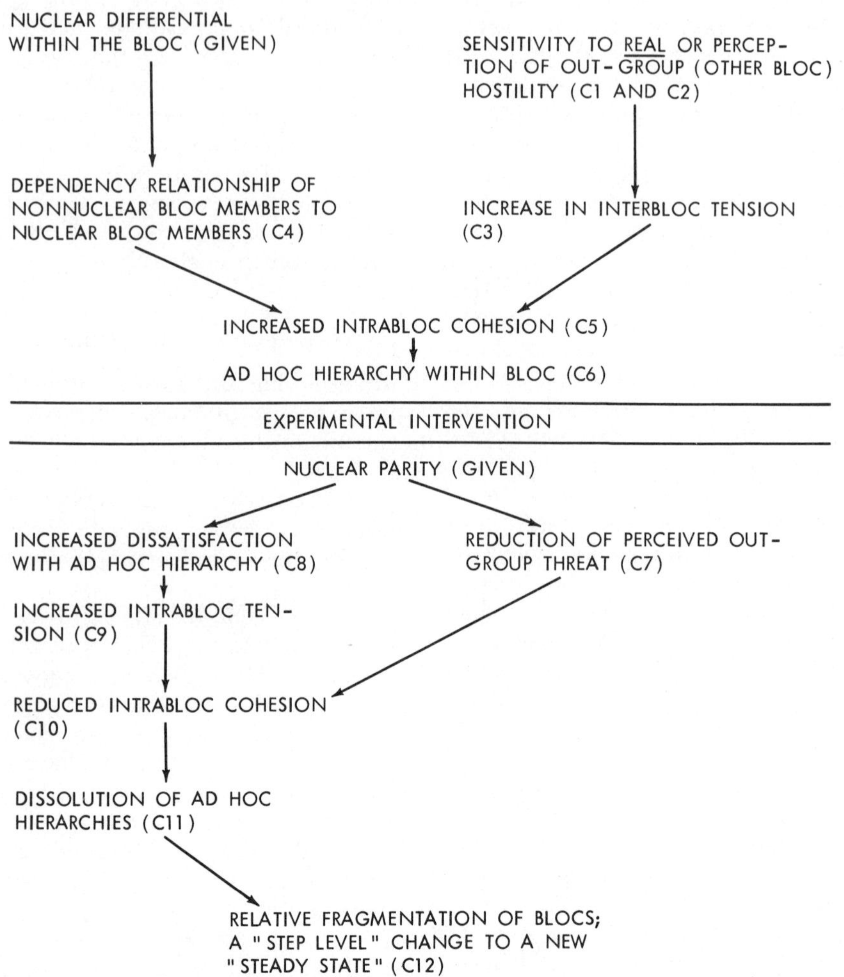

FIGURE 1. *Hypothesized linkings for INS No. 8. The numbers preceded by "C" indicate conditions in a chain of conditions through which the "steady state" A is hypothesized to pass in its transformation into the "steady state" B.*

among conditions. The hypothetical model is summarized as Fig. 1.

Figure 1 contains, in effect, a set of twenty-three difference and correlational hypotheses (corresponding to the conditions and linkages) which were explored with data derived from INS-8. The results of that exploration are summarized as Fig. 2, a model of the empirical findings.

An examination of Fig. 2 puts us in a position to answer our more general research question: Is the international system different before and after the spread of nuclear weapons? The answer to this question is an unqualified yes.

A comparison of Figs. 1 and 2 provides a means of gauging the confirmation of the detailed theoretical model. In the binuclear system, all of

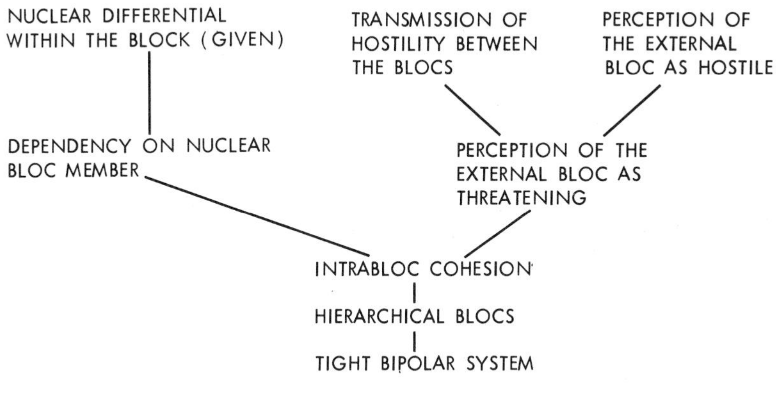

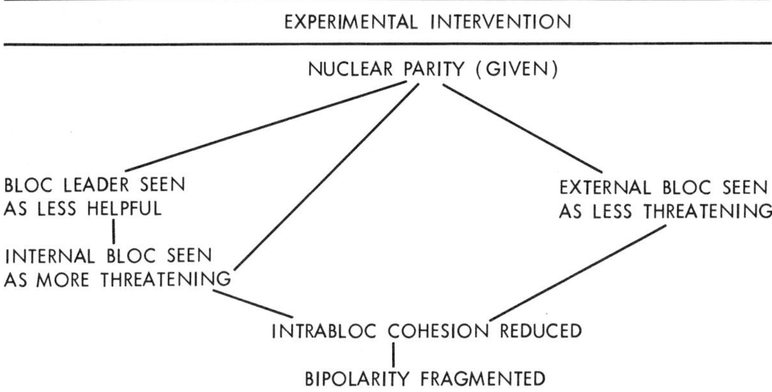

FIGURE 2. *Reformulation of the theoretical model in light of the experimental findings.*

the predicted conditions were established, but two of the predicted linkages (C.3 → C.4 and C.4 → C.5) were not.

The binuclear system was comprised of two hierarchical, cohesive bloc alliances. The nations of the external bloc were perceived as more hostile and threatening than the nations of the internal bloc. The communication between the blocs contained a greater level of expressed hostility than the communication within the blocs. The nonnuclear nations expressed dependency upon the nuclear bloc leader, a dependency which tended to be related to out-group hostility and threat. The dependency on the bloc leader and the hierarchical ordering of the blocs stemmed from both military and economic insufficiencies; the economic insufficiency continued into the postspread situation. In sum, the binuclear system was tightly bipolar.

Four key elements of the prespread system were different after the spread of nuclear capability: (a) threat external to the bloc was reduced, (b) threat internal to the bloc was increased, (c) the cohesiveness of the blocs was reduced, and (d) the bipolarity was fragmented. All of these add up to step-level changes in the cold-war system along lines predicted by the theoretical model.

We can now return to the propositions abstracted from the literature: The results of these experiments would tend to support the insights of Burns (1958 and 1961) and Tucker (1962) and cast doubts on those of Hilsman (1959), Morgenstern (1961), and Kissinger (1961). Beyond confirming the breakdown in the cold-war alliance system, the data produced in these experiments tend to support a model which explains the occurrence of this phenomenon.

The experiments which yielded the data upon which this report is based were conducted in 1960 (within five months of France's first nuclear detonation). In the years that have passed since 1960, French relations vis-à-vis the United States have tended to confirm the model's general prediction; whether the detailed predictions of the theoretical model would also be confirmed by this development is a matter which can be discovered only through extensive research; hopefully, as a result of this study, we now have a clearer idea of the international and domestic phenomena on which to focus such research.

Bibliography

Brody, R. A., "Deterrence Strategies: An Annotated Bibliography," *Journal of Conflict Resolution*, **4,** 443–457, 1960.

Brody, R. A., "Some Systemic Effects of the Spread of Nuclear Weapons Technology: A Study through Simulation of a Multi-Nuclear Future," *Journal of Conflict Resolution*, **7,** 663–753, 1963.

Brody, R. A., and R. Noel, *Inter-Nation Simulation Participants' Manual*. Evanston, Ill.: Program of Graduate Training and Research in International Relations, 1960.

Brown, H., and J. Real, *Community of Fear*. Santa Barbara: Center for the Study of Democratic Institutions, 1960.

Brzezinski, Z., *The Soviet Bloc: Unity and Diversity*. Cambridge, Mass.: Harvard University Press, 1960.

Burns, A. L., "Military Technology and International Politics," *Yearbook of World Affairs*, 1961. London: Stevens and Sons, Ltd., 1961, pp. 185–203.

Burns, A. L., "The New Weapons and International Relations," *Australian Outlook*, **12,** 32–42, 1958.

Frank, J. "The Great Antagonism," *Atlantic Monthly*, **202,** 58–62, 1958.

Guetzkow, H., "The Use of Simulation in the Study of Inter-Nation Relations," *Behavioral Science*, **4,** 183–191, 1959.

Guetzkow, H., C. Alger, R. Brody, R. Noel, and R. C. Snyder, *Simulation in International Relations: Developments for Research and Teaching*. Englewood Cliffs, N. J.: Prentice-Hall, Inc., 1963.

Guetzkow, H., R. Brody, M. Driver, and P. Beach, *An Experiment on the N-Country Problem through Simulation*. St. Louis, Mo.: The Social Science Institute, Washington University, 1960.

Guetzkow, H., and H. Simon, "The Impact of Certain Communication Nets upon Organization and Performance in Task-Oriented Groups," *Management Science*, **1,** 233–250, 1955.

Hilsman, R., "On NATO Strategy," *in* Wolfers, A., ed., *Alliance Policy in the Cold War*. Baltimore: The Johns Hopkins University Press, 1959, pp. 149–183.

Iklé, F., "*N*th Countries and Disarmament," *Bulletin of the Atomic Scientists*, **16,** 391–394, 1960.

Kaplan, M., *System and Process in International Politics*. New York: John Wiley and Sons, Inc., 1957.

King, J. E., Jr., "Collective Defense: The Military Commitment," in: Wolfers, A., ed., *Alliance Policy in the Cold War*. Baltimore: The Johns Hopkins University Press, 1959, pp. 103–145.

Kissinger, H. A., *The Necessity for Choice.* New York: Harper and Row, Publishers, 1961.

Knorr, K., ed., *NATO and American Security.* Princeton, N. J.: Princeton University Press, 1959.

Miller, W. L., "The American Ethos and the Alliance System," *in* Wolfers, A., ed., *Alliance Policy in the Cold War.* Baltimore: The Johns Hopkins University Press, 1959, pp. 31–48.

Modelski, G., *The Communist International System.* Princeton, N. J.: Center for International Studies, 1960.

Morgenstern, O., "The *N*-Country Problem," *Fortune,* March, 1961, p. 136 ff.

Morgenthau, H. J., "Alliance in Theory and Practice," *in* Wolfers, A., ed., *Alliance Policy in the Cold War.* Baltimore: The Johns Hopkins University Press, 1959, pp. 184–212.

Newcomb, T. M., "Autistic Hostility and Social Reality," *Human Relations,* **1,** 69–86, 1947.

Osgood, R. E., *NATO: The Entangling Alliance.* Chicago: University of Chicago Press, 1962.

Rosecrance, R., ed., *The Dispersion of Nuclear Weapons.* New York: Columbia University Press, 1964.

Tucker, R. W., *Stability and the Nth-Country Problem.* Washington, D. C.: Institute for Defense Analyses, 1962.

Wolfers, A., ed., *Alliance Policy in the Cold War.* Baltimore: The Johns Hopkins University Press, 1959.

PART FIVE

Nonmilitary Restraints and the Peaceful Resolution of Controversy

INTRODUCTION

Most theories about factors (forces) that reduce the likelihood of war focus on military restraints of the kind discussed in Part IV. Yet there are many nonmilitary factors that seem to reduce the attractiveness and therefore the likelihood of violent conflict. Some take the form of nonmilitary restraints, which stay the hand of statesmen who might otherwise resort to violence. Others encourage the peaceful resolution of controversy.

As in the case of military restraints, the bulk of the literature on nonmilitary factors is speculative. Furthermore, on some topics that fall under this rubric, a systematic literature is almost nonexistent. Accordingly, the editors of this volume have, at points in the discussion, inserted relevant hypotheses of their own. A number of pioneering empirical research efforts are also cited at appropriate points.

Nonmilitary Restraints Against the Use of Violence

A variety of nonmilitary factors can be cited that deter a state from military attack by reducing the perceived value of winning a war or increasing the perceived likelihood or disutility of unfavorable outcomes associated with war. These include anticipated destruction of the fruits of war, international bonds, world public opinion, and international norms. Some of these restraints also operate at an earlier stage of conflict, when the alternative of violence is not under consideration, discouraging states from adopting harsh tactics toward one another that might foster a conflict spiral leading to war.

Anticipated Destruction of the Fruits of War

Violence is sometimes eschewed in the pursuit of a goal because it appears that the use of violence, per se, will defeat that purpose. The purpose can be defeated in a number of ways. If the object sought is physical, e.g., industrial capacity or manpower, it may be destroyed in the course of military combat. Alternatively, the other state may destroy or make unusable some of its own material wealth to avoid confiscation. In addition, to the extent that the object sought involves cooperation from citizens of the other state, violence may be inappropriate. Angry people do not make particularly good factory workers or military allies. The cost of maintaining order among the citizens of an angry state is often not commensurate with the value of the cooperation obtained, as many of the former colonial powers discovered. Finally, the use of violence is especially inappropriate if the goal is ideological conversion of the adversary, since attitudes are not easily changed by force.

International Bonds

It is possible to cite three kinds of *bonds* with another state that may act to discourage the use of violence against it: similarity, past cooperation, and functional dependence. In addition to restraining states from the choice of a violent alternative, these international bonds can also have a pacifying effect at earlier stages of conflict, when the alternative of violence is not under consideration, by restraining states from adopting harsh tactics toward one another. Hence, they can reduce the likelihood of a conflict spiral leading to war of the kind described in Part III of this volume.

Similarity of race, culture, or ideology may to some extent restrain a state from the use of violence or reduce the level of violence employed. An empathic mechanism is probably involved: The more similar the citizens of the other state, the more likely are they to be seen as fellow human beings and the less likely are they to be characterized as an enemy which deserves harsh punishment. However, the importance of similarity as a restraining force should not be overestimated; fraternal wars are fairly common.

Past Cooperation. Cooperation between states can engender friendly feelings among their citizens that later act to inhibit the use of violence. In the words of Levi (1964, p. 23), "The peaceful behavior and attitudes that have become habitual as a result of direct mutual dependencies are likely to carry over into all behavior patterns." The longer and more important the period of cooperation is, the more effective and durable such feelings are likely to be. Again, the importance of past cooperations as a restraint should not be overestimated; yesterday's friend can become tomorrow's enemy, especially when the national leaderships want it that way. But this factor also seems to deserve mention.

Functional dependence on another state can be said to exist when that state has the capacity to be useful in some way and there is reason to believe that it can be induced to be useful. Dependence produces a fear of alienating the other state and hence induces restraint against the use of violence. Sources of dependence include existing trade and aid agreements, the existence of a common enemy, etc. Of course, every restraint has its breaking point; and, in this case, functional dependence is only effective to the extent that the goals that can be achieved if the other state cooperates are more valuable than the goals that can be achieved through war. Nevertheless, functional dependence is probably a very important restraint against war.

While carrying great potential for preventing violence, dependence on another state can sometimes have quite the opposite effect. If the other state fails to cooperate in the expected way, considerable hostility is likely to be generated, especially if there has been an agreement to cooperate or a history of cooperation. For example, current Chinese hostility toward the Soviet Union seems to derive in part from promises broken by the latter state. Such hostility enhances the probability that violence will be employed. In addition, dependence on another state can sometimes motivate military action against that state if it is felt that the needed object can be more cheaply captured by force than wooed by good behavior.

Research on International Responsiveness. The restraining effect of international bonds can be thought of as one element of a more general responsiveness toward the needs of the other state. Russett (1962) has recently established a link between international bonds and responsiveness, in an empirical study of the United States Congress and the British Parliament. He found that legislators who had economic or personal ties with another state showed greater responsiveness toward that state in their voting or speaking than did other legislators. Whether this effect was due to feelings of friendliness or functional dependence is not clear, but the study shows the importance of international bonds. Russett's research grew out of a comparative case study by Deutsch et al. (1957), in which responsiveness was found to have been a critical prerequisite for the development of political integration between states in a number of historical instances.

International Stability As a Result of Functional Interdependence. The point was made above that dependence on another state can act as a restraint against the use of violence and other harsh tactics in dealing with that state. It follows that international stability (in the sense of the absence of war) is, at least in part, a function of the degree of interdependence among all states.

A similar point has often been made regarding the integrative effect on society of multiple group memberships among its people (Coleman, 1957). If person *A* is associated with person *B* in one group and person *C* in another, he is dependent on these people and, therefore, not too likely to advocate the use of harsh tactics against them. The more people with whom he associates, the more peaceful he will be. The more people in a society who hold multiple group memberships and the more diverse the membership of its groups, the more stable that society will be.

Paradoxically, a certain amount of conflict within a society that is characterized by multiple group memberships may enhance stability (Ross, 1920). If labor and management contain both Catholics and Protestants and there is some conflict along religious lines, industrial conflict should be less acute since men on both sides of industry will be loath to antagonize their coreligionists on the other side because they are dependent on these coreligionists for support in the religious struggle. Similarly, in such circumstances, industrial conflict can mute religious conflict. The healthiest situation may be one in which both kinds of conflict exist at a low level, each preventing the other from escalating to a high level. That multiple group membership among states and a certain mount of conflict between groups of states may be healthy in international relations is suggested by Alger (1961 and Selection 14).

From the viewpoint of interdependence, the greatest enemy of stability, in both domestic and international society, is *bipolarity*. In a bipolar system, the units (people or states) are divided into two great camps (blocs) with considerable interdependence within each camp but little between camps. In a bipolar system, considerable tension often develops between the camps, and the use of violence is not always effectively restrained.

Bipolarity can be broken down in two ways:

1. By increasing opportunities for contact and cooperation between members of the opposing camps. Alger (1961 and Selection 14) has suggested that United Nations membership has this effect by offering members of opposing blocs the opportunity to find common interests in such issues as allocation of the United Nations budget.

2. By destroying the dominant position of the leader of one or both camps. International blocs are usually organized around a single, dominant state. In addition to encouraging bloc solidarity, the leader often discourages the members of his bloc from developing meaningful contacts with members of the opposing bloc. Functional interdependence can develop across bloc lines only if the position of the leader is weakened. The preeminance of a bloc leader is often based on superior military capacity, with the leader providing protection to other members in exchange for compliance with his wishes. His position will be weakened to the extent that other bloc members develop sufficient military capacity to protect themselves.

In a recent simulation study, Brody (1963 and Selection 12) has demonstrated the validity of the latter point. His study suggests that proliferation of nuclear weapons in a bipolar world will create greater interbloc communication and hence lower interbloc tension.

This discussion of stability harkens back to a traditional proposition in the balance of power literature, that stability is a function of the number of independently powerful states. As mentioned in the introduction to Part IV, this proposition is usually justified on the assumption that the existence of a greater number of states permits the development of a greater variety of alliances and thereby increases the likelihood that a would-be aggressor will be confronted with an unbeatable coalition. Deutsch and Singer (1964) suggest a different justification based on the notion of multiple group membership. The more independently powerful states there are in a system, the more groups of varying membership can be formed and the less likely a schism into two hostile camps becomes on any international issue.[1]

World Public Opinion

World public opinion has often been cited in popular writing as a deterrent to war and to the use of other harsh tactics that may place states on the road to war. However, this phenomenon has seldom been carefully analyzed by scholars. According to the popular notion, one state is sometimes restrained from the use of violence or other harsh tactics against another because it anticipates disapproval from third states. World public opinion should not be confused with military action or threats of such action on the part of third states, which have already been treated in Part IV of this book on the balance of power and nuclear deterrents. A possible example of the force of world public opinion can be found in American reluctance to invade Castro's Cuba, which can be explained as partially founded on a fear of alienating other Latin American states.

Determinants of the Effectiveness of World Public Opinion. The effect of world public opinion is certainly due, at least in part, to interdependence among states. Each state knows that it jeopardizes the cooperation of other states by arousing their hostility. The more dependent a state is on the rest of the world, the greater is the danger in alienating world public opinion.

Dependence on other states would not be so compelling if these states could be forced to cooperate. For example, if threats of violence could be used by larger states to force smaller states to trade, the opinions of these smaller states would not be worth so much. However, in a bipolar world such as the modern one, the likelihood that large states will threaten small ones is diminished because of the fear that the latter will defect to the opposing bloc; and, hence, the effectiveness of world public opinion is probably strengthened.

Determinants of the Vigor of World Public Opinion. A distinction needs to be made between the *effectiveness* of world public opinion, i.e., its capacity to dissuade, and the *vigor* of world public opinion, i.e., the extent to which it can be mobilized and amplified. The vigor of world public opinion against war has grown markedly over the past fifty years (Lerche, 1956).

One reason for this vigor lies in the danger that war poses to all states. In former times, it was possible for one state to ignore a war between two others as irrelevant to its welfare. But modern nuclear weapons, with their great explosive power and broad fall-out regions, make this no longer possible.

In addition, international organizations such as the United Nations enhance the vigor of world public opinion by providing unique forums for the mobilization of world public opinion. Most smaller states are unwilling to censure larger ones

---

[1]The assumption that multipolarity leads to international stability is not universally shared among international relations scholars. Waltz (1964) has argued that a bipolar world is more stable because the responsibility for deterring aggressive action is diffused in a multipolar world. See also Rosecrance (1966).

unless they know that other states will join them in this move. A forum, such as those at the United Nations, provides a setting in which many states can take a *simultaneous* stand against an aggressor and thereby provide assurance to each individual state that it does not stand alone in its condemnation. The conviction that other states will join oneself in condemning aggression is probably also strengthened by the existence of formal norms, i.e., international agreements, against war. More will be said about norms in the next section.

While agreeing that world public opinion (or as he calls it "neutralist policy") against war has grown in importance over the past few decades, Rosecrance (1963) has argued that the vigor of this opinion may be somewhat declining today because of a growing recognition by many neutral states of their great dependence on the major powers and a consequent decreasing willingness to run the risk of alienating these powers by condemning their use of harsh tactics in international conflict.

International Norms

The final kind of restraint to be examined in this section derives from international norms against the use of violence. A *norm* is a generally accepted rule of behavior. Norms may be *formal*, i.e., written down, or *informal*, i.e., generally accepted but not written down and sometimes not even verbalized. Formal norms in international affairs are mostly embodied in treaties and are called *international law.*

Although there has been sentiment against war in all ages, war was not formally proscribed until the signing of the Kellogg-Briand Pact in 1928, in which all parties agreed to "condemn recourse to war for the solution of international controversies, and renounce it as an instrument of national policy." More recently, signatories of the United Nations Charter have agreed to "refrain in their international relations from the threat or use of force against the territorial integrity or political independence of any state." Provisions in some regional pacts, such as the Inter-American Treaty, also proscribe war among the signatories.

Informal norms that limit the use of violence are harder to identify but nevertheless clearly exist. These usually develop on a bilateral basis, through a process called *encapsulation* by Etzioni (1964). An example might be the tacit agreement between the United States and the Soviet Union not to become involved in overt hostilities against one another.

States do not always comply with international norms. But it is amazing how often they do comply, given the absence of a central authority with a monopoly of violence. Several authors (e.g., Larsen, 1961; Fisher, 1962; and Iklé, 1964) have examined the reasons for compliance with a norm. Their suggestions can be listed under six main points: (a) fear of retaliation from the state that is injured when the norm is broken (a state that is injured is, of course, likely to retaliate whether or not a norm is involved; but retaliation will usually be greater when a norm is violated in order to discourage norm violation at a later date from the same or other states); (b) fear of censure by world public opinion, which is usually especially sensitive to the breaking of a norm because of the bad example it sets to other states and on other norms; (c) fear that one's own compliance will set a bad example for other states and cause them to feel freer to break the same or another norm at a later date; (d) fear of losing one's reputation for living up to treaty obligations and thus one's "credit rating" in future negotiations; (e) normal institutional resistance to changing policies, in this case based on earlier official acceptance of the norm in question; (f) the feeling that it is morally right to conform to international law.

Fisher (1962) has also analyzed the process by which informal norms come into existence.

Although the effectiveness of most kinds of international norms is generally acknowledged (see Brierly, 1958), questions have been raised about the capacity of antiwar norms to restrain states against the use of violence. It is usually argued that states will ignore international norms in matters that touch their basic interests, such as issues of war and peace (Falk, 1962; Hoyt, 1961). This argument fails to come to grips with the reasons for compliance listed above. To the extent that world public opinion, the promulgation of a bad example, or loss of national credit rating are things to be feared, the existence of a norm may well deter an attack in an area of considerable national interest, *if the rationale for launching the attack is not overwhelming*. Even if the only basis for conforming is a moral sense of commitment to a norm, the existence of a norm may tip the balance against the resort to violence if other arguments for and against violence are *evenly balanced*, however deep the interests touched.

The Peaceful Resolution of Controversy

War usually grows out of a controversy or dispute between states with seemingly incompatible goals.[2] One side begins the war in an effort to further its end of the dispute or to prevent the other side from making gains, and the other is forced to respond.

Disputes that might otherwise lead to war can sometimes be resolved peacefully through negotiation, mediation, arbitration, or other third-party action. Hence, the use and success of these approaches are relevant to the prevention of war. The successful resolution of controversy through one of these approaches does not inevitably lead away from war. In the words of Iklé (1964, p. ix), it can sometimes "exacerbate hostilities, strengthen an aggressor, prepare the way for his attack, and erode the legal and moral foundations of peace." But it probably more often leads to peace than to war.

This section will mainly be concerned with negotiation but will take up third-party intervention briefly at the end.

By *negotiation* is meant verbal communication between parties aimed at finding an agreed course of action. A distinction is sometimes made between *true* and *false* negotiation. True negotiation takes place when both parties are genuinely inter-

[2]Occasionally, as was stated in the introduction to Part II, war develops from conflict-oriented goals, e.g., the perpetuation of a military elite whose position is guaranteed by conflict per se. But, more commonly, it results from some kind of dispute.

ested in reaching a settlement and are willing to make some concessions in the interest of such a settlement; false negotiation occurs when one or both are uninterested in a settlement and use the dialogue for other purposes, such as propaganda or delay. This distinction is probably too sharp in application since both sets of motives are often present; but it can be said that the present section will deal only with the true, i.e., nonpropagandistic, aspects of negotiation.

A good deal of research has been done on international negotiation, but most of it is descriptive rather than theoretical in approach. Interesting exceptions to this generalization can be found in Iklé (1964) and Sawyer and Guetzkow (1965). Three fascinating theoretical treatments of collective bargaining in industry have recently appeared (Douglas, 1962; Stevens, 1963; Walton and McKersie, 1965). In addition, some interesting laboratory research has been published on negotiation (Kelley, 1966; Siegel and Fouraker, 1960; Thibaut and Faucheux, 1965).

When and Why Do States Negotiate?

Very little has been written about the forces that determine *whether* states will embark on negotiation. It seems reasonable to suppose that hostility reduces the likelihood of international negotiation, just as it reduces the likelihood of interpersonal communication (Newcomb, 1947). The attractiveness of negotiation is probably a positive function of its apparent likelihood of success, which may in part be due to earlier favorable experience with negotiation. The attractiveness of alternatives other than negotiation must also be considered. However, these theoretical ideas do not cover much ground.

The determinants of *when* negotiation begins have also received comparatively little attention. A particularly interesting question concerns the forces that govern whether negotiation comes early or late in a controversy. Some controversies begin with negotiation and only move to war (or other extreme forms of conflict behavior) if negotiation fails. In other cases, there is little sentiment for negotiation until a war has been fought.

From the vantage point of the policy maker, there are arguments favoring both early and late negotiation. Early negotiation can be justified by the restraints that exist against the use of violence. It costs more to fight than to talk; hence, war should be elected only if negotiation fails. Late negotiation can be justified in another way. Demands presented in negotiation are often backed up by the implicit or explicit threat of war. If there is ambiguity about the outcome of war between the two states involved in a controversy, it may not be possible to determine whose demands are to be taken more seriously. Hence, negotiation is a futile exercise until a test of comparative strength has been made on the battlefield.

Whether the arguments for early or late negotiation win out probably depends on the circumstances. It seems reasonable to suppose that the rationale for early negotiation will seem stronger, the greater the restraints are against war. Hence, negotiation is more likely to come early in a controversy, the greater the potential destruction from war, the more vigorous world public opinion against war, the stronger the bonds between parties to the controversy, the more stable the distribution of power, etc. The rationale for late negotiation will seem stronger the greater the ambiguity concerning who can win a war.

What Determines the Success of Negotiation?

The likelihood that negotiation will end in agreement is mainly a function of the probability that concessions will be made by one or both parties. Forces that block concession include hostility and, where an agreement depends for its execution on good faith, distrust. Distrust and other psychological states are discussed by Pool in Selection 13. The likelihood of concessions is probably, in part, also a function of the degree of interdependence between the two parties. By making concessions, one party builds good will with the other; by holding out, good will is lost. Hence, concessions are more likely to be made, the more important it is to gain the other party's good will because of dependence on that party for the satisfaction of some need (Pruitt, 1962).

In many cases, negotiation can be described as a two-stage process, having an early stage, in which each side attempts to persuade the other to make concessions, and a later stage, in which an effort is made to locate and move jointly toward common ground (Stevens, 1963). The probability that agreement will be reached in the second stage depends, in part, on the tactics used in the first. In particular, it depends on the use of the tactic of committing oneself firmly to a position in an effort to persuade the other party that it must move if the negotiation is to succeed. If either party commits itself too rigidly to a position that is not acceptable to the other, it may not be able to make adequate concessions in the second stage and a stalemate may result. One party's overcommitment is sometimes a product of the other's seeming lack of rigidity in the first stage.

The success of negotiation may also depend on the size of the elements involved. Fisher (1964) has suggested that negotiation moves most rapidly when the issues, parties, and precedents are "fractionated" down to the smallest possible size.

Third-Party Intervention in Controversy

There are a number of ways in which third parties can exert influence on controversies. They may put pressure on the principals to negotiate or make concessions. In addition, they may participate actively in five ways described by Lerche (1956): (a) *good offices*, where the third party expedites negotiation by providing a meeting ground or transmitting communications; (b) *inquiry*, where the third party investigates the facts underlying a dispute; (c) *mediation*, where the third party proposes a solution and attempts to persuade the principals to accept it; (d) *arbitration*, where the third party proposes a solution that is manditory on the principals as a result of prior agreement between them; and (e) *judicial settlement*, where the World Court acts as arbiter. (See also Young, 1967.)

Third party actions can contribute to the success of negotiation in a number of ways. Third parties may be able to discover alternatives that have eluded the principals. By dragging out their inquiries and recommedations, they may provide a breathing spell in which hostilities dissipate and the parties become more capable of communicating and making concessions to one another. By providing a meeting place, pressuring the principals to sit down together, or carrying messages, they can facilitate communication, the heart of negotiation. Third parties are sometimes able to exert sufficient pressure on one or both principals for concessions to be made. In addition, a third party proposal can sometimes provide a graceful basis for one party to climb down, without appearing weak, from an overly rigid position developed in an earlier stage of negotiation.

Substitutes for Negotiation

Negotiation is not always a practical approach to international controversy. States may not be willing to converse or, if willing, may be so mistrustful or lacking in responsiveness that agreement cannot be reached. Under such circumstances, tacit agreements may develop (Schelling, 1957), or it may be possible for one of the states to make unilateral moves that reduce the other state's hostility or increase its trust and responsiveness to the point at which negotiations can be fruitful. A series of proposals for unilateral moves that might be taken by the United States to lessen tension in the East-West controversy has been made by Osgood (1959, 1962 and Selection 15), who suggests that these moves may start a benevolent circle of mutual conciliation comparable in form but in a direction opposite to that of the arms race.

Conclusion

Aside from the voluminous writings on international law, which are mostly not of a theoretical nature (in the sense of theory described in the introduction to Part I), there is a paucity of scholarly literature on nonviolent restraints against international conflict and on the peaceful resolution of international conflict. As usual, empirical work is scarce; but, in addition, there is little theoretical material. Hence, the contents of this chapter may seem "thinner" than the contents of some of the earlier introductory chapters, with more emphasis on lists of variables and less theoretical analysis. Clearly, there is room here for a great deal more research. In contrast to the study of military restraints, which are not found at all levels of society, a comparative theory of nonviolent restraints might well be developed which would be applicable to many different forms of conflict. For example, third parties appear in the resolution of almost any kind of conflict, from marital conflict to international conflict. Insight into the role of third parties can be derived from studying almost any social phenomenon, and a theory of this phenomenon might well be developed that would cut across all of the theoretical and applied fields of social science.

References

Alger, C. F., "Non-resolution consequences of the United Nations and their effect on international conflict," *Journal of Conflict Resolution*, **5**(2), 128–145, 1961.

Brierly, J. L., *The Basis of Obligation in International Law, and Other Papers.* Oxford: Clarendon Press, 1958.

Brody, R. A., "Some systemic effects of the spread of nuclear weapons technology: a study through simulation of a multi-nuclear future," *Journal of Conflict Resolution,* **7**(4), 663–753, 1963.

Coleman, J. S., *Community Conflict.* New York: The Free Press, 1957.

Deutsch, K. W., S. A. Burrell, R. A. Kann, M. Lee, M. Lichterman, R. E. Lindgren, F. L. Loewenheim, and R. W. Van Wagenen, *Political Community and the North Atlantic Area.* Princeton, N. J.: Princeton University Press, 1957.

Deutsch, K. W., and J. D. Singer, "Multipolar power systems and international stability," *World Politics,* **16**(3), 390–406, 1964.

Douglas, A., *Industrial Peacemaking.* New York: Columbia University Press, 1962.

Etzioni, A., "On self-encapsulating conflicts," *Journal of Conflict Resolution,* **8**(3), 242–255, 1964.

Falk, R. A., "Revolutionary nations and the quality of international legal order," *in* M.A. Kaplan, ed., *The Revolution in World Politics.* New York: John Wiley and Sons, Inc., 1962.

Fisher, R., "Constructing rules that affect governments," *in* Q. Wright, W. M. Evan, and M. Deutsch, *Preventing World War III.* New York: Simon and Schuster, Inc., 1962.

Fisher, R., "Fractionating conflict," *in* R. Fisher, ed., *International Conflict and Behavioral Science.* New York: Basic Books, Inc., 1964.

Hoyt, E. C., "The United States reaction to the Korean attack," *American Journal of International Law,* **55**(1), 45–76, 1961.

Iklé, F. C., *How Nations Negotiate.* New York: Harper and Row, Publishers, 1964.

Kelley, H. H., "A classroom study of the dilemmas in interpersonal negotiations," *in* Kathleen Archibald, ed., *Strategic Interaction and Conflict.* Berkeley, Calif.: University of California Press, 1966.

Larson, A., *When Nations Disagree.* Baton Rouge, La.: Louisiana State University Press, 1961.

Lerche, C. O., *Principles of International Politics.* New York: Oxford University Press, Inc., 1956.

Levi, W., "On the causes of peace," *Journal of Conflict Resolution,* **8**(1), 23–35, 1964.

Newcomb, T. M., "Autistic hostility and social reality," *Human Relations,* **1**(1), 69–86, 1947.

Osgood, C. E., "Suggestions for winning the real war with communism," *Journal of Conflict Resolution,* **3**(4), 295–325, 1959.

Osgood, C. E., *An Alternative to War or Surrender.* Urbana, Ill.: University of Illinois Press, 1962.

Pruitt, D. G., "An analysis of responsiveness between nations," *Journal of Conflict Resolution,* **6**(1), 5–18, 1962.

Rosecrance, R. N., *Action and Reaction in World Politics.* Boston: Little, Brown and Co., 1963.

Rosecrance, R. N., "Bipolarity, multipolarity and the future," *Journal of Conflict Resolution,* **10**(3), 314–327, 1966.

Ross, E. A., *The Principles of Sociology.* New York: Century Company, 1920.

Russett, B. M., "International communication and legislative behavior: the Senate and the House of Commons," *Journal of Conflict Resolution*, **6**(4), 291–307, 1962.

Sawyer, J., and H. Guetzkow, "Bargaining and negotiation," *in* H. Kelman, ed., *International Behavior.* New York: Holt, Rinehart and Winston, 1965.

Schelling, T. C., "Bargaining, communication, and limited war," *Journal of Conflict Resolution,* **1**(1), 19–36, 1957.

Siegel, S., and L. E. Fouraker, *Bargaining and Group Decision Making.* New York: McGraw-Hill Book Company, 1960.

Stevens, C. M. *Strategy and Collective Bargaining Negotiation.* New York: McGraw-Hill Book Company, 1963.

Thibaut, J., and C. Faucheux, "The development of contractual norms in a bargaining situation under two types of stress," *Journal of Experimental Social Psychology,* **1**(1), 89–102, 1965.

Walton, R. E., and R. B. McKersie, *A Behavioral Theory of Labor Negotiations.* New York: McGraw-Hill Book Company, 1965.

Waltz, K. N., "The stability of a bipolar world." *Daedalus,* **3,** 881–909, Summer, 1964.

Young, O. R., *The Intermediaries: Third Parties in International Crises.* Princeton, N. J.: Princeton University Press, 1967.

13

ITHIEL DE SOLA POOL

Deterrence as an Influence Process

A theoretical discussion which is designed to foster a broader-than-usual approach to deterrence theory. Deterrence has usually been attributed to the nature of military preparations but is here defined as a special case of influence. Various nonmilitary modes of influence are proposed, including modifying what comes to the adversary's attention and providing information to the adversary.

Deterrence is a special case of influence.

We know a fair amount about pressure, persuasion, propaganda, bargaining, fear, and other mechanisms of influence. An extensive literature treats of the processes whereby human beings influence each other. Clearly, any theory of deterrence should be either congruent with existing theories of influence or should specify the reasons for its divergence.

There are many complex ways in which one human system may influence another. It is well to distinguish these different modes of influence, though in life they overlap. These modes of influence are:

1. Generating trust and positive affect
2. Generating fear
3. Modifying what comes to the influencee's attention
4. Modifying the salience of different things to him
5. Providing information
6. Modifying certainty
7. Providing a behavioral model to the influencee
8. Changing the objective environment
9. Changing the influencee's resources

Generating Trust

The influencing of people by generating confidence and good relations has been abundantly studied by social psychologists, particularly those in the fields of human relations and group dynamics. Such psychologists, living in a democratic society and generally having liberal predispositions, have

An excerpt from a technical publication of the same name, TP 3879 of the U.S. Naval Ordnance Test Station, China Lake, California, November, 1965. Reprinted by permission of the author and the U.S. Naval Ordnance Test Station. An extensive set of footnotes, including many references, that are included in the original had to be omitted in this version because of space limitations. The author is Professor of Political Science at the Massachusetts Institute of Technology.

focused on persuasion in relatively noncoercive environments such as those of voluntary associations, social cliques, and classrooms. There they have found that constructive and stable changes are produced under conditions of positive reinforcement, low tension levels, equalitarian relationships, and democratic leadership.

These are important findings. They apply to environments which all of us would like to see prevailing throughout the world. They apply to environments which actually do exist through a large part of human life and not only in the democratic West.

With due allowances for cultural differences, the principles of group behavior can be usefully applied by a foreman in Japan, India, or Russia as much as in the United States. Even in the most totalitarian society, much of life consists of courteous human interaction among friends, neighbors, co-workers, etc. Democratic and equalitarian principles are at least in part valid interpretations of universal human nature. With proper qualifications, psychologial insights about persuasive relations in informal groupings may have relevance to dealing with Soviet diplomats or even with Khrushchev. The question at issue is what are the proper qualifications, and this has been very little studied.

One obvious qualification is that the principles for generating trust have been derived in situations where a modicum of affection or trust is found in the group already. The family, for example, though not voluntary, shares strong bonds of affection. Even arbitrarily chosen subjects from a sophomore class approach each other with the assumptions of civility common to secondary contacts in a free society. Such subjects are not in a state of terror of each other. In that situation, identifications result from pleasantness, not aggression. Contrast this to the situation in a concentration camp where Bettelheim found the victims identifying with the aggressors.[1]

In short, while the principles of how to persuade by trust are important, we need to know more about their limitations (1) in extreme environments and (2) where institutional structures demand distrust and competition. We must avoid assuming that the principles of democratic human relations are applicable before we give due consideration of their interaction with other modes of influence.

Generating Fear

We have just noted that most psychological experiments seem to show fear to be a relatively ineffectual force for persuasion. People repress or deny unpleasant facts. But practical experience seems a better guide here than do research results achieved under quite limited or artificial circumstances. Common-sense evidence includes the experience that men at war quickly learn how to protect themselves when live bullets start coming. Or one might cite the penal system. Fear of "cops" does lower driving speeds. Or, turning to strategic matters, American policy has certainly been affected by our assessment of Soviet strength. Two years ago, when we believed a missile gap existed, there was much more urgency at high governmental levels about disarming and controlling nuclear weapons than there is now when (rightly or wrongly) we believe ourselves to have overwhelming strategic superiority. If at some point in the future we again become convinced that

[1]Bettelheim, B., "Individual and mass behavior in extreme situations," *Journal of Abnormal and Social Psychology*, 38 (1943), 417–452.

the Russians could destroy us, we may become much more receptive to difficult compromises.

The entire peace movement is a reflection of the persuasive power of fear. The disarmers may feel that the public is blind in not being as anxious as they. But the fact that thousands of persons have taken an antinuclear position is evidence of the impact of fear.

It is only a platitude, however, that fear influences people. The important question is how, when, and under what circumstances. The research literature is not too helpful here, so let us spell out some speculative hypotheses.

1. Fear will be effective when the danger is seen as certain to face one in a finite time period. If the danger is only a possibility, then one may use the mechanism of denial. Unless the worst is seen as certain to occur, one can hope for the best and defer worrying about the worst until it happens.

2. Fear will be effective upon people whose role it is to concern themselves with the danger. If one has a job as a fireman, or doctor, or undertaker, or policeman, or strategic planner, one will develop an objective way of taking account of the danger; whereas if one has no such responsibility to force one to think about it, one may indulge in denial.

3. Fear will be effective if it has been present in the background for some time, and if the persuader's short-run action is to give relief. Thus, police interrogators have long known that a way to get a confession is suddenly to be kind to a man after terrorizing him for a long period.

4. Fear will be effective if the intimidated person is allowed to establish good rationalizations for yielding.

If these principles are valid, then the American deterrent posture of building a large ballistic missile force without indulging in threats is a very good one. The message conveyed by that force-in-being is addressed to professional diplomats, statesmen, and soldiers who are not likely to miss its import. It provides a background against which to act in a generous or friendly fashion at some future time. If force is overwhelming, no psychic energy will be given to fruitless seeking of ways to safely disarm it by surprise instead of accepting its intended message. If the force is not verbally brandished (as it was in an unfortunate Stewart Alsop *Saturday Evening Post* article), the foe can invent many good reasons for not feeling defeated by it.[2]

So regarding one mode of influence—generating fear—the American posture has much to commend it. It uses fear in a fairly effective way. But fear is only one mode of influencing an enemy. Before we accept the present posture as optimal we must consider what it does in each other mode of influence. But before we change our posture we must also consider how such changes would affect the use of this mode of influence.

Modifying what Comes to the Influencee's Attention and Modifying the Salience of Different Things to Him

These two modes of influence are so much alike that they can be discussed together.

Along with the dissemination of information, the most frequent result of propaganda campaigns is to change attention and saliency. Propaganda is sometimes described as an attempt to change attitudes, but that is something it seldom achieves. Studies of voter

[2]Alsop, S. "Kennedy's grand strategy," *Saturday Evening Post*, vol. 235, No. 13 (March 31, 1962), 11–16.

behavior have demonstrated how, in American electoral campaigns, few people get converted in their views; but many are redirected in their attention or have the saliency of different issues changed for them, and this affects their actions.

It is the same in world politics. Khrushchev turns the Berlin heat on and off without changing any American belief about Communism or about Berlin or about anything; but the result is marked changes in American actions, such as mobilizing or demobilizing reserves. An agricultural problem drastically reduces both the Chinese and Russian proneness to foreign adventure. The Israeli-Franco-British adventure in Suez saved the Russians many of the embarrassing international consequences of their actions in Hungary and vice versa.

A deterrence policy characteristically seeks certain changes in saliency and attention. It seeks to reduce the saliency to an enemy of those objectives which are of maximum salience to us. If a vital goal for us is to deter any Soviet attack on Western Europe, then it is helpful to us to keep Europe relatively unimportant to Russia, for example, by keeping the Sino-Soviet conflict acute. Similarly, it is helpful to focus political rivalry on the race for economic development.

Note that these two examples of how to de-emphasize a Soviet focus on Europe included one that used antagonistic actions and one that sublimated hostility. Both routes are possible. Naturally, one prefers to find "the moral equivalent of war" in constructive activities such as the science race. But it is also perfectly possible to lower the salience of conflict in one area by creating conflict in another. Thus, in this sense, we defend Laos and South Vietnam against Communist China insofar as we keep the situation in the Formosa Straits unstable.

Providing Information

Changes in the perception of the external environment can change the conclusion of means-end calculation without changing the calculator's goals or values one whit.

For example, as long as the United States did not have accurate and complete information about the number and types of Soviet missiles, we had to assume the worst and build up our forces accordingly. The acquisition of reliable intelligence now allows us to confine our program to appropriate levels. At any time the Soviets could have restrained the American arms program by releasing credible information on the size of their stockpile and on their development program. They chose instead to work a bluff, exaggerating their forces. American policy responded to facts as misperceived due to the bluff. Successful intelligence ultimately broke the bluff and permitted a modified policy. Note that in all of these changes there was no change in basic American goals or values. The only changes were in perceptions of the facts.

The provision of information—and for similar reasons the focusing of attention—is a mode of influence particularly suitable to deterring Soviet aggression. There are reasons why:

1. Information is something people accept even from a hostile source. The experiments of Hovland and others on the "sleeper effect" have shown that, while initially people accept or reject information according to their attitude to the informant, with the passage of time, the source tends to be forgotten

and the information acquires a life of its own.[3]

2. The Soviet elite are avid consumers of foreign information. Their doctrine discourages receptiveness to friendly gestures or overt verbal persuasion by the capitalist foe. It also steels them against threats. But on the other hand it requires them to take realistic account of changed circumstances and balances of forces. They pride themselves on cold realism in assessing the objective facts. This claim is valid, but only partly, because the facts the Soviet leaders attend to are so thoroughly screened. Ideology, censorship, and conformism mean that information—whether pleasant or unpalatable—is likely to be noted only if it is credible in terms of their world view.

Aside from a substantial body of theory on the conditions of credibility, social science research on persuasion by information suggests rather forcefully that facts do not speak for themselves. A fact is capable of many interpretations. Its significance is seldom unambiguously conveyed unless made explicit. A fact plus an explanation of its significance are more likely to communicate than either the fact alone or the interpretative generalization alone.

Deterrent information may fail if it does not conform to that principle. If it consists only of a warning statement or only of a particular weapons action each unlinked to the other, it may not communicate as intended.

A common instance of a military fact that does not communicate without interpretation is the first move in a planned series. A Soviet move to assume a larger role in a Southeast Asian Guerrilla area could be either a move to forestall the Chinese or a move to step up pressure against us; yet we would not know which. An American buildup of conventional NATO forces or of mobile retaliatory forces could be a first step toward a later reduction of more provocative forces, but unless unambiguously labeled, it could be interpreted as an over-all force buildup.

This is a point which cannot be overstressed since, to the actor who knows his total plan, the significance of the first moves may seem glaringly obvious. It is hard for him to avoid overestimating how much he is communicating. Redundance and more redundance is usually necessary.

Modifying Certainty

It is well to introduce a distinction between two kinds of information communicated in the course of an influence process: namely, the distinction between the substantive facts themselves and estimates of their probable occurrence. For the statistically inclined the distinction can be expressed as the difference between communicating the first moment of a distribution and communicating its second moment. The Russians deterred us from more vigorous action in Laos by somehow communicating to us that they did not want to push to the limit there. But that information was ambiguous. They had two separate decisions to make: first whether to give us the information that compromise was possible, and second what degree of certainty to provide us with on that matter. They chose, and probably skillfully, to give us the information in such a fashion that we could never be sure whether it was real or whether we were being mousetrapped.

[3]Hovland, C. I., Janis, I. L., and Kelley, H. H. *Communication and Persuasion*, New Haven, Conn.: Yale University Press, 1953.

We are blurring a further distinction here, the distinction between degree of probability and degree of certainty. The relation of these concepts is one of the profoundest and most controversial in the philosophy of science. We prefer to avoid such issues here. Both those things, in whatever way they are related, are manipulable, and apart from the content of the information.

A large part of the art of deterrence, as of influence in general is the manipulation of certainty rather than the manipulation of the substance of the facts. Certainty is often much easier to affect than net conclusions. Our net image of the Soviet regime is that it is hostile to us. Their occasional good-will maneuvers are not likely to change our net judgement, but these maneuvers do have the effect of causing some doubt as to whether our assumptions are right and thus generate confusion. They reduce American confidence in our understanding of them and leave us without a sense of easy predictability. On this matter the situation is largely symmetrical. We probably also have a wider latitude of influence on their certainties than on their net conclusions.

The literature on the psychology of decision-making under uncertainty is extensive. Learning from consistent stimuli is much faster than learning from stochastic ones. But the problem in deterrence is only partly that of teaching. It is also one of maintaining certain motivational states. It is important in planning deterrent strategy to be clear which objective is being served, teaching facts or affecting confidence. Raising certainty may help if the objective is to teach a conclusion; lowering it may help if the objective is to compel caution and indecision.

Providing a Behavioral Model to the Influencee

All the facts in the world do not tell a person how to act. He needs to be guided by the example of how some ego-ideal acts when faced with similar facts.

Oddly enough, the United States is to a considerable extent such a model for the Soviet Union and indeed for the whole world.

The Soviet Union is essentially an imitative society. All the vital ideas in the socialist world are imports from the West. Marxism is itself a radical version of popular democratic doctrines that permeated Europe in the first half of the 19th century. With one partial exception, the changes which the Russians have introduced are either also Western importations or they are failures. The one partial exception is Bolshevik party organization. The notion of the disciplined political machine which Lenin introduced was his adaption of American and European party machines and bureaucratic organization, but it was an extreme version, and unfortunately it worked. Since this 1905 idea, Bolshevism has produced no interesting innovations. Stalin transformed central planning into the key concept of Communism, but the idea of a planning board with a development plan was a completely Western notion discussed in detail by all wings of opinion in England and Germany in the 1920s. When Khrushchev defined socialism to Sukarno as "calculation, nothing but calculation," he underlined that Russian Communism has been nothing but a way of introducing a Western industrial society.

Whatever the Soviets have tried to

add that is non-Western has failed. There are three such elements, any one of which if it had succeeded would have made the "Soviet experiment" something other than perverted Westernization. The first was total control over man—Stalin's attempt at creating a society well characterized by Orwell and Milosz. But the total police state is a failure, hated by everyone in the bloc and verbally repudiated in Khrushchev's secret speech, in the "thaw," and in Polish and Yugoslav revisionism. The "new Soviet man" has not appeared.

The Soviet Union is still a totalitarian tyranny, but one thing has become clear: Totalitarianism is not a successful stable system of human organization. It is preserved with great effort against continuous resistance. It shows no prospect of becoming a new historic form of civilization capable of lasting for hundreds of years. It is a fragile system unable to get human beings to internalize its values in "1984" fashion.

The second novel and non-Western attempt of Soviet Communism was aimed at the destruction of religion. That too has failed, with religion still continuing to attract many young Russians.

The third great leap out of the Western tradition was the attempt to substitute communal living for peasant farming—the collective farms in Russia and, in an even more extreme form, the communes in China. This has been the greatest failure of all. To the extent that collectivism has been pushed, the farm problem has been made insoluble.

While the few original Soviet ideas have been unsuccessful, Communism in Russia has been effective as a way of rapid Westernizing. The goal is admittedly to overtake the U.S. Admiration for American achievements has always permeated the Soviet elite. And it has been Western ideas, be they jazz or abstract art, or input-output analysis, or survey research, which have excited Russian intellectuals.

Even in the military field, Russian strategic thinking has, to a substantial degree, followed American strategic thinking, generally with a 1- or 2-year time lag. The Americans developed the doctrine of deterrence. The Russians learned it. We recognized the importance of hardening. The Russians are beginning to see it. We developed a mobile Polaris system. The Russians are moving toward it.

Providing the Russians with ourselves as a model is one more way in which we influence Soviet behavior. Whatever major commitments we make are likely to be partial models for the Russians. It would be nonsense to say that everything we do will be copied. The imitation is partial and selective. But anything we do in a major and successful way creates a pressure within the Soviet Union to try the same.

Changing the Objective Environment

We have already noted how dependent any set of calculations is on the perceptions of the real world which go into it. Changing the facts is obviously a way to change perceptions of them. Making a deterrent invulnerable, adding strength at any level, or changing force structures are obvious ways of affecting the opponent's calculations.

Changing the Influencee's Resources

One kind of change in the objective environment needs special treatment.

That is the denial to the opponent of resources to carry out undesirable actions. The American economy is sufficiently larger than the Soviet economy so that an arms race in one area may serve to deny to the Soviets the resources they need in another. It is hard for the Soviets to sustain a full-scale moon program, conventional forces, missile hardening and mobility, and passive defense. Pushing our opponents into preferred ones of these programs is a realistic measure against their adopting others.

Summary

While the practice of deterrence has been relatively sophisticated, the literature about it has tended to look at it in very oversimplified ways. Among the many mechanisms involved in influence, it has tended to look at but one at a time. Indeed, the writings about deterrence by psychologists have tended to look at only one mode of influence, namely, generating trust, while the writings of some strategic writers have considered only the influence of threats. Unfortunately, it is often true that what has a desired action in one mode of influence is damaging in another. That is further complicated by considerations of timing.

It is necessary to distinguish short-run and long-run results of each mechanism and to consider feedback. Fear today may be a condition of trust tomorrow. A model may be copied only after a time lag.

So whenever we consider a proposed deterrent action, we should test it against the gamut of ways in which it may operate:

1. What does it do to the development of the adversary's trust in us and in our intentions?
2. What does it do in causing them to fear undesired courses of action, and is that fear so managed as to maximize its constructive consequences?
3. To what topics does it shift whose attention and interest and with what action effects?
4. What added information does it provide to the adversary, and how will that information be used in his calculations?
5. How does it affect his confidence in his own estimates of the situation?
6. What effect will our action have by way of example, if and to the extent that we are taken as a model by the adversary?
7. In what way does the action change the environment; and will the adversary, in taking account of those changes, act in ways we like?
8. Does the action deny to the adversary any resources for acting in undesired ways?

14

CHADWICK F. ALGER

Non-resolution[1] Consequences of the United Nations and Their Effect on International Conflict[2]

An analysis of the informal functions of the United Nations. The author proposes that participation in the United Nations reduces in various ways the likelihood that a state will become involved in war. Derivations from the sociological theory of conflict are employed extensively in the analysis. Much of the information on the experience of delegates to the United Nations is derived from an extensive series of interviews and observations made by the author during a number of visits to United Nations headquarters.

Introduction

Secretary-General Hammarskjold, on a number of occasions, admonished us to broaden our scope of inquiry when assessing the influence of the United Nations on international relations. For example, in the introduction to his Fourteenth Annual Report to the General Assembly in August, 1959, he declared that there is a tendency to overestimate the significance of votes on General Assembly resolutions in comparison to other consequences of Assembly meetings:

> . . . whatever legal standing the Charter may provide for the results of the votes, the significance of these results requires further analysis before a political evaluation is possible. This observation applies to the composition of majorities and minorities as well

A slightly abridged version of an article by the same name in the *Journal of Conflict Resolution,* **5,** 128–145, 1961. Reprinted by permission of the author and that journal. The author is Professor of Political Science at Northwestern University.

[1]Resolution here refers to resolutions passed by United Nations bodies; it is not used in the sense of conflict resolution.

[2]This paper is based on field work at the United Nations in 1958 and 1959 which was supported by funds from the Carnegie Corporation in New York. Helpful criticism of an earlier draft was received from Harold Guetzkow and James A. Robinson of Northwestern University, William A. Scott of the University of Colorado, Keith S. Petersen of the University of Arkansas, and several United Nations diplomats who will remain anonymous.

as to the substance of the resolutions. These resolutions often reflect only part of what has, in fact, emerged from the deliberations and what, therefore, is likely to remain as an active element in future developments [9, p. 10].

It is the purpose of this article to discuss some potential non-resolution consequences of the United Nations—in particular, the General Assembly. It is also a goal of this article to show how these non-resolution consequences may significantly affect international conflict.

Some Non-Resolution Consequences of the Assembly

Six non-resolution consequences of the General Assembly have been selected for discussion here. They will be presented in the following order: (1) The impact of Assembly experience on participating national civil servants and nationals from other occupations; (2) The development of personal friendships among delegates across national lines; (3) The accentuation by the specialized committees of expert in contrast to purely political factors; (4) The formation of cooperating groups of nations that do not conform to normal political alignments; (5) The extension of the active interest of participating nations to additional geographic areas and to a broader range of international problems; (6) The new information and new sources of information that become available to participants. These factors affect the international system outside the General Assembly and also affect subsequent international relations within the General Assembly, a part of the system.

1. Impact of Assembly Experience on Delegates

The additional personnel that come to the United Nations for the General Assembly come from other overseas posts, foreign offices, other government departments, parliaments, and private life. For three months they are separated from their normal environment and have what is for many a quite intensive experience that places them in an extraordinarily different communications network. For some this experience is repeated for several years in succession. From posts in which most viewpoints on international relations that are encountered are from the perspective of one nation, they come to a community where they are constantly subjected to many perspectives. In addition, they are in the company of many people, members of the secretariat and others, who look at the system as a whole rather than from the perspective of one nation.

The parliamentary framework of the General Assembly provides an atmosphere that is quite different from that to which most of the delegates are accustomed, since most of them are governmental bureaucrats. For these bureaucrats to become delegates requires that they move away from a rather stationary existence behind a desk that provides, if not isolation, considerable restraints on the access to them by persons not in their own bureaucracy. But in the Assembly, where they become mobile delegates operating most of each day away from a protective bureaucratic shell, they are directly accessible to other delegates. As has already been indicated, the lobbyist, journalist, and scholar can approach them directly as they pass from meeting hall to lounge, to dining room, and back to meeting hall in the relatively open society of the General Assembly. Although the extent of this non-delegate contact may not be great for some delegates, there is little doubt that the sources of intellectual stimulation of most delegates greatly extends that provided by the bureaucrat's incoming box and appointment calendar.

It may also be significant that delegates who participate in the General Assembly return to their normal posts with first-hand knowledge of United Nations procedures. They will be more competent to use these procedures intelligently. In the General Assembly, parliamentary diplomacy has developed into a phenomenon quite different from traditional bilateral diplomacy and is more complex than it was in the smaller League of Nations. Through participation in the General Assembly many national officials are learning parliamentary diplomacy through personal experience. This suggests the hypothesis that those who have mastered this particular kind of procedure for policy implementation are more likely to use it in the future than those who find such procedures unknown, unintelligible, and highly unpredictable.[3] This would include not only temporary delegates but permanent mission officials as well, most of whom move on to other diplomatic posts after a few years' service at the United Nations.

2. Friendships Across National Boundaries

The informality of social relations among the delegates impresses the observer who watches them in the corridors, lounges, restaurants, and meeting rooms of the United Nations. This informality may partially be attributed to the large number of persons involved. As hundreds of delegates surge into the Delegates' Lounge, the dining room, and the cafeteria following committee sessions, the social restraints associated with traditional diplomatic interchange give way to more informal patterns of behavior. Events such as the concert (followed by dancing and dinner) given by the Secretary-General and the President of the General Assembly in the 1958 session have an atmosphere of informality unexpected for such occasions. The formal attire of the perhaps two thousand persons in attendance was not matched by their informal conduct as they stood in line for Scotch and champagne, attempted to dance on the crowded dance floor, queued up for the buffet dinner, and then searched for a table at which to eat—some resigning themselves to standing up. And as the evening drew to a close there was another line to be faced as delegates obtained their coats from the check room.

In addition to the role of numbers, social interaction among delegates is encouraged by the physical environment offered by the United Nations Headquarters buildings. When one is enmeshed in this environment in the midst of the delegates he is tempted to rank the architect of the United Nations buildings along with the writers of the Charter in importance. The intensity of interaction of members of the General Assembly is heightened by the proximity of all of the arenas of delegate activity while they are on the United Nations premises. The General Assembly Hall, committee rooms, dining room, and lounge are all close to each other. A relatively few hallways connect the main centers of activity and dele-

[3]In an attempt to assess the impact of Assembly experiences on delegates, the writer interviewed delegates to the Fourteenth General Assembly who had not served before. Delegates from thirty countries were interviewed both before and near the end of the Assembly. This data is now being analyzed. In another United Nations field study for Northwestern's International Relations Program, Gary Best studied the difference between diplomacy conducted at the site of an international organization and diplomacy in a national capital. Permanent Mission personnel from all member nations were interviewed in this study (2).

gates pass and re-pass each other frequently as they go about their tasks. One inhabitant of this system who desires to see another member on a particular day need not make a formal appointment nor look for him very energetically, for he will encounter him a number of times during the day.

Social interaction among the delegates is also encouraged by delegation receptions, with each delegation holding at least one and usually two receptions during the Assembly session. The uniformed attendant, calling out the names of the guests as they arrive, is reminiscent of the diplomatic heritage of the Assembly. Each national delegation to the Assembly must perform the representational functions of a foreign embassy as well as play parliamentary aspects of its role. It is perhaps diplomatic tradition that determines the nature of other social functions such as concerts in the General Assembly Hall, and occasional plays and other cultural events. All of these occasions add to the wide variety of situations in which members of the General Assembly encounter each other.

The sustained interaction of the delegates as well as the variety of the occasions on which they confront each other provides opportunities for the development of friendships across national boundaries that surpass those of normal diplomatic intercourse. As a result, delegates have networks of personal friends on other delegations. These networks provide opportunities for inter-nation communication that are more flexible than formal channels. The maintenance of these friendships places certain obligations on delegates, such as alerting friends to changes in policy or gradually adjusting them to change. Two United Nations delegates have themselves described the role of personal friendships:

> Seldom is any vote changed by personal relations because persons, unless very senior, have little influence over national policies. It is possible however to foster a better understanding and appreciation of national positions as a result of social contacts and sometimes to affect subsequent formal exchanges and in the long run voting patterns. . . . In many eyes the personal relationships established at the United Nations have as much, if not greater, importance than the formal decisions which are reached [8, pp. 39 and 47].

3. Participation of Experts

One of the factors that contributes to the intensity of personal friendships is the camaraderie that develops among groups of delegates who are experts in the same fields. Since most delegates spend their time on one committee that is handling one kind of issue, it is advantageous to nations to assign delegates to these committees who are experts in the subject matter being discussed. It is also the case that delegates assigned to these committees without previous claim of expert knowledge become experts, at least in the context of their own delegations, on the matters being considered. In addition to frequent similarities of professional training, the experts on a particular committee spend long hours together in their committee, giving them a common fund of knowledge and shared experience. For those who return to the same committee for several years common bonds are intensified. These bonds facilitate the work of the committees and at times become so pronounced as to create rivalry between committees.

Thus, it is hypothesized that the specialized committees not only create a need for experts in the conduct of assembly business but also serve as a training ground for additional experts and reinforce the dedication of experts to the norms of their profession. A corollary of this hypothesis is that delegation positions in the Assembly and recommendations to home governments are affected by the professional norms of participating experts in international law, human rights, international economics, and so on.

4. Shifting Majorities

One important aspect of the perspective of this analysis is that it probes below the level of nation behavior in international organizations to the individual level. It has been suggested that it makes a difference who the individuals that participate are and that the effects of participation upon these individuals are important. Furthermore, it is important in the General Assembly that the simultaneous consideration of a number of issues requires nations to play a number of roles simultaneously. Coordination of the seven committee voices of a national delegation is not always easy, particularly since different issues often require cooperation with a different set of allies. It is contended that the variety of voting alignments across committees in the General Assembly introduces new elements into diplomacy within the United Nations and eventually outside as well.

In the political committees, the United States and the Soviet Union are the main protagonists, with their political allies aligning on the appropriate side and primarily some Afro-Asian nations playing a mediating role. NATO, the Warsaw Pact, SEATO, the Central Treaty Organization, OAS, and a scattering of bilateral treaties mirror basic alignments on key political questions. But in the economic committee, it is the haves against the have-nots, with Latin Americans joining the Afro-Asians in a drive for an increase in multilateral economic programs. Often the Soviet Union votes with this group as does the Netherlands and Norway of the NATO bloc. On the social and humanitarian committee, Afro-Asian Moslems and European and Latin American Catholics cooperate on questions relating to birth control. On the trusteeship and non-self-governing territories committee the colonial nations and the newly independent countries are the main protagonists. On a matter before the legal committee related to ocean shipping, the maritime nations are lined up against non-maritime members. Finally, on the budgetary committee the lines of conflict are sometimes drawn with virtually all member nations on one side and the Secretariat on the other, as the committee assumes the typical parliamentary attitude toward the expenditures of executive officials.

Thus as one moves from committee to committee and issue to issue, a variety of alliances is encountered. It is contended that the General Assembly, because of its varied agenda, provides opportunity for and stimulus for cooperative effort that often runs in opposition to political alignments based on organizations other than the United Nations. This cooperative effort opens up new lines of communications. It requires joint effort not only in the public sessions of committees but also in small working parties who negotiate final wordings of resolutions, and in bilateral conversations, at the United Nations and perhaps also in national capitals. These lines of communication can then be used for other purposes. These alignments and new communications routes become elements in subsequent diplomacy in the United Nations and in diplomacy conducted outside the United Nations.

5. Expansion of Nation Concern

The scope of the agenda of the General Assembly also has the effect of expanding the area of concern of participant nations. Participation in deliberations on an average of over seventy agenda items causes each nation to extend, in terms of both geography and subject matter, the range of items with which its diplomacy is directly involved. Most countries vote on almost all of these items and this requires that most of them take positions on matters that they would not have had to take stands on otherwise. It also requires public assertion of positions which might otherwise have been taken in private. Furthermore, private positions must usually be changed—if not in principle at least in emphasis and perhaps in explanation of motives—before they are made public.

It is hypothesized that this expansion of nation concern, along with the extension of the requirements for public declaration of policy, affects policy positions already held. When a nation is required to play a role in an agenda of items that covers the world, it assumes obligations that modify roles played in narrower arenas. For example, the extended participation in world affairs that the United Nations requires of the newly independent nations may be very important. After decades of foreign rule, in the first years of independence nations are inclined to be self-centered, to self-consciously assert their independence in relations with other nations and to assume little responsiblity for the state of the international system as a whole. The addition of so many independent units to the international system which is now taking place could heighten instability. The fact that United Nations participation prevents the isolation of these nations and extends their responsibilities may be diminishing the instabilities that they create in international affairs.

6. Availability of New Information

The public debates in the General Assembly and private discussions as well provide member nations with a large volume of information on international affairs. For at least some of the smaller nations, the volume of reports sent home from their United Nations mission is greater than that from any other foreign post. Statements by participants on their nation's policy and its underlying rationale comprise a substantial portion of the voluminous documentation of the United Nations. In the "general debate" that opens the annual sessions of the General Assembly, virtually every nation of the world declares its position on what it considers to be the most important international questions. In the course of committee debate most nations participate in the "general debates" on each of the some seventy items on the agenda. Following each vote in the committees a number of nations feel the need to explain their votes. Then, when each item comes to the plenary session, nations that feel the most strongly about it may again take the opportunity to explain their positions.

In addition, there are, of course, constant explanations of positions in discussion by delegates outside the committee and plenary sessions. During the variety of occasions for delegate interaction there is considerable opportunity for detailed explanation of national positions and reasons for maintaining them. This not only includes occasions when delegates can take the initiative in making the policy of their government clear, but also occasions in which delegates can acquire information. In such cases the United Nations environment may be quite important. Much opportunity is offered for a delegate himself, or through a friendly delegate, to get information without betraying the significance of the discussion of the matter. For this reason it is hypothesized that much information is available at the United Nations with virtually no cost. Information may be obtained without revealing explicit intentions or interests to the degree that this is required to cross the more restrictive barriers of diplomacy in a national capital. A diplomat from a European country who has been at the United Nations for several years told the writer: "On the whole, this is probably the best place in the world to pick up information on other governments."

In addition, the Secretariat and special committees and visiting missions of the General Assembly collect and distribute reports on a great number of international problems. These reports, along with records of Assembly debates and other documents, provide voluminous documentation that covers virtually all international problems. To an extent never the case heretofore, a common body of documentation available to all defines the nature of major problems, supplies extensive documentation on positions of conflicting parties, and furnishes detailed background information. This documentation is, of course, more important to some nations than it is to others. For smaller nations and nations not directly involved in some issues, United Nations information sources may provide virtually all of the data on which national positions are based. This suggests the hypothesis that the growth in dependence on documentation shared by all tends to give nations a more similar view of the world.

Non-Resolution Consequences of the General Assembly and International Conflict

Are these non-resolution consequences of the General Assembly intriguing but inconsequential by-products of international relations in this community? Or do they have significance for important problems in international relations? An attempt will now be made to demonstrate that non-resolution consequences of the kind just discussed are potentially significant for what is with considerable unanimity cited as the most important problem in international relations and also as *the* problem of our age: international conflict. The primary purpose for this exploratory exposition is to show that research on non-resolution consequences is not only justified but urgently needed. In decisions so crucial as those involved in the creation of and participation in international organizations, it is not prudent for men to know only vaguely the consequences of their acts when more precise knowledge is obtainable.

To ask the relationship between the non-resolution consequences of the General Assembly and international conflict is to ask a question that international organization scholars have not attempted to answer, except by occasional impressionistic and anecdotal accounts. This does not mean, however, that the scholar who attempts to answer this question must start from scratch. There is knowledge in the social sciences—in the literature on organizations, communications, and conflict, for example—which is useful. Possibly because the study of international organizations has become primarily the domain of political scientists, we are inclined to look at these organizations only as particular kinds of political institutions. But human behavior in international organizations is also a special case, for example, of organizational behavior, communication, and social conflict. Knowledge from these areas of social science can be usefully applied in the study of international organizations along with knowledge gained from the traditional foci of the political scientist. In the exploration of the potential relationship between the non-resolution consequences of the General Assembly and international conflict that follows, knowledge is drawn from outside the international relations area whenever possible.

The ensuing discussion indicates five kinds of ways in which the non-resolution consequences already described may have an effect on international conflict. (1) Change in the traditional patterns of inter-nation communication may affect conflict. Particularly relevant here are the changes in these patterns that personal friendships, extended national interest, and the effects of Assembly experience on delegates bring. (2) There may be a relationship between conflict and new kinds of information that the Assembly makes available. It is asserted that relationship occurs because of the greater predictability of the behavior of other nations that this information allows. (3) The third and fourth examples discuss how Assembly participation places both the nation and the individual in a more varied set of roles than before that may bind each to a larger community. In the case of the nation, the new kinds of alignments that Assembly activity brings and extended national interest are important. (4) In the case of individuals cross-pressures are encouraged by the involvement of professional norms and personal friendships. (5) Finally, the possibility is discussed that conflict in the Assembly may itself be a non-resolution consequence that substitutes for conflict elsewhere.

1. The Channeling of Information

When relations among nations are looked at as a communications system, sharp differences are discerned between the part of this system that is within an organization such as the General Assembly and that which is conducted through more traditional channels. Bilateral communications outside an international organization are conducted through the elaborate and, for the most part, extremely formal mechanisms of diplomacy. The restraints that diplomatic practices have placed on inter-nation communication have helped not only to create conditions in which there are significant areas of national ignorance about the policies and intentions of other nations, but the cost of obtaining information to eliminate ignorance has often been high. Formal requests for information may betray ignorance, reveal intentions, or expose areas of concern. These costs must be weighed against the value of the information—if it is even available. Within the General Assembly, however, a portion of the restraints on inter-nation communication are eliminated. The sustained social interaction in a variety of kinds of situations, in the context of a common institution, stimulated by such elements as personal friendships and camaraderie of experts, breaks down these restraints.

Do the new kinds of communications opportunities that the General Assembly permits have any relationship to international conflict? James March and Herbert Simon, in their recent volume summarizing the literature on organizational behavior, suggest that there is a body of knowledge that will give some insight on this question. Studies of organizations have indicated that "the greater the channeling of information-processing, the greater the differentiation of perceptions within the organization" (12, p. 128). By channeling of information they mean limiting the number of organization members to whom any given bit of information is transmitted. Related to the proposition on the channeling of information is another which indicates its relevance to our discussion. It states that differences in the perception of reality are one of the major factors contributing to intergroup conflict (12, p. 121).

The converse of the March and Simon propositions offer stimulating hypotheses when applied to the General Assembly. It is hypothesized that the community of diplomats in New York, largely because of their participation in the General Assembly, is an element in the international communications system where the circulation of information is more diffuse and the patterns of its distribution more complex than in the remainder of the system. Therefore it is further hypothesized that the General Assembly tends to give officials who participate in it a more similar perception of reality than they have before they participate. The information that these persons supply to the remainder of the international system when they report home and when they move on to other posts tends to give all member nations a more similar perception of reality. Thus, as a network of communications routes that supplement and sometimes by-pass traditional diplomatic patterns of communication, the General Assembly tends to lessen the intensity of conflict by causing member nations to have more similar perceptions of the world.

2. Predictability

As a consequence of the opportunities that the General Assembly provides for the relaxation of the communications restraints of traditional diplomacy and because of the new information available in the Assembly, it is hypothesized that participating nations know more about the capabilities and intentions of other participating nations than they would without this institution. In other words, it is contended that an organization such as the General Assembly makes the world more predictable for its members. Is there a relationship between predictability and conflict? Robin M. Williams, Jr., in a work on conflict among ethnic, religious, and racial groups in the United States, suggests that "disruption of stable expectations of interpersonal conduct tends to be productive of intergroup conflict" (14, p. 57). Karl Deutsch has asserted the importance of predictability in the development of an international community as follows: "Insofar as members of a stable political community must be able to expect more or less dependable interlocking, interchanging, or at least compatible behavior from each other, they must be able, at least to that extent, to predict one another's actions" (6, p. 53).

The General Assembly may not only make the world more predictable to its members as a result of opening new routes for communication and creating an environment in which nations must give extensive explanations of their policies. This extensive requirement that nations explain policies publicly may tend to make these policies more stable. Conformity with predetermined plans should be greater after these plans have been revealed publicly before most nations of the world than when dissemination has been more restricted. This would seem to be particularly true if these plans have become the basis for multilateral action within the United Nations. The reader may have noted that this is the reverse of a proposition often found in international organization literature which asserts that public debate in bodies such as the General Assembly may intensify conflict by making positions more rigid and thereby eliminating the openness of conflicting parties to compromise. But the importance of predictability to conflict suggests that public commitment may not always be a deterrent to conflict reduction. It would be valuable to know more about the conditions under which each of these seemingly contrary propositions holds true.

3. Overlapping Conflict Systems

This discussion has emphasized ways in which General Assembly processes may tend to diminish the intensity of some international conflicts. It is true, of course, that at times participation intensifies conflict between parties. In some cases, however, there may be potential beneficial effects for the stability of the system as a whole when conflict between traditional allies is intensified as a result of their being required to take a public stand on an issue on which they disagree; this may tend to relax, to some degree, tension between traditional foes who might then find themselves on the same side of an issue. For example, debate on colonial problems sometimes intensifies conflict between NATO allies when some members of NATO find themselves unable to support their allies on colonial issues. This conflict is accompanied by cooperative effort by some NATO members with nations who oppose them on other issues.

The literature on conflict often refers to the salutary effect of overlapping conflicts that in a sense tend to cancel each other out. Edward A. Ross, a sociologist writing several decades ago, described this process:

> Every species of social conflict interferes with every other species in society . . . save only when lines of cleavage coincide; in which case they reinforce one another. . . . A society, therefore, which is ridden by a dozen oppositions along lines running in every direction may actually be in less danger of being torn with violence or falling to pieces than one split just along one line. For each cleavage contributes to narrow the cross clefts, so that one might say that *society is sewn together* by its inner conflicts [13, p. 164–5, author's emphasis].

A mechanism whereby a "society is sewn together" by its conflicts is that of multiple group affiliations of its members which add an element of interdependence to the relations of conflicting groups. The committees of the General Assembly may be looked upon as multiple group affiliations required of the national delegations of the Assembly. Political allies find themselves at cross-purposes in economic and trusteeship committees and political enemies may at times be surprised to discover that they are allies on other issues. In the 1958 Assembly, for example, a resolution was passed urging the establishment of an international capital development fund in which the alignment was basically most NATO nations and a few more developed members of the British Commonwealth against the rest of the world. This was a significant departure from the usual alignment of the Latin American nations and others with the United States on political issues.

Multiple group affiliations bring cross-pressures that tend to restrain the pursuit of the goals of any one affiliation. It has been noted, for example, that workers in so-called "isolated" industries such as miners, sailors, fishermen, lumbermen, and sheep-tenders tend to back political extremists. This is believed to be caused by the fact that members of these groups do not have the multiple affiliations that integrate other members of society into the broader community (11, pp. 95–6). Does the broader scope of participation that the General Assembly requires of nations serve to integrate them into a wider community and thereby modify extremist tendencies of nations formerly more isolated?

As an example we might ask whether there is any indication that the Soviet Union is to some extent integrated into the United Nations community by its multiple committee participation. Thomas Hovet, in a study of bloc voting in the General Assembly, has compiled figures that are useful. In roll call votes that Hovet classifies "collective measures, regulation of armaments, etc.," the Soviets have voted with the majority only 18.4 per cent of the time. On resolutions devoted to human rights and self-determination, however, they have voted with the majority on 50 per cent and 45 per cent of the roll call votes respectively. As a result of these percentages, and others less high, the Soviets have an over-all concurrence with majorities of 39.1 per cent (10, p. 68–70). Although the Soviet Union and its allies are, to a considerable degree, isolated from the remainder of the United Nations community, we hypothesize that the overlapping system of conflicts tends to integrate them into this community. Sharing voting victories on some items makes the Assembly seem less like an institution devised solely for the frustration of Soviet ambitions and makes success in additional areas seem more feasible and worth striving for through parliamentary means. And communication is easier with delegates who, on occasion, are on your side than with delegates who constantly oppose you.

4. Individual Personalities and Conflict

As indicated earlier, study of nation participation in international organizations has rarely probed below the nation as a unit of analysis. Simultaneous with the widely held belief that individuals can change the ultimate fate of nations very little, there is the assumption that decisions of importance are made in foreign offices—delegates in international organizations being merely agents for the implementation of these decisions. United Nations delegates do, nonetheless, have a role in shaping policies that they advocate for their governments. In some cases delegates operate under general instructions with the freedom to design specific policies within this framework. However, whether the delegate's instructions be general or specific, the competence of delegates in pursuing national objectives in international bodies determines the kinds of choices that foreign office officials will have available in forming future policy. Furthermore, the delegate in an international organization selects and arranges information that is sent to the foreign office and often makes policy recommendations. The information and recommendations supplied by delegates may play a prominent role in the development of instructions that are sent back to the delegate.

Assuming that the individual delegate does have a role in the development of his nation's policies makes the effect of the General Assembly environment on delegates of some interest. Does the fact that the General Assembly to some degree consists of small international communities of experts and that personal friendships across national boundaries are encouraged have effects that are related to the role of the Assembly in international conflict? The literature on social conflict tells us that the introduction of personal factors in social relations tempers conflict. Lewis Coser, for example, suggests that the "elimination of the personal element tends to make conflict sharper, in the absence of modifying elements which personal factors would normally introduce" (5, p. 118). This is a special case of the so-called cross-pressure hypothesis that has found its way into political studies in surveys of voting behavior (1, p. 283; 3, p. 183). Persons who have opposing forces acting on them that engender internal conflict and indecision in voting situations have been found to be less strongly committed politically. It is not our suggestion, of course, that the cross-pressures brought to bear on General Assembly delegates will necessarily cause them to change votes or do about-faces on policy choices. The development and maintenance of personal friendships and the norms of fellow-experts may, however, alter the way in which delegates perceive situations, determine the types of contacts and sources of information available to them, and eventually affect the picture of the situation that they relay home. It is hypothesized that the development of personal friendships tends to temper the intensity of conflict which delegates feel exists between their nation and nations with whose delegates they develop friendships. Devotion by delegates to the norms of their fellow-experts on Assembly committees may produce the same effect. Those who bemoan the existence of intercommittee rivalry should not overlook the fact that it is likely caused by inter-nation cooperation!

5. General Assembly Conflict as a Substitute

There is a tendency to consider all conflict as negative in its consequences. Such a perspective may prevent the perception of transformations in conflicts that are taking place. It has already been indicated that conflicts among members of a subsystem may make the over-all system more stable if they tend to criss-cross a bipolar cleavage that is threatening stability. It is also possible that conflict in one form may serve as a substitute for a more violent variety.

Lewis Coser's book, *The Functions of Social Conflict*, offers a stimulating analysis of the potential positive values of conflict. In discussing the valuable information which conflict allows the antagonists to obtain about each other, Coser asserts:

> Conflict consists in a test of power between antagonistic parties. Accommodation between them is possible only if each is aware of the relative strength of both parties. However, paradoxical as it may seem, such knowledge can most frequently be attained only through conflict, since other mechanisms for testing the respective strength of antagonists seem to be unavailable [5, p. 137].

Earlier Coser tells us that "if alternative means are not available or are believed to be unavailable, the only way to a reappraisal of the contending parties' power is to use the 'weapon of last resort'" (5, p. 136). Does the General Assembly at times provide a suitable alternative means for appraisal of relative strength that may make the resort to "weapons of last resort" unnecessary? It may be seen that the process here is somewhat akin to that earlier described wherein the Assembly contributes to predictability by providing more reliable information on the capabilities and intentions of opponents in conflict. But an element is added; in this instance we ask whether Assembly action might provide a substitute for other kinds of action.

Inis Claude seems to suggest that the General Assembly and the Trusteeship Council of the United Nations may be serving as arenas of final conflict over colonial questions. He reports that the most significant thing about the role of the United Nations in colonial affairs is not that it "has become the registrar of the triumphant surge of dynamic anticolonialism, but rather that it has become the scene of conflict, the prize ring within which the battle over the future of colonialism has been fought" (4, p. 361). In some quarters, United Nations efforts in colonial questions are judged a failure because all members are not speaking with one voice in the solution of these problems. But this conflict might be enacted in a more violent way were United Nations councils not available as a battleground. Are battles of parliamentary diplomacy substitutes for more violent battles elsewhere? It is imperative that we know much more than we do about instances in which this is the case. It is not necessarily true that an Assembly that does not reach agreements on major conflicts has been a total loss. It is crucial that we learn under what kinds of conditions conflict is amenable to transformation from violent conflict to a conflict of parliamentary diplomacy.

Conclusion

Some non-resolution consequences of the General Assembly have been discussed with the purpose of providing direction for research that will give more complete understanding of the effect of the United Nations and other international organizations on relations among nations. It has been asserted that perceptivity to such effects may be intensified by looking at these organizations in the context of the entire international system rather than looking at them as complete systems in and of themselves. It has also been suggested that one is more perceptive to the non-resolution consequences of the General Assembly if he recognizes the fact that nations may not be the only units whose Assembly participation merits analysis. It may be significant that each nation is playing a role in seven committees simultaneously. And aspects of the behavior of individual delegates may merit consideration.

In assessing the relationship between the non-resolution consequences of the Assembly and international conflict, literature outside political science and outside international relations has been cited. This was done to show the relevance of bodies of knowledge from other areas of human behavior to the study of international organizations. The intellectual barriers that surround academic departments have cut off this study from resources outside its home base—political science. Indeed, it is only recently that the main stream of political science has begun to affect the study of international organizations. If the great gain of the past decade has been a more general recognition that there is politics in international organizations, perhaps the advance of the coming years will be the acknowledgment that people are to be found there as well.

There seem to be significant patterns of interaction in the United Nations about which we as yet know very little. These patterns were not devised by those who built the organization at San Francisco, and the writer believes that in many cases they have not been implementations of conscious planning. Often they have been the products, it would seem, of widely scattered individual decisions. They have been born out of the daily agony of individual practitioners trying to stave off cataclysm by accomplishing the seemingly impossible. Often the practitioners are so busy with their individual acts that they do not see the over-all patterns. And sometimes when they do see them they do not have time to contemplate their significance. It is up to the social scientist, building on the insights that the practitioner can give, to discern their significance in terms of their effects on international relations and the relationship of these effects to the long-range goals of international organizations.

Up to the present time, the underlying patterns have been neglected because scholars and practitioners have tended to concentrate on the explicit organizational mechanisms for conflict resolution. Changes in the basic interaction process that international organizations may effect have been overlooked. It remains to be seen whether changes have been effected that are measurable, but we may be stumbling into unplanned consequences of organizational building that equal in importance those that are planned. Ernst Haas has concluded, as a result of his study of the European Coal and Steel Community, that international "institutions are crucial causative links in the chain of integration" (7, p. 450). They not only handle their explicitly assigned tasks but become the causes of other new factors that affect relations among their members. Haas reports that "our European lesson drives home the potential role of institutional forces in rechanneling and realigning previous group loyalties and expectations" (7, p. 457).

Furthermore, international organizations may spur integration in a given system through making the relationships between units in the system more complicated. This may occur by the initiation of new kinds of cooperative efforts among nations that run contrary to normal political alignments, the involvement of some nations in problems that they would have ignored were they not required to act in the organization, the establishment of new channels of cooperation for governmental experts, and the establishment of new and more intense friendships among officials across national boundaries.

The creation of international organizations may thus have a two-level effect: one effect being the organization's success at attaining goals for which it is established and the other being basic changes in the international system in which it is established. A closer study of the latter may be a requisite for making international organizations more effective in the achievement of explicit goals. For example, advocates of revision of the United Nations Charter might well look at their proposals not only as revisions of Charter mechanisms but also as revisions of basic patterns of internation relations. Those who voice a desire for more orderly and neatly organized General Assembly processes might also give careful consideration to the potential effects of their proposals. What would be the effects of cutting the size of the General Assembly Committees? What would be the impact of reducing the number of items on the agenda? On the other hand, more sophisticated knowledge about the non-resolution consequences of the Assembly might show opportunities for changes in procedures that could have effects as significant as Charter revision but that require neither Charter revision nor seem threatening to those sensitive to inroads on national sovereignty.

In the introduction to his Fourteenth Annual Report to the General Assembly, Secretary Hammarskjold made two recommendations for changed procedures. He asked for regular meetings of the Security Council in executive session and for the development of international economic policies in short special meetings at the ministerial level, within or under the aegis of the Economic and Social Council. How prepared are international organization scholars to predict the consequences of such innovations? Such predictions cannot be made from the data ordinarily used for international organization research: verbatim records of meetings, resolutions, handouts to the press, and journalistic accounts. These documents are only partial reflections of the consequences of the operation of political institutions. If he is to contribute anything to questions such as these beyond what the insightful practitioner and journalist can offer, the political scientist must collect other types of data and include it in his analysis. Scholars of international organizations have hardly begun the work which could enable them to provide knowledge beyond that which practitioners and journalists can supply. Under the existing documentary material above the surface lies an iceberg of unknown dimensions. Here may be unanticipated consequences of international organizational building which could make these organizations self-destructive. On the other hand, there may be elements which could be utilized to advantage.

References

1. Berelson, Bernard R., Paul Lazarsfeld, and William N. McPhee, *Voting*. Chicago: University of Chicago Press, 1954.
2. Best, Gary. "Diplomacy in the United Nations." Doctoral thesis, Northwestern University, 1960.
3. Campbell, Angus, Gerald Gurin, and Warren E. Miller, *The Voter Decides*. Evanston, Ill.: Row, Peterson and Co., 1954.
4. Claude, Inis L., Jr., *Swords into Plowshares*. New York: Random House, 1956.
5. Coser, Lewis, *The Functions of Social Conflict*. Glencoe, Ill.: The Free Press, 1956.
6. Deutsch, Karl, *Political Community at the International Level*. Doubleday Short Studies in Political Science, No. 1, Garden City, N.Y.: Doubleday, 1954.
7. Haas, Ernst, "The Challenge of Regionalism," *International Organization, 12*, 440–58, 1958.
8. Hadwen, John, and Johan Kaufmann, *How United Nations Decisions are Made*. New York, 1958. (Mimeographed document prepared by two United Nations delegates.) Rev. published, Leyden, Netherlands: A. W. Sijthoff, 1960.
9. Hammarskjold, Dag. "Introduction to Fourteenth Annual Report to the General Assembly on the Work of the Organization from June 16, 1958, to June 15, 1959," *United Nations Review*, **6**, 8–18, 1959.
10. Hovet, Thomas, Jr., *Bloc Politics in the United Nations*. Cambridge, Mass.: Center for International Studies, Massachusetts Institute of Technology, 1958.

11. Lipset, Seymour Martin, "Some Social Requisites of Democracy: Economic Development and Political Legitimacy," *American Political Science Review*, **53,** 69-105, 1959.

12. March, James, and Herbert Simon, with Harold Guetzkow, *Organizations*. New York: John Wiley and Sons, Inc., 1958.

13. Ross, Edward Alsworth, *The Principles of Sociology*. New York: Century Co., 1920.

14. Williams, Robin, *The Reduction of Intergroup Tensions*. New York: Social Science Research Council, 1947.

15

CHARLES E. OSGOOD

Calculated De-escalation as a Strategy

A proposal for a strategy for resolving international conflicts under conditions that do not lend themselves to the negotiated settlement of issues. This strategy involves unilateral tension-reducing activity on the part of one of the participants.

Calculated De-Escalation as a Strategy

About seven years ago, at the height of tensions in the nuclear confrontation between the United States and the Soviet Union, several proposals for the control and gradual reduction of tensions in international relations appeared. One of these was a policy paper of mine bearing the improbable title, *Graduated and Reciprocated Initiatives in Tension-reduction.* I soon discovered that no one, including myself, could remember the title, even though it stated the essence of the policy proposal clearly and succinctly. Later I discovered that the initials spelled out G-R-I-T, which was appropriate, because grit is exactly what its execution requires.

GRIT is a strategy of calculated de-escalation of international tensions. It is the application of *interpersonal* communication and learning principles to *international* relations—where the communication is more by deeds than by words and where what is learned is mutual understanding, trust, and respect. The fullest development of this approach, as a policy, has been presented in two books of mine: *An Alternative to War or Surrender* (University of Illinois Press, 1962) and *Perspective in Foreign Policy* (Pacific Press, 1966).[1]

This strategy can be thought of as running Herman Kahn's escalator in reverse. Steps in military escalation are *unilaterally initiated*; we do not negotiate with the North Vietnamese about

An excerpt from "Escalation and de-escalation as political strategies," *Phi Kappa Phi Journal*, **47,** 3–17, 1967. Reprinted by permission of the author and The Honor Society of Phi Kappa Phi. The author is Professor of Psychology and Research Professor in the Institute of Communications Research at the University of Illinois.

[1]The latter volume applies the GRIT strategy to the Vietnam War and United States relations with the Peoples Republic of China.

increasing the tempo of our bombing or moving it closer to Hanoi and the Chinese border—we just do it. But each step we take threatens the opponent into *reciprocating* with aggressive steps of his own. Steps are *graduated* to the extent that the escalation is calculated and controlled, that risk-taking is counter-balanced by prudence, and that the political objectives are limited. But military escalation is deliberately *tension-increasing*. Now, let us reverse just one of these features—change tension-production to tension-reduction—and see what we discover as a strategy.

We would have a situation in which nation A would devise patterns of small steps, well within its limits of security, intended to reduce tensions and carefully designed so as to induce reciprocation from nation B. When reciprocation is obtained, the margin for risk-taking is widened and somewhat larger steps can be taken. The direct effect of this process is damping of the escalation in mutual tensions and lessened chances of expanded war; the psychological side-effect is increased mutual confidence and trust. Both nations are gradually learning how to behave in a nuclear age.

The Carrot and the Stick

The rules we want each opponent to learn are these: (1) if he tries to change the status quo by force, we will firmly resist and restore the status quo; (2) if he tries to change the status quo by means which reduce tensions, we will reward him by steps having similar intent; (3) if he tries to take advantage of initiatives we make in his favor, we will shift immediately to firm and punishing resistance; (4) if, on the other hand, he reciprocates to our initiative with steps of his own having similar intent, we will reward him with somewhat larger steps designed to reduce tensions. This is what I mean by *calculated* de-escalation. My colleagues in psychology will recognize this strategy as the familiar process of deliberately *shaping* behavior, here being suggested for use on an international scale. Needless to say, we have to follow the same rules if we expect others to learn them, and this is precisely what we have *not* been doing in Vietnam.

Is it possible to simultaneously maintain our national security and yet behave in such a way as to induce reciprocation from a hostile opponent? In the book already referred to, I tried to spell out in some detail how this could be done; here I can merely state the criteria without elaboration. *To maintain security*: (a) we retain during the process our capacity to inflict unacceptable nuclear retaliation should we be attacked at that level; (b) during the process we retain capacities for conventional military resistance adjusted to the level of tension existing; (c) we graduate our tension-reducing initiatives according to the degree of reciprocation obtained from any opponent; (d) we diversify our initiatives both as to nature and as to geographic locus of application; and (e) our initiatives are unpredictable by the opponent as to their nature, locus and time of announcement. *To induce reciprocation*: (a) we persistently communicate our sincere intent to reduce and control international tensions; (b) our initiatives are publicly announced at some reasonable interval prior to their execution and identified with the general policy; (c) each announcement includes explicit invitation to reciprocation, but with form not necessarily specified; (d) announced initiatives are executed on schedule regardless of any prior commitment by the opponent to reciprocate; and (e) planned patterns of initiatives are continued over a considerable period of time, regardless of reciprocations given or even of tension-increasing events elsewhere.

It should be noted carefully that this strategy includes the "stick" as well as the "carrot." We retain a minimal but sufficient nuclear deterrent as well as appropriately graded conventional forces, so that we can effectively resist military escalations by others. But we *think* of these capabilities not simply as a deterrent but rather as a security base, enabling us to take the persistent, calculated steps necessary to move toward a less dangerous world. If any opponent misinterprets our initiatives as a sign that we are "going soft," and makes an aggressive probe to test his interpretation—as the Soviets did in Cuba—then we shift promptly to the "stick"; we resist firmly, and punishingly if necessary, yet calculatedly, using precisely that level of force required to restore the status quo. As a matter of fact, such probes provide the most effective kinds of learning experiences—for both sides. This was the lesson I think the Soviet Union learned from the Cuban Missile Crisis; unfortunately we may have learned the wrong lesson—that "When Good Guys get tough, Bad Guys back down."

It seems perfectly clear that a political policy of tension escalation, calculated or otherwise, can only hamper or even make impossible successful negotiation. It creates an atmosphere of resentment and distrust in which honest negotiations cannot be undertaken; and worse, we can hardly expect those who have been bombed into negotiation to honor any agreements reached. All I can do is to ask you to ask yourselves if you would feel any deep sense of obligation to commitments made under the pressure of superior force. Calculated de-escalation, on the other hand, is explicitly designed to create and maintain an atmosphere of mutual trust within which agreements of increasing significance become possible. Most people earnestly desire peace—though they do not have even the vaguest conception of what this might refer to—and part of this is the ultimate elimination of weapons of mass destruction (nuclears). It is my firm conviction that, given the existing system of competing nation-states, only some form of calculated tension de-escalation can create the conditions under which a progressive sequence of negotiated agreements leading to this end could be undertaken.

De-escalation vis-a-vis the Soviet Union

Is all this an idealist's pipe-dream when set against the cold facts of a harsh real world? Not at all. We have been quietly following this kind of policy vis-a-vis the Soviet Union for nearly three years, even since the Cuban Missile Crisis—which may have been a learning experience of the right sort for both sides. We didn't eliminate any of our overseas bases when Khrushchev demanded them as a bargain for Cuba, but later we denuclearized bases in both Turkey and Italy on our own (reciprocative) initiative. There have been reciprocative moves in reducing the production of fissionable materials, in cutting back military budgets, and in many other areas. The Soviets have even created their own name for it—*the policy of mutual example*!

Have the predicted psychological side-effects—reduced tensions and increased mutual trust—occurred? Each reader can be his own judge as to whether or not the Russian Bogey has been cut down somewhat in size over the past three years, even though the Soviet Union remains the major threat to our security by virtue of its nuclear capability. We apparently felt enough trust to send Ambassador-at-large Averell Harriman to Moscow in a fruitless attempt to gain their mediation in a negotiated settlement in Vietnam last summer. I would argue that the Soviet Union would not have maintained its posture of relative neutrality with respect to Vietnam (in actions, if not in words) for so long a period had we not been successful in modifying the harshness of our image in their eyes. Our national image is now shifting in the opposite direction, however.

PART SIX

The Incidence of War: Statistical Evidence

INTRODUCTION

The four preceding parts of this volume have focused on causal theory concerning the forces that impel states toward or away from war. The theoretical concepts presented in these sections have served as vehicles for discussing, and in some cases reprinting, much of the significant empirical literature that exists on the causes of war. But, in the end, a few interesting empirical studies remain that do not fit into the earlier scheme because their theoretical implications remain unclear. These are all comparative case studies[1] involving large samples of states or wars. They deal with such issues as the frequency of various kinds of war, the distribution of war over time, and the relationship between the incidence of war and measurable variables such as the distance separating states or the incidence of internal conflict. Such studies are not unrelated to theory. Theory has sometimes entered into the choice of variables examined in these studies. Furthermore, the facts uncovered in these studies will have to find a place in the theory of international conflict as it emerges and may well play some heuristic role in the development of this theory. Rather, one might say that the theoretical relevance of these studies has not yet been realized. They are discussed in a separate section because it would be misleading to assign them to one or another of the four theoretical classifications.

A number of statistical studies have been performed to relate the incidence and magnitude of war to gross variables such as era or nationality. These studies are mainly presented in Sorokin (1937), Wright (1942), and Richardson (1960). Only a few of these studies have yielded interesting results. Sorokin, after present-

[1]The comparative case study method of research is discussed in the introduction to Part I.

ing evidence to refute theories of periodicity and linear trend over time, rather apologetically reports that his only finding is that states are involved in larger and more frequent wars in periods of greater economic strength. Richardson finds, not surprisingly, an inverse relationship between the distance separating two states and the frequency of wars between them. More interestingly, Richardson reports that the frequency of wars involving a given state is a positive function of the number of neighbors on its borders. Wesley (1962 and Selection 17) has constructed a mathematical model that explains the inverse relationship that is found between the frequency and size of war on the one hand, and the number of people dwelling outside but near a state's borders, on the other.

In addition to searching for correlations with other variables, Richardson looked for regularities in the statistics on incidence and size of war per se and achieved considerable success in this effort. In one study, he calculated the number of years in a period from 1820 to 1929 when there had been no war, one war, two wars, etc., and found a very close fit between these frequencies and those predicted by the Poisson distribution from probability theory. In another study, he found a simple relationship between the frequency and size of war, which implies that "there is some constant probability that (each) war will end before the total number of its victims has increased by some specific percentage" (Harsanyi, 1962, p. 690). These studies are related to recent research by Horvath and Foster (1963) in which a probability model was shown to fit data on the frequency of war alliances of various sizes.

The discovery that the incidence of war and certain features of war follow the laws of probability should not be taken as evidence that war is a mysterious and unalterable affliction. Rather, an analogy can be made to airplane accidents, the frequency of which also follows the laws of probability. Many of the causes of airplane accidents have been discovered and removed, materially reducing the probability of such accidents per passenger mile.

References

Harsanyi, J. C., "Mathematical models for the genesis of war," *World Politics*, **14**(4), 687–699, 1962.

Horvath, W. J., and C. C. Foster, "Stochastic models of war alliances," *Journal of Conflict Resolution*, **7**(2), 110–116, 1963.

Richardson, L. F., *Statistics of Deadly Quarrels*. Pittsburgh, Pa.: The Boxwood Press, 1960.

Sorokin, P., *Social and Cultural Dynamics*, Vol. 3. New York: American Book Company, 1937.

Wesley, J. P., "Frequency of wars and geographical opportunity," *Journal of Conflict Resolution*, **6**(4), 387–389, 1962.

Wright, Q., *A Study of War*. Chicago: University of Chicago Press, 1942.

16

R. J. RUMMEL

Dimensions of Foreign and Domestic Conflict Behavior: A Review of Empirical Findings[1]

A review of the literature involving the use of factor analysis on historical data concerning internal and international conflict. The literature suggests that these two kinds of conflict are unrelated, which calls into question a number of familiar hypotheses concerning aggressive regimes and diversionary wars.

Introduction

Conflict between people singly as individuals or collectively as nations is a clash of desires. It is a *situation* in which two or more parties *perceive* mutually exclusive values or goals.

A conflict situation may involve a physical or violent clash between the parties in an attempt to overcome the other. War and revolution are examples of this. Where conflict behavior exists, however, it is generally less violent and more demonstrative, exemplified in such traditional acts as diplomatic protests or naval "maneuvers." Often a conflict situation involves no overt conflict behavior. The perception of mutually exclusive goals or values exists, but for reasons such as the overwhelming strength of one of the parties (e.g., U.S.S.R. versus Finland) or the dampening of overt behavior by outside interests (e.g., NATO leaders and the UN intervening in the 1964 controversy between Turkey and Greece over Cyprus), little or no conflict behavior may occur.

Overt conflict behavior, consequently, is a sufficient but not a necessary condition for the presence of a conflict situation. When conflict behavior occurs, a situation of conflict necessarily exists, but conflict situations may exist without overt conflict behavior. The distinction is important when one is analyzing foreign and domestic conflict. The usual approach is to study this conflict as manifested in

---

Especially prepared for this volume. The author is Associate Professor of Political Science at the University of Hawaii.

[1]This paper was prepared in connection with research supported by the National Science Foundation under contract NSF-GS-536. I want to thank Richard Chadwick, Phillips Cutright, George Modelski, Dean Pruitt, Stuart Nagel, Anatol Rapoport, and Pitirim Sorokin for their comments on an earlier draft of this paper.

wars, revolutions, and guerrilla warfare. But concentration on such behavior restricts the analysis only to conflict situations in which this behavior is manifested. Unwarranted conclusions may follow. For example, without realizing that overt conflict behavior may be manifested in only a small number of conflict situations, one might generalize from a finding that contemporary wars are a result of ideological conflict to "all contemporary international conflict is ideological." With the above caveat in mind, the remainder of this paper will be confined to discussing the results of empirical analyses of conflict *behavior*.

Dimensions of Conflict Behavior

As mentioned above, the kinds of conflict most often studied are war, revolution, and guerrilla warfare.[2] The last phenomenon has grown as a research topic only in the last few years. Books on war and revolution are innumerable, but none exists on troop movements, mobilizations, accusations, border incidents, threats,[3] riots, demonstrations, general strikes, etc. On diplomatic protests, there is one work (McKenna, 1962).

Paucity of interest in all but the most violent forms of conflict behavior makes it difficult to relate conflict literature to questions of current interest. Are certain conflict behaviors related so that a nation undertaking threatening troop movements is also making diplomatic protests, accusations, threats, and recalling or expelling ambassadors? Does all conflict behavior, domestic and foreign, cluster together so that, when a nation has revolutions, riots, demonstrations, etc., it is also engaging in threats, troop movements, etc.? If conflict behavior forms one cluster in this fashion, then the occurrence of any one conflict act by a nation indexes and presages the occurrence of others. On the other hand, do conflict acts form into separate clusters of behavior? Do domestic-conflict acts, e.g., occur together but without being correlated with foreign-conflict behavior? Do warlike acts of conflict take place apart from—independent of—a group of conflict acts that are associated with the normal diplomatic friction among nations? These questions pertain to the *dimensionality* of conflict behavior within and between nations.

A conflict-behavior *dimension* represents a number of conflict acts that are highly correlated with each other. If conflict behavior grouped into separate clusters of conflict acts, then each cluster would be represented by a dimension. These separate dimensions would then delimit variables that form galaxies of relationships, with each variable more correlated with others in its cluster than with any of those in other clusters. Multiple dimensions of this sort, e.g., may be seen in the voting behavior of United States senators, where one dimension in their voting could be that of liberal-conservative, another of Democrat-Republican.

A nation may be given a score on a dimension to index the degree to which its conflict behavior is of the kind defined by the dimension. As discussed below, e.g., there appears to be a war dimension of conflict behavior that represents the co-occurrence of such

[2] For a brief discussion of foreign and domestic conflict-behavior literature, see Rummel (1963), Tanter (1966), and Haas (1964).

[3] It should be noted, however, that Schelling (1960) is very much concerned with threats in his work. Threats are also of central concern in the research of the Stanford studies on conflict and integration, although in the context of expression and perception of hostility. See Zinnes (1963).

conflict behavior as war, mobilization, troop movements, and threats. A nation would be high or low on this dimension as it manifested this behavior.

Determining dimensions of conflict behavior between and within nations has a number of values. First, the delineation of these dimensions allows one to identify *basic* conflict acts, i.e., those most highly related to other conflict behavior, that may therefore be used to index and predict them. Secondly, such dimensions allow explicit comparing and contrasting of nations on their conflict behavior. Without these dimensions, nations would have to be compared on each conflict act, as legislators would have to be compared on each vote; the identification of dimensions reduces the labor to a comparison of only the basic variables identifying each dimension.

Finally, the research payoff of establishing such dimensions should be mentioned. If one is concerned with determining the correlates of conflict behavior—its conditions and causes—it is necessary to know what dimensions exist to avoid misinterpreting one's findings. For example, assume there exist three dimensions of conflict behavior, say *A*, *B*, and *C*, that are unknown to the researchers. Assume also that he is concerned about the relationship between foreign-conflict behavior and power. Now, he may pick the number of wars of a nation as his conflict variable, or he may use an index that is a combination of several conflict acts. Assume that he selects the number of wars as his variable. Assume also that war is highly intercorrelated with a set of conflict acts forming a cluster represented by *only one* of the dimensions *A*, *B*, or *C*. Then the presence or absence of a relationship (except a near-perfect relationship) found between war and power *says little about the relationship of power to the other dimensions of conflict behavior.*[4] Thus, important conditions or causes of conflict behavior may be overlooked.

On the other hand, assume the researcher selects the approach of combining several conflict acts into an index. He may then unknowingly choose acts that are parts of different clusters and thus represent different dimensions. This would result in a confounding of his index and would place a severe limitation on the meaningfulness of the results. Power might be highly related to a nation's position along each of the conflict-behavior dimensions *A*, *B*, and *C*. As a result of forming an index out of multidimensional acts, however, *he may find no relationship where one exists or he may find a relationship opposite to that which exists between power and the conflict behavior the index is meant to represent.*

The primary goal of this paper is to discuss in nontechnical terms the results of several studies on the dimensionality of domestic- and foreign-conflict behavior.[5] Some of this work has been published; other studies are currently being prepared for publication. All apply factor analysis to the conflict behavior of a large number of nations. Following the discussion of these findings, a final section will attempt to tie them together and present some propositions. First, however, the nature of the method employed to delineate dimensions of behavior should be mentioned briefly.

---

[4]If the relationship between war and power were perfect or near perfect, i.e., war could be completely or almost completely predicted from a nation's power, then power would have the same relationship to the other conflict acts and clusters of conflict acts—dimensions—that war has.

[5]This review of findings is of the studies completed by October, 1964.

Factor Analysis

Factor analysis is a mathematical tool for identifying the clusters (dimensions) of relationships (correlations) that exist among a large number of variables.[6] Each of the factors resulting from a factor analysis (simple-structure multiple-factor solution) indicates which variables enter into the cluster it represents, which variable is most representative of the cluster, and how much of the total relationship among all the variables analyzed is contained in the cluster. A complex web of relationships among a large number of variables can be reduced, therefore, to a small number of dimensions (continua) that can be used for description and analysis. Factor analysis is useful for *mapping* an empirical domain, where the basic relationships and concepts are unknown.

Factor Analysis Involving Conflict Behavior

The first factor analysis including conflict-behavior data was published in 1949 by Raymond Cattell (Cattell, 1949). The study involved a factor analysis of data for 69 nations on 72 variables, such as population size, area, telephones per capita, and real standard of living. Included among these variables were data on number of riots (which includes local rebellions), revolutions, assassinations, wars, and foreign clashes, from 1837 to 1937. The results showed that variables representing domestic-conflict behavior had little relationship to the foreign-conflict behavior variables.[7] No dimension coming out of the analysis was able to delineate a cluster containing variables of both domestic- and foreign-conflict behavior. The two foreign-conflict behavior variables (war and foreign clashes), on the other hand, came out positively related on the same dimension, which indicates that nations with a large number of wars, during 1837 to 1937, also had many foreign clashes; those with few wars had few foreign clashes. Another dimension identified riots and assassinations as related to each other positively. Revolutions, however, came out on a factor by itself (in the conflict-behavior variables) and, thus, was little related to any of the other conflict acts within and between nations.

Because the 1949 study involved a large number of nations for which data were lacking, Cattell and associates carried out a second analysis eliminating the 29 nations with the most missing data (Cattell et al., 1951). As a consequence of the more than one-third reduction in the number of nations covered, the relationships among the conflict-behavior variables changed. A factor identifying a cluster including war and foreign clashes was still extracted from the data, but riots also appeared in this same cluster. Thus, when the analysis was made more specific to developed Western nations, as it was by his exclusion of 29 nations,[8] the number of riots was found to be related to foreign-conflict behavior.

[6]For the technical details of factor analysis, see Harman (1960). For more elementary texts, see Fruchter (1954), Cattell (1952), and Rummel (1967). Cattell's introductory chapters are especially recommended to the student without any statistical background.

[7]It is assumed that the reader has no statistical or mathematical background. Those interested in the technical details, such as the correlations and factor loadings, may wish to consult the studies mentioned.

[8]"In dropping 29 countries, we must recognize . . . that our factors will be true only of the species of 'modern, industrial nations' which now chiefly comprises our population" (Cattell et al., 1951, p. 410).

The relationship between assassinations and riots was discovered to be different also. Where, in the 1949 study, nations high in assassinations were also high in riots, in the 1951 reanalysis, assassinations were found much less related to riots, representing now a different dimension. Revolutions, however, remained on a dimension different from the other conflict-behavior variables in both the 1949 and 1951 studies.

In a third study, Cattell and Gorsuch (1965)[9] worked with a completely new set of data, 51 variables for data collected on 52 nations (8 of which were colonies) for the mid-1950's. The conflict-behavior variables included were foreign political clashes and riots (defined to include rebellions). In the results, these two were identified with different dimensions. Insofar as one measure was of foreign-conflict behavior and the other of domestic, the results indicate an independence between internal- and external-conflict behavior for this different time period also.

In 1963, the results of three factor analyses of conflict-behavior data for 77 nations for 1955 to 1957 were published (Rummel, 1963). The first of these factor analyses was on 13 foreign-conflict behavior variables: antiforeign demonstrations, diplomatic protests, negative sanctions, severance of diplomatic relations, expelling or recalling ambassadors, expelling or recalling officials of less than ambassadorial rank, accusations, threats, military action, war, mobilizations, troop movements, and the number killed in foreign-conflict behavior.

Three clusters of relationships among these variables were revealed, the largest of which appeared to represent a *war* dimension both in terms of the number of variables and strength of relationship. Central to this cluster were the number killed, wars, accusations, threats, and military action. The second cluster included mainly the two expulsion-recall variables and troop movements. Severance of diplomatic relations, antiforeign demonstrations, and negative sanctions formed the third cluster. These last two clusters seemed to involve *diplomatic* and *belligerent* dimensions of foreign-conflict behavior respectively and were labeled thus.

These three dimensions, *war*, *diplomatic*, and *belligerent*, were found to be independent of each other. This means, e.g., that the warlike conflict behavior of nations, in 1955 to 1957, did not necessarily occur along with belligerent kinds of behavior and vice versa. Moreover, diplomatic-conflict behavior, apparently representing moves on the diplomatic chessborad, occurred sometimes with and sometimes without warlike or belligerent behavior of a nation.

The second factor analysis was applied to data on nine measures of domestic conflict: assassinations, general strikes, guerrilla war, riots, revolutions, demonstrations, major government crises, purges, and the number killed in all forms of domestic conflict. Here, three clusters also appeared. The largest of these involved riots, demonstrations, and major government crises, variables that generally represent a spontaneous, unplanned kind of conflict behavior. Accordingly, this cluster was named a *turmoil* dimension. The second dimension was mainly of purges, revolutions, and the number killed in domestic conflict; the third dimension was of guerrilla warfare and assassinations. Both of these dimensions represent organized-conflict behavior, i.e., behavior that is planned with definite objectives and methods in mind. The

[9]The results are also given in Gorsuch (1962).

difference between the two is that the second includes overt organized-conflict behavior of a revolutionary character, while the behavior delineated by the third dimension is covert. Accordingly, the second and third dimensions were named *revolution* and *subversion* respectively.

Since the separate factor analyses of domestic- and foreign-conflict behavior say nothing about dimensions that might be common to both kinds of behavior, a third factor analysis was calculated for all 22 conflict-behavior variables.[10] Six clear clusters of relationships were delimited, but not one involved both foreign-conflict and domestic-conflict behavior variables—a clear indication for the 1955 to 1957 data that dimensions of conflict behavior stopped at the border, that the dimensions changed as the focus moved from internal- to external-conflict behavior.

Using the same variables, but with new data collected on 83 nations for 1958 to 1960, Raymond Tanter (1966) replicated the above three factor analyses. For his foreign-conflict behavior data, Tanter identified the same three clusters of relationships, the *war*, *diplomatic*, and *belligerent* dimensions. The results of the domestic-conflict behavior analysis were slightly different, however. While the separate spontaneous-conflict and planned-conflict behavior clusters that appeared in the 1955 to 1957 data were also found, the planned-conflict behavior that, in the 1963 study, resolved into overt and covert (revolutionary and subversion) clusters merged into one *internal-war* dimension. As mentioned, the *turmoil* dimension was also found to exist in the 1958 to 1960 domestic-conflict behavior data. Tanter's factor analysis of the combined 22 domestic- and foreign-conflict behavior variables produced some clusters which differed from those in the factor analysis of the combined 1955 to 1957 data. Nonetheless, the finding still revealed no cluster involving both domestic and foreign variables. In the 1958 to 1960 conflict behavior of nations, the dimensions also stopped at the border.

In another study by Tanter (1965), 1955 to 1957 and 1958 to 1960 data for each nation were added to give 1955 to 1960 conflict data for 75 nations on the same 9 and 13 domestic- and foreign-conflict behavior variables. Again, the same three analyses were computed. As a result of the factoring of the foreign-conflict behavior data for 1955 to 1960, the same three *war*, *diplomatic*, and *belligerent* dimensions were identified. In the case of domestic behavior, the *turmoil* and *internal-war* dimensions also emerged. When the 1955 to 1960 data were analyzed for the 22 variables together, the results still lacked a cluster of relationships that exhibited both domestic- and foreign-conflict behavior variables.

Another study dealing with this same set of data should be mentioned. Richard Chadwick (1963) carried out a factor analysis of a smaller number of domestic- and foreign-conflict behavior variables together for the years 1955, 1956, and 1957. In the 1955 analysis, the first cluster was exclusively foreign-conflict behavior and the second and fourth clusters were exclusively domestic. A remaining cluster, the third, involved both domestic and external behavior—riots, antigovernment demonstrations, and expelling or recalling diplomats. In the analysis of 1956 data,

[10]Two measures of possible systematic data error, censorship and world interest in a nation, were included to gauge the reliability of the findings. The result of the error analysis was to give greater credence to the dimensions emerging from the three factor analyses of the 1955 to 1957 data than would otherwise be the case. The Tanter study (1966), discussed below, similarly weighed the effect of systematic error.

two of the four clusters were exclusively domestic or foreign. The third cluster involved antigovernment demonstrations, expelling or recalling diplomats, and threats; in the fourth cluster were major government crises and antiforeign demonstrations. In the 1957 analysis, the second of the five clusters identified had both internal and external behavior—riots and antiforeign demonstrations. For the annual data, then, the overall results suggest there is a common dimension generally involving turmoil-like behavior (riots and demonstrations) and diplomatic or belligerent types of foreign-conflict behavior (expelling or recalling diplomatic officials and antiforeign demonstrations). This common dimension is lost, however, when annual data are aggregated.

In addition to the Rummel (1963), Tanter (1965, 1966), and Chadwick (1963) studies, one additional factor analysis has been done on a large number of domestic-conflict variables Rummel, 1966a). The conflict data in this case were on 113 countries for 1946 to 1959 and were reported by Harry Eckstein (1962) on measures of internal warfare, turmoil, rioting, large-scale terrorism, small-scale terrorism, mutiny, coup, plots, administrative action, quasi-private violence, and total number of unequivocal plus equivocal acts of violence. A thirteenth measure, extended violence, was derived from his tables and also included in the factor analysis. Three clusters of relationships were identified. The first involved a cluster of riots, turmoil, and small-scale terrorism, the same *turmoil* dimension found in the Rummel (1963) and Tanter (1965, 1966) studies. The second cluster involved mutinies, coups, plots, and administrative actions (purges); the third brought together warfare (e.g., guerrilla war) and extended violence. These two clusters were quite similar to the *revolution* and *subversion* dimensions found in the Rummel (1963) study.

Discussion

To the author's knowledge, and with one exception,[11] the eight factor analyses just reviewed comprise all the factor analyses involving two or more domestic- or foreign-conflict behavior variables completed by October, 1964.[12] The results of these studies point to a number of conclusions on the dimensionality of conflict behavior.

First, domestic- and foreign-conflict behavior clearly fall on different dimensions in all studies with the exception of Chadwick's analysis using annual data. Consequently, although the empirical evidence appears to be almost overwhelming in favor of no common domestic- and foreign-conflict behavior dimension, this conclusion should be tentative until additional studies on annual, monthly, weekly, and even daily data are completed. With this qualification in mind, it is proposed on the basis of most of the results that domestic- and foreign-conflict activities generally represent independent behavior.[13] Some nations have much domestic-conflict behavior but no foreign; others have much

---

[11]An M.A. thesis involving a factor analysis of over twenty domestic-conflict behavior variables has been recently completed at San Diego State College under the direction of Ivo K. Feierabend.

[12]This is the date when the final draft of this paper was completed for this volume. Since then, additional studies have been completed (Rummel, 1965, 1966b) that do not alter significantly the conclusions presented here. [Later research challenging the conclusion that domestic and foreign conflict are unrelated will be found in J. Wilkenfeld, "Domestic and foreign conflict behavior of nations," *Journal of Peace Research*, 1968, 56–69. Ed.]

[13]Pitirim Sorokin also came to this conclusion as a result of his graphical analysis of wars and revolutions over a number of centuries (Sorokin, 1937).

domestic- and much foreign-conflict behavior; still others have no domestic-conflict behavior and no foreign; finally, some have no internal conflict but high external. The implication of this finding is that *there are no common conditions or causes of domestic- and foreign-conflict behavior*; the genesis of domestic- and foreign-conflict behavior must be different. Hence, rapid industrialization, underdevelopment, totalitarian regimes, or unstable political systems cannot be the general cause of both, as is often asserted. Such conditions may serve as *necessary* causes, producing the required atmosphere for conflict behavior, but the *sufficient* condition setting off the behavior differs as one goes from internal to external conflict behavior.[14]

Turning to domestic conflict per se, the seven studies that involved two or more domestic-conflict behavior variables resulted, with one exception, in riots and revolutions appearing in different dimensions. The exception is the analysis of the 1956 data by Chadwick, in which the two variables appeared in the same cluster. The evidence in all the other studies, however, including Chadwick's 1955 and 1957 data analyses, indicates that riots, as representative of the *turmoil* dimension, and revolutions, as representative of Rummel's *revolution* and Tanter's *internal-war* dimensions, occur independently of each other. Turmoil does not necessarily occur with revolutions or guerrilla warfare, and vice versa.

Secondly, *turmoil* appears as a dimension in all the studies in which several domestic-conflict behavior variables were used. The consistency of its appearance strongly argues for the reliability of the dimensions. Moreover, in all the studies with the exception of Chadwick's, the division in the internal-conflict behavior among the dimensions was between spontaneous behavior, represented by *turmoil*, and the programmed, planned behavior, represented by revolutions and guerrilla warfare. Whether planned-conflict behavior is unidimensional, as an *internal-war* dimension, or bidimensional, as *revolution* and *subversion* dimensions, is ambiguous however.

As to foreign-conflict behavior, the Rummel-Tanter studies suggest three dimensions, *war*, *diplomatic*, and *belligerent*. As the author has written elsewhere (Rummel, 1963), the meaning of this tridimensionality is that a particular conflict act need not presage more provocative or violent acts. Instead, it may be an almost automatic diplomatic reaction—expelling an official for spying, applying pressure on a country by recalling one's ambassador, or discontinuing aid shipments—to a relatively minor situation. Conflict behavior also may be evidence of contained hostility, enmity sufficient to bring the people to the streets condemning the other country and sufficient to cause diplomatic relations to be severed, boycotts to be imposed, and perhaps frequent and spontaneous border clashes, but contained hostility since mobilization does not occur and war is not declared. War may, indeed, escalate from such situations, but the findings to date are that war generally occurs independently of them.

[14] If A is a sufficient condition for B (i.e., whenever A happens, B occurs) and B is independent of C (i.e., when B happens, C occurs only sometimes), then A cannot be a sufficient condition of C. This logically follows since there are times when A happens (and B thus happens) and C does not take place. For A to be a sufficient condition of both B and C, they must be perfectly related, always co-occur. In the sciences, one looks for high and not perfect relationships since human or instrumental error or other variables will obscure the relationship, but the logic still applies.

Propositions

A review of the findings of a number of factor analyses which employ two or more domestic- or foreign-conflict behavior variables results in the following propositions:

1. Domestic- and foreign-conflict behavior generally are independent of each other; they share no common dimension of conflict behavior.
2. A spontaneous kind of conflict behavior, *turmoil*, is a major dimension of domestic-conflict behavior.
3. Independent of a turmoil dimension, domestic-conflict behavior also involves planned behavior represented by *revolution* and *subversion* dimensions or these dimensions merged into one *internal-war* dimension.
4. Foreign-conflict behavior occurs along *war*, *diplomatic*, and *belligerent* dimensions.

Refercences

Cattell, Raymond B., "The dimensions of culture patterns of factorization of national characters," *Journal of Abnormal and Social Psychology*, **44,** 443–469, 1949.

Cattell, Raymond B., *Factor Analysis*. New York: Harper and Brothers, 1952.

Cattell, Raymond B., H. Bruel, and H. Parker Hartman, "An attempt at a more refined definition of the cultural dimensions of syntality in modern nations," *American Sociological Review*, **17,** 408–421, 1951.

Cattell, Raymond B., and Richard L. Gorsuch, "The definition and measurement of national morale and morality," *Journal of Social Psychology*, **67,** 77–96, 1965.

Chadwick, Richard, "An analysis of the relationship of domestic to foreign conflict behavior over the period 1955–1957." First-Year Paper, Northwestern University, Evanston, Ill., 1963 (ditto).

Eckstein, Harry, "The incidence of internal wars, 1946–1959," Appendix I of *Internal War: The Problem of Anticipation*, Report submitted to the Research Group in Psychology and the Social Sciences, Smithsonian Institution, Washington, D. C., January 15, 1962.

Fruchter, Benjamin, *Introduction to Factor Analysis*. New York: D. Van Nostrand Company, Inc., 1954.

Gorsuch, Richard L., "National morale, morality, and cultural integration," unpublished M.A. thesis, University of Illinois, Urbana, 1962.

Haas, Michael, "Some societal correlates of international political behavior," Ph.D. Dissertation, Stanford University, Palo Alto, Calif., 1964.

Harman, Harry H., *Modern Factor Analysis*. Chicago: University of Chicago Press, 1960.

McKenna, Joseph C., *Diplomatic Protest in Foreign Policy*. Chicago: Loyola University Press, 1962.

North, Robert C., Richard A. Brody, and Ole R. Holsti, "Some empirical data on the conflict spiral," *Peace Research Society (International) Papers*, **1,** 1–14, 1964.

Rummel, Rudolph J., "Dimensions of conflict behavior within and between nations," *General Systems* (Yearbook of the Society for General Systems Research), **8,** 1–50, 1963.

Rummel, Rudolph J., "A field theory of social action with application to conflict within nations," *General Systems* (Yearbook of the Society for General Systems Research), **10,** 183–211, 1965.

Rummel, Rudolph J., "Dimensions of conflict behavior within nations, 1946–1959," *Journal of Conflict Resolution*, **10,** 65–73, 1966a.

Rummel, Rudolph J., "Attribute and behavioral patterns of nations," Paper presented before the Computers and the Policy-making Community Institute, Lawrence Radiation Laboratory, Livermore, Calif., April, 1966b.

Rummel, Rudolph J., *Applied Factor Analysis*. Evanston, Ill.: Northwestern University Press, 1967.

Schelling, Thomas C., *The Strategy of Conflict*. Cambridge, Mass.: Harvard University Press, 1960.

Sorokin, Pitirim, *Social and Cultural Dynamics*, Vol. III. New York: American Book Company, 1937.

Tanter, Raymond, "Dimensions of conflict behavior within and between nations, 1955–1960." *Peace Research Society (International) Papers*, **3,** 159–183, 1965.

Tanter, Raymond, "Dimensions of conflict behavior within and between nations, 1958–1960," *Journal of Conflict Resolution*, **10,** 48–64, 1966.

Zinnes, Dina Antje, "Expression and perception of hostility in interstate relations," Ph.D. Dissertation, Stanford University, Palo Alto, Calif., 1963.

17

JAMES PAUL WESLEY

Frequency of Wars and Geographical Opportunity[1]

A mathematical demonstration that the relationship empirically observed between the frequency and size of a war may be a function of the geographical opportunity for interaction between populations. This illustrates the use of mathematical models to summarize and explain empirical findings.

It will be shown here that the relationship between the frequency of wars and the size of wars may be derived on the basis of geographical opportunity alone. It is, of course, reasonable to expect geographical opportunity to affect the frequency of wars, since the frequency of wars between neighboring countries is greater than the frequency of wars between countries widely separated geographically. A man is much more likely to quarrel with his next-door neighbor than with someone several houses removed. Interactions of all sorts, both constructive as well as destructive, are more frequent between people in adjacent areas than between those widely separated geographically.

If war is more likely between neighboring countries, then the frequency of wars experienced by a particular country should correlate with the number of neighbors the country has. Lewis Fry Richardson (1960, p. 176), showed that this was indeed the case. He found that the number of external wars between 1820 to 1945 with more than 7,000 war dead correlated with the number of frontiers for the 33 countries he investigated.

This correlation, while demonstrating that the effect of geographical opportunity exists, does not indicate the precise magnitude of the effect. To evaluate the situation more accurately it is possible to proceed as Richardson did (p. 291). It may be noted that wars of a given size will usually be fought where the population of the smaller side sustains a loss of at most some fraction k of its population. Thus, the

---

Reprinted from the *Journal of Conflict Resolution*, **6,** 387–389, 1962, by permission of the author and that journal. The author is Associate Professor of Physics at the University of Missouri at Rolla.

[1]This work was completed during the tenure of a Special Fellowship from the National Institute of Mental Health, United States Public Health Service.

smallest population that can generally be expected to engage in a war with a total of n war dead is $n/2k$, it being assumed that both sides suffer about the same number of casualties, $n/2$. If the population of the world is broken up into cells whose populations are each of this minimum size, then there will be at most s potential belligerents that might engage in a war with n war dead where

$$s = 2kW/n, \qquad (1)$$

where W is the world population.

In terms of geographical opportunity it may be assumed that only neighboring cells will go to war against each other. Richardson (p. 290) compared the number of common boundaries or frontiers between neighboring cells with the frequency of wars of different sizes and failed to obtain precise agreement with observation. The *number* of boundaries is not, however, the proper measure of geographical opportunity, for if two countries share a *long* common boundary they will have greater opportunity for interaction than if they share only a *short* common boundary. The measure of geographical opportunity for war is, therefore, taken here as the length of frontiers or boundaries between the population cells. This measure is in population units and does not involve actual physical length. A long physical frontier between two countries with low population densities might afford the same geographical opportunity as a short frontier between two countries with high population densities. The opportunity for interaction as measured here by the length of the boundary between population cells is proportional to the number of individuals residing near a common boundary.

If A is the total land area of the earth, then each cell may be assumed to occupy an area $a = A/s$. The perimeter of each cell is proportional to $a^{1/2}$. Summing over all of the s cells then gives a total perimeter about all cells which is proportional to $s^{1/2}$,

$$P \propto s^{1/2}. \qquad (2)$$

From equations (1) and (2) the total perimeter P about all s cells is seen to be proportional to $n^{-1/2}$,

$$P \propto n^{-1/2}. \qquad (3)$$

It is now postulated that the rate at which war dead are generated is proportional to the geographical opportunity as measured by P, equation (3). If df/dn is the frequency of wars producing war dead in the range from n to $n + dn$, then the rate at which war dead are produced in wars of this size is given by

$$n\, df/dn. \qquad (4)$$

Equating this rate of generation of war dead, equation (4) to the geographical opportunity, equation (3), the result is found to be

$$n\, df/dn \propto n^{-1/2}. \qquad (5)$$

In terms of logarithms equation (5) may also be written in the form

$$\log_{10} (df/d \log_{10} n) = C - 0.5 \log_{10} n, \qquad (6)$$

where C is some constant. This relation is precisely the same as the empirical relation already established by Richardson (1960, p. 148 and p. 292) whose summarized data for wars between 1820 and 1945 are reproduced in Table 1.

The constant C was chosen as 3.84 so that the theoretical curve would coincide with observation for wars involving 5×10^3 to 5×10^4 war dead.

It cannot be claimed that the derivation of the distribution formula, equa-

TABLE 1

Frequency and Magnitude of Wars

War dead n	*Magnitude* $\log_{10}n$	*Number of wars* $\frac{df}{d\log_{10}n}$	*Observation* $\log_{10}\left(\frac{df}{d\log_{10}n}\right)$	*Theory* $C - 0.5\log_{10}n$
10^3	3	$\geq$198	$\geq$2.30	2.34
10^4	4	70	1.84	1.84
10^5	5	24	1.38	1.34
10^6	6	6	0.78	0.84
10^7	7	2	0.30	0.34

tion (6), in terms of geographical opportunity alone is the only derivation possible. An investigation involving some direct measure of the geographical opportunity (such as a correlation of frequency of wars between two countries with the number of roads across their common frontier) is probably required to settle the matter.

Reference

Richardson, L. F., *Statistics of Deadly Quarrels*. Pittsburgh, Pa.: The Boxwood Press, 1960.

PART SEVEN

Toward an Integrated Theory and Cumulative Research

INTRODUCTION

Taken together, the introductions to the first six parts of this book constitute a wide-ranging summary of the theoretical and empirical literature on the causes of war. The heart of this summary is found in the introductions to Parts II and III, which deal with forces (factors) that move states toward war, and the introductions to Parts IV and V, which deal with forces that lead away from war.

A diverse picture emerges from these four introductions. Many theories are presented, embracing a large number of forces which appear either to induce or prevent large-scale international violence. Each theory is plausible as an explanation for certain aspects or certain kinds of wars, and some are even supported by evidence. But most of the theories are incomplete and tenuously related to one another. A comprehensive, valid theory of war is not yet in hand.

The existence of diverse approaches and explanations is not altogether unwelcome. There is much to be said for early specialization in scholarship, leading to the development of miniature *islands of theory* (Guetzkow, 1950), in areas amenable to research, which can eventually be linked together into an integrated whole. Several subfields of physics took this path to success.

Nevertheless, in the midst of building islands of theory, it seems wise to lift one's head occasionally and survey the broader environment in an effort to determine how the islands might eventually be bridged together. This part of the book will deal with broader, more integrative perspectives that provide bridges between some of the discrete concepts and hypotheses presented earlier. The three perspectives presented in this introduction represent three different "levels" of analysis: (a) the psychological processes involved in the decision to go to war, (b) the comparative characteristics of stable and unstable international systems, and (c) the dynamics of movement toward and away from war. Other perspectives are presented in the readings that follow this introduction.

The Decision to Go to War

According to this perspective, the decision to go to war is part of a problem-solving sequence, in which national policy makers generate and weigh a variety of definitions of the situation and alternative courses of action (Brody, 1966). The occasion for decision is most often the perception that another state's goals are incompatible with one's own, i.e., that another state threatens national goals or that an opportunity exists to advance one's own goals at the expense of another state. The alternatives generated are mostly forms of *conflict behavior*, i.e., courses of action designed to destroy, injure, deprive, thwart, or otherwise control the other state (Mack and Snyder, 1957). For example, at a given time, policy makers might be considering the following alternatives: (a) initiating negotiations with another state, (b) appealing to the United Nations for action against that state, (c) instituting an economic blockade against that state, and (d) initiating violence, e.g., bombing its capital. An additional alternative that is always explicitly or implicitly under consideration is inaction, i.e., doing nothing.

The decision that is made among the alternatives facing policy makers will be influenced by both *rational* and *irrational* considerations. By rational considerations are meant those that turn on an inventory and weighting of the possible consequences emanating from each alternative. By irrational considerations are meant emotional states. The former kind of considerations will be taken up first and at greatest length since they encompass most of the factors discussed in earlier parts of the book.

A schematic and admittedly oversimplified version of the process of rational decision making will be presented in this section, which nevertheless seems adequate for the present purpose. To the extent that policy makers are acting rationally, they will develop an intuitive estimate of the expected gain and expected cost associated with each alternative. Expected gain can be thought of as the sum, over all positively valued consequences of an alternative, of the utility of that consequence multiplied by its subjective probability. Expected cost can be thought of as the sum, over all negatively valued consequences, of the disutility of that consequence multiplied by its subjective probability. These definitions of expected gain and cost are too mathematical to be fully descriptive of what goes on in the mind of the policy maker, which is why we said that policy makers develop *intuitive estimates*.

To the extent that the decision is informed by rational considerations, it will be based on these intuitive estimates. That alternative will be chosen for which the expected gain *most outweighs* the expected cost or, where expected cost is greater than expected gain for all alternatives, for which the expected cost *least outweighs* the expected gain. In more precise mathematical terms (which are probably overly precise but provide a handy way of talking about the decision function), we might say that the alternative will be chosen for which the expected gain minus the expected cost is greatest.

Most of the factors discussed in other parts of this volume can be thought of as determining the expected gains and costs associated with various alternatives, including most notably the alternative of going to war. These forces will be italicized in the paragraphs below. A summary of the points made below is presented in Table 1.

TABLE 1

Examples of Forces Determining the Expected Gains and Costs Associated with Violent and Nonviolent Alternatives

Some determinants of the expected gain associated with violent alternatives (i.e., war)	
Forces enhancing the utility of consequences associated with the choice of violence	Forces increasing the subjective probability of achieving favorable consequences from the choice of violence
Goals that are seen as incompatible with those of the other state Perceived threat from the other state	Own military strength in comparison with that of the other state Likelihood that goals will be destroyed as a result of violence (negatively related to expected gain from violence)
Some determinants of the expected cost associated with violent alternatives	
Forces enhancing the disutility of unfavorable consequences associated with the choice of violence	Forces increasing the subjective probability that negative consequences will result from the choice of violence.
Destructive force possessed by the other state Inherent cost of waging war Strength of international norms against war Effectiveness of world public opinion Dependences on the other state or third states that are likely to condemn the use of violence	Capacity of the other state to penetrate own defenses Vigor of world public opinion
Some determinants of the expected gain associated with nonviolent alternatives (including inaction)	Some determinants of the expected cost associated with nonviolent alternatives (including inaction)
Trust Mediation (Both enhance the subjective probability of successful negotiation)	Costs of inaction (e.g., costs associated with accepting a first strike from another state that is seen as sure to attack eventually)

Note: According to the model, violence will be elected when the expected gain minus the expected cost from violence is greater than the expected gain minus the expected cost from all nonviolent alternatives including inaction. The lists of factors are incomplete. A more thorough analysis of the nonviolent alternatives would include a variety of alternatives and a finer breakdown into determinants of utility and subjective probability, as shown for the alternative of initiating violence.

The expected gain for any form of conflict behavior is a function of the importance of the *goals* at stake and the *perceived incompatibility* of these goals with those of the other state. The stronger these factors are, the more likely are all forms of conflict behavior, including the initiation of violence, to be chosen in preference to no action. Since threat perception is tantamount to a perception of goal incompatability, the likelihood of choosing conflict behavior in preference to no action is also a function of the degree of *perceived threat.*

One element of the expected gain associated with the use of violence is the subjective probability that violence will achieve the goals at stake. The stronger one's own *military preparations* appear to be in comparison to those of the adversary, the greater will be this subjective probability and, hence, the greater the likelihood that violence will be chosen in preference to other alternatives. The more probable it seems that one's goals will be *destroyed as a result of the use of violence* (e.g., that the adversary will destroy some of his productive capacity), the less likely is violence to be chosen.

The expected cost associated with use of violence is a function of what have been called restraints in earlier portions of this volume. The disutility of outcomes associated with violence will be greater (and, hence, the likelihood of employing violence will be lower), the greater the *destructive force* possessed by the other state, the greater the *inherent cost of war*, the stronger international *norms against violence*, the greater the *effectiveness of world public opinion*, and the greater the *dependence* on the other state or third parties who oppose the use of violence. The subjective probability of negative outcomes will be greater (and, hence the likelihood of going to war will be lower), the greater is the other state's *capacity to penetrate one's own defenses* and the greater is the *vigor of world public opinion.*

The decision about whether or not to employ violence also rests on the expected gains and costs associated with other nonviolent alternatives. Forms of conflict behavior can usually be located on a scale of *extremity.* More extreme forms of conflict behavior exert more pressure on the adversary but also elicit greater resentment from him and often from third parties (Miller, 1964). In addition, more extreme forms are often inherently more costly. An example of the way a set of alternatives might be ranged on a scale of extremity will now be given:

(less extreme)	argument and negotiation	nonviolent
	political pressure	
	economic sanctions	
	military threats	
	limited military operations	violent
(more extreme)	all-out military operations	

The restraints against less extreme forms of conflict behavior are usually milder because of lower resentment and inherent cost. Hence, the expected cost of such alternatives is smaller, and, on this basis, one might expect states to opt for less extreme forms of conflict behavior.

However, the expected gains from less extreme forms of conflict behavior must also be considered; and, if they do not measure up to that achievable through violence, violent alternatives may be chosen despite their greater expected cost. Negotiation is a nonviolent form of conflict behavior. The expected gain from negotiation is a function of the subjective probability that it will end successfully. Hence, factors that enhance the progress of negotiation, such as the existence of *trust* between states or the activity of *mediators*, reduce the likelihood that violence will be employed.[1]

Finally, it is necessary to consider the expected gain and cost associated with *inaction*. It is entirely possible for a violent alternative to be chosen whose expected *cost* greatly outweighs its expected gain if all of the other alternatives including inaction are less acceptable. In other words, all forms of restraint against violence will fail if the status quo and other remedies look sufficiently unfavorable; hence, the importance of giving an adversary some concessions in a controversy which he cannot win, in order to avoid his turning to violence.

The picture presented so far in this section is one of a single actor, a unitary rational decision apparatus, devising many alternatives and carefully calculating and weighing their expected gains and costs. Such a picture, though useful, is not altogether warranted for four reasons:

1. Irrational or emotional forces, such as *hostility*, usually play a part side by side with rational forces. Hostility usually operates subtly by inclining a policy maker to the choice of more extreme forms of conflict behavior, because these satisfy more fully his impulse to harm the adversary, and by removing those restraints that arise out of role obligations to the adversary. The greater his hositility, the more acceptable become extreme forms of conflict behavior, including violence.
2. A *climate of opinion* about the adversary may develop which rules out certain alternatives before they are even considered. For example, after an extended period of conflict, the alternative of negotiation may seem so alien to national elites that they fail to give it careful consideration despite its actual promise as a means of resolving the conflict.
3. An atmosphere of *crisis*, which increases the general level of tension for a policy maker, can also affect his decisions by limiting the number of alternatives under consideration and distorting his estimates of the probable outcomes of action.
4. The decision-making apparatus almost always consists of a collection of people, rather than a single intelligence. It is true that national decision makers are sometimes so like-minded on an issue that they can be treated theoretically as a single actor. But such is by no means always the case. A theory of corporate or political decision making, in which contributions from various groups are integrated into a final decision, is needed to supplement the version just presented.

Stable and Unstable International Systems

Decision-making analyses of international affairs focus on the events internal to a single state at critical moments of choice. Systems analyses, on the other hand, focus on the distribution of various properties among a group of states and the interactions and relations among these states.[2]

---

[1]If negotiation is successful, it can also reduce the probability of war by diminishing the *perceived incompatibility of goals* on both sides.

[2]A thorough exposition of the use of systems analysis in the study of international relations will be found in McClelland (1966).

The best-known systems analyses of international conflict are the theories of balance of power and stable deterrence discussed in Part IV of this volume. Both deal with the effect on military stability of the distribution and nature of military capability. Recently, a few systems analysts have borrowed an idea from the sociology of community integration and proposed that the likelihood of war is an inverse function of the strength and universality of ties among the states in a system (see Part V).

Actually, it should be possible to construct an omnibus systems theory employing most of the forces discussed in this book. Most of these forces can be thought of as characteristics of states or of the relations between states. Hence, the distribution of these characteristics is relevant to the general stability of an international system.

One approach to constructing such a theory would be to start with a set of hypotheses about *trade-off functions* between pairs of variables in relations between two states, i.e., hypotheses that take the following form: The more (less) there is of *X*, the less of *Y* is needed to reduce the likelihood of violence to a certain level.[3] As an illustration, we might talk about the relationship between a variety of other variables and the military strength objectively needed for *adequate restraint* of another state from the use of violence.[4] For convenience of expression, the state whose military strength is at issue will be referred to as "we." Again, concepts used in earlier introductory sections will be italicized.

We need less military strength to restrain them adequately:

1. The more *compatible* their *goals* are with ours.
2. The greater their *trust* is in us (and, hence, the less likely they are to seek power at our expense and to engage in preventive war).
3. The more *friendly* their citizens are toward ours.
4. The less military advantage they can gain from *striking first*.
5. The greater the distance is and more formidable the natural barriers are between them and us.
6. The less *military strength* they have.
7. The more *dependent* they are on our good will (e.g., for the continuance of trade or common defense against an enemy or to prevent us from joining their adversary).
8. The stronger *international norms* are against the use of violence.
9. The more vigorous and effective *world public opinion* is against war.
10. The more adequate are the *mechanisms for the peaceful settlement of disputes*.

"Adequate restraint" of another state must be arbitrarily defined. For example, it might be set at a 1 per cent probability of attack from that state per year.

---

[3]The use of trade-off functions assumes the validity of some sort of *compensatory model* for the combination of the different variables employed in this book. For a discussion of this and other kinds of basic combinational models, see Coombs (1964).

[4]The notion of *military strength* used here is synonymous with the term *power* as used in the introduction to Part IV. The editors of this volume recognize that this variable is a long way from operationalization today but feel that its use in this illustration can be justified because of the great familiarity of the concept.

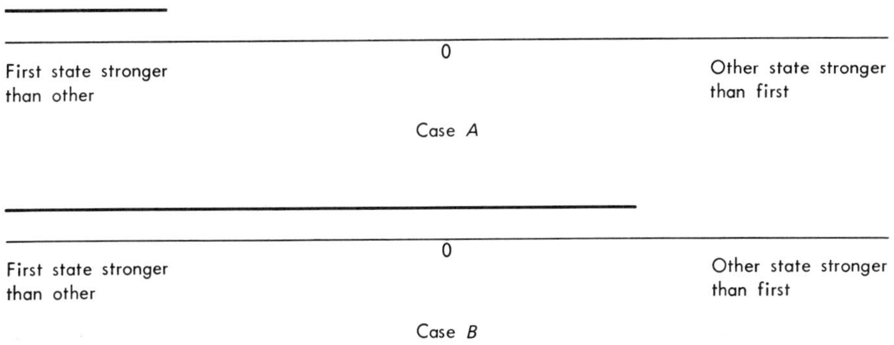

0

First state stronger than other

Other state stronger than first

Case *A*

0

First state stronger than other

Other state stronger than first

Case *B*

FIGURE 1. *Levels of relative military strength at which the other state is at least adequately restrained from attacking.*

Like military strength, adequate restraint is taken as objectively measurable rather than as an element of the thinking of any state (the state that is trying to deter). We may think that another state is not adequately restrained when, in reality, it is. This concept refers to the nature of reality.

A diagram may help to illustrate what is meant by the level of military strength needed for adequate restraint of another state. The dimension in Fig. 1 refers to the relative strength of two states ("first" and "other"). At the zero point, the two states have equal strength. To the left of this point, the first state is stronger; to the right, the second is stronger. The metric of the dimension cannot be specified precisely until more is known about the measurement of military strength (see Knorr, 1956) and the relationship between military strength and degree of restraint.

The heavy line above the dimension covers all levels of relative strength at which the other state is adequately (or more than adequately) restrained. (The right-hand end of this line refers to the minimally adequate level of relative power.) If the relative power of the two states lies anywhere along this line, citizens of the first state can feel reasonably secure. In case *A*, certain factors, such as the perceived incompatibility of goals or the lack of adequate ties, are conducive to violence on the part of the other state. The first state needs a preponderance of military strength to deter the other adequately. Case *B* refers to a situation in which the other state has relatively little incentive for aggression or aggression would be difficult or costly. The other state is, therefore, adequately restrained over a much broader range of relative military strength. Indeed, it is adequately restrained when stronger than the first state.

The diagrams shown in Fig. 1 are concerned only with restraints on the other state. A systems theorist would prefer a model that specifies the conditions of *stability* between the two states, i.e., the conditions under which *both* are adequately restrained. Such a model can be constructed by adding to these diagrams lines referring to the conditions under which the *first* state is adequately restrained from

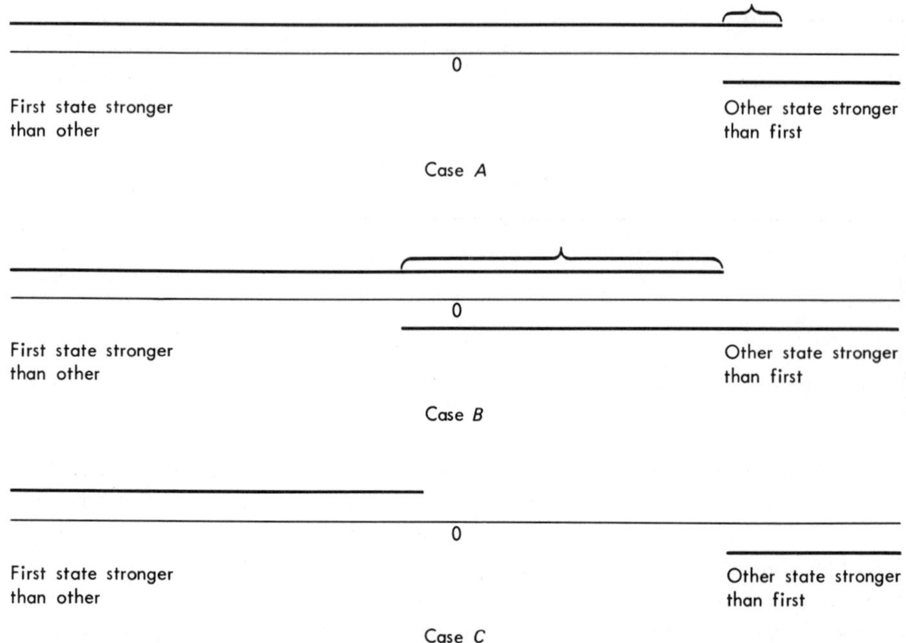

FIGURE 2. *Levels of relative military strength at which each state is at least adequately restrained from attacking. The upper line pertains to restraint of the other state and the lower line to restraint of the first state. Both states are adequately restrained in the region where the lines overlap (shown by a bracket) if such a region exists.*

attacking the *other*, as shown in Fig. 2. Once again, the upper heavy line refers to the conditions under which the other state is adequately restrained from attacking the first. The lower heavy line refers to the conditions under which the first state is adequately restrained from attacking the other.

The region in which these two lines overlap can be interpreted as the *range of relative military strength at which both states are adequately restrained.* The situation is stable when relative military strength is within this region. The width of this *region of stability* is presumed to be *inversely* related to the probability of achieving military stability or the persistence of stability once it is achieved, since a narrower region is less likely to be occupied.

Case *A* might refer to the relationship between a highly revisionist first state, bent on conquest, and a satisfied but somewhat hostile other state. Stability can be achieved but is unlikely to persist because of the narrowness of the region of stability (the range within the bracket). Case *B* might refer to the relationship between two relatively satisfied states separated by a high mountain range in the era of foot soldiers. Stability is practically guaranteed by the width of the region of stability. Case *C* might represent two states which are highly suspicious of one another and for both of which there is considerable advantage in striking first.

The absence of a region of stability indicates that there is *no possibility* of achieving adequate bilateral restraint.[5,6]

Similar trade-off functions and figures could be used to analyze the level of other kinds of forces needed to ensure adequate bilateral restraint, e.g., the level of trade between two states needed to outbalance mutual suspicions. As the model develops, it might be possible to accommodate more than two states within the framework, so that eventually the stability of an entire community of states could be determined.

The analytical diagrams just presented provide a framework within which it may be possible at least partially to resolve the disagreement posed by Claude (1962) between the *equilibrium* theorists, who claim that the most stable distribution of military strength is one in which potential antagonists are equal in strength, and the *preponderance* theorists, who claim that stability is achieved only when certain states have a preponderance of strength (see the introduction to Part IV). Our analysis suggests that the answer to this riddle, at least in the short run, depends on other factors. When, as in case *A* of Fig. 2, the other state is highly motivated for war or relatively poorly restrained by nonmilitary factors, the first state may need a preponderance of strength if stability is to be maintained. On the other hand, when the situation resembles case *B*, where motivation for war is low and nonviolent restraints are high, stability may be achieved with equal military strength (equilibrium) or a small preponderance *in either direction.*

This analysis does not deal with changes over time in the distribution of military strength or changes in the region of stability (see the next section of this introduction). Hence, it does not fully answer the riddle posed by Claude, who appears to use a somewhat broader definition of stability that includes the long run as well as the short run. But it does suggest that no simple determination can be made between the arguments of the advocates of equilibrium and preponderance. Each position seems to be correct under certain circumstances.

A link can easily be drawn between the systems analysis presented in the present section of this introduction and the kind of decision-making analysis presented in the last. Trade-off functions of the kind listed above follow logically from knowledge of the forces affecting decision makers (plus the assumption of a compensatory model for the combination of variables). For example, knowledge that the other state's decision makers are less likely to attack us the greater our military strength is and are less likely to attack us the more they depend on our good will leads to the

[5]The greater the probability of attack at which a state is considered adequately restrained, the longer are the lines in this kind of diagram and, hence, the wider is the region of overlap. It follows that the lines in case *C* of Fig. 2 might overlap if adequate restraint were defined as 5 per cent probability of attack per year instead of 1 per cent. Hence, with this new definition, stability might be potentially achievable.

[6]No position is taken in this analysis concerning the fashion in which the various factors interact in determining the probability of resort to violence, i.e., the length of the lines in Figs. 1 and 2. For example, the degree of restraint imposed by military inadequacies may be *additive* with that imposed by world public opinion, or these factors may combine in some other way.

logical deduction of trade-off function 7, that we need less military strength to deter them adequately the more dependent they are on our good will. These trade-off functions in turn imply the diagrams shown in Figs. 1 and 2. To put it another way, decision-making analysis permits estimation of the probability that a state will resort to violence under various conditions. Knowledge of such probabilities underlies the kind of analysis shown in Fig. 2.

Movement Toward and Away from War

The decision-making and systems analyses presented earlier in this chapter attempt to answer a very limited question: Given the following conditions, (e.g., the level of hostility and amount of interdependence) what is the probability of war? They do not go further and ask why these conditions change so as to increase or decrease the probability of war. We need also to ask such questions as: How do decision makers get into a situation in which the resort to violence has greater expected gain minus expected loss than any other alternative? How do changes occur in the width of regions of stability (Fig. 2) and in the location of systems with respect to these regions? The following brief discussion will address such issues in the context of some of the ideas presented in the introduction to Part III concerning movement toward war.

The point was made in that introduction that changes in relations between states sometimes take the form of a conflict spiral (North, Brody, and Holsti, 1964). First one state becomes less trusting, more hostile, and harsher in its policies, then the other changes along similar lines, then the first again, etc. Such spirals make war progressively more likely by intensifying the conditions that lead to war. However, conflict spirals are not the only pattern of movement in the relations between states. Sometimes, instead, we have *benevolent spirals* (see Osgood, 1962, and Selection 15), which move in the opposite direction from conflict spirals; and sometimes both kinds of spirals slow down and stop moving[7] or even change directions.

The points just made lead to two kinds of questions about change in the relations between states: Why does change persist in the same direction during a conflict spiral or a benevolent spiral? Under what circumstances do these spirals stabilize or change direction?

The first question can be answered in terms of the interdependence of the basic elements of relations between states discussed in various parts of this book: goals, perceptions of goal incompatibility, hostility, military strength, willingness to adhere to norms, dependence on the other state, etc. The interdependence takes two forms: (a) Each element affects its counterpart in the opposing state, which produces an effect once again in the first state, etc. For example, increases in *our* hostility lead to actions and verbalizations that may cause an increase in *their*

[7]Pruitt (1965, in press) has suggested that what looks superficially like stability in the relations between two states usually turns out to be an alternating succession of small-scale benevolent and conflict spirals which stay within a relatively constant range.

hostility, which may eventually add to our hostility. Thus, the conflict spiral deepens. Or reduced hostility on our part may reduce their hostility, which may eventually cause ours to decline further in a benevolent spiral. (b) One kind of element affects another. For example, increases in our hostility may cause us to break certain treaties thereby reducing our dependence on them and theirs on ours, which makes each of us willing to use harsher tactics, which increases mutual suspicion, which makes it harder to resolve conflicts, which heightens the sense of threat on both sides, which enhances the vigor of the pursuit of power, etc. Or reduced hostility on both sides increases mutual trust, which makes it possible to negotiate treaties that make us more interdependent and, hence, less likely to resort to harsh tactics, etc.

The second question, concerning the slowing down and dissipation of benevolent and conflict spirals, can be answered by explaining why one or both states fail to match *in intensity* the other's recent friendly or hostile moves. Take the case of a conflict spiral. Such a spiral can slow down only if one or both states begin to underreact to the other's hostile move, i.e., to respond to provocations with less-intense counterprovocations. Various factors may produce such an underreaction. For example, during a conflict spiral, a state's resources for further conflict may dissipate to the point where it cannot feasibly react at full strength to the other's most recent provocations. In addition, as relations between two states deteriorate in a conflict spiral, policy makers or other elites in one or both states may become alarmed about the direction in which the conflict spiral is carrying them. These men begin to counsel moderation and make an effort to diagnose and resolve the issues underlying the conflict. As a result, their state begins to underreact, and the spiral begins to slow down or even reverse. One might liken the activities of such men to a household thermostat. They go into action when relations with the other state deteriorate beyond a point and, thereby, make possible a return to the prior level of friendship.[8]

The analysis at the end of the last paragraph offers a vehicle through which the restraints discussed in Parts IV and V can be introduced into the discussion of movement toward or away from war. The motives underlying the activities of people who counsel moderation in the middle of conflict spirals are probably closely related to the motives that restrain national leaders from initiating violence: fear of war, a conviction that war cannot be won, anticipated destruction of the fruits of war, cultural ties or a sense of obligation to the other state, dependence on the good will of people in the other state, world public opinion, and international norms. To put the point in another way, these restraining forces probably operate not only at the point where a decision is being made about whether or not to go to war but also at earlier points during incipient conflict spirals and so cause these spirals to dissipate and arrest movement toward the brink of war.

---

[8]This analysis is closely related to one presented by Russett (1962), who argues essentially that war is more likely in a conflict spiral, the less time such people have to mobilize their energies to resist further deterioration. Russett's views are more fully presented in the introduction to Part III.

References

Brody, R. A., "Cognition and behavior: a model of inter-state relations," *in* O. J. Harvey, ed., *Experience, Structure and Ambiguity*. New York: Springer Publishing Company, 1966.

Claude, I. L., *Power and International Relations*. New York: Random House, 1962.

Coombs, C. L., *A Theory of Data*. New York: John Wiley and Sons, Inc., 1964.

Guetzkow, H., "Long range research in international relations," *American Perspective*, **4,** 421–440, 1950.

Knorr, K., *The War Potential of Nations*. Princeton, N. J.: Princeton University Press, 1956.

Mack, R. W., and R. C. Snyder, "The analysis of social conflict—toward an overview and synthesis," *Journal of Conflict Resolution*, **1**(2), 212–248, 1957.

McClelland, C. A., *Theory and the International System*. New York: The Macmillan Company, 1966.

Miller, R. C., "Some comments on power on the inter-nation level," *Background*, **7**(4), 195–200, 1964.

North, R. C., R. A. Brody, and O. R. Holsti, "Some empirical data on the conflict spiral," *Peace Research Society (International) Papers*, **1,** 1–14, 1964.

Osgood, C. E., *An Alternative to War or Surrender*. Urbana, Ill.: University of Illinois Press, 1962.

Pruitt, D. G., "Definition of the situation as a determinant of international action," *in* H. C. Kelman, ed., *International Behavior: A Social Psychological Analysis*. New York: Holt, Rinehart and Winston, 1965.

Pruitt, D. G., "Stability and Sudden change in interpersonal and international affairs," *Journal of Conflict Resolution*, in press.

Richardson, L. F., *Arms and Insecurity: a Mathematical Study of the Causes and Origins of War*. Pittsburgh, Pa.: The Boxwood Press, 1960.

Russett, B. M., "Cause, surprise and no escape," *The Journal of Politics*, **24**(1), 3–22, 1962.

18

CLARK C. ABT • MORTON GORDEN

Report on Project Temper[1]

A description of a computer simulation of international conflict. This simulation is essentially an integrative theory which, with the aid of a computer, generates a series of events over time. This theory employs a decision-theoretical model to link together many observations and smaller theoretical "islands" that have been developed by other scholars.

The Need for an Integrated International Conflict Model

An effective choice among alternatives requires a perception of the full range of alternatives available, an understanding of the nature of these alternatives, and an estimate of the consequences of the choice of any alternative for future freedom of action and overall objectives. Effective choice is becoming increasingly difficult for national decision makers and policy planners under current conditions of global and protracted political conflict, rapidly devastating military technology, and large government bureaucracies.

The global scope of the considerations and perceived consequences of national decisions has enormously increased the quantity of information that must be assimilated, before decision reflecting the overall problem of national policy can be made with confidence. At the same time that the global consequences of major national decisions have been recognized, the time available for effective decision making has in many cases been compressed by a rapidly reacting and vastly powerful military technology. Where months might have been available for study of alternative strategies in World War II, contemporary weapons require a capacity for decisions concerning the most vital matters of national survival within hours. When the difficulties of these increases in the amount of information that must be assimilated and analyzed and the decreases in the time available for planning and decision making are compounded by the reduced effectiveness of communications within

---

Especially prepared for this volume. Clark C. Abt is President of Abt Associates, Inc., in Cambridge, Massachusetts. Morton Gorden is Associate Professor of Political Science at the University of Pennsylvania.

[1]Project TEMPER was initially funded by the Raytheon Company and has received continued support from the U.S. Department of Defense.

a large government bureaucracy that actually tends to increase response time (or decrease coordination or both), the possibility for effective choices of national policy is degraded.

Experiments have indicated that there is an increasingly narrowed perception of alternatives under such stressful conditions as data saturation and time limitation. Thus, just when there is a need for the highest quality of decision making, the stressful nature of crises requiring a decision tends to degrade decision making to a few narrow and unimaginative alternatives.

Because of the much *increased amount* of information that must be considered before decisions having global consequences can be made and because there is *less time* now available for such consideration, a requirement exists for *a means of rapidly relating a given national-policy problem to all major alternatives available within the constraints of traditions and resources and, after the alternatives have been identified, of rapidly examining their global effects and consequences.* Most policy planners can identify the major available alternatives in a given crisis within a few hours. What they cannot do in less than months (when it may be too late) is thoroughly examine the branching trees of possible consequences that grow out of each alternative. Means must be found to *store the trees of consequences* that can be developed over many months in *anticipation* of sets of alternatives arising out of typical crises, in such a way that the salient characteristics of alternatives may be retrieved from storage within hours. An integrated model of global military, political, and economic interactions programmed for storage in and rapid readout from an electronic computer could satisfy this requirement.

A computer simulation of such an integrated model could thus serve the function of uniquely high-speed analysis of alternatives that is essential to rational decision making within very limited time spans. Routines for identifying specific consequences that are desired or to be avoided may be introduced, and the relative frequency and sensitivity of such critical outcomes can be examined rapidly for alternative policies and plans. By the application of clearly defined measures of effectiveness and cost in their major military, economic, political, and cultural elements, the relative payoffs and risks of alternative policies and plans may also be determined more precisely than by means of verbal comparisons. The relative rating of alternatives can never be more precise than the precision of the input assumptions and may even lose some precision in processing through the model simulation, but it is very likely to be more precise than traditional means of analysis applied very rapidly. An integrated military-political-economic conflict-model computer simulation can exercise the most sophisticated analytical considerations, that would require months to apply to each alternative, in minutes of computer operating time and a few hours for analyzing the printed output, simply because it stores the sophisticated analytical methods and can apply them with great speed.

Perhaps an even more important application of an integrated international-conflict-model computer simulation than very high speed analysis of alternative courses of action is experimentation with the objective of identifying otherwise unanticipated alternatives and consequences. The very activity of developing the elements and their interrelations for an integrated model of global military, political, and economic interactions requires the precise formulation of concepts to be exercised in the model. The very activity of programming the model for computer simulation—i.e., the writing of detailed instructions for the computer to follow in dynamically simulating the model relations—forces decisions to be made concerning the detailed nature of the model. Thus, hidden assumptions long dormant can be revealed and, once revealed as assumptions, can be altered to determine quasi-experimentally what other assumptions might lead to. It can only be done quasi-experimentally because the model is not completely similar to the real world. Nevertheless, this sort of experimentation is likely to be more rigorous and thorough than that taking place in a single human mind in the course of analysis and much less hypercritical and expensive than if carried out in the real world.

Experimentation with alternative strategies by computer simulation could be more thorough than personal mental experimentation alone because it is inherently accessible to many more persons. Any one analyst's mental experimentation with alternatives will usually omit some of the alternatives and consequences most obnoxious to that analyst (by the psychological mechanism of denial). But, if a number of people, by developing the model and examining and modifying the input assumptions regularly, attempt to "store" their own special biases in the model simulation, the relative weighting of probabilities of outcomes may be somewhat distorted, but a number of computer runs is nevertheless likely to reveal the *full spectrum of outcomes* as a result of incorporating the *full spectrum of biases*.

It may be asked why it is necessary to experiment with different national military, political, and economic policy alternatives, when empirical data are available from world history for an evaluation of the consequences of alternative policies. Historical studies are certainly useful, but they are not by themselves an adequate basis for evaluation because of the much increased rate of technological change. Technology, and particularly military technology, is so significant and so rapidly changing a factor in national policy decisions that there is inadequate experience with its status at any given time to provide a statistically satisfactory source of analysis. There has never been a general nuclear war (with both sides possessing nuclear weapons). We are already at a point where we must deal with the strategic consequences of thermonuclear-armed ballistic missiles with mission-cycle times of less than an hour, when we have not even had any experience (happily!) with a general war conducted with jet bombers and atomic weapons. Thus strategic essentials have changed more rapidly than has the accumulation and analysis of empirical historical data on alternative possibilities. In the past, many local and some general wars were fought with essentially the same weapons and supported by the same societies and economies, so that it appeared that historical studies might indicate probable outcomes of alternative strategies. Since 1945, and ever increasingly, we must anticipate the future by synthesizing simulations of those of its elements we can predict and accept the uncertainty due to those we cannot. But to extrapolate from the experiences of the past, except for the most universal abstract and generalized concepts, would be absurd because the conditions obtaining in that past have changed so much.

It may be worthy of a generalization that, *as the rate of technological change increases, the only theoretical method having any hope of providing a basis for planning is one exploiting the evolving technology itself as a basis for anticipation of possibilities.* Developing a computer simulation of an integrated international-conflict model can hardly be considered keeping up with technological change in itself, because its utility is still completely dependent on the quality of its inputs. However, once developed to the point of rationally processing its inputs, it may be modified by the addition of goal-seeking and goal-changing processes that will make possible an increasing degree of "learning" and corrective adaptation. Computer simulations may someday improve themselves beyond the quality of the data inputs and eventually even beyond the problem structuring. Today computer simulations of integrated international-conflict models may be compared to the newborn babe, helpless without constant attention, providing chiefly esthetic delight (and much cleaning up behind the scenes), and absorbing more resources than they produce. In the near future—the next few years—computer simulation of such models may be considered like small children having the beginnings of simple rational behavior that is plausible without being in any way productive of new knowledge. (At this stage, an economic submodel might produce "brilliant" strategies such as, "Buy low, sell high!") In the more distant future—perhaps in three or four years—such model simulations might have capabilities analogous to adolescents: considerable mastery of fundamentals, even occasional creative insights and contributions to knowledge, although these are mostly in the realm of drawing fresh attention to important but neglected problems, and, unfortunately, considerable erratic behavior tending to gross exaggerations. At this point the model simulations would be useful for exercising the imaginations and judgment of planners and decision makers but would still not deserve to be taken too seriously in their conclusions. Finally, in perhaps ten years, such devices might achieve a measure of early maturity: sound behavior with infrequent delinquency, solid production of new but only rarely startling knowledge, diligent self-improvement through acquisition of sophisticated experience and new formal techniques.

After that, it is difficult even to speculate without raising egregious connotations of the lesser science fictions, but, perhaps in a generation or two, such devices could begin to solve some really tough problems beyond current human capability, at a rate fast enough to apply the solutions.[2]

The Intellectual Basis

In describing the development of an integrated international-conflict model, it seems important to state first the principal theoretical influences at the time of the theory's conception because some aspects of the TEMPER model theory are similar to many current international relations (IR) theory concepts.

A description of the major influences on the development of the TEMPER theory requires a brief summary of how TEMPER deals with global international conflict in primarily political, military, and economic variables. Nation actors are treated as highly aggregated decision-making units that attempt to minimize the discrepancy between their ideal state and reality by allocating political, military, and economic resources within acceptable costs. The two super-

[2]This same forecast was made some three years ago, and some of its short-term aspects seem to recede like a mirage, always about to be solved, never quite nailed down.

powers and their allies, the United States and its allies and the U.S.S.R. and its allies, compete for the political loyalty, economic cooperation, and military alliance of the neutral nations, much as in Parsons' article on the possibility of an international two-party system, with the United States and U.S.S.R. in the party roles and the uncommitted developing countries in the role of the electorate.[3]

Where deterministic sequences of cause and effect are unknown or uncertain, probabilistic relations are employed. Qualitative variables such as ideological preferences are expressed and processed numerically by index scales. Differences among nations are expressed as different values of common variables much as Brzezinski and Huntington compare United States and Soviet political power as differences in some common variables.[4] As in Herbert Simon's notion of replacing the "optimizing" with the "satisficing" decision process,[5] TEMPER decision making, operating with limited time and knowledge, tries to find acceptable but not necessarily optimum responses to perceived problems.

Obviously many concepts in contemporary IR theory are not dealt with in TEMPER or dealt with in a very highly aggregated form. For example, the probably critical internal domestic decision-making process that precedes decisions as initiations, escalations, and terminations of military conflict are collapsed in TEMPER to rationalistic balancing calculation of the relative costs of peace, war, escalation, and termination. While the calculation includes political and economic as well as military factors, it does not even attempt to simulate the complex internal intrigues and organizational interactions described in the historically oriented studies of policy decisions by Butow, Kecskemeti, Whiting, Wohlstetter, and Abt.[6]

TEMPER theory, having been originally intended for foreign-policy research, highly aggregates the domestic sources of, constraints on, and operations of foreign-policy formulation in order to allocate most of its theoretical structure to the comprehensive exercise of internation relations. Increasingly, this seems an error of judgment to the writers. On the other hand, constraints on the number of variables and their relations were imposed by the need for a practical computer simulation (i.e., one whose running time on the largest machines was shorter than the average failure interval and short enough to permit multiple runs within budget constraints). These constraints forced a choice among the alternatives of concentration on domestic bases of foreign policy, foreign-policy interactions, or some of both. The second alternative that was chosen still seems to offer a more comprehensive theoretical frame-

---

[3]Talcott Parsons, "Polarization of the World and International Order," *in* Quincy Wright, W. M. Evans, and Morton Deutsch, eds., *Preventing World War III*. New York: Simon and Schuster, Inc., 1962.

[4]Zbigniew K. Brzezinski and Samuel P. Huntington, *Political Power:* US/USSR. New York: The Viking Press, Inc., 1964.

[5]Herbert A. Simon, *Models of Man: Social and Rational*. New York: John Wiley & Sons, Inc., 1957.

[6]Robert J. C. Butow, *Japan's Decision to Surrender*. Stanford, Calif.: Stanford University Press, 1954. Paul Kecskemeti, *Strategic Surrender*. Stanford, Calif.: Stanford University Press, 1958. Allen S. Whiting, *China Crosses the Yalu: The Decision to Enter the Korean War*. New York: The Macmillan Company, 1960. Roberta Wohlstetter, *Pearl Harbor: Warning and Decision*. Stanford, Calif.: Stanford University Press, 1962. Clark C. Abt, *The Termination of General War*, unpublished Ph.D. thesis, Cambridge, Mass.: Massachusetts Institute of Technology, 1965.

work for exercising and evaluating foreign-policy interactions than any other single theory. Unfortunately, this framework is similar to other attempts at comprehensiveness in its lack of rigor and detailed realism.

The principal theoretical influences on the initial and persisting TEMPER model were of two types: a theorist's personal contact with the principal TEMPER designer, and the impact of a theorist's written works. In the first type, four persons stand out: Professor Karl W. Deutsch, the senior author's teacher in undergraduate courses in political philosophy at Massachusetts Institute of Technology; Robert G. Porter, an operations analyst and systems engineer who was the senior author's supervisor and taught him the technique of flow-charted analysis of command and control systems at the Raytheon Company; Professor Thomas C. Schelling, whose seminar on arms control and many discussions of conflict behavior provided much of the stimulation for the theoretical effort; and Colonel William M. Jones (USAF retired, now at the RAND Corporation), a sophisticated military planner and war gamer who had the vision for a wider view of national security than of weapons management alone and who taught the writers much about the military decision-making process.

In the category of written influences, the works of W. Ross Ashby, Charles J. Hitch, Herman Kahn, Morton A. Kaplan, Robert Osgood, Nicholas Rashevsky, Lewis F. Richardson, Thomas C. Schelling, Claude E. Shannon, and Quincy Wright predominate.

Ashby's *Design for a Brain*[7] stimulated some of the TEMPER decision-making concepts, particularly the idea that homeostasis among political forces is the condition for stability. Hitch's *Economics of Defense in the Nuclear Age*[8] and his other writings at the RAND Corporation suggested the possibility of cost-effectiveness criteria for decisions' being applied not only to weapon system selection but also to overall policy selection, if only the various political, economic, and military utilities could be expressed commensurably. Herman Kahn's *On Thermonuclear War*[9] and earlier RAND reports clarified the nature of strategic deterrence and general nuclear war capabilities and limitations as they affect military bargaining. Morton Kaplan's *System and Process in International Politics*[10] reinforced the concepts of national decision making suggested by Ashby in a more abstract context, by treating international relations as a set of processes in a system of specific actors with specified characteristics and interrelations. Robert Osgood's *Limited War*[11] clarified the political factors tending both to escalate and to contain such conflicts, by suggesting specific military decision-making modes developed for TEMPER.

Rashevsky's *Mathematical Biology of Social Behavior*[12] and Richardson's *Arms and Insecurity*[13] both suggested at least the possibility (and also the theoretical attractiveness) of mathe-

[7]W. Ross Ashby, *Design for a Brain*, 2nd ed., New York: John Wiley and Sons, 1960.

[8]Charles J. Hitch and Roland McKean, *The Economics of Defense in the Nuclear Age*. Cambridge, Mass.: Harvard University Press, 1960.

[9]Herman Kahn, *On Thermonuclear War*. Princeton, N.J.: Princeton University Press, 1960.

[10]Morton Kaplan, *System and Process in International Politics*. New York: John Wiley and Sons, 1957.

[11]Robert Osgood, *Limited War*. Chicago: University of Chicago Press, 1957.

[12]Nicholas Rashevsky, *Mathematical Biology of Social Behavior*. Chicago: University of Chicago Press, 1951.

[13]Lewis F. Richardson, *Arms and Insecurity*. Chicago: Quadrangle Press and Pittsburgh, Pa.: Boxwood Press, 1960.

matical expressions of large-scale social processes. While universal formulas for arms races and other global phenomena were found to be a false lead, the approach appeared to offer useful results on a more disaggregated level.

Schelling's *The Strategy of Conflict*[14] analyzed the issues of military bargaining, not so much in Kahn's rationalistic style of systems analysis, but rather from the psychological point of view of decision-makers' perceptions, expectations, and priorities and suggested the need for distorted mutual perceptions and a mixture of cooperation and conflict in the bargaining among nations. Shannon's *Mathematical Theory of Communication*[15] and the work of other communications theorists indicated the behavioral (input-output) equivalence of two different networks, if the values of individual elements could be adjusted, which suggested that a common formal network could represent the behavior of quite different national entities if the elements of that network could be varied to correspond to the different degrees that particular variables are present in different nations. Quincy Wright's *A Study of War*[16] provided a rich factual background on the variety of international conflicts and the multiplicity of their causes. These, then, were the intellectual sources of the TEMPER model theory.

Theoretical Assumptions

The fundamental theoretical assumption about world conflict on which the TEMPER Model is based is that the overall nature of the current world conflict and the national strategies designed for dealing with it are best described in the comprehensive terms of global military, political, and economic interactions. In terms of an engineering analogy, overall system design is best accomplished by the systems approach, which considers all the major elements and their interactions, rather than the components approach, which refines details in isolation from context. In terms of operations research, optimization over the major trade-offs obtains a more efficient result than suboptimization of each of the elements involved. In terms of a military analogy, a balanced plan taking account of all major operations is superior to one that provides exhaustive detail on one operation and nothing on the others. In sum, a comprehensive examination of the dynamics of global conflict can profit from identifying the major elements and relating them in proportion to their importance, without regard to such artificial geographic and disciplinary limits as exist in area studies and specifically military, political, and economic studies. The balance of power, the balance of political loyalties, and the balance of trade are very much related, and the theory of global strategy on which TEMPER is based attempts to relate them.

Any theory is an attempt to explain phenomena, usually in a way sufficiently simplified to permit experimentation by manipulation of the variables to achieve specific results. A theory of cold and limited war and global conflict should explain at least some of the major events that occur, in the sense of identifying combinations of factors that, under specified conditions, result in these events. The events we are most concerned with explaining are international conflicts such as

[14]Thomas C. Shelling, *The Strategy of Conflict*. Cambridge, Mass.: Harvard University Press, 1960.

[15]Claude E. Shannon and W. Weaver, *Mathematical Theory of Communication*. Urbana: University of Illinois Press, 1949.

[16]Quincy Wright, *A Study of War*. Chicago: University of Chicago Press, 1942, 2 volumes.

political warfare (threats), economic warfare (embargos), and shooting war and international agreements such as military alliances, trade, aid, and military intervention in support of an ally.

The specific results we should like to achieve experimentally by manipulating the variables are enhancements of the military security and economic standards of, first, the free nations of the West and, eventually, all nations, by an avoidance or limitation of wars, technological advancement, and economic growth. The variables to be manipulated to these ends include technological factors such as productivity, economic factors such as investment, military factors such as deterrence and local defense, and political factors such as a nation's alliances and ideological propensity toward expansionism.

Each of the technological, economic, military, and political factors is itself the product of some aspect of some or all of the other factors. For example, the technological factor of unit productivity is the result of the economic factor of investment in research and development, as well as that of previous technology. The economic factor of investment is determined in part by the results of the competition among domestic consumption, government spending (including military procurement and operations), and foreign aid and trade for the gross national product, which is itself the result of the previous GNP plus growth from investment. The military factor of the balance of strategic power is determined in part by the political factors of allied and potential enemy intentions, the economic factor of government spending, and the technological factor of the relative combat effectiveness of weapons. The political factor of a nation's propensity to expand is also the result in part of technological advancement, economic productivity, relatively strong military capabilities, and how these factors interact with the same factors of other nations as well as those of ideology. Because of these functional interrelations, *no purely economic, military, or political theory or model can explain comprehensively the nature of international conflicts*.

A second fundamental assumption of the theory is that *all nations possess sufficient formalistic similarity for their behavior to be described by the identical set of variables*. Thus all nations have some degree of technology; an economy consisting of investment, production, and consumption; some actual or potential military force; and political loyalties and aversions. The relative weight of these variables may differ from nation to nation, as, e.g., the state of technology or the degree of political unity may vary from nation to nation, but the variables will be the same. In other words, it is possible to identify standard characteristics shared by all nations, the different values of which will identify their differences.

This is really not such a novel idea, being commonly applied to the comparison of national population, area, wealth, and military power. What is perhaps somewhat new is that a standard set of variables should also be used to describe the ideological, political, and decision-making aspects of different nations. This is made possible because the theory is intended to describe realistically only the external behavior of nations toward each other along with the most aggregated internal operations. It is not intended necessarily to describe realistically how the behavior is determined by detailed domestic interactions. In terms of an engineering analogy, the theory is intended to be an "equivalent circuit" to international behavior that will produce certain outputs from certain inputs, much as a real nation will but not necessarily by means of the same internal structure.

A third fundamental assumption of the theory is that *each nation acts like a homeostatic device that seeks an equilibrium between an ideal conception of itself in relation to the world and the perceived discrepancies from this ideal produced by real world dynamics*. The nation is assumed to behave in such a way as to correct the discrepancies it perceives between its ideals and the real state of the world by appropriately allocating its resources.

A fourth fundamental assumption of the theory is that *nations do not perceive the real world exactly as it exists, but rather in a way that is incomplete and distorted by their own preconceptions, values, and experiences*. Thus, e.g., they tend to be sensitive to (to amplify) external threats that have done them damage in the past.

A fifth fundamental assumption of the theory is that *nations will attempt to reduce the discrepancies between their ideals and reality in the most obviously effective way*, again on the assumption that the acceptability of the cost and the effectiveness of a given solution is that which is perceived. Thus if a discrepancy can be reduced only by introducing other and greater discrepancies between equally important ideal and real values, no action will be taken.

A sixth fundamental assumption of the theory is an instrumental necessity for the realization of cost-effective decision making. This is that *all costs and all degrees of discrepancy-reducing effectiveness can be reduced to common, commensurate units*.

Finally a seventh basic assumption or set of assumptions is that nations can reduce economic, military, and political discrepancies between ideal and reality by the following six types of behavior:

1. Ideal modification (sour grapes response —since it wasn't feasible, it couldn't have been desirable)
2. Resource allocation
3. Political action
4. Military maneuver
5. Military (combat) action
6. International bargaining (including formal negotiation and tacit bargaining)

In summary, the seven basic assumptions of this theory of cold and limited war conflict are: (1) geographic and functional comprehensiveness and integration, (2) formalistic similarity (identical variables) among substantively different nations, (3) homeostatic national behavior that attempts to reduce discrepancies between ideals and reality, (4) imperfect national perception of intentions and actualities, (5) reduction of discrepancies between ideals and reality by the most efficient means within acceptable costs, (6) availability of commensurate units of measurement for previously incommensurate costs and degrees of effectiveness, and (7) reduction of discrepancies between ideals and reality by the most efficient of at least the six alternative means of ideal modification, resource allocation, political action, military maneuver, military action, and international bargaining.

A Description of the Temper Model[17]

The Temper Structure

The Actors, Nation Groups. Within the model, there are different actors

[17]Limitations on space preclude a fuller description. Examples are offered in place of a complete presentation. A more complete discussion of TEMPER theory can be found in a comparison of international relations theory and

called *Nation Groups*. Each one is a sovereign decision-making entity with a distinctive data base defining its characteristics. The composition of a Nation Group as a representation of reality is set according to the needs of the particular experimental run. A run may use situations which define the Nation Group as an aggregate of real world nations acting in concert or a Nation Group defined as a single real world nation. The model provides space for thirty-nine different Nation Groups. In addition, multiple combinations for alliances of Nation Groups are possible. In this way, substantial flexibility is achieved so that one Nation Group may be the single geopolitical entity of the United States, while another may be an aggregate of European real world nations, and they may both act together in an alliance.

What They Can Do. The Nation Groups are provided with the capability of functioning in a broad range of situations at a level of detail deemed appropriate for the uses of the model. Each Nation Group, once its national characteristics are set in the data base, can recognize problems of a domestic nature, problems with its neighboring states, and problems with foreign powers elsewhere in the world. Thus, if we should like to design a run in which the European powers were an integrated Nation Group, we could have the decision makers of the group occupied with setting a national budget and procurement policy; advancing national goals, including territorial aspirations; and guarding the military and political security of their areas. These model decision makers would have to pay attention to domestic demands and pressures as well as to foreign-policy problems which require interacting with the enemy and with members of their alliances. The model decision makers operate in a complex environment where many cold-war problems demand solution and the solutions are often interdependent and in need of integration.

For each of the problems faced by the aggregated European Nation Group, there is a set of solutions appropriate to the problems. The players can alter the internal expenditure pattern to solve economic problems. They can bargain with their enemies to reduce the threat from the outside. They can alter the state of conflict by escalating or de-escalating. They can make threatening gestures to force an enemy to back down. They can do all or part of these actions at different times. All this can be done, resources being available, by the Nation Group.

However, problems will often be of sufficient magnitude so that allies will have to be called in to aid in the execution of policy. The European Nation Group may decide that the United States is necessary for the guaranteeing of the security of the area and may invite the United States to participate on European soil. Likewise, the Europeans may decide that some problems can be handled independently and that the alliance should not be called to function. The United States may also refuse to grant requests if her own national problems prevent alliance participation or if her own views deviate from those of her allies. Throughout model runs, the relations between the United States and European Nation Group may deteriorate, improve, or remain stable. The alliance may be tested over a

TEMPER in Morton Gorden, "International Relations Theory in the TEMPER Simulation," *in* Harold Guetzkow, ed., *Simulations in the Context of International Relations Verbal Theory* (forthcoming). The TEMPER model is continually developing so that this account may be slightly different from the currently operating version.

broad set of situations, and a record of performance kept.

How They Act—The Simulation Structure. Space—Space and time must be organized within the computer to allow the desired operations to take place. A structure is provided to implement the situations. The structure which will be described below is not the only possible vehicle to carry the burden of the model. It is the result of considerable experience and prior implementation. This experience has left us with an inheritance which is emminently usable but bears some historical traces which are currently necessary for economies of implementation, if not for design functions.

Computer storage space is organized to include four basic spatial units of interaction: the Bloc; the Nation Group; and two types of Conflict Regions: Land and Naval. There are three Blocs in TEMPER: West, East, and Neutral. The Blocs may each have thirteen Nation Groups, each of which has a communication structure with the other Nation Groups within the Bloc. This permits the formation of alliances among all Bloc members or any set of Bloc members. The Bloc appears in the model primarily as a structural support for alliance communications and interactions.[18] The three Blocs of up to thirteen members each provide the thirty-nine Nation Groups.

The Conflict Regions represent geographic areas which encompass one, two, or three Nation Groups, usually one from each of the three Blocs. Their function is to provide a structure which simulates geographic contiguity. The Nation Groups within a Conflict Region have conflict potential with each other. Conflict between two nations which are not contiguous within one Conflict Region may be carried out either with intercontinental strategic weapons, or by permission granted to an ally by the Nation Group present.

One ally may then stage through another to engage in military conflict with a member of an opposing Bloc. This can only be done, however, with the permission of the Nation Group present, which also becomes engaged in the conflict. The spaces provided allow the thirteen Land Conflict Regions as settings for situations. In addition to these Land Conflict Regions, there are seven Naval Conflict Regions,[19] a total of twenty Conflict Regions.

Time—Time is organized in the model to carry out the simulated actions which are to be run. Real time is collapsed into an abbreviated form, which allows ten years of simulated play in less than one hour of real time. Runs can be any length, ranging from ninety days to ten years of simulated time. The limit of ten years is self-imposed for many reasons, the chief one being that the value structure which is attached to each Nation Group (its ideology and cultural character) is subject to significant changes over periods longer than a decade. If the model were to run for longer than a decade, a much larger set of subroutines would be needed to make the culture dynamic.

Different model functions are also fitted into a time framework to help simulate reality. There is, e.g., a yearly budget which annually requires the decision makers to allocate their funds.

[18]There are some residual Bloc functions in economic and psychological areas which have not yet been programmed into the Nation-Group format. TEMPER originally had only three interacting Blocs, and computer space limitations have prevented a complete change-over at this time.

[19]The current simulation has only two.

There are procurement cycles, major international negotiations, and other functions which occur periodically to ensure their inclusion in model play. Time thus plays a role of setting bounds on the simulation and generates the need for periodic decisions by subroutines and, in the case of the man-machine game, human players.

Figure 1 illustrates the submodel structure for each Nation Group as the operations are carried out in computer space and time.

The Interaction of Submodels

The preceding sections have described TEMPER at a level of detail sufficient to communicate an overview. It will be useful to explore the simulation in a bit more detail to recognize the importance of an integrated view of international interaction.

Each Nation Group has a data base which includes the initial conditions for starting the simulation. The resources and motives for the allocation of these resources are initial parameters which set the character of the run. A change of data base to simulate new Nation Groups and a change in motives can set a basic strategy which the model will simulate in ten years of model time. It should be emphasized that the user has wide latitudes at the outset of each run in the choice of geography and political characteristics of the Nation Groups. The simulation then takes this data base and arranges it in playable order and allows the simulation to begin.

The Nation Group must first become aware of the state of the world through a status report prepared in the Psychological-Political Submodel. All of the information which each Nation Group receives about its enemies is biased to distort the information.

Having perceived opponents and having distorted the information accordingly, threat is computed. The military strategic threat is formed by estimating the opponents' nuclear war capability and intent and the danger of accidental war with which all Nation Groups in the Bloc are threatened. The military tactical threat is a measure of the enemy tactical capability and intent in local situations in each Conflict Region. The political threat is measured as the amount of political influence lost. The economic threat represents fear that the enemy is achieving a monopoly in certain strategic raw materials and is winning over the economies of neutral Nation Groups by economic relations. An unfavorable balance of payments also increases economic threat.

Within the Psychological-Political Submodel, protagonists and antagonists are now defined and the threat which each poses to the other has been calculated. The model now requires a dynamic element to drive and direct the Nation Groups. Each Nation Group has a series of motives which perform the driving function and which restrain it from using particular means to achieve larger ends. For example, each Nation Group has a set of initiatives necessary to set it in motion. The vague concepts of "initiatives" must be translated into quantitative form in order to render them workable in a mathematical model. Therefore, the driving force of internal initiative is measured by its desired economic growth rate, while its external initiative is expressed by the amount of assistance which it gives to others.

Some of the motivations act as constraints, as in the case of allowable limits placed on government control

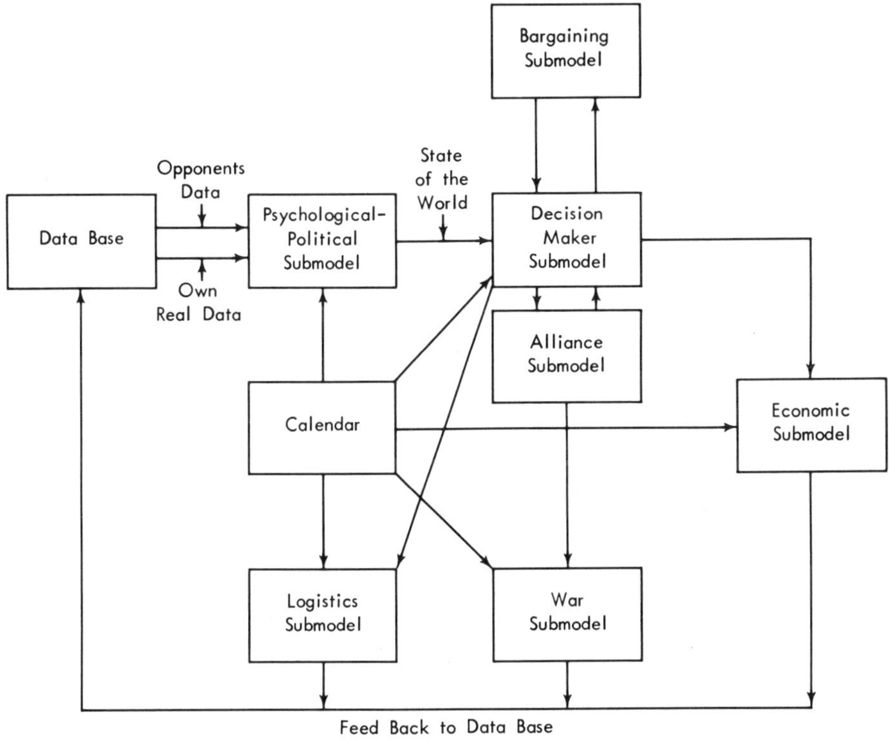

FIGURE 1. *Computer simulation submodel block diagram.*

over the Nation-Group's economy. In the case of the West Bloc members, the restrictions on government control are important, while less so in the other Blocs. There are also constraints in dealing with friends and enemies, implemented in the form of reluctance to use threatening military or psychological operations to solve problems which might be dealt with by less provocative means.

Some cultural motivations provide both constraints and incentives, as in the case of the satisfaction index. Each Nation Group must invest a certain amount of resources in the consumer sector in order to satisfy the demands of the population for consumer goods. When there are no threats to divert resources from the consumer sector, demands become a driving function for output; but when threats require resources, the driving function becomes a restraint put on each Nation-Group's ability to divert resources from the consumer sector to other areas.

The model now includes a set of resources for each Nation Group, the threats posed, and a set of driving functions and constraints to direct the allocation of resources. Given its goals and resources, the model tries to maximize the gains for each Nation Group according to the ideals which it holds. However, ideals or motives are greater than resources in the real world, and the Nation Groups must now adjust their goals to reality and reality to their goals. The adjustment of goals and reality to each other takes place in the Decision-Maker Submodel which must deal with the information prepared and made available by the Psychological-Political Submodel each time cycle of the simulation.

The Decision-Maker Submodel must define the problems to be solved, select and sort the problems for consideration, select the best solution among possible alternatives, and give commands to allocate resources for solution of problems.

The definition of problems takes place by comparing the ideal values of variables and parameters with their real status. The discrepancies dictate the nature of the problems to be solved. The problems are classified according to intensity and according to their domestic or foreign origins. Domestic problems are recognized each ninety days and their intensity is measured by the dollar difference between the ideal state and the real. The intensity of Nation-Group foreign problems, considered weekly, is also measured as a dollar discrepancy and is further magnified by the importance of the Conflict Region under consideration. The intensity is further amplified by the addition of a threshold on the rate of change to identify a rapidly growing discrepancy as a crisis. Crises are given priority (assuming no wars) in the problem recognition operation in order that they may be solved first and make first demand on available resources.

Nation-Group problems are thus recognized and sorted into appropriate areas of model responsibility and arranged in a hierarchical order by intensity for consideration by the problem-solving capabilities of the model. Once the entire range of problems is recognized and ordered, the appropriate solutions for each of them is considered.

Solutions to problems are chosen on the basis of the least costly of the available effective solutions. The Decision Maker does not optimize, but rather "satisfices," for the array of solutions is examined and the least expensive of the ones which work are selected until the problem is solved. It is possible to under- or overallocate resources to some degree for, even after several tries, the Decision Maker may not find some completely appropriate response to the problem of harmoniously integrating his behavior.

To solve problems caused by foreign enemies the Decision Maker can call on four possible alternatives. He can maintain the status quo, employ psychological threats of retaliation, military action, or bargaining.

Doing nothing, accepting the status quo, is the standard against which other solutions are measured. Only those solutions which are cheaper than the status quo are admissible.

The possibility of threatening military retaliation to force the enemy to decrease his threat is also considered. The calculated cost includes the risk of damage by nuclear war. The effectiveness is measured by how recent the last threat was and how credible the enemy finds the threat. If repeated bluffs have not been carried out or if the threat is used too often, it will not be effective.

Military action is also a possible solution. Escalation is considered and the military cost is calculated. The propensity for use of military coercion sets a different attack-utility threshold for each Nation Group. A variable risk-gain ratio sets different costs on the use of military force appropriate to the values in the Nation-Group's culture.

All of these military actions are a graduated response, and the Decision Maker will take the least costly response necessary to meet his need. Escalation and de-escalation are all called for in limited degrees, which may range up or down from a reinforcement of a garrison or a forward deployment of troops to a large-scale conflict with limited use of nuclear weapons.

Bargaining represents another possible solution. Bargaining one's own advantage for an advantage of the enemy may be a "satisficing" solution, and it will then be chosen.

The Bargaining Submodel must perform three functions to aid the Decision Maker in his choice of problem solutions. It must first identify problem areas which are amenable to bargaining. It must second decide on the terms of the bargain, how much of what is to be bargained. It must third compute the cost of the bargain as a problem solution to ensure that it is not more costly than the problem itself.

All bargains dealing with foreign affairs or domestic budget allocations to carry on the cold war, be they formally negotiated or tacitly agreed upon, are considered in the same bargaining structure. The object of bargaining must first be decided upon. Party *A* will select his most difficult problem. He will then scan the table of his perception of his opponent's problems. If *A* has an excess of resources in an area where he believes *B* has a problem, he will consider offering the excess as a bargaining lever to aid in the request that *B* remove the pressure on *A* in *A*'s problem area. The first function of the Bargaining Submodel, identification of what is bargainable, is thus carried out.

Terms for the bargain must next be set. The bargainable item is tested by *A* to see how much of the excess he can offer without endangering his position. He must then also determine how much he must ask his opponent to give up. The offer of the excess and the request for an opponent's withdrawal of pressure, after passing the tests of Nation-Group security, are made to the opponent.

The opponent must then calculate whether or not he can accept the offer by *A* and the request for withdrawal of pressure on *A*. If the offer is acceptable, and it may not be, owing to *A*'s misperception of *B*'s needs, *B* considers the offer and puts it through a test to see if it is worth more than *B*'s maintaining his pressure on *A*; *B* may also make a counteroffer to get better terms. If *B* stands to gain by accepting the bargain, he accepts *A*'s offer and request.

The second function of the Bargaining Submodel, setting the terms of the bargain, is thus completed. Next, each side must prepare the cost of carrying out the bargain and present the array of available bargains and costs to its Decision Maker as possible alternate solutions to problems.

In addition to the cost of the terms, there is a cost of prolonged bargaining failure. The time, energy, resources, and good faith lost in refusing a bargain is an opportunity cost added to the price of the terms of the next successive bargain.

Thus, a list of bargaining costs is presented to the Decision Maker to add to his array of possible solutions. With the total lists of various solutions, the Decision Maker makes his choice of the least expensive workable solution. If doing nothing is the cheapest solution, that will be accepted. Whenever Psychological action is cheaper than the status quo, it will be selected. Military action, if cheaper than the status quo, is then considered as an attractive solution and will be taken in conjunction with Psychological pressure. Where bargaining is possible, it will be taken as a solution.

Having chosen the proper solution for the particular problem in question, the Decision Maker must then go to the problem of next highest intensity, and the process is repeated.

Having chosen the appropriate response, the Decision Maker must then command an allocation of resources to deal with the problems as he has seen fit. The War and Economic Submodels allocate these resources and the Logistic Submodel ships them.

The Economic Submodel keeps an accounting of the costs of procurement and maintenance of different types of forces and their location. Strategic and tactical forces must be depreciated, replaced, and deployed. Each Nation Group can procure forces needed to help solve his own foreign problems. He forms force-needs schedules and receives the effective forces for his use.

The War Submodel sends forces of opposing Blocs into combat on the decisions of the Decision-Maker Submodel. The decision may be the result of power opportunities unrestrained by inhibiting motivations factors, the result of self-defending actions arising from aggressions, or the result of accident or misunderstanding. Combat outcomes are determined probabilistically according to relative quantities and qualities of engaged forces. Combat effectiveness factors are derived from three types of terrain, availability of air support or superiority, offensive or defensive operations, conventional or nuclear weapon usage, and other factors.

Other typical economic capabilities include the allocation of Nation-Group resources among domestic consumption, domestic investment, domestic government expenditure, and foreign economic relations. Industry and agriculture are distinguished, and industrial products are partitioned among heavy industry, light industry, military-ordnance industry, and weapon- and space-systems industry products. Levels for military forces, and industrial and agricultural products are set on order from the Decision-Maker Submodel. Annual economic growth is a function of capital investment, and the return from investment is a function of threatening world conditions.

The Logistics Submodel makes land forces available for shipping either at home (indigenous forces) or to allies (exogenous forces). These forces include tactical air wings, ROAD divisions—combined infantry—armor tactical units, paramilitary groups, and nuclear army divisions. The submodel also handles other aspects of the traffic of military forces between allies.

At any one time, however, some of these diverse capabilities may not be at the disposal of the Decision Maker to carry out the selected response. It may be that the Economic or the Logistic Submodels cannot accommodate the decision reached by the Decision-Maker Submodel. If the chosen solution is to escalate in a given Conflict Region, and the Decision Maker commands such action, it is possible that the Logistics Submodel will report back that it is impossible to send forces because there has not been sufficient previous procurement. The same phenomenon may occur with the Economic Submodel, which will show that the resources are not available to engage in a major effort which one of the problems has required. These failures to be able to respond to the Decision-Maker's choice result in the problem coming up once more for solution. The function of the operations submodels is to react to the feasibility of a given action. The selection of alternatives must include an integrated view of the economic capacity, military capability, and political willingness of the Nation Group. If the submodels responsible for carrying out the decision are not able to meet the criteria of feasibility because provision has not been made in advance, the state of the new world is not changed to mediate the problem.

In the event that the chosen solution is also feasible, the operations submodels will carry out the command of the Decision Maker and act to modify the real world in the desired direction. At this point the cycle begins again. The modified real world is taken into account in the newly formed data base of the model, and the data base then feeds into the cycle with new data resulting in different problems demanding new solutions.

In the event that the domestic resources could not handle the problem and the Nation Group could not afford to take military action or threaten unilaterally, the Decision Maker considers calling on alliance members for assistance. He scans the members of his Bloc as listed in the Alliance Submodel, and chooses those who have professed an interest in his Conflict Region. They receive a request for forces and decide whether or not to honor the request. Meeting the request is a function of the interest that the ally has in the Conflict Region and the risk which he suffers from engagement. Interest is determined by weighted sum of the allied forces already staged in the region, the geographic position relative to the ally and a common enemy, the resources of the region, and the past history of allied agreement. If interest is sufficient, the ally checks the availability of his own resources and sends off a reply offering aid commensurate with his interests and capability.

The offers of aid are then processed by the requesting Nation-Group's Decision Maker, and, if the offers are substantial enough to solve his problem, he acts with the allies' offers.

Each ally is given credits or debits according to the value of his contribution or refusal. A score is kept, and allies who continuously refuse to help are eventually dropped from alliances within the Bloc. If a Nation Group is particularly unwilling to express common interests with anyone in the Bloc, his score drops to a point at which he must withdraw from the Bloc.

The foregoing alliance relations apply to members of the Western and Eastern Blocs. The Neutrals, who are the object of competition between the two other Blocs, can make requests of either West or East. Similar considerations apply in the winning over of the Neutrals into either of the other camps.

In this fashion, Nation-Group action can be augmented by alliance cooperation. Alliances may form or break as they are tested by the model situations. Nation Groups may leave their Blocs and be put into the Neutral category for the operation of a new game. One important dimension of success or failure in the integrated planning for a cold war can be seen in the alliance records of Bloc operations.

The structural description has proceeded from an initial view of the status of the Nation Group to its problem definition and solution sets, including acting with allies. Such a structure gives wide latitude for users. It is possible to put different substance into the structure by adjusting Nation Groups and their characteristics at the outset. The user can also request output in a printed, cathode-ray tube, or slide format to view the different outcomes of his settings. In this way, the user may explore a range of possibilities and have rapid feedback on the results of his decisions.

Summary

We have described the need for an integrated global political-military-economic model of international conflict. The intellectual basis and the theoretical assumptions of such a model, TEMPER, have been outlined, as well as some of the logic and major operations of the model itself. The TEMPER model has thus been examined from the aspects of requirements, assumptions, functions, and operations.

The original and sustained objective of the TEMPER Model is the exploration of global cold-war and limited-war conflict among the major political power blocs of the era since World War II. Cold-war conflict includes political and economic activities, as well as military preparations and maneuvers threatening various uses of force. Limited-war conflict also includes important political and economic aspects. Cold- and limited-war conflict have been studied most in a piecemeal fashion by analyses in depth concerned with one particular geographic area or one particular type of operation. Unfortunately, studies of specific areas and operations can only contribute to but not accomplish an integrated global, cross-functional evaluation. For the development of national and alliance strategies, all major geographic areas and functional aspects must be considered together. Technology and alliance politics have so interconnected geography, politics, economics, and military factors that at least one important task in national policy formation is examination of how these factors interact on a global scale. This is what requires the global and interdisciplinary scope of the TEMPER Model.

Has this effort been worthwhile? As designers of the model, we are strongly in the affirmative, principally because of what we have been able to learn about international conflict and large-scale social-system simulation from the effort of model design. The users are the Joint War Games Agency of the United States Joint Chiefs of Staff and the National Military Command Systems Support Center of the U.S. Defense Communications Agency. They will have to speak for themselves concerning the utility of this man-machine model. Thus far, social scientists carrying out research on international conflict have not had operating access to the model simulation owing to its being in development. Even if access were available, however, we suspect that most researchers in the field would prefer to design their own models rather than use someone else's, and that would match our own intuition, which is that one learns most by doing, i.e., designing and testing the model, rather than observing its operation.

To widen the accessibility of such integrated, complex conflict-model simulations is perhaps the next most important task. Such models are unlikely to be improved until they can be given detailed examination and test operation by many social scientists. This requires major improvements in displays, computer input-output systems, and man-machine gaming techniques. Until wider access is provided to such models, their principal beneficiaries in knowledge are likely to remain their designers.

19

THOMAS W. MILBURN

Intellectual History of a Research Program

A report on Project Michelson, a Government research program (1959 to 1966) which was designed to generate scientific knowledge about strategic deterrence and international stability. Many research projects were funded through this program, including those reported in this volume by Holsti, Brody & North; Robinson, Hermann & Hermann; Naroll; Raser & Crow; and Pool. A committee of scholars which advised this project performed an integrative function with respect to theory and research on these topics.

The following is a brief intellectual case history of the evolution of Project Michelson, a cross-disciplinary behavioral science research program[1] on the nature of strategic deterrence, one form of influence process in international relations.

The Background Situation

In 1958 the most widely accepted premise of American military policy was the massive retaliation doctrine, which held that the U.S. should prepare to fight and win a nuclear war with the Soviet Union. This doctrine required the development of a nuclear capacity for massive destruction of Soviet territory, cities and ordnance. It implied the policy of counterforce, i.e., targeting primarily enemy missiles and other military installations, in the hope of being able to disarm an enemy or blunt his attack. These measures were presumed to be able to serve a variety of military and political purposes (missions): deter a Soviet attack on the U.S. or its allies, prevent limited wars, and pose an obstacle even to strong "provocation" by the Soviet Union. Hence, the massive retaliation doctrine proposed a multi-mission strategy.

A few Americans[2] questioned this

Especially prepared for this volume. The author is Professor of Psychology at De Paul University.

[1]Run by the U.S. Navy, this program involved some 35 scholars and their research assistants, included well over 100 separate studies and investigations and cost about a million dollars.

[2]These included Buzzard *et al.* (1956) and Nitze (1956). A little later, others asking similar questions included Backus (1959) and Milburn (1959).

doctrine and proposed instead a minimum or finite deterrent strategy. This viewed nuclear weapons as retaliatory forces, to be used in the event of a nuclear attack, and whose deployment was intended primarily to deter such an attack. Targeting of cities instead of weapons was recommended, and a *limit* was seen to the amount of nuclear force that would be necessary to deter or to respond appropriately, i.e., in a graduated fashion. Proponents of this strategy rejected the multi-mission approach, arguing that non-nuclear methods would prove more effective as a means to deter and control lesser conflicts and provocations. Three arguments were employed in defense of the minimum deterrent strategy: (1) A series of careful analytical studies suggested that cities could be destroyed more readily and with considerably less force than was earlier believed. This is because the destruction of cities in modern industrial nations essentially can be equated with the resultant collapse of these nations as political entities. Hence, it was argued that the U.S. could deter the Soviet Union with far less nuclear capacity than had been thought necessary. (2) The adoption of such a strategy would therefore save money. (3) A stalemate was developing, involving nuclear parity and hence a "no-win" condition in which neither party could escape unscathed from a nuclear war. The crux of the argument put forward by advocates of the minimum deterrent strategy was that criteria for effective deterrence could prove quite different from criteria for fighting and "winning."

The counterarguments of the massive retaliation advocates can be summarized as follows: (1) Destroying cities is immoral, so threatening cities is immoral. (2) We "really" deter an antagonist (e.g., the Soviet Union) through his *rational*[3] estimate of our probable surviving capacity for long-range destruction after his nuclear attack. Since this estimate is an indeterminate amount, likely to be affected by his optimism or pessimism, we must overprepare. (3) A multi-mission capability will prove less expensive in the long run, because it will take care of several kinds of missions that would otherwise have to be prepared for separately.

The advocates of minimal deterrence retorted with the following counter-counterarguments: (1) True minimal deterrence implies threatening cities, but threatening is *not* attacking, and if threats are credible (i.e., believable) they need never be carried out. (2) A multi-mission force may be less expensive, but it is also less workable because it is *less credible.* Nobody, including ourselves, could believe that we would attack, say, the Soviet Union, to inhibit a Communist attack by indigenous forces in Malaysia. Other capabilities and strategies are needed to handle this kind of threat. (3) A minimal deterrence strategy should lead to more stable relations between the U.S. and the U.S.S.R.

In the fall of 1958, the director of a Navy analysis group which had been estimating minimum requirements for physical destruction of industrial cities by nuclear means asked a psychologist (the author) for an estimate of the psychological, sociological, and political correlates of such damage. How much physical damage would be

[3]Rationality implies behaving consistently with a particular decision rule. Most of the prominent decision rules imply that a man should choose that alternative which will gain for him the most in comparison to what he loses. It is not usually considered rational merely to cause the opponent to lose more than one loses oneself. There is, of course, no guarantee that human beings, even national leaders, will act rationally.

required to produce sociological and political disaster for a nation? This was a difficult question. There was a meager literature on disaster, and even those sections dealing with the nuclear attacks on Hiroshima and Nagasaki did not provide much insight into how people and countries might behave following heavy nuclear attacks (e.g., Iklé, 1958). Disasters of a truly national scope have been rare in modern times. They have generally tended to occur to a single city at any given time, rather than to an entire nation. Help converges on the devastated city from surrounding cities. But in the case of a nuclear attack upon a whole nation, such help could not be obtained, and rural areas would be held back from giving aid by fallout.

Conscious of these arguments, the author began briefly to explore the disaster literature. It soon became evident that most existing works on disaster tended to *underestimate* the effects of a nuclear conflict. Focusing as they did mostly upon economic factors, they estimated only the lower limit of the damage that might occur.[4]

If the magnitude of a problem is overwhelming, and the resources for its solution, are of equally dismaying paucity, it may be more fruitful to redefine the problem, to ask different questions. It occurred to the author that the most significant issue was not the degree of disaster that might, with sufficient provocation, be inflicted on an enemy, but rather what the opponent *perceives* as most likely to be destroyed in any specific set of circumstances. The essential question was, How does he evaluate what he stands to lose? The opponent's perceptions and evaluations should influence or even dictate our decisions about military policy.

This represented a new set of assumptions, an overturning of the earlier "givens" of the problem. These assumptions would lead to the use of learning and decision theories to conceptualize the topic; and, to the extent that deterrence could be regarded as a broad influence process, literature from political science, sociology, psychology, and economics could all be brought to bear on the problem. Thus a study which began as a literature review of the effects of disaster and an analytical attempt to view their estimated consequences (to "think about the unthinkable") led to an interdisciplinary research program on deterrence as a broad influence process.

The Inyokern Meeting

The Inyokern Meeting, which was held at China Lake, California, in June 1959, stimulated and led to

[4]Much disaster compressed by nuclear weapons into a small time period would permit less time to adapt and adjust to it. Moreover, as anthropologist Anthony Wallace has suggested, disasters disorganize not only property and organizational structures, but also those cognitive mazeways by which men live their lives (Wallace, 1956). Men grow disoriented, concretized in their thinking, become little inclined or able to be ingenious or innovative. Survivors may feel guilty and apathetic. They often throw out existing governments and for a time become most conservative.

Nuclear disasters would also produce many mutations of viruses and microbial bacteria to attack a populace whose resistance to these, already lowered by much radiation, would be further depleted by a consequent inability to generate effective antibodies. Additionally, eighty to ninety percent of the people with intellectual and leadership skills in finance, engineering, medicine, law, and so on, tend to live and work in or near the likeliest targets—the cities—and thus are most likely to be destroyed. Without a gigantic field experiment that no sane or civilized, modern nation would be willing to undertake, there is no actual way of telling precisely how bad the aftereffects of a nuclear war would be (Iklé, 1958).

Project Michelson. The basic purpose of this meeting was to explore the premises underlying the concept of strategic deterrence for their congruence with some of the "harder" (i.e., better-documented) findings from the behavioral sciences. Another purpose was to inventory the current state of theory and research concerning international conflict in light of empirical knowledge in the behavioral sciences. The men who attended this meeting came from many academic disciplines but shared interests in the application of social and behavioral science to the problems of international conduct and in the relevance of new military technology to these problems.[5]

The international relations literature, which has blossomed during the past few years, was in a state of relative underdevelopment in 1959.[6] The behavioral contribution to this literature had scarcely begun to be made. It was far less evident then than now that convergences might be found among empirically based concepts and research results. Efforts to make a critical evaluation of the concept of deterrence caused the group to look at the processes and tactics of international influence, which led in turn to an analysis of inadequacies in the current theoretical and knowledge bases of the field of international relations. It was particularly clear that there were major inadequacies in our understanding of the psychological processes underlying national behavior.

The participants at Inyokern interested themselves in exploring the unexamined premises at the base of some of what was then current thinking about military policy. One such premise seemed to be that we were "good" and our adversaries "bad" *and* that they must recognize themselves as bad, that the bad knuckles under to the good. Another was that whatever will destroy will also deter, that power equals persuasion.

Bearing in mind that an overarching U.S. goal was to prevent World War III, were there widely held yet unexamined *psychological* premises concerning national behavior that were worth examining? What were the roles of national goals? What were Soviet, American, European, and Chinese goals? How did these relate to probable responses to various U.S. initiatives? How might we most effectively develop processes to discourage nuclear attacks upon the U.S.? What were the difficulties and possibilities involved in our encouraging the Soviet Union, say, to move its energies in ways consonant with both its own and U.S. goals?

In addition, might not effective deterrence be a function of the way the world, as a truncated community, was organized and of the way power centers were arranged within it? Vul-

---

[5]Participants in the Inyokern Meeting included, by primary field of training, political scientists R. C. Snyder (chairman), Ithiel de Sola Pool and R. C. North; physicists L. T. E. Thompson, T. E. Phipps and William B. McLean; economists C. E. Lindblom and Henry S. Rowen; mathematician F. E. Bothwell; sociologist David Gleicher; psychologists Raymond A. Bauer, Donald N. Michael and Thomas W. Milburn (initiator of meeting and, later, director of Project Michelson); and anthropologist John Gillin.

Some of their other areas of expertise included: disaster, Gillin; passive defense systems, Michael; Soviet Union, Bauer and Gleicher; China (PRC), North; news media and public opinion, Pool and Michael; decision making, Snyder; systems analysis, Lindblom and Rowen; defense problems, Bothwell, Phipps, Pool, McLean, Thompson and Rowen. Dr. Thompson was first Technical Director at NOTS (the U.S. Naval Ordnance Test Station at China Lake), consulted widely for the government, and was also vice president of United Aircraft. Dr. McLean was current Technical Director of NOTS.

[6]See Singer (1965).

nerability, as long as it was mutual vulnerability, might develop into a national, and international, asset. The answer was not immediately obvious, and ideally would depend upon an understanding of our values and those of our adversaries, as well as of our respective national psyches. And of course careful and thorough systems analysis would be needed. Moreover, what would *future* alliance structures (and the world they circumscribed) be like, or future technologies?

The reader will note that these are not trivial questions; it is not always clear what are our values and goals. For example, are these to be inferred from our behaviors, our preferences, our expenditures or our ideals? At sufficiently high levels of abstraction, e.g., the "good life," men of all nations share similar values.

In much of the proceedings, the meeting addressed itself to questions of how one achieves the most objective answers to these questions, i.e., answers least distorted by the perceptual filters of our wishes or our fears, our expectations or our ideologies. It also discussed the nature of rationality and, particularly, the limits on the appearance of rational behavior.

In order to fill some of the gaps in the International Relations literature, the members of the Inyokern Meeting attempted to sketch out a framework of what they knew and what they needed to know about discouraging and encouraging processes of influence relevant to the prevention of World War III. They developed the ideal of graduated nuclear response and discussed the fact of mutual hostageship. They generally agreed that demands and promises (or threats) must be commensurate. A message which demands little but promises great cost to the opponent for failure to comply is likely to be perceived and treated as incredible. Similarly, the message which demands a great deal but gives little evidence of willingness to pay a commensurate price for obtaining it, is not likely to be treated as credible. Clearly, greater demands require a show of greater force. The Inyokern group suggested, therefore, that limited war and related provocations might most effectively be handled through limited war forces.

The participants realized that new research methods had to be developed in order to examine more thoroughly those political and psychological mechanisms which were important to an understanding of international relations and relevant to the stabilization of these relations. The development of such new methods could be considered an intellectual risk, calling for venture capital of a sort only rarely available (e.g., from Carnegie Corporation, AF-OSR, ONR or NSF). The meeting surveyed our knowledge of deterrence in order to determine its psychological and philosophical underpinnings, and so to be better able to examine inaccurate myths that handicap our understandings of ourselves and others.

In exploring problems of strategic policy, the group developed a frame of reference which included looking at some traditional topics—national goals, the role of force—and some areas of ignorance, e.g., what strategies would go with what values, what were Soviet and Chinese values. This frame of reference involved a decision-making approach generally untypical of international relations theorists at that time. Out of the discussions came much thinking and questioning. For example: what is it we are really trying to accomplish through a deterrent relationship? (Not everything, surely, because we have other instrumentalities and actions suited to many purposes. However, we would like to influence the Soviet Union—through appropriate actions and through new military technology, employed in appropriate strategic and political ways—*not* to attack the U.S.) What can be the first and second order consequences of influence attempts? Whom would we influence—the people, the State, their chief decision makers? Do the Soviets internalize a conflict between rationality and emotionality? Does rapid technological change lead to changes in modal personalities? From this line of questioning evolved the need to implement empirically the concept of "Other's Perceptions" (enemy's perceptions).[7]

In concerning themselves with influence, the meetings reviewed and extrapolated from the disaster literature and discussed the psychological antecedents of credible communications (a function of Actor's actions) and *meaningful* ones (a function of Other's experiences). What is necessary to establish credibility—several things, e.g., congruence between declaratory and action policies; consistency of a message with past messages; congruence of value of the deterred action to us with the cost we threaten to inflict; congruence between risk and stake threatened and risk and stake deterred. What parts and kinds of our messages and actions are most likely to inhibit, which most likely to provoke, attack? What are the virtues of leaving American declaratory policies consistent with action policies, and what are the disadvantages? The meetings achieved some consensus and some dissensus concerning the way things ought to be. There was disagreement over the nature of U.S. values and over questions concerning what was needed or feasible. The participants made queries and recommendations, with respect to both policy and to needs for scientific investigation. For example, should we work for the graduated deterrence option or for the counter force? (The meeting supported graduate deterrence fairly wholeheartedly.)

Several unpublished papers came out of the Inyokern Meeting: one on Soviet goals, values and tactics; one on American goals and values; one on tactics appropriate to the discouragement of aggression; one concerning the nature of positive influence; and one examining the problems inherent in using a policy of deterrence based on reward and threat, rather than on threat alone.

A major input was the paper, "What Constitutes Effective Deterrence?" (Milburn, 1959), which was used to interest potential participants in coming to the meeting, and written to lay a basis for defining problems in behavioral science terms. This essay strove to find a basis for deciding upon a minimum level of available military force needed to deter an aggressor. It also considered some factors that might cause the level to fluctuate. The paper conceptualized deterrence, albeit overrationally, in terms of decision and learning theory. The disadvantageous side effects of punishment (less is known of threat) were described, as well as the virtues of "rewarding" an opponent for movement in directions consonant with U.S. and overarching values.

These papers developed the notion that a combination of reward and threat might be far less costly, and might also avoid the unfortunate side

---

[7]A threat is not effectively a threat unless Other perceives and responds to it as such. Similarly a reward is not an effective reward unless Other perceives and responds to it as a reward, in which case Other increases the intensity and frequency with which he engages in the rewarded class of behavior.

effects of threat and punishment. Positive influence implies that we might change the direction in which the Soviet society operates, a function of the extent to which we could change or control values of relevance to them. We might, it was suggested, examine Soviet culture, organizational settings, organizational roles and ideology, to extract convergences in research findings for an understanding of Soviet values, goals, and possible responses.

It was assumed that the behavior of any person and any group ordinarily has several causes; consequently we could reduce the effects of error in any set of observations through combining that set with other independent sets of observations. We assumed that each of the several conceptual worlds in which a decision maker lives (ideological, cultural, organizational, psychological) affects him to some extent; and since these worlds are overlapping, they have a combined effect on behavior. We did not suppose that a society's culture is independent, say, of ideology, but rather that the *observations* and *measurements* on which inferences regarding culture are based might be independent of those on which inferences concerning ideology are based. Either kind of observation or measurement might serve as a basis for prediction or generalization. To the extent that independent observations are involved, a greater sampling has to be taken from a total relevant domain of knowledge, on the basis of which deductions might be made. Also to be avoided are some of the errors implicit in, or built into, each of the modes of observation employed, variations of measurement associated with method. Despite the claims of scholars in a variety of disciplines, none of them has produced unshakable evidence that his field alone pursues the Truth. Where similar inductions are supported by independently gathered information, more faith can be placed in those inductions. After all, the observers examine the identical total entity, though each concentrates on what his discipline defines as worth abstracting from the total, active, living world. In different ways, and in different categories, they all investigate the same world.

Two studies were initiated on the basis of the above rationale, using scholars from different disciplines with different methods. One concerned Soviet values (Angell, 1963) and took a new look at the Soviet operational code (Singer, 1964). The other was a psychological laboratory attempt to capture the attitudes, beliefs, and values of players likely to come to mutual gain or mutual destruction through a version of Prisoner's Dilemma, a non-zero sum game. It was assumed that the results of these two studies would complement each other (Ratoosh, 1961).

To some extent, the first studies in a research program tend to set the style, and often the tempo, of an entire program. It therefore seems worthwhile to describe the first two studies in more detail so that they might serve as indicators of further researches which lack of space makes impossible to include here.

It seemed useful to study Soviet values and the Soviet operational code (as a set of value-action imperatives) compared with American analogs primarily to assess what to threaten—and so as to enable the U.S. more readily to inhibit and not to provoke dangerous, large-scale Soviet military actions. We also wanted to understand Soviet goals, compared and contrasted with American ones, so that we might more effectively be able to "reward" the Soviets for actions consonant with their goals and values, but dissonant with a strategy of a large-scale nuclear attack on the U.S. or a *heating up* of the cold war. We wanted, moreover, to estimate not only possible Soviet intentions but also possible responses of the Soviet Union to various kinds of U.S. actions—as tests of predictions made to probe our understandings of how Soviet perceptual filters of U.S. actions worked. We were fairly sure that the Soviets did not see us as we saw ourselves. So, how did they see us—and what were the systematic distortions in their perceptions of us (or in ours of them, we might have asked)? And we needed to be able to compare these results with other ones of Russian national character, of the Soviet operational code, and of the Soviet ideal man (Gorer, 1949; Leites, 1951, 1953).

We wanted to achieve results on the basis of an objectively arrived-at sampling plan. The plan would sample the contents of several systematically chosen relevant literatures addressed to elites along preselected categories, and utilize various reliability checks—all so that behavioral validity checks would be feasible.

Consequently, Angell and Singer began a systematic analysis of values contained in journalistic material directed to six roughly comparable Soviet and American elites. (Material on American elites was included to provide a basis for comparison.) It was hoped that Angell and Singer would be able to ascertain and describe the positions of periodicals aimed at elites (military, political, etc.) in the Soviet Union with respect to certain values, and compare these with the value positions of analogous elites in the U.S.

The U.S.-Soviet confrontation, a relationship chronically pathological during the 50's and early 60's, was a non-zero sum game. It inescapably involved elements of cooperation as well as competition. It was not a case of pure conflict at all, but a situation containing elements of both conflict and cooperation in which both sides had potential for concurrent loss or gain, though the latter possibility seemed less likely. In terms of the values which could be destroyed or maximized, both sides could win, or both could lose.

Thomas Schelling (1960) had written persuasively of the extent to which the cold war and various other limited conflicts might be considered non-zero sum games wherein tacit bargaining or communication of intent by one's actions could play an important role. The game theorist likes to suggest decisions or behaviors men will adopt if they are rational; the psychologist wants to know how men will behave whether rational or not. It seemed worthwhile, therefore, for someone to study certain personality and situational variables experimentally in a non-zero sum game. It was felt that research of this sort might help to validate or disaffirm some of the hypothesized relations suggested by Schelling. The economist tends to postulate rationality in his human subjects: they will behave in a certain way because they are rational. The psychologist wishes at least to observe behavior, and at best to produce it from environmental manipulations.

Roughly in concert with the studies of Soviet values and operational code, a parallel laboratory investigation of personality, style, value and attitudinal factors which influence style of play of Prisoner's Dilemma (a mixed motive game in which a player has to choose between increasing his own immediate gain or increasing the total gain of both players) was begun by psychologist Philburn Ratoosh (1961).[8]

Though their methods differed (content analysis vs. laboratory experiment), the Angell and Singer investigation was related to that of Ratoosh in that similar propositions were tested. It was assumed that one could verify propositions more completely by using scientific methods maximally different from one another. In content analysis, one has a sense of relating to a specific current or historical reality, one in which we cannot unambiguously test causal propositions; whereas in the experiment one maximizes the general (abstract) nature of the arrangement so that one may hope to grasp causal relationships between some very few variables. (The comparison, however, proved more suggestive than immediately useful.) Similarly, the results of historical data such as that of Raoul Naroll might be compared with abstract games and political simulations such as the Inter-nation Simulation of Harold Guetzkow, not merely so that either research technique might "validate" the other, but so that both might verify or at least test similar propositions.

[8]The prisoner's dilemma has proved a simple, successful, and, in the last few years, widely used example of a non-zero sum (or "non-constant sum") game, i.e., a decision situation susceptible to rational analysis. Most "games" as decision situations are constant-sum in the sense that the losses for one player are wins for the other, and vice versa. Such games are simple analogs of ubiquitous interdependent human relations or situations which are not pure conflict affairs but also necessitate some coordination, if not cooperation, between players (or experimental subjects), since outcomes are possible in which both players can win or both lose. Rationality in such situations may yield different outcomes depending upon whether it is defined for the individual or the group (i.e., includes consideration of outcomes for one or both).

One can imagine an error term or a bias (error variance) associated with any method and hope to arrive at a closer approximation of truth through searching for convergences among findings from very different methods. That way, the systematic, methods-associated bias of each would tend to cancel the other out. Such was the general rationale for Michelson, in terms of which many of the relations between separate investigations were built.

The Formative Period

It was a fortunate time in the social sciences. Lincoln Bloomfield had developed Polex, a form of political exercise through which he studied crises, employing scenarios of threatening situations with experts on areas or strategy playing through the problems. Harold Guetzkow had invented Inter-nation Simulation, a man-machine simulation of a world in which internal relations were programmed on a computer while external relations were played out by human players. Daniel Lerner was about to replicate his survey of the opinions of European elites; he had interviewed panels of leadership in England, France and Germany since 1954. Charles Osgood was about to investigate meanings in twenty non-American cultures, in an attempt to replicate in each culture findings based on his new technique for the measurement of the structure of connotative meaning, the semantic differential. Political scientist Robert C. North, from what had started as a 1958–1959 faculty seminar on conflict at Stanford University, had undertaken a thorough investigation of freshly available archival documents which dealt with events in the crises leading to World War I.

North's scholarly and behavioral (Ford Foundation-supported) case study of factors operating during the six weeks preceding hostilities (which later he compared and contrasted with events in the Bosnian Crisis of 1908 and 1909) focused on the outbreak of an "accidental war." Although it was not immediately realized, he was beginning to study a particular crisis situation from a point of view which would enable him and others to study and compare several crises. His rigorous content analysis of communications between the five capitals seemed exciting and promising from the start.

Meanwhile, a Navy Polaris Steering Committee concerned with research and exploratory development of new technology developed an interest in exploring the nature of strategic deterrence, having in mind, initially, the development of relevant background information and, eventually, criteria for choosing from among future weapons systems those which were potential successors to Polaris. After reviewing several proposals from different organizations, the Polaris Committee supported the plans from the Naval Ordnance Test Station. Enough money became available to implement research recommendations of the Inyokern Meeting of June 1959. (It might be noted in passing that the proposal for this investigation of the nature and antecedents of effective deterrence had, for selling purposes, to be divided into background and more operationally relevant studies.)

The model which appears in Figure 1 began to take shape as the basis for explorations, i.e., for planning research, rather than as an ideal analytical tool. This model is conceptualized in terms of inputs (or independent variables), i.e., actions by the U.S.; outputs (dependent variables or results); the appearance of war (+) or its disappearance (−); the growth of war (🡅) or its de-escalation (🡇); and several kinds of intervening variables. These last provided bases for studying factors relevent to the understanding of how situations such as crises, alliance systems and factors such as culture or ideology all could function as perceptual filters which could transform U.S. actions into effects quite different from what we had intended. History, various forms of strategic gaming, cross-cultural investigations, the psychological laboratory and various forms of simulation for sampling the total conceptual space more adequately, could all now be employed. Aside from the notion of reducing the error variance associated with a particular method or technique of observation, a purely serendipitous advantage emerged from the multi-method approach: that some policy makers might now see specific kinds of data as being more persuasive than others, because they matched better their own experience and training. Should it turn out that consistencies or convergences in the findings could indeed be produced, then historical data might persuade the historians, and simulation data persuade the engineers; and each might find the results of the methods used by the other more acceptable in this context.

It became possible to develop a more cohesive research strategy for an entire program, a research program which became known as "Project Michelson," named for Albert Michelson, the first U.S. Nobel prize winner in physics. The program was named for him because he had sought to measure what had been considered absolute or ineffable, e.g., the speed of light, the elasticity of the earth; and we too, who had to communicate to physicists, were attempting to introduce

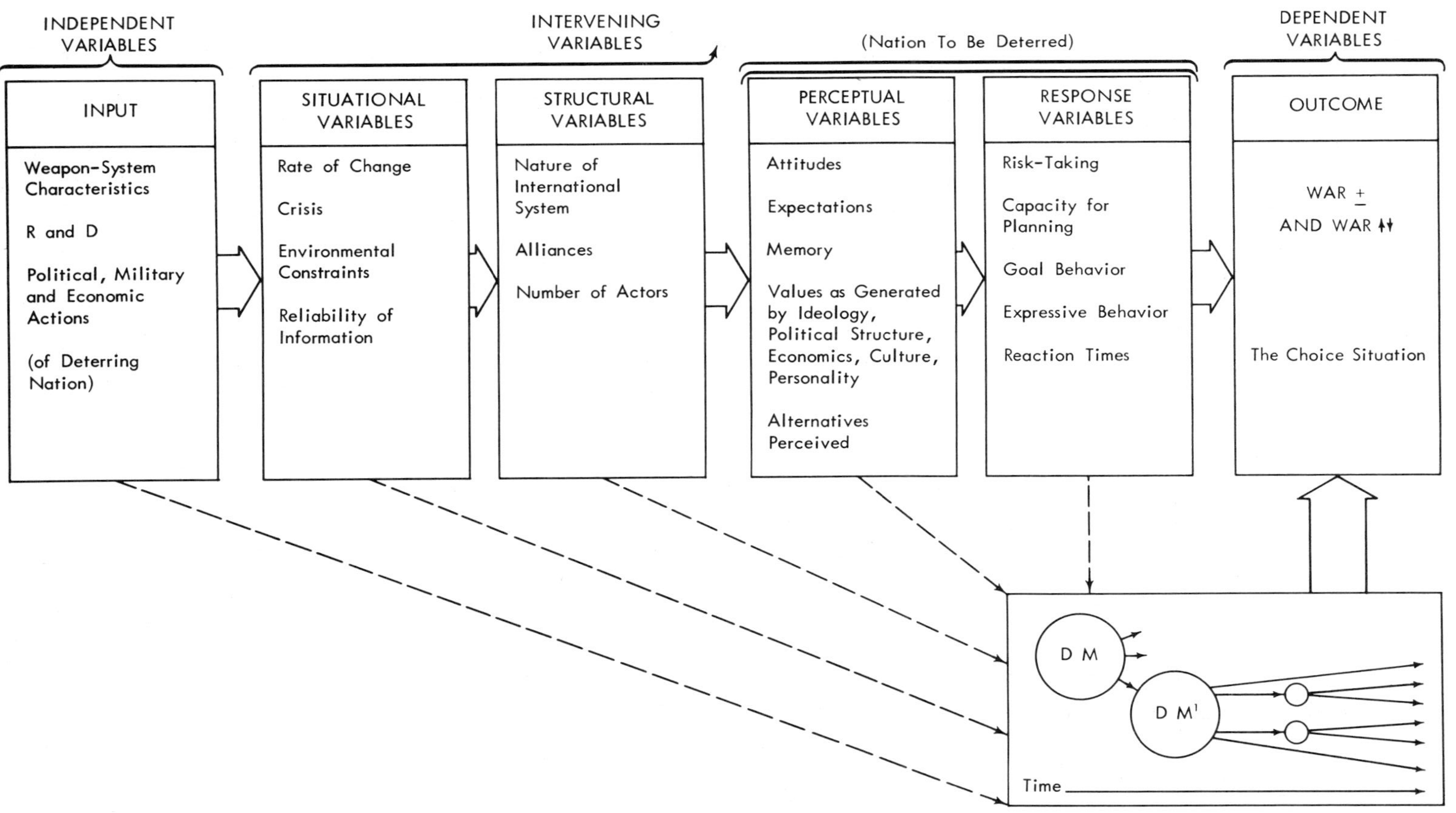

FIGURE 1. *The Project Michelson conceptual model.*

more rigor into the study of phenomena which must seem to physicists equally unmeasurable.

A structure for evaluating the program and pointing out promising directions was developed. This was the Project Michelson Advisory Committee. It consisted of an audience of experts from government, including the Department of Defense and the State Department, and from academia, who met once or twice a year from 1961–1965. Some participants in the Inyokern Meeting served on the committee. The Advisory Committee often proved an important source of change in the Project Michelson premises.

For heuristic reasons, it was assumed that American, Soviet, and Chinese goals could be pinpointed and understood. With these goals in mind, some predictions of the behavior of these countries could be made. Because American leadership valued alliances with European allies, it could be assumed that the attitudes of those allies toward weapons systems, as well as toward deterrence and defense, would prove of interest to the research team. In pursuing these interests, it became evident that methods did not exist for generating comparable forms of data cross-historically and cross-culturally. Existing forms of simulation or gaming were very primitive indeed. New modes would simply have to be developed, as would others called for by the rationale of the research.

It was then that the dialogues of the Project Michelson research team began to include such matters as are diagrammed in Figure 1, e.g., situational variables, structural variables and perceptual variables. (Certain studies had to be tailored to be within reach of these classes of categories, or dovetailed to fit an independent or dependent variable category. This figure, which evolved from several earlier conceptualizations of the problem, depicts U.S. actions as *inputs* and Soviet responses as *outputs*. It emphasizes the prominent roles of various classes of intervening or mediating variables, e.g., situational ones such as crises; structural ones such as the cohesiveness of the Western as contrasted with that of the Eastern bloc; and perceptual ones, based upon anticipations and fears of the Soviet leadership, as these might be shaped by ideology, culture, and modal personality, as well as the specific personality structures of particular leaders. The schema later provided a basis for planning research studies and a pattern of research. Some studies, concerning the nature of crises (Hermann, 1964), for example, were seen as contributing to the general class of situational variables. Other studies provided a propositional inventory, e.g., a survey of the strategic literature (Snyder, 1961) yielding 212 hypotheses which were related to relevant social and behavioral science theories and findings and which served to interrelate classes of variables.

Results of this preliminary effort provided one basis for Inter-nation Simulation exercises by Harold Guetzkow and his colleagues, which would throw light on possible changes in future worlds, and also provided a source of hypotheses which could be tested by Raoul Naroll in his cross-historical and cross-cultural studies. Naroll aimed particularly to achieve methodological rigor in his studies; and he developed data quality control techniques for acceptance or rejection of data for analysis.

It seemed appropriate also to describe possible relevant future situations, among them one concerning arms control. Louis Sohn began then his extremely successful prediction of Soviet arms control positions. Ithiel de Sola Pool analyzed the role of political context and its impact on mode and style of communication and of the relevance of communication theory for specifying the conditions of credible deterrent messages, presumptively both tacit and formal communications. Daniel Lerner collected current data concerning the values and attitudes of European elites, which were deemed relevant to the study.

Viewed in retrospect, the project Michelson conceptual model (Figure 1) provided a more explicit rendering of premises than had been possessed earlier, but it was still vague in many ways. While it was helpful as a tool for the integration of research, as a theoretical framework it contained a number of flaws. No provision was made for interaction between the variables; and it was doubtful that the variables would always operate in the left to right direction delineated in the model. In fact, the model may have prevented seeing deterrence as a function of interactions of the world community; or as a function of the quality of interaction between two, or among several, nations. Though systems experts have emphasized the merit of including feedback loops for learning and memory in a model of this sort, none was included here, this model seeming complicated enough without them. The model also gave little attention to affect (i.e., emotion) except as it might appear in time of crisis. It now seems likely that affect acts as an amplifier or as an inhibitor of perceptions and actions, particularly in periods of crisis.[9] In non-crisis situations the lack of concern with affect might be more reasonable, but that remains an empirical question. Though many hypotheses were built and tested, the model itself, as a whole and single entity, was never tested. In fact, no statement was ever formulated in sufficiently operational language to make possible the testing of the entire model. In that sense, no validated theory of deterrence was developed; nor was any related theory of influence in international relations evolved from which a theory of deterrence might be extrapolated. However, key building blocks, e.g., the role of crisis, were identified and shaped. Deficiencies were identified in existing analytical tools and empirical evidence, and actions were taken to remedy them. It should be remembered that during this period not even an *untestable* model of deterrence appeared in the literature.

Testing of the model would have included the testing of linked chains of hypotheses and interlocking hypotheses, as well as attempts to predict from the model to several (rather than one) dependent variables—all across various methods. An early Project Michelson model of deterrence (prior to Figure 1) had started with a concept of the rational behavior of a single decision maker whom it would be advantageous to try to influence. It was supposed that this decision maker might first be considered to act in a rational manner, on the basis of a minimum or least-regret strategy, and that custom, law, ideology, culture, habit, and neurosis would all act to reduce the alternatives available from some possible set to a much smaller grouping resulting from these. The earlier model was also a *multi-method* and *multi-observation point* model, since it assumed that actual international behavior is overdetermined. That model, however, was more

[9]Tomkins (1962, 1963) has developed an empirically based theory of the nature of the affects.

static and less complete than the one which appears in Figure 1.

Knowledge for Action

In the summer of 1962, the Project Michelson Advisory Committee brought together a group of scientists to integrate and apply the results of prior studies up to that time. These included Professors R.C. Snyder, Ithiel de Sola Pool, C.E. Osgood, Wilbur Schramm, and R.C. North, as well as other specialists on various individual topics such as content analysis, political and military gaming and the study of personality. There Pool wrote "Deterrence as an Influence Process," an impressive refinement of the definition of deterring as influence, in which he articulated and compared two influence models: an economic model and a psychological (persuasive) model. He suggested ways in which they interrelate, and are both applicable to deterrent situations. There Snyder performed a *tour de force* in reviewing and integrating the results of the several efforts at stating or validating hypotheses to that date. At the same time, North and Osgood began another kind of integration, across differentiation units and levels of complexity, i.e., person, group, institution, nation, in which they sought to apply a revised version of Osgood's mediational learning theory model to groups and to international relations.

The above efforts concentrated upon the development of new insights into, and new knowledge of, deterrence and other influence processes. These, in turn, entailed the application of relevant social and behavioral science knowledge. At the same time, because of the interests of some of the investigators, and especially because of the increasing interest of the sponsors, there was concern for the development of guidelines for action. In his review of the literature of strategic hypotheses in 1961, Snyder had proposed a set of decision rules derived from an inventory of strategic propositions. Essentially, this was an attempt to explore certain influence strategies and tactics as possible applied tools of national security. During the Summer Study of 1962 he revised these decision rules so as to increase their potential utility for action.

Pool developed and applied a large number of criteria for evaluating various technological modes. He subdivided his criteria according to the nature of the situation, e.g., crisis or non-crisis. In a meeting at China Lake in 1965, Glenn Paige, Edwin Shneidman, Jan Triska and some others sought to spell out decision rules for the management of crises.[10]

---

[10]A crisis may sometimes be exploited through the crystallization of values which crises produce, and through the cohesiveness and sense of urgency which they develop within organizations. However, since crises tend to be characterized by a need for innovations, a high degree of threat, and a need for action which is high relative to the time available for decision, the existence of crisis rules for management can be readily imagined. The capacity to delay response with military force, the hypothesized merit of which was explored in two sets of studies by Crow and Raser, conceivably would be extremely valuable in crises because it would provide more time for key decision makers to innovate. On the other hand, contingency planning should, merely by having been done, reduce the need to innovate. The prime need in times of crises is to seek to defend against, or at any rate to handle, the most dangerous-appearing threat first, even though the existence of that risk might be uncertain. A good example of this kind of action is the hospital situation in which a patient shows ambiguous symptoms characteristic of both an extremely dangerous, rare disease and a far less dangerous, frequently occurring one. A first rule of internists is to work as though it were actually the more dangerous

The final meeting of the Project Michelson Advisory Committee was held at Pearl Harbor in the fall of 1964. By that time, relations with the Soviets seemed more stable and less sensitive to disturbance than earlier. Moreover, by then, the related problem of the proliferation of nuclear weapons scarcely appeared to be the responsibility of the Department of Defense. The problems for the immediate future at that time appeared to be those of limited and sublimited war, particularly the sort of actions supported by the Communist Chinese (PRC). Plans for future research should, therefore, emphasize the Far East; and should examine the conflict there more carefully than at any time before. It would be difficult to say how much of a role the conflict in South Vietnam played in the change in the *Zeitgeist*. However, that conflict was growing; and we tended to respond to its existence by more emphasis on *coup d'état* and limited war, not on Southeast Asia.

During the last year of the studies, no less attention was given to the application of scholarly criteria for evaluating the studies. However, more attention was paid to applying the findings to policy problems.

By the time Project Michelson concluded in 1965, the personnel acquired an awareness of the need to focus the efforts of behavioral science toward developing an understanding of motives and intentions, likely behaviors and likely responses of potential adversaries. This is an area in which there tends to be too little systematic and objective information, as contrasted with the evaluation of capabilities of opponents. The behavioral sciences might eventually prove to be useful in evaluating morale, and political and sociological stability and growth.

disease, even though some of the side effects of the treatment may not be altogether pleasant for the patient and unnecessary to the less severe condition.

Summary and Conclusions

In 1958 some operations analysts (systems analysts working at operations research), physical scientists by training, invited a psychologist to look at a model of physical damage they had developed and validated, in order that their model might be enriched by social science inputs. Their invitation led to a paper "What Constitutes Effective Deterrence?" (Milburn, 1959) which was then employed to interest behavioral scientists in participating in the Inyokern Meeting. Redefinition of the problem was essential and finally led the Inyokern group to want to deal with influence and communication systems as well as their perceptual and motivational underpinnings.

The participants explored some of the consequences of premises relevant to behavior, e.g., premises about the perception of intentions or the nature of influence processes at different levels of societal complexity. In particular, they emphasized the role of Soviet (and Chinese) goals, perceptions, and perceptual filters of culture, ideology, and situation in determining Soviet reactions to what Americans might regard as actions clearly intended to discourage or encourage certain classes of action. Americans have several goals relevant to strategic deterrence by which they hope to prevent World War III; so they would combine discouraging some kinds of action with encouraging others—"the stick and the carrot" method. International influence efforts can also be thought of in communication terms, although not in terms of words alone, since nations also employ tacit communications. Tacit communications, e.g., those involving the movements of troops or artillery in or out of attack or defense range, are blunt and often ambiguous ways of revealing intended actions. They also indicate the degree to which one's intended actions are contingent upon the behavior of one's adversary. During crises, tacit communications alone can prove singularly inadequate although they may appear to validate declaratory communications.

It should be remembered that the international relations literature in 1959 consisted more of essays than of reports reflecting empirical work, i.e., systematic and objective studies. Moreover, while strategic deterrence had been official U.S. policy, there were, at that time, few behavioral scientists contributing to that policy.[11] Early in the Michelson effort there continued the effort to redefine deterrence as a set of influence attempts rarely identical in their effects to the amount of physical damage they might be able to produce before or after a nuclear strike upon the U.S. As the program progressed, empirical results led to increasing emphasis on (1) the conditions under which the use of a deterrent force might provoke rather than deter an attack upon the U.S., (2) the differences between Soviet and U.S. perceptions of self and adversary, (3) the development of Sino-Soviet differences and enmity, and (4) the differences between the perception of an opponent's capabilities and intentions during particular crises as contrasted with remissions in the pathology of the cold war relationship. This last point, that crises tend to influence systematically the perceptions and behaviors of the parties to them, both provoker and provoked, thus reducing the likelihood of considered, rational responses to one another's actions, led to the consideration of decision rules of interest to men of policy.

The several major consequences of Project Michelson can be divided in various ways. The inputs that made significant contributions toward policy included a specific contribution, Daniel Lerner's report on attitudes of the French elites toward deterrence and defense, which led to the cancellation (quite fortunate, as it turned out) of a large weapon system. A more general contribution to policy-relevant thinking was made through an integration of crisis research by Robinson, North, Naroll, and a System Development Corporation crew of systems analysts. Louis Sohn's materials proved useful in preparing for Arms Control and Disarmament negotiations with the Soviet Union. Nearly every study—the entire effort—contributed in important ways to Project Seabed, a summer study (1965) organized to make recommendations concerning follow-on efforts for the Polaris program, a major U.S. strategic weapon system.

Certain large-scale scholarly programs in the field of international relations were stimulated by Project Michelson, e.g., those at Stanford University, Massachusetts Institute of Technology, Northwestern University, and the University of Michigan. Despite its relatively modest budget, Project Michelson pushed along the development of a wide range of scholarly activities. The fruit of these activities is documented in a series of technical reports and summarized in three progress reports (see the Appendix). Also several integrational meetings were

---

[11]Among the few who were making contributions were William Kaufmann, Ithiel de Sola Pool and Thomas C. Schelling.

held which stimulated new approaches to content analysis, to the study of the personalities of key world leaders, and to various forms of simulation and gaming. The project supported efforts to compare different forms of gaming, such as Guetzkow's Inter-nation Simulation and Bloomfield's expert political exercises. It supported the development too of several forms of new behaviorally oriented theory and method in the field of international relations. These include Snyder's critical review and propositional inventory of the deterrence literature in the light of social science findings; O'Sullivan's content analysis of the Soviet strategic literature in contrast to that of the U.S.; Naroll's development of a sample of independent historical cases, which could be used for statistical tests of a number of hypotheses about deterrence; an attempt to employ the intuitive wisdom of behavioral scientists to look at gaps in substantive knowledge (Milburn and Milburn, 1966); and others mentioned briefly in the body of this essay. Efforts were made to evaluate, and, where it seemed practicable, to "validate" by some criteria nearly all of the techniques or methods under development.

Perhaps the most important accomplishment of Project Michelson was its demonstration that programmatic interdisciplinary and interuniversity research can be accomplished. Investigators from various disciplines in the behavioral sciences can collaborate, even at a distance. Even diversely trained scholars can work together; e.g., they can generate a common conceptual language and, at least to some extent, an integrated yet complex intellectual product. A closely related accomplishment was the demonstration that a dialogue between scholars and policy makers can be achieved, such that applied and even basic research in the behavioral sciences can make an impact on policy and strategy.

References

Angell, R. C. A comparison of Soviet and American values and foreign policies. *Studies in Deterrence V*, China Lake, California: U. S. Naval Ordnance Test Station, November 1963. (NOTS TP 3168.)

Backus, P. H. Finite deterrence, controlled retaliation, *United States Naval Institute Proceedings*, LXXXV (1959), 23–29.

Buzzard, A. W., Sir John Slessor, and R. Lowenthal, "H-Bomb: Massive retaliation or graduated deterrence," *International Affairs*, London, XXXII (1956), 148–165.

Gorer, G. Some aspects of the psychology of the people of Great Russia. *American Slavic and East European Review*, VIII (1949), 155–166.

Hermann, C. F. Crisis decision making: A simulated exploration of crises in international politics. Unpublished doctorial dissertation, Northwestern University, 1964.

Iklé, F. C. *The Social Impact of Bomb Destruction*. Norman, Oklahoma: University of Oklahoma Press, 1958.

Leites, N. *The Operational Code of the Politburo*. New York, 1951.

Leites, N. *A Study of Bolshevism*. Glencoe, Illinois: The Free Press, 1953.

Milburn, T. W. What constitutes effective deterrence? *Journal of Conflict Resolution*, III (1959), 138–145.

Milburn, T. W., and Milburn, J. F. Predictions of threats and beliefs about how to meet them. *American Behavioral Scientist*, IX (1966), 3–7.

Ratoosh, P. Experiments in nonconstant-sum games. University of California, Berkeley, August 1961. (Mimeo.)

Schelling, T. C. *The Strategy of Conflict*.

Cambridge, Massachusetts: Harvard University Press, 1960.

Singer, J. D. Soviet and American foreign policy attitudes: a content analysis of elite articulations. *Studies in Deterrence VII*, U. S. Naval Ordnance Test Station, Jan. 1964. (TP 3226.)

Singer, J. D. *Human Behavior and International Politics.* Chicago: Rand McNally, 1965.

Snyder, R. C. Deterrence weapon systems and decision making. *Studies in Deterrence III*, China Lake, California: U.S. Naval Ordnance Test Station, Oct. 1961. (TP 2769.)

Tomkins, S. *Affect, Imagery and Consciousness.* Vols. I and II. New York: Springer, 1962, 1963.

Wallace, A. F. C. *Human Behavior in Extreme Situations: A Survey of the Literature and Suggestions for Further Research.* Washington, D. C., National Academy of Sciences—National Research Council, Committee on Disaster Studies, 1956.

Wohlstetter, A. The delicate balance of terror. *Foreign Affairs*, XXXVII (1959), 211–234.

Appendix:

Selected List of Project Michelson Studies

Angell, R. C. *Studies in Deterrence V.* A study of the values of Soviet and of American elites. NOTS TP 3168, November 1963.

Bloomfield, L. P. Detex I: A political-military exercise on strategic deterrence in a Southeast Asian crisis, 1964.

———. Detex II: A political-military exercise on Naval Communications during a nuclear crisis, 1964.

———. Detex III: On MLF and NATO —some preliminary observations.

Bloomfield, L. P., and Whaley, B. The political-military exercise: A progress report on the state of the art, 1964.

Bloomfield, L. P., Whaley, B., Ordeshook, P., and Scott, R. H. Exdet III: A student-level experimental simulation on problems of deterrence, 1965.

Bloomfield, L. P., Barringer, R. E., and Whaley, B. A survey sutdy of the MIT political-military gaming experience, 1965.

Brody, R. A. Deterrence strategies: An annotated bibliography. *Journal of Conflict Resolution*, IV (1960), 443–457.

Crow, W. J. A study of strategic doctrines using the Inter-Nation Simulation.

———. Simulation runs with Latin Americans.

———. Simulation: The construction and use of functioning models in international relations.

Crow, W. J., and Raser, J. R. Capacity to delay response: Macro-analysis of experimental results from Inter-Nation Simulation runs.

Crow, W. J., and Solomon, L. N. A simulation study of strategic doctrines, 1962.

———. The use of the Inter-Nation Simulation in experiments.

De Grazia, S., and Stecchini, L. C. *Studies in Deterrence XI.* The coup d'état: Past significance and modern technique. NOTS TP 3807.

Halperin, M. H. *Studies in Deterrence IX.* Deterrence and local war. NOTS TP 3174, May 1963.

Hermann, C. F. Crises in foreign policy-making: A simulation in international politics.

———. Prediction considerations of possible relevance in validating Inter-Nation Simulation.

Hermann, C. F., and Hermann, Margaret G. On the possible use of historical data for validation study of the Inter-Nation Simulation, 1962.

———. The potential use of historical data for validation studies of the Inter-Nation Simulation: The outbreak of World War I as an illustration, 1963.

———. *Studies in Deterrence X.* Validation studies of the Inter-Nation Simulation. NOTS TP 3351, 1964.

Hermann, Margaret G. Some relationships among self-esteem, defensive behavior, and decision-making under stress, 1963.

Higgs, L. D., and Weinland, R. G. Project Michelson Preliminary Report, 1 February 1963. NOTS TP 3154.

———. Project Michelson Status Report I, 1 February 1964. NOTS TP 3448.

Holsti, O. R., and North, R. C. An adaptation of the "General Inquirer" for the systematic analysis of political documents. Studies in international conflict and integration.

———. The General Inquirer System applied to Sino-Soviet Relations. Studies in international conflict and integration.

———. Perceptions of time, perceptions of alternatives, and patterns of communication as factors in crisis decision-making. Studies in international conflict and integration, October 1964.

———. Soviet perceptions of strategic weapon system characteristics. Quarterly Progress Report No. 2. Studies in international conflict and integration.

Ike, N. Records of the Liaison Conferences, Nos. 19 to 66.

La Forge, R. Media content and elite values: A critical review of the Angell study. Oregon Research Institute Monograph, April 1962.

La Forge, R., and Starr, R. Critical review of "Soviet and American foreign policy attitudes: A content analysis of elite articulations," NOTS TP 3226.

Lerner, D., and Gorden, M. European community and Atlantic security in the world arena. Boston, Massachusetts: MIT, Center for International Studies, 1961.

———. Strategic thinking of the European elites. Boston, Massachusetts: Center for International Studies, 1961.

Milburn, T. W. (NOTS). *Studies in Deterrence I.* Design for the study of deterrent processes. NOTS TP 2781, April 1964.

———. *Brief Report on the Inyokern Meeting: Some First Steps Toward a Theory of Deterrence.* Behavioral Science Group, China Lake, California, June 1959. (Mimeo.)

———. *Capacity to Delay Response.* April, 1963.

———. The concept of deterrence, some logical and psychological considerations. *J. Social Issues,* XVII (1961), 3–12.

———. What constitutes effective deterrence? *Journal of Conflict Resolution,* III (1959), 138–145.

Milburn, T. W., and Snyder, R. C. *Problems in the Utilization of Positive Influence in International Affairs.* Behavioral Sciences Group, China Lake, California, June 1959. (Mimeo.)

Naroll, R. How Russians think.

———. Notes on capacity for delayed response.

———. On deterring the Soviets.

———. System in tension: Great Russian elite informal social values.

———. Thwarting disorientation and suicide: A cross-cultural survey.

———. Two stratified random samples for a cross-cultural survey.

———. Warfare, peaceful intercourse and territorial change: A cross-cultural survey.

———. Waterways and territorial change.

———. (See Technical Progress Report

403 NOTS TP 3863 for complete citations.)

North, R. C. Interim Report: Attitudes of the People's Republic of China toward the Seventh Fleet, Taiwan, and United States bases in Japan . . . . Studies in international conflict and integration.

———. Perceptions of time, perceptions of alternatives, and message volume as factors in crisis decision-making (Final Report). Studies in international conflict and integration.

———. Time as a factor in crisis decision-making: The 1914 case. Studies in international conflict and integration.

North, R. C., and Triska, J. F. The measurement of international tensions: A review of methodological problems (Final Report). Studies in international conflict and integration.

———. U.S.S.R.-Chinese relations: Cohesive and conflictual aspects (Final Report). Studies in international conflict and integration.

North, R. C., Triska, J. F., Holsti, O., and Zaninovich, M. G. The analysis of international tension (Final Report). Studies in international conflict and integration.

Osgood, C. E., and North, R. C. From individual to nation: An attempt to make explicit the usually implicit process of personifying international relations, May 1963.

O'Sullivan, T. C., Jr. Analysis of Soviet strategic writings. Advanced Systems Studies Department.

———. Factor analysis of the interrelation of variables as identified in the literature of stability and deterrence—An experiment in methodology.

———. Further analysis of U.S. and Soviet writings.

Phelps, J. FBM submarine deployment options as instruments of arms control and crisis management.

———. *Studies in Deterrence VI.* Human communication and deterrence. NOTS TP 2841, September 1963.

Pool, I. de S., and Whaley, B. *Studies in Deterrence XII.* Deterrence as an influence process. NOTS TP 3879.

Pruitt, D. G. Three experiments on decision-making under risk.

———. Two factors in international agreement.

Ratoosh, P. Experiments in nonconstant-sum games. August 1961. (Mimeo.)

Robinson, J. A. Memorandum No. 1 for Project Michelson: Some relations of crisis to selected decision process and outcome variables.

———. Memorandum No. 4 for Project Michelson: "Short term" deterrence problems: Crisis decision-making and weapons systems.

Robinson, J. A., and Hermann, C. F. Memorandum No. 5 for Project Michelson: A validity problem: Crises in simulated foreign policy organizations.

Singer, J. D. *Studies in Deterrence VII.* Soviet and American foreign policy attitudes: A content analysis of elite articulations. NOTS TP 3226, January 1964.

Snyder, R. C. A preliminary attempt to identify crucial empirical foci of inquiry concerning deterrence.

———. Project Michelson Summer Workgroup (CASBS)—A Progress Report.

———. *Studies in Deterrence III.* Deterrence, weapon systems, and decision-making. NOTS TP 2769.

Sohn, L. B. *Studies in Deterrence IV.* The prospects for future arms-control negotiations. NOTS TP 2770, October 1964.

Solomon, L. N. Annotated bibliography on deterrence propositions. Progress Report No. 1.

———. Annotated bibliography on deterrence propositions: Research relevant to problems of inter-nation relations.

Triska, J. F. Pattern and level of risk in Soviet foreign policy-making: 1945–1963. Final Report. Stanford Studies of the Communist System.

Wright, Q. *Studies in Deterrence II.* Prevention of the expansion of limited wars and preservation of international order with special reference to the role of seaborne weapon systems. NOTS TP 2668.

20

HAROLD GUETZKOW

Simulations in the Consolidation and Utilization of Knowledge About International Relations[1]

A series of proposals for ways in which future integration can be provided for research on international politics. The author, who originated the Inter-Nation Simulation, suggests that future research be guided by the goal of developing more adequate simulations of international politics. He suggests the formation of committees and secretariats for this purpose.

In the last decade and a half, important gains have been made in the number and quality of research studies in the field of international relations, evidenced by such empirical pieces as those assembled by J. David Singer (1967) and by the essays constituting this book (Pruitt and Snyder, 1969). If the trend continues, there will be an increasing need for ordering and integrating the knowledge generated in such studies—and an opportunity for the application of the findings, in on-going decisions by policy-makers of the world. During this same period of time, a capability to simulate complex international processes was created by the development of a variety of simulation formats (Guetzkow, 1966a) and by the invention of simulation languages (Naylor, *et al.*, 1966, Chapter 7).

This essay explores the potentiality of using simulations as devices for ordering theories and for integrating empirical findings. Buttressed by verbal deliberations on the one hand and by mathematical formulations on the other, can simulations implement the ability of decision-influencers to use such theories and findings in interna-

Especially prepared for this volume. Published by permission of the author and Northwestern University. The author is Fulcher Professor of Decision-Making in the Departments of Political Science, Psychology and Sociology; Co-Director of the International Relations Program; and Director of the Simulated International Processes Project at Northwestern University.

[1]This paper was prepared as part of the activities of the Simulated International Processes project (Advanced Research Projects Agency, SD 260) conducted within the International Relations Program at Northwestern University.

tional policy-making? At the end of this presentation, a proposal is developed to illustrate one way in which work with simulations might be organized for the consolidation and utilization of knowledge about international relations.

Simulations as a Format for Theory

Over the past centuries it has been customary to express political, economic, social, and psychological theory in words—in the vernacular of the times, after the demise of Latin as the *lingua franca*. With the development of mathematics, scholars possessed a vehicle by which they might express their loose verbal formulations with more explicitness, separating their assumptions from the derivations which follow as consequences of their analyses (Alker, 1965). But both of these formats for the development of theories have shortcomings. The serial nature of verbal exposition, with one thought following another on the written page, imposes serious limitations. Likewise, the intractability of many mathematical systems, once non-linear formulations are involved, seriously handicaps the investigators. Building upon both verbal and mathematical expositions, contemporary scholars are exploring the usefulness of simulations as devices for handling complex materials, both theoretical and empirical (Dawson, 1962; Naylor, *et al.*, 1966; Evans, *et al.*, 1967, Chapter 1, pp. 1–15). In the social sciences, a simulation may be conceived as "an operating representation in reduced and/or simplified form of relations among social units [i.e., entities] by means of symbolic and/or replicate component parts" (Guetzkow, 1959, p. 184).

Simulations in international relations attempt to represent the on-going international system or components thereof, such as world alliances, international organizations, regional trade processes, etc. Clark Abt and Morton Gorden (1968) and their associates have represented such processes as perception, homeostasis, and bargaining, through a digital computer simulation called TEMPER, a *T*echnological, *E*conomic, *M*ilitary, *P*olitical *E*valuation *R*outine. Harold Guetzkow and his associates (Guetzkow, Alger, Brody, Noel, and Snyder, 1963) have developed man-machine constructions (sometimes called "games") in which the decision-making processes are handled by human participants serving as surrogates for the international actors, whilst national processes are formulated through some thirty equations, the computation of which serves to represent the capabilities and consequences of the decision-making. Lincoln P. Bloomfield and his associates (Bloomfield and Whaley, 1965), following earlier developments by Hans Speier and others at the RAND Corporation (Goldhamer and Speier, 1959), used the "political exercise" in which crisis gaming among area experts is monitored by a "control team" which serves to umpire moves developed in response to an on-going scenario. This "all-manual" (as distinguished from the "all-computer") format is now used intensively at high levels within some parts of the United States government (Giffin, 1965). Because the control team operates principally in terms of intuitive verbal theory as it directs the progress of the game, allowing and disallowing particular international behaviors and imposing consequences on the various countries' teams, this simulation style in the long run may not prove as useful a format for the consolidation of knowledge as will man-computer and all-computer simulations. Further, it seems that, as the state of the computer arts becomes more adequate and our knowledge about international affairs grows more explicit and is grounded on a better data-base, man-machine constructions will be replaced by all-computer simulations. Already this has occurred, for example, in the development of formulations about legislatures, which moved from James S. Coleman's all-manual game (Coleman, 1963) to the all-computer simulation of voting in the Eighty-eighth Congress by Cleo H. Cherryholmes (1966) and Michael J. Shapiro (1966).

Consolidating Knowledge About International Relations Through Simulations

As we move into the latter third of the Twentieth Century, it seems feasible to catalyze the consolidation of our knowledge about international affairs through the use of simulations. Verbal efforts to present holistic integrations of extant knowledge are found in the textbooks of international relations. Yet, their contents are theoretically vague and their data bases are largely anecdotal as Denis G. Sullivan points out (Sullivan, 1963; especially his "Conclusions," pp. 305–313). Mathematical formulations, such as those by Lewis F. Richardson (1960), are more partial in scope, even though they are explicit in structure and systematic in their grounding in data. When an attempt is made to be comprehensive, as occurred in the work of Rudolph J. Rummel (1966), the mathematical theory tends to be at a metalevel, more statistically theoretical than substantively explicit.

How can simulations be used as vehicles for accumulating and integrating our knowledge, both in its theoretical and its empirical aspects, building upon the contributions of those who work in ordinary language as well as of those who use the language of mathematics?

Simulations may serve in three ways as formats through which intellectuals may consolidate and use knowledge about international relations: (1) Simulations may be used as techniques for increasing the coherence within and among models, enabling scholars to assess gaps and closures in our theories; (2) Simulations may be used as constructions in terms of which empirical research may be organized, so that the validity of our assertions may be appraised; (3) Simulations may be used by members of the decision-making community in the development of policy, both as devices for making systematic critiques, through "box-scoring" its failures and successes, and as formats for the exploration of alternative plans for action.

(1) Simulations in the Differentiation and Amalgamation of Theories in International Relations

Simulations of the international system are frameworks into which both verbal and mathematical formulations may be incorporated, therein combining something of the rigor of a mathematical model (which an all-computer simulation is) (Guetzkow, 1965) with the comprehensiveness of a verbal inventory (Snyder and Robinson, 1961 [*sic*]). Quincy Wright (1955) noted years ago in his *Study of International Relations* that our knowledge of international affairs develops in fragments. What is examined piecemeal, however, must eventually be reassembled, especially if the knowledge is to be used in policy work, where problems come as wholes. Once differentiated, our findings must be amalgamated.

The appearance of "handbooks" in the social sciences, consisting of chapters which attempt integrative summaries of bodies of literature, such as the one developed by Herbert C. Kelman (1965) on *International Behavior*, dramatizes how knowledge tends to be developed segmentally, composing "islands of theory" (Guetzkow, 1950, pp. 426, 435, 438, *et passim*). The contributors to a handbook single out a componential process within international affairs, such as "Bargaining and Negotiation" (Sawyer and Guetzkow, 1965), foci which are sometimes differentiated in much detail elsewhere, as in this case in the exciting verbal treatments by Fred Charles Iklé in *How Nations Negotiate* (1964) and by Arthur Lall in *Modern International Negotiation* (1966). In parallel, a body of quasimathematical work may develop, as in this same instance is found in the Theory of Games (Shubik, 1964). Within a simulation, aspects of both streams of theory may then be consolidated as a nodule or a modular—as each subroutine of a simulation is sometimes designated—as was done by Otomar Bartos in developing a negotiating routine for international trade in which he used the rubics of J. F. Nash's mathematically formulated "solution" (Sherman, 1963).

The "reader," exemplified in the influential compilation of *International Politics and Foreign Policy* (Rosenau, 1961), uses juxtaposition as a tool for the integration of knowledge. But, a more closely articulated and systematic integration of components is now possible through the use of simulation. As Paul Smoker and John MacRae demonstrate in their reconstruction of the Inter-Nation Simulation to explore the Vietnam situation, it is possible to take an already existing model of international affairs and incorporate additional and revised components within the existing framework (MacRae and Smoker, 1967, see Appendix, pp. 11–23). For example, in this Canadian/English simulation of the Vietnam situation, the collaborators were able to use Smoker's earlier work (Smoker, 1965) with the Richardson model in a rigorous development of polarization as dependent upon both trade and defense (MacRae and Smoker, 1967, pp. 16–17, *cf.*, "The Computer Model" columns) in defining "National Security"—an important feature heretofore absent from the Inter-Nation Simulation.

Simulations, especially those of the all-computer variety, demand a clarity that is unusual in theory building (Guetzkow, 1965, pp. 25–39) in the specification of the entities involved, in the exact involvement of variables used to describe the entities, and in the explicit formulation of the relations among both entities and variables. Once these components of theory have been assembled into a simulation, gaps within the framework become more readily apparent. One reason Walter C. Clemens (1968) elucidated the shortcomings of TEMPER with ease is found in its high level of explicitness (Guetzkow, 1966a). As more and more effort is put into amalgamating part-theories, there will be an increasing need for a standard language within which to construct each such "island of theory," so that they may be readily incorporated into larger, more encompassing constructions.

Despite the difficulties involved, as one of the central architects of TEMPER knowingly testifies (Gorden,

1967), with improvements in simulation languages (Naylor, *et al.*, 1966) it will be possible to articulate one modular with another more easily, if they are all built originally in a common computer language. Then there may be a division of labor among scholars, in which each may work on his components with a thoroughness worthy of his specialization. Then, when his "islands of theory" are placed within a simulation, the researcher may become aware of the broader issues that are relevant to his area of focus.

The complexities of theory, which are impossibly cumbersome when the ideas are formulated verbally in textbooks (Scott, 1967) and intractable when the ideas are structured as models (Orcutt, 1964, pp. 190–191), may become more amenable when simulations are used to organize the division of labor more coherently among the scholars working within international affairs, providing for a differentiation of effort as well as for an amalgamation of findings.

(2) Simulations as Vehicles in the Validation of Theories in International Relations

Simulations of the international system are devices through which empirical findings may be organized, so that the validity of their theoretical contents may be assessed. With the coming increase in the number of "data-making" studies (Singer, 1965, pp. 68–70) of the "real world," as reference materials are sometimes designated, there is need for consolidation of these empirical findings, as well as integration of our theories. Theory of all kinds—be it verbal, verbal-mathematical, or simulation—needs to be validated. As Charles F. Hermann has pointed out, it is important for many purposes to determine the degree of correspondence between the simulation model and the reference system (Hermann, C. F., 1967, p. 220), whether interested in the variables and parameters of the model (*ibid.*, p. 222), in the similarity or dissimilarity of the array of events produced in both simulation and the world (*ibid.*, p. 222–23), or in determining whether the same hypotheses hold in both model and reference systems (*ibid.*, pp. 223–24). When policy work is based on explicitly formulated theory, it is possible to judge the adequacy of policy alternatives more adequately if the extent of its validation is known.

Man-machine and all-computer simulations, especially, provide a systematic, somewhat rigorous technique for the appraisal of the validity of theory. Richard W. Chadwick (1966) has shown how correspondences between hypotheses embodied as assumptions about the functioning of national political systems may be checked out against empirical data gathered from the reference system of years centering on 1955. For example, he found that, although the likelihood of a decision-maker to continue in office is assumed in the simulation to be a function both of the latitude the decision-maker has in constructing his policies and the extent to which his supporters are satisfied with the consequences of his policies, the hypothesis holds in the international reference system of 1955 only with respect to the latter (Chadwick, 1966, p. 11).

Guetzkow (1967) was able to examine over twenty studies in which one or more operations in simulations of international processes were each paralleled by an empirical finding. These ranged from correspondences in the form of anecdotes about events [such as the fact that a conference, called by Lord Grey of England in the prelude to World War I and never assembled, proved to be the vehicle by which the issue was resolved by the participants in the Hermanns' adaptation of the Inter-Nation Simulation representing European developments in the summer of 1914 (Hermann and Hermann, 1967, pp. 407–8)] to correspondences between relationships among variables [such as the linear function between national consumption standards and the satisfaction of the groups which validate the officeholders (Elder and Pendley, 1966, p. 31)]. In his summary of particular comparisons of simulation outputs with data from the reference system, Guetzkow found there was "Some" or "Much" congruence in about two-thirds of the fifty-five instances available from the twenty-three studies, providing a kind of "box-score" on the simulations. These findings, taken in conjunction with achievements being realized through simulation in other parts of the social sciences (Guetzkow, 1962a), foreshadow the fruitfulness of cumulating findings on the validity of theory as it has been integrated within an operating simulation model.

Simulations are not only apt vehicles for making studies of the systematic, rigorous validations of theory. When used for such purposes, they also heuristically spin off ideas for revising theory about international processes. For example, in the man-computer format Dina A. Zinnes demonstrated an inadvertant error in the construction of the Inter-Nation Simulation: by omitting the buffer role of embassies between the home nation's foreign office and the foreign offices of other nations, a "small groups" effect was elicited, in which a cycle of even more hostility leading to less communication leading further to even more hostility exacerbated itself (Zinnes, 1966, pp. 496, 498–99). This effect was not found in the relations among the European capitals in the summer of 1914. Now it is possible to reconstruct the simulation so as to avoid this so-called "autistic hostility" phenomenon (Newcomb, 1947). Another example of the way in which validation study of simulation theory aids in its revision is found in Robert E. Pendley and Charles D. Elder's re-definition of the meaning of "officeholding" in the programmed components of the Inter-Nation Simulation (INS) in terms of contemporary verbal theory and data on the stability of regimes and governments. After comparing ways in which the simulation and the reference system behave, they conclude that "INS theory is a fairly good predictor of stability, but that it is the stability of the political system rather than stability of particular officeholders that the theory explains" (Pendley and Elder, 1966, p. 25).

Thus, simulations are useful devices through which efforts in the validation of their theoretical soundness may be organized when outputs of simulations are compared with corresponding characterizations in the reference system. Further, in the very process of making the comparisons one has a heuristic tool through which verbal and mathematical speculation can be grounded empirically to provide a base for the revision of simulation theory. Unless simulation theory is validated, it would seem unwise to use it for "decision-making" in the policy-making community.

(3) Simulations in the Utilization of Knowledge for Policy-Making in International Affairs

Were a body of consolidated knowledge about international affairs available, it would seem that simulations might aid in the utilization of that knowledge —for monitoring on-going events as well as for the construction of "alternative futures." The myriad of actors within the international system—be they members of planning units in foreign ministries, entrepreneurs in businesses operating overseas, or officials within governmental and nongovernmental international organizations—base their decisions for actions upon their assumptions of the ways in which this system functions, combined with their assessments of its present state. Simulations may increase the adequacy with which knowledge about international affairs is utilized in the conduct of foreign affairs, by providing explicit theories as to how the system operates, as well as by providing a continuously up-dated data-base. A somewhat comprehensive list of "Some Areas of Knowledge Needed for Undergirding Peace Strategies," presented elsewhere (Guetzkow, 1962b, pp. 90–91), runs the gamut of such topics as "initiative and coordination within national security decision machinery" and "international communications." Simulations, geared to the policy problems confronting the public and private decision-makers of the world, can serve in two ways as aids in the utilization of this knowledge: (a) in being a framework within which the antecedents and consequences of on-going policy decisions can be examined, and (b) in being a way of considering alternative futures of the international system, either as contingencies or as ends whose paths-to-achievement may be plotted.

(a) "*Box-Scoring*" *Policy Decisions.* In the hurly-burly of organizational life, there is seldom time for explicit analyses of the effectiveness of "hits" and "misses." Seldom does the decision-maker systematically sort out the way the antecedents in his decision situations eventuate in their consequences. Yet, today there are increasingly adequate techniques of both verbal and mathematical varieties available, which help in structuring knowledge so that it may be used more effectively in decision processes. For example, the verbal analyses involved in program-planning and budgeting procedures now being urged throughout government (Chartrand and Brezina, 1967) are becoming more and more sophisticated in their specification of the means-ends chains involved in cost-benefit analyses (Grosse, 1967). With the mathematization of "optimizing techniques" within operations research (Carr and Howe, 1964), miniature theories are being constructed about the assessment of the influence of factors upon outcomes. These verbal and mathematical sources of explication are making it feasible to construct on-going simulations of policy processes of decision-making, as illustrated in extant all-computer models of budgetary processes of municipalities (Crecine, 1965). In the arena of international relations, it also would seem possible to use simulations as vehicles for the explication of decision-making processes, thereby "box-scoring" policy-making.

Suppose a policy-planning group in a country's disarmament and arms control bureau were interested in making an analysis of the relations among antecedents and consequences of their policy decisions with respect to the nation's postures in a multilateral "standing group" operating in Geneva. It might then erect a simulation of the international system and run it parallel with the policy deliberations. For example, it might combine a negotiation exercise (Bonham, 1967) within the context of a man-computer simulation of international processes (Smoker, 1967), tailored to fit conditions of the moment. Were there disagreement within the staff, two or more alternative simulations could be explored, changing the parametric weighting given to particular variables, and even substituting one nodule for another, allowing them to "compete" as to adequacy. Through such a double-nested simulation, it would be possible to examine developments at two levels—in terms of (1) the on-going conference situation in Geneva, and (2) the changes in the overall international political scene itself. In examining the immediate situation, they could simulate the action of the committee of principals within the foreign policy machinery of the government itself, along with responses of opposite numbers, of allies, and of non-aligned nations—once policy proposals were activated in the international arena. In examining the context of the work of the multilateral group, one would simulate the arms race within regions as well as globally, including the impact of the failure to achieve a non-proliferation treaty as well as the consequences of already agreed-upon treaties, such as the test-ban.

One operation of the simulation might be molded to be strictly congruent with on-going policies. Then the developments—both antecedents (in structure and process) and consequences (in outcomes and feedbacks)—could be "box-scored," as the events of the international system unfolded week-by-week, month-by-month. In fact, were alternative simulations operating simultaneously a few weeks or months ahead of the decisions of this committee of principals, their outputs might be used for policy development within the arms control and disarmament agency, were they satisfied with the extent of the validity of these simulation results.

Such a "box-scoring" procedure would demand an explication of the theories (which now are often being used without clear formulation by the policy-makers of the assumptions involved), so that an appropriate simulation (with its competing variations) might be adapted from extant models in forms useful for policy problem-solving. Further, in requiring the tallying of successes and failures, the procedure would eventuate in a careful validation of the simulation. The modulars composing the antecedent processes as postulated by the policy-makers would be assessed as to whether they yield their predicted consequences in the "real world." Note that these two steps are the same two procedures involved in the consolidation of knowledge by basic researchers concerned with international affairs, as outlined in the previous sections of this essay: (1) the amalgamation of verbal and mathematical theory in a simulation's constructions, and (2) its validation through empirical confrontations.

To use simulation as an instrument for policy development would be to have a powerful tool by which the ever increasing richness of theory and data might be brought to bear upon decision-making in international affairs by the policy-influencers of the world throughout the remainder of this century. But such "box-scoring" procedures would not only be of aid to the policy-makers; the applied work would have important feedbacks into research. It would provide a vehicle by which the thinking of outstanding political leaders might be fed back into the academic community, so that its work might benefit from the creativity of the policy community. Further, on-going comparisons between expectations and realities, made week-by-week over the years, would highlight congruences and incongruences between the simulation model—in its many variations—and central aspects of the reference system.

(b) *Exploring Alternative Policy Futures.* Simulations are an important heuristic in their potential for representing alternative, future state of affairs which to date have been non-existent (Boguslaw, 1965). As knowledge is consolidated through simulation, enough confidence may be gained eventually to use such constructions for the systematic exploration of alternative futures (de Jouvenel, 1963, 1965). Although, certainly, theory should be data-based, simulations must not be "data-bound" (Guetzkow, 1966b, pp. 189–91).

Efforts to use simulations for the exploration of possible futures are in their infancy. An example in miniature of such pioneering in an all-computer format is found in the U.S. Department of State's analysis by computer of the consequences of various voting arrangements within the United Nations. The simulation was applied to "178 key votes that took place in the General Assembly between 1954 and 1961," the weighting being based on population and contributions to the UN budget. Richard N. Gardner reports that while the weightings "would have somewhat reduced the number of resolutions passed over U.S. opposition, they would have reduced much more the number of resolutions supported by the United States and passed over Communist opposition. The same conclusion was reached in projecting these formulas to 1970, having regard to further increases in membership" (Gardner, 1965, p. 238). Using a man-computer format, Richard A. Brody experimented in the summer of 1960 with the effects of the proliferation of nuclear capabilities upon alliances (Brody, 1963). Working from an inventory of some thirty-six verbal propositions in the literature about the "Nth country problem," Brody designed a variation of the Inter-Nation Simulation so that consequences of an antecedent spread of nuclear weapons technology among nations might be studied. Brody found a "step-level change in the 'cold war system'" after the spread of nuclear capability: Threats external to each bloc were reduced, and threats internal to each block were increased, accompanied by a decrease in bloc cohesiveness; the original bipolarity of the system was fragmented (Brody, 1963, p. 745). A final example, employing the manual technique of the political-military exercise, is found in the recent exploration by Bloomfield and his colleagues of the "possible future employment of United Nations military forces under conditions of increasing disarmament" in the context of the U.S. proposals of April 18, 1962, on General and Complete Disarmament (GCD) (Bloomfield and Whaley, 1965). After investigating four hypothetical crises—indirect aggression and subversion in Southeast Asia, a colonial-racial civil war in a newly independent African nation, a classic small-power war in the Near East, and a Castro-type revolution in Latin America—Bloomfield draws a set of policy inferences, including the notion that "disarmament planning might well consider whether an appropriate plateau for the GCD process can be found somewhere" (*ibid*, p. 864).

The use of simulation for sketching alternatives may prove in the long run to be a useful implement in the reconstruction of our international system, should we ever devote enough resources toward the generation and consolidation of knowledge so as to give us the validity to make such constructions viable. In the creation of unprecedented alternative futures (Huntington, *et al.*, 1965), can we manage with verbal speculation alone —or with mathematical formulations only? Perhaps, as we gain experience in amalgamating modulars which have been grounded in empirical findings, we will, someday, have the ability to construct futures which are more than visionary.

These are the goals, then: to develop simulation theory, in the context of verbal speculation and mathematical constructions about the structures and processes involved in international affairs; to apply a variety of criteria in the validation of such theory, depending upon the purposes for which it is intended; to use for decision-making the knowledge which has been consolidated for purposes of policy development, both in terms of short run "box-scoring" and in the long run for the creation of alternative futures. If such is the potential, the query becomes, "How can we accelerate our rate of accomplishment in achieving these goals?"

Accelerating the Consolidation and Utilization of Knowledge about International Relations through Standing Colloquia

Let this essay conclude with a proposal for acceleration in the study of international relations through the establishment of *colloquia* centering on simulations, so that there may be a continuous dialogue between theory builders, empirical researchers, and policy developers. Perhaps the time is now appropriate for a more integrative, long range effort than is possible alone through doctoral dissertations, textbooks, collections of juxtaposed readings, handbooks of summary pieces, substantive inventories developed for special occasions, and *ad hoc* conferences and committee reports. Given the pace of the explosion of knowledge within the international relations area (Platig, 1966, pp. 3–11), which the foregoing efforts are yielding, it seems imperative that a technique of potential efficacy be explored to hasten a tighter, more cumulative articulation of this knowledge.

There now are some fifteen to twenty sites throughout the world at which simulations of international affairs are being conducted. These operations vary widely in their magnitude and quality, as well as in their styles. Only a few of these will nurture their activities into full-fledged centers worthy of adequate, continuous support.

One or more such units probably will operate within a university setting, with its efforts undergirded by the relevant disciplines and its output available to all throughout the world. Such university-related centers would provide training in simulation for scholars and professionals interested in foreign affairs. With the recent emergence of the autonomous research organization, it is difficult to believe that such "think-tanks" (Reeves, 1967)—be they of a "for profit" or a "non-profit" variety—will not give serious attention to simulation work. Perhaps some of the international companies will develop their considerable knowledge, obtained in commercial operations overseas, through special corporate staffs concerned with the simulation of the international system in which they operate, with some focus on the role of the non-governmental organizations. In the decades ahead, at least a dozen or so units concerned with simulation may be established within agencies of different governments in the world. In developing their foreign policies toward each other, there may emerge a common core of data and theories, even though each foreign office—just like each international company—will probably develop for its own exclusive use a simulation base of secret contents. Little wonder, then, that the international organizations—most appropriately perhaps the United Nations Institute for Training and Research—will need to lead the development of simulation models, so that all countries, regardless of their resources in the social sciences, may have access to a universal model for the exploration of the antecedents and political consequences of their policies. Because of the exemplary work the United Nations Secretariat has done on its statistical services in decades past, a universal data-base for simulation work is already well advanced.

Within the last five years there has been a considerable growth in bodies of empirical data which have been and are being generated through elections, interview surveys, and the like (Bisco, 1966). Perhaps now is the time to develop somewhat analogous *standing colloquia*, so that those developing theory—be it verbal or mathematical in style—may consolidate their work. Were one such colloquium staffed with a secretariat, perhaps it could provide a means by which theorists could relate with more intimacy and rigor to the data-gatherers and data-makers. In addition, such a colloquium would provide a forum in which policy-influencers might have their formulations dialogued. It may turn out that just as a number of data consortia are developing throughout the world, there may be more than one colloquium—different modes of simulation and different purposes may demand different kinds of colloquia for varying styles of collaboration. For example, already it seems that those interested in the uses of simulation for education and training are centering their efforts in ways different from those using simulations as vehicles for theory construction and validation (Coleman, Boocock, and Schild, 1966).

How might a colloquium implement collaboration among four to five simulation centers located in different parts of the world? Through a working director—who would probably need to be a young, flexible theorist of some distinction—the secretariat of the colloquium might develop an integrated model of the international system, as was suggested above (*cf.*, *supra*, (1), pp. 4–7). In the process of constructing the model over a period of some five to ten years, periodic sessions with theorists—regardless of the mode in which they work—would be convened, so that a consolidation of fruitful and adequately verified components of theory might be incorporated into the colloquium's simulation. The staff of the colloquium would compare the assumptions underlying extant simulations and design experiments for assessing the importance of the differences. To obviate the need to operate its own simulation in its early years, it might invite three or four simulations already in operation—perhaps on sub-contract—to address the same inquiry, so that systematic comparison among the various alternative models might be made, in the style pioneered by Hayward R. Alker, Jr. and Ronald D. Brunner (1967).

Without attempting to operate its own data consortium, how might the staff of the colloquium manage to ground its model in the findings from such research? It might review the empirical literature to assess the extent to which components of its model are being validated. It might then develop recommendations, in the mode of inventories, as to where further empirical work was needed, coordinating the execution of such research so that there would be close matching between simulation and reference materials (*cf.*, *supra*, (2), pp. 7–9). With an ever increasing volume of research being generated through Programs of Area Study as well as in the more traditional Centers of International Studies (Snyder, 1968), the staff of the colloquium might usefully provide a liaison service, so that the developing simulations throughout the world would be more closely articulated with outpourings in empirical research, both of a qualitative and quantitative variety. In fact, just as a member of the colloquium's secretariat might be designated to work with the verbal theory of the more speculative scholars in order to incorporate their ideas into the simulation, so might a special staff member be assigned the task of developing the theory which emerges from empirical studies into a form that could be phrased as modular sub-routines for use in the colloquium's simulation. In fact, it is easy to understand how the colloquium might pay special attention to achievements in simulation in other parts of the social sciences, too, so that full advantage could be taken of developments in the field of artificial intelligence (for the development of foreign policy decision-making models) and in the field of organizational simulation (for the development of inter-nation system models), for example.

In all the activities of the colloquium, policy-related professionals would be involved intimately so that their decision-makers—be such located in foreign offices, in international corporations, or in international organizations—might develop operations in tandem with those evolving in the colloquium. Were some consensus to emerge through the good offices of the colloquium, various simulation groups throughout the two hemispheres might exchange modules, as well as use each other's data-bases—on perhaps multilateral as well as bilateral bases. Which centers will effect a collaboration so that their competitive efforts will become cooperative, too—as in the fashion of the SSRC/Brookings Economic Quarterly Model of the United States (Duesenberry, *et al.*, 1965)? It is exciting to imagine the officers of inter-parliamentary unions of the regions of the world contracting with colloquia for systematic exploration of some items on their agenda, so that their deliberations might be grounded in the fruits of social sciences, as such are represented in the consolidation of knowledge about international affairs through simulations.

Collaboration among simulation centers will be accelerated mightily with the coming of world-wide computer systems, which might be shared by centers comprising a core group which has proven its ability to work together in an integrative way. Through the leadership of the Western Behavioral Sciences Institute, John Raser and his overseas colleagues—from Japan, Mexico, and Norway—already are gaining experience in the practicality of cooperation in cross-cultural research involving man-computer simulations (Solomon, Crow, and Raser, 1965). Should the work of the colloquium be successful, such centers would operate in a common computer language, making possible the integration of their work. Should the efforts of the colloquium be achieving its goals, the same group of centers would be sharing data-bases using common variables, all commensurable with each other. Eventually the colloquium's function would be merely that of coordinating the operation of a communication-by-satellite system of validated simulations. Then, the policy-makers of the world might all join freely such an international net, building our world futures through cooperative endeavor.

As Hans J. Morgenthau asserts, "What is decisive for the success or failure of a theory is the contribution it makes to our knowledge and understanding of phenomena which are worth knowing and understanding. It is by its results that a theory must be judged . . ." (Morgenthau, 1967, from "PREFACE to the Fourth Edition). Will the use of simulation as a vehicle in the consolidation and utilization of knowledge in international relations enable us to develop theory whose results will give us a better world than the one we've lived in for the last quarter century, whose policy roots have been dominated by the babel of theory posed in ordinary tongues?

Summary

What is simulation's potential for the consolidation and utilization of knowledge about international affairs? Although all-computer and man-computer simulations, as well as all-manual political exercises, may be employed as devices for training participants, simulations may also be used as a way of positing theory and deriving its consequences. Simulations may be used as a tool for the integration of widely used verbal theory, as well as for theory which is developed in mathematical language. Simulations encourage explicitness in formulation and permit the coherent amalgamation of subtheories into interactive, holistic constructions of great complexity. Further, using simulation as the format for formulating theory enables systematic and rigorous work to be achieved in the validation of its interrelated parts, feeding back heuristically into reformulations of aspects of the model which are less than congruent with the empirical materials. Finally, data-grounded simulations may aid in the development of policy, both in terms of its evaluation as well as in terms of its creation. By monitoring on-going events with simulations operated in parallel, "box-scores" can be derived for appraising the adequacy of unfolding policies. By using these same simulations as devices for the examination of alternative futures, modification in short term policies can be made and long-run forecasts can be mounted.

In conclusion, a proposal is made for acceleration of the consolidation and utilization of knowledge about international affairs through the establishment of standing colloquia. Analogous to the growing consortia being developed throughout the world for amassing and retrieving political data, it is proposed that special standing colloquia be developed among scholarly and governmental centers, so that competing simulations, along with their verbal theories and mathematical formulations, might be used integratively as ways of coordinating the development and use of knowledge about international relations.

References

Abt, Clark, and Morton Gorden. "Report on Project TEMPER." In Dean G. Pruitt and Richard C. Snyder (Editors), *Theory and Research on the Causes of War.* Englewood Cliffs, New Jersey: Prentice-Hall, Inc., *1969.*

Alker, Hayward R., Jr. *Mathematics and Politics.* New York: The Macmillan Company, *1965.*

Alker, Hayward R., Jr., and Ronald D. Brunner. "Simulating International

Conflict: A Comparison of Three Approaches." Mimeo. New Haven, Connecticut: Yale University, July, *1967*.

Bisco, Ralph L. "Social Science Data Archives: A Review of Developments." *American Political Science Review*, 40, 1 (March, *1966*), 93–109.

Bloomfield, Lincoln P., and Barton Whaley. "The Political-Military Exercise: A Progress Report." *Orbis*, 8, 4 (Winter, *1965*), 854–870.

Boguslaw, Robert. *The New Utopians: A Study of System Design and Social Change.* Englewood Cliffs, New Jersey: Prentice-Hall, Inc., *1965.*

Bonham, G. Matthew. "Aspects of the Validity of Two Simulations of Phenomena in International Relations." Ph. D. Dissertation. Cambridge, Massachusetts: Department of Political Science, Massachusetts Institute of Technology, *1967.*

Brody, Richard A. "Some systemic effects of the spread of nuclear-weapons technology: a study through simulation of a multi-nuclear future." *The Journal of Conflict Resolution*, 7, 4 (December, *1963*), 663–753.

Carr, Charles R. and Charles W. Howe. *Quantitative Decision Procedures in Management and Economics.* New York: McGraw-Hill Book Company, *1964.*

Chadwick, Richard W. "An Empirical Test of Five Assumptions in an Inter-Nation Simulation, about National Political Systems." Evanston, Illinois: Simulated International Processes project, Northwestern University, August, *1966.*

Chartrand, Robert L., and Dennis W. Brezina. "The Planning-Programming-Budgeting System: An Annotated Bibliography." Washington, D. C.: The Library of Congress Legislative Reference Service, April 11, *1967.*

Cherryholmes, Cleo H. "The House of Representatives and Foreign Affairs: A Computer Simulation of Roll Call Voting." Ph. D. Dissertation. Evanston, Illinois: Department of Political Science, Northwestern University, August, *1966.*

Clemens, Walter C. "TEMPER and International Relations Theory: A Propositional Inventory." In William D. Coplin (Editor), *Simulation Models of the Decision-Maker's Environment.* Chicago: Markham Publishing Co., *1968.* Presented at Wayne State University Symposium, Detroit, Michigan, May 10–13, 1967.

Coleman, James S. "The Great Game of Legislature." *The Johns Hopkins Magazine*, (October, *1963*), 17–20.

Coleman, James S., Sarane S. Boocock, and E. O. Schild (Editors). *In Defense of Games. American Behavioral Scientist*, Part I, 10 (October, *1966*); *Simulation Games and Learning Behavior. American Behavioral Scientist*, Part II, 10 (November, *1966*).

Crecine, John P. "A Computer Simulation Model of Municipal Resource Allocation." Ph. D. Dissertation. Pittsburgh, Pennsylvania: Carnegie Institute of Technology, *1965.*

Dawson, Richard D. "Simulation in the Social Sciences." In Harold Guetzkow (Editor), *Simulation in the Social Sciences: Readings.* Englewood Cliffs, New Jersey: Prentice-Hall, Inc., *1962*, 1–15.

De Jouvenel, Bertrand (Editor). *Futuribles: Studies in Conjecture.* Geneva, Switzerland: Droz, *1963* and *1965.*

Duesenberry, J. S., G. Fromm, L. R. Klein, and E. Kuh (Editors). *The Brookings Quarterly Economic Model of the United States.* Chicago: Rand, McNally & Co., *1965.*

Elder, Charles D., and Robert E. Pendley. "An Analysis of Consumption Standards and Validation Satisfactions in the Inter-Nation Simulation in Terms of Contemporary Economic Theory and Data." Evanston, Illinois: Department of Political Science, Northwestern University, November, *1966*.

Evans, George W., II, Graham F. Wallace, and Georgia L. Sutherland. *Simulation Using Digital Computers*. Englewood Cliffs, New Jersey: Prentice-Hall, Inc., *1967*.

Gardner, Richard N. "United Nations Procedures and Power Realities: The International Apportionment Problem." *Proceedings of the American Society of International Law*, 59th Meeting (April, *1965*), 232–245.

Giffin, Sidney F. *The Crisis Game: Simulating International Conflict*. Garden City, New York: Doubleday & Company, Inc., *1965*.

Goldhamer, Herbert, and Hans Speier. "Some Observations on Political Gaming." *World Politics*, 12, 1 (October, *1959*), 71–83.

Gorden, Morton. "Burdens for the Designer of a Computer Simulation of International Relations: The Case of TEMPER." In Davis B. Bobrow (Editor), *Proceedings of the Computers and The Policy-Making Community Institute*. Englewood Cliffs, New Jersey: Prentice-Hall, Inc., *1967*. Presented at the Institute held at Lawrence Radiation Laboratory, University of California, Livermore, California, on April 4–15, 1966.

Grosse, Robert N. "The Application of Analytic Tools to Government Policy: The Formulation of Health Policy." In William D. Coplin (Editor), *Simulation Models of the Decision-Maker's Environment*. Chicago: Markham Publishing Co., *1968*. Presented at Wayne State University Symposium, Detroit, Michigan, May 10–13, 1967.

Guetzkow, Harold. "Long Range Research in International Relations." *The American Perspective*, 4, 4 (Fall, *1950*), 421–440.

Guetzkow, Harold. "A Use of Simulation in the Study of Inter-Nation Relations." *Behavioral Science*, 4 (*1959*), 183–191.

Guetzkow, Harold (Editor). *Simulation in the Social Sciences: Readings*. Englewood Cliffs, New Jersey: Prentice-Hall, Inc., *1962a*.

Guetzkow, Harold. "Undergirding Peace Strategies through Research in Social Science." In Gerhard S. Nielsen (Editor), *Psychology and International Affairs: Can We Contribute? Proceedings of the XIV International Congress of Applied Psychology*, Volume I. Copenhagen, Denmark: Munksgaard, *1962b*, 88–96.

Guetzkow, Harold. "Some Uses of Mathematics in Simulations of International Relations." In John M. Claunch (Editor), *Mathematical Applications in Political Science*. Dallas, Texas: The Arnold Foundation, Southern Methodist University, *1965*, 21–40.

Guetzkow, Harold. "Simulation in International Relations." In *Proceedings* of the *IBM Scientific Computing Symposium on Simulation Models and Gaming*. York, Pennsylvania: Maple Press, *1966a*, 249–278.

Guetzkow, Harold. "Transcending Data-Bound Methods in the Study of Politics." In James C. Charlesworth (Editor), Monograph 6, *A Design for Political Science: Scope, Objectives, and Methods*. Philadelphia: The American Academy of Political and Social Science, December, *1966b*, 185–191.

Guetzkow, Harold. "Some Correspondences Between Simulations and 'Realities' in International Relations." Evanston, Illinois: Northwestern University, *1967*. In Morton Kaplan (Editor), *New Approaches to International Relations*. New York: St. Martin's Press, *1967*.

Guetzkow, Harold, Chadwick F. Alger,

Richard A. Brody, Robert C. Noel, and Richard C. Snyder. *Simulation in International Relations: Developments for Research and Teaching.* Englewood Cliffs, New Jersey: Prentice-Hall, Inc., *1963.*

Hermann, Charles F. "Validation Problems in Games and Simulations with Special Reference to Models of International Politics." *Behavioral Science*, 12, 3 (May, *1967*), 216–231.

Hermann, Charles F., and Margaret G. Hermann. "An Attempt to Simulate the Outbreak of World War I." *American Political Science Review*, 61, 2 (June, *1967*), 400–416.

Huntington, Samuel P., Ithiel De Sola Pool, Eugene Rostow, and Albert O. Hirschman. "The International System." In *Working Papers* of the *Commission on the Year 2000* of *The American Academy of Arts and Sciences*, Volume V. Boston: The American Academy of Arts and Sciences, *circa 1965.*

Iklé, Fred Charles. *How Nations Negotiate.* New York: Harper and Row, *1966.*

Kelman, Herbert C. (Editor). *International Behavior: A Social-Psychological Analysis.* New York: Holt, Rinehart and Winston, *1965.*

Lall, Arthur. *Modern International Negotiation: Principles and Practice.* New York: Columbia University Press, *1966.*

Macrae, John, and Paul Smoker. "A Vietnam Simulation: A Report on the Canadian/English Joint Project." *Journal of Peace Research*, 1 (*1967*), 1–25.

Morgenthau, Hans J. *Politics Among Nations: The Struggle for Power and Peace.* New York: Alfred A. Knopf, *1967* (Fourth Edition).

Naylor, Thomas H., Joseph L. Balintfy, Donald S. Burdick, and Kong Chu. "Introduction to Computer Simulation." In their *Computer Simulation Techniques.* New York: John Wiley and Sons, Inc., *1966*, 1–22.

Newcomb, Theodore M. "Autistic Hostility and Social Reality." *Human Relations*, 1 (*1947*), 69–86.

Orcutt, Guy H. "Simulation of Economic Systems: Model Description and Solution." *Proceedings* of the *Business and Economic Statistics Section, American Statistical Association, 1964*, 186–193.

Pendley, Robert E., and Charles D. Elder. "An Analysis of Office-Holding in the Inter-Nation Simulation in Terms of Contemporary Political Theory and Data on the Stability of Regimes and Governments." Evanston, Illinois: Department of Political Science, Northwestern University, November, *1966.*

Platig, Raymond E. *International Relations Research: Problems of Evaluation and Advancement.* New York: Carnegie Endowment for International Peace, *1966.*

Pruitt, Dean G., and Richard C. Snyder (Editors). *Theory and Research on the Causes of War.* Englewood Cliffs, New Jersey: Prentice-Hall, Inc., *1969.*

Reeves, Frank. "U. S. Think-Tanks: The New Centers for Research and Thought, and Their Growing Impact on American Life." A series of five articles in the *New York Times*, June 12–16, *1967.*

Richardson, Lewis F. *Arms and Insecurity.* London: Stevens and Sons, Ltd., *1960.*

Rosenau, James (Editor). *International Politics and Foreign Policy: A Reader in Research and Theory.* New York: The Free Press, *1961.*

Rummel, Rudolph J. "A Social Field Theory of Foreign Conflict Behavior." Prepared for Cracow Conference, 1965. *Peace Research Society* (*International*) *PAPERS*, 4 (*1966*), 131–150.

Sawyer, Jack, and Harold Guetzkow. "Bargaining and Negotiation in International Relations." In Herbert C. Kelman (Editor), *International Behavior: A Social-Psychological Analysis.* New

York: Holt, Rinehart and Winston, *1965.*

Scott, Andrew M. *The Functioning of the International Political System.* New York: The Macmillan Company, *1967.*

Shapiro, Michael J. "The House and the Federal Role: A Computer Simulation of Roll Call Voting." Ph. D. Dissertation. Evanston, Illinois: Department of Political Science, Northwestern University, August, *1966*

Sherman, Allen William. "The Social Psychology of Bilateral Negotiations." M. A. Thesis. Evanston, Illinois: Department of Sociology, Northwestern University, *1963.*

Shubik, Martin (Editor). *Game Theory and Related Approaches to Social Behavior.* New York: John Wiley and Sons, Inc., *1964.*

Singer, J. David. "Data-Making in International Relations." *Behavioral Science,* 10, 1 (January, *1965*), 68–80.

Singer, J. David (Editor). *Quantitative International Politics: Insights and Evidence in World Politics. International Yearbook of Political Behavior Research,* Volume VI. New York: The Free Press (Macmillan), *1967.*

Smoker, Paul. "Trade, Defense, and the Richardson Theory of Arms Races: A Seven Nation Study." *Journal of Peace Research,* II (*1965*), 161–176.

Smoker, Paul. "International Processes Simulation." Evanston, Illinois: Simulated International Processes project, Northwestern University, *1967.*

Snyder, Richard C. "Education and World Affairs Report." New York: *1968.*

Snyder, Richard C., and James A. Robinson. "The Interrelations of Decision Theory and Research and the Problem of War and Peace." *National and International Decision-Making.* New York: Institute for International Order, *1961* (*sic*), 16–25.

Solomon, Lawrence N., Wayman J. Crow, and John R. Raser. "A Proposal: Cross-Cultural Simulation Research in International Decision-Making." La Jolla, California: Western Behavioral Sciences Institute, June, *1965.*

Sullivan, Denis G. "Towards An Inventory of Major Propositions Contained in Contemporary Textbooks in International Relations." Ph. D. Dissertation. Evanston, Illinois: Department of Political Science, Northwestern University, *1963.*

Wright, Quincy. *The Study of International Relations.* New York: Appleton-Century-Crofts, *1955.*

Zinnes, Dina A. "A Comparison of Hostile Behavior of Decision-Makers in Simulate and Historical Data." *World Politics,* 18, 3 (April, *1966*), 474–502.

Postscript: Retrospect and Prospect

While it is not feasible to produce a definitive overview of the vast material surveyed in this volume, it may be useful to offer some tentative impressions as well as projections of intellectual developments into the future.

To repeat an earlier stricture, good theory about international conflict does not come easily and the accumulation of reliable knowledge in this area must necessarily be fairly slow. Nevertheless, it is encouraging to note a sharp increase over the last decade in both the quality and the tempo of research. Our theoretical and empirical tools have improved markedly, and our research output has increased substantially. Some of what seem to be the most significant advances will now be reviewed.

Advances in Theory

Over the past decade, our theories have become more explicit, richer (i.e., more complex), and more broadly based in the social and behavioral sciences. Consequently, our explanations of war are beginning to become more satisfactory, and small steps have been taken toward an improved capacity to predict.

A central feature of this theoretical improvement has been the increasing number of operationally definable and measurable variables that have been employed in the construction of hypotheses. The use of such variables enhances clarity and makes it possible to perform empirical tests of the adequacy of theory. Operationally definable psychological variables have been particularly prominent in recent years, e.g., *perception*, *cognition*, *motivation* and *communication*. Instead of the vague psychological formulations of the past—e.g., "human nature" makes war inevitable—we have begun to develop a capacity to account clearly for deliberate acts of national violence and for "rational errors" made by decision makers. Other new[1] concepts, which have been identified and combined in various conceptual models, include *decision making*, *crisis*, *coalition*, *value salience*, *deterrence*, *threat*, *tacit bargaining*, *information overload*, *trust*, *system* and *subsystem*, *responsiveness*, and *stability*.

Other Advances

Three basic trends are evident in the material presented in this volume. In the first place, there has been a most encouraging increase in the sheer number of tested research tools and techniques which can be used in the study of international conflict. *Case studies* are now often preceded by the development of explicit theoretical frameworks, and rigorous comparisons of two or more cases are now often made. *Laboratory experiments* are now being employed, including simulational and gaming studies of such phenomena as negotiation and crisis decision making. Notable progress has been made in the field of *computer simulation of international processes*. *Statistical studies of historical data* are not only becoming more numerous, but are accompanied by important developments in data-generating and datahandling techniques, such as *content analysis* and *factor analysis*. Greater use of *mathematics* in connection with all of these approaches is now evident. Important advances have been made in *cross-cultural* and *cross-sectional* methodologies. Finally, extensive efforts are under way to *validate* these and other methods. All in all, this battery of methodological possibilities constitutes an imposing gain over the situation ten years ago.

A second trend to be noted is toward a better coordination of theory building and empirical research. No longer do we find two noncommunicating groups of scholars, one engaged in intuitive, armchair speculation and the other collecting data without benefit of theoretical insight or purpose. Researchers are now committed to the integration of theory and research technique. When they build theory, they try to bear in mind the problems involved in testing it. When they analyze data, they do so in order to improve theory.

Finally, it is clear that the research enterprise is becoming more cumulative and that researchers are more frequently and effectively communicating to one another their aims, procedures and findings. In the United States, an *ad hoc* group has developed, consisting of many of the major leaders mentioned in this volume. This significant development increases the likelihood that variables, concepts, measures, and tactics of inquiry will be comparable and complementary between research groups and that research plans and findings will receive early and rigorous criticism. A *research community* in the area of international conflict appears to be in the making.

---

[1]Obviously not all the concepts listed here are new to the social and behavioral sciences. The term "new" refers to significant usage in research and theory-building focused on international conflict.

Unfinished Business

It would be strange, not to say suspicious, if much did not remain to be done in the field of research on the causes of war. Each section of this book describes some "islands of theory" which are in various stages of development. Each of these islands needs further theoretical and empirical development and new islands need to be discovered. In addition, in order to gain greater intellectual control over the necessary and sufficient conditions antecedent to the employment of violence, we need to build bridges between the islands. Several approaches to building such bridges were described in Section VII, but much more needs to be done. Decision-making perspectives and the international system perspective must be conceptually and empirically linked. One kind of linkage will come through research on comparative foreign policy making, another through systematic comparisons of key decisions under different degrees of system stability. In order to move from correlations to causality, we shall have to achieve more precise specifications of the contribution of single variables in a multi-variate cluster and of how the values of variables change under changing relationships among them.

If this is an awesome agenda, let us remember that we are better able than ever before to attack it with some hope of progress.

Author Index

Subject Index